Praise for *Advanced Web Metrics with Google Analytics, Second Edition*

Web analytics has become an essential part of every online marketer's toolkit. But you can't just rely on the flood of data alone—you need to interpret it, and in many cases, fine-tune reports to accurately reflect your own goals and objectives. The second edition of Brian Clifton's Advanced Web Metrics with Google Analytics *is a comprehensive roadmap to helping you get the most from your metrics—an indispensable guide to helping you take your online marketing campaigns to the next level.*
> —CHRIS SHERMAN, Executive Editor, Search Engine Land

The field of web analytics has evolved very quickly both in terms of the tools as well as best practices. Fortunately, Brian Clifton has done the hard work for us in updating his excellent first book so this second one is the must-read for anyone looking to get the most value out of Google Analytics and web analytics more broadly.
> —ASHLEY FRIEDLEIN, CEO, Econsultancy

Advanced Web Metrics *is a unique book that combines high-level management advice and nitty-gritty detail in an easy to understand and, above all, useful way. It's great for web managers, analytics specialists, and marketers alike.*
> —DAN DRURY, Director, Bowen Craggs & Co., and Author of the *Financial Times* Index of Corporate Website Effectiveness

If you're looking for a practical, tactical guide in how to implement and think about web marketing optimization, look no further. Brian Clifton spells it out by industry, by job function, by Key Performance Indicator, and more.

Brian has been studying and consulting on web optimization since the inception of online marketing. He provides an in-the-trenches look at making the most of a free but powerful tool that every web owner should get to know. This is the hands-on guide to what you need to know that answers questions like:

So what do I do with all this web data?

How do I use all these reports?

How do I measure the impact of promotion codes and discounted pricing?

How can I make sure I'm going to earn my bonus?
> —JIM STERNE, Founding Director and Chairman of the Web Analytics Association

In a time when companies are aggressively trying to do more with less, Brian delivers an arsenal of real-world examples and techniques for wringing more opportunities from our website and marketing campaigns. Guarantee your future employment—buy, read, and implement all of the techniques of this outstanding book.
> —BILL HUNT, Coauthor, *Search Engine Marketing Inc.*

Advanced Web Metrics with Google Analytics™

Second Edition

Brian Clifton

Wiley Publishing, Inc.

Senior Acquisitions Editor: WILLEM KNIBBE
Development Editor: TOM CIRTIN
Technical Editor: ALEX ORTIZ
Production Editor: DASSI ZEIDEL
Copy Editor: LINDA RECKTENWALD
Editorial Manager: PETE GAUGHAN
Production Manager: TIM TATE
Vice President and Executive Group Publisher: RICHARD SWADLEY
Vice President and Publisher: NEIL EDDE
Book Designer: FRANZ BAUMHACKL
Compositor: MAUREEN FORYS, HAPPENSTANCE TYPE-O-RAMA
Proofreader: JEN LARSEN, WORD ONE NEW YORK
Indexer: ROBERT SWANSON
Project Coordinator, Cover: LYNSEY STANFORD
Cover Designer: RYAN SNEED
Cover Image: ISTOCKPHOTO

Library of Congress Cataloging-in-Publication Data

Clifton, Brian, 1969–

  Advanced Web metrics with Google Analytics / Brian Clifton.—2nd ed.

    p. cm.

  Includes bibliographical references and index.

  ISBN 978-0-470-56231-4 (pbk.)

  1. Google Analytics. 2. Web usage mining. 3. Internet users—Statistics—Data processing. I. Title.

  TK5105.885.G66C55 2010

  006.3—dc22

                        2009052154

Dear Reader,

Thank you for choosing *Advanced Web Metrics with Google Analytics*. This book is part of a family of premium-quality Sybex books, all of which are written by outstanding authors who combine practical experience with a gift for teaching.

Sybex was founded in 1976. More than 30 years later, we're still committed to producing consistently exceptional books. With each of our titles, we're working hard to set a new standard for the industry. From the paper we print on, to the authors we work with, our goal is to bring you the best books available.

I hope you see all that reflected in these pages. I'd be very interested to hear your comments and get your feedback on how we're doing. Feel free to let me know what you think about this or any other Sybex book by sending me an email at nedde@wiley.com. If you think you've found a technical error in this book, please visit http://sybex.custhelp.com. Customer feedback is critical to our efforts at Sybex.

Best regards,

Neil Edde
Vice President and Publisher
Sybex, an imprint of Wiley

"Advanced web metrics is about doing the basics very well and applying it in a clever way"

—Sara Andersson, CEO, Search Integration AB

Acknowledgments

As for the first book, writing this second edition has been both very rewarding and very hard work. The second edition started off as a list of straightforward updates, yet turned out to be a complete rewrite of content—such is my obsession with producing what I hope is a worthy book.

I have never considered myself a natural writer. Endlessly agonizing over every sentence, I would yearn for perfection, or at the very least adequacy. The first book, written while working twelve hours a day at Google, took me eighteen months to finish (mainly written on trains and planes or in various hotel rooms across Europe or in the US). This time I got myself organized and even more obsessive (if that were possible) and completed the second edition in six months. The relief of my much-supportive partner, Sara, friends, and family is almost palpable.

Yet the process of writing remains enjoyable. In fact, I am already looking forward to my next writing project, though I am undecided as to what that should be! However, I am not a one-man band, and many people have happily contributed their time to make this book even better than the first.

First, special thanks go to Alex Ortiz-Rosado, Nick Michailovski, and Tomas Remotigue, all of Google, who have significantly contributed to my knowledge and understanding of the internal workings of Google Analytics over the years. All worked late and on their own time to sanity-check and expand on the technical aspects of this book. Alex is my much-appreciated technical editor. His eagle eye for detail and patience at explaining some of the more complex intricacies of Google Analytics have enabled me to write a much more comprehensive book.

Significant feedback, help, and brainstorming were also freely provided by Shelby Thayer, a web analytics practitioner, enthusiast, advocate, and all-round nice person working for Penn State University. Shelby kindly proofread and commented on every page of this book, ensuring content relevance and continuity.

Thanks also go to Leonardo Naressi and Eduardo Cereto of Direct Performance for their expertise and advice with Flash event tracking; Ophir Prusak of POP, who provided detailed explanations and workarounds when integrating Google Analytics with Website Optimizer; Dan Drury and Abdurashid Atahanov of Bowen Craggs & Co. Limited for their input on effective KPI strategies within large corporations; Neal McGann and Andre Wei of VKI Studios for sharing their experience of Website Optimizer; Jeremy Aube of ROI Revolution for his continuous support of the GAAC community; Sara Andersson for her generous advice and strategic thinking regarding integrating offline and online marketing and for sharing her ideas on search marketing, social media engagement, and life in general; Avinash Kaushik for reviewing this book and for honoring me by writing the foreword; Mikael

Thuneberg, Nikki Rae (Fresh Egg Ltd.), Eran Savir (Kampyle), Ravi Pathak (Tatvic), and Eyal Eldar (easynet (seperia) Ltd.) for providing case study content to include with Chapter 12; and all members of the Google Analytics Authorized Consultants (GAAC) network for their stimulating discussions, experiences, and thoughts when implementing Google Analytics for their clients.

Last but not least, many thanks to the Wiley publishing team: Willem Knibbe, whose enthusiasm for this topic meant that I was always going to produce a second edition of this book; Tom Cirtin, who kept the structure and cohesion going in a straight line throughout; Dassi Zeidel, Linda Recktenwald, and Jen Larsen, and the many other people at Wiley who work tirelessly in the background to help create and polish what I hope you will consider is an enjoyable and informative read. Ultimately this was my mission, for what potentially can be a very dry subject.

That's quite a long list, with people from all over the world (at least seven countries) helping to shape, expand, and improve the content provided. I hope I have remembered everyone.

About the Author

Brian Clifton, PhD, is an internationally recognized Google Analytics expert who consults on website performance optimization for global clients. Coming from a web development and search engine optimization (SEO) background, he has worked in these fields since 1997. His business was the first U.K. partner for Urchin Software Inc., the company that later became Google Analytics.

In 2005, Brian was the first person with web measurement experience to join Google Europe. As former Head of Web Analytics for Google Europe, Middle East, and Africa, he defined the strategy for adoption and built a team of pan-European product specialists. He is now CEO and Senior Strategist for Omega Digital Media.

Brian received a BSc in chemistry from the University of Bristol in 1991 and a PhD in physical and theoretical chemistry in 1996. Further work as a postdoctoral researcher culminated in publishing several scientific papers in journals, including *Molecular Physics*, *Colloids and Surfaces*, and *Langmuir*. During that time, he was also an international weightlifter, representing Great Britain at world and European championships.

Studying science at university during the early nineties meant witnessing the incredible beginnings of the Web. In 1991, Tim Berners-Lee, a scientist working at the CERN laboratory in Switzerland, launched the first web browser and web server to the academic community, thereby sowing the first seeds of the World Wide Web.

Although the communication potential of the Web was immediately clear to Brian, it took a little while for ideas to formulate around business opportunities. In 1997 he left academia to found Omega Digital Media, a U.K. company specializing in the provision of professional services to organizations wishing to utilize the new digital medium.

Since leaving the field of chemical research (and weightlifting), Brian has continued to write—either on his blog, Measuring Success (www.advanced-web-metrics.com/blog), as a guest writer on industry forums, or via whitepapers.

Brian holds the title of associate instructor at the University of British Columbia for his contribution to teaching modules in support of the Award of Achievement in Web Analytics. You can also hear him speak at numerous conferences around the word, where he discusses data-driven online strategies and site optimization. Brian was born in Manchester, United Kingdom, and now lives in Sweden.

Contents

Foreword

Let's get one thing out of the way first. This is an excellent book.

If you are standing in a bookstore scanning this Foreword, rush to the checkout counter and buy it right away. You are not going to regret it. I promise.

If you have already purchased this book and are just starting to read it, then let me assure you that you are in for a delightful treat. How often do you hear that about a book about numbers?

I am thrilled that Brian has updated *Advanced Web Metrics*. That's because the core reason I personally love the Web, and I do *looove* the Web, is that it is in a constant state of evolution. It stands to reason then that key web analytics solutions like Google Analytics also evolve.

In just the last year Google Analytics has released really wonderful features like Intelligence (which applies control limits, statistical algorithms, forecasting, and sensitivity analysis to help identify key insights), Custom Variables (now you can collect metadata about your site and visitors in a way that was impossible before), an open API (now the sky's the limit when it comes to you being able to analyze, interpret, and display your data in unique ways), and so much more. Notice that I am not even mentioning my beloved analytical technique, Advanced Segmentation!

Especially because you have so much power at your disposal, Brian's book is key to your success.

Five years ago, when working at Intuit, I postulated the 10/90 rule. It states, simply, that for every $100 you have to invest in making intelligent decisions on the Web, you should invest $10 in technology and $90 in people. On reflection, that rule is even more true today. You can use a portfolio of free tools for web analytics, surveys, competitive intelligence analysis, and pretty much anything else you want to do. What these tools don't come with is the expertise and skills required to use them to the fullest potential that they all promise.

That is where Brian comes in.

Brian has spent a lifetime in the field of web analytics (okay, okay, lifetime as thought of in Internet years!). He has deep expertise by being a practitioner. He has worked at Google and helped influence Google Analytics while he was working with some of the largest companies in the world to help them measure what they thought was impossible to measure. In the last couple of years, through his consulting practice, he has made that last quest his full-time job.

I cannot think of anyone better to gently walk us down the path of morphing from Reporting Squirrels to Analysis Ninjas. *Advanced Web Metrics with Google Analytics* starts at an easy clip, explaining the basics, getting you acquainted with the new world of data. It then steps up slowly but steadily to a crescendo, where you are truly dancing with the data.

I have had the privilege of writing two web analytics books, and *I* learned so much about Google Analytics by reading Brian's book. I am confident you are in for a similar experience.

Let me close with this thought: Getting access to data in our world is easy. Taking that data and revolutionizing how your business makes decisions, makes money, and makes your customers happy are not easy.

This book will make that not-easy journey easier.

Good luck!

Avinash Kaushik
Author, Web *Analytics 2.0 and Web Analytics: An Hour a Day*
Analytics evangelist, Google

Introduction

Although the birth of Web took place in August 1991, it did not become commercial until around 1995. In those early days, it was kind of fun to have a spinning logo, a few pictures, and your contact details as the basis of your online presence. My first website was just that—no more than my curriculum vitae online at the University of Bristol. Then companies decided to copy (or worse, scan) their paper catalogs and brochures and simply dump these on their websites. This was a step forward in providing more content, but the user experience was poor to say the least, and no one was really measuring conversions. The most anyone kept track of was hits, which nobody ever really understood, though they were assumed (incorrectly) to be visits.

Around the year 2000, fueled by the dot-com boom, people suddenly seemed to realize the potential of the Web as a useful medium to find information; the number of visitors using it grew rapidly. Organizations started to think about fundamental questions such as "What is the purpose of having a website?" and considered how to build relevant content for their online presence. With that, user experience improved. Then, when widespread broadband adoption began, those organizations wanted to attract the huge audience that was now online, hence the reason for the rapid growth in search-engine marketing that followed.

Now, with businesses accepting the growing importance of their online presence, they are prepared to invest. But how much money and resources should an organization put into this? For example, should the site cater to ten languages, accept five currencies, and run in four browser types from visitors with six different operating systems, including mobile? How should the site be marketed, which channels are most effective, and can we predict the return on investment for the next campaign?

Answering such questions requires data and hence a measurement tool. Put simply, this is what web analytics tools, such as Google Analytics, allow you to do—study the online experience, in order to improve it.

But what can be measured, how accurate is this, and how can a business be benchmarked? In other words, how do you measure success? Using best-practice principles I have gained as a professional practitioner, this book uses real-world examples that clearly demonstrate how to manage Google Analytics. These include not only installation and configuration guides but also how to turn data into information that enables you to understand your website visitor's experience. With this understanding, you can then build business action items to drive improvements in visitor acquisition (both online and offline), conversion rates, repeat visit rates, customer retention, and ultimately your bottom line.

Who Should Read This Book

As a great friend and mentor to me once said, "Advanced web metrics is about doing the basics very well and applying it in a clever way." I wish I had thought of that phrase! It epitomizes everything about my approach to web analytics and this book. Thus, I have attempted to make this book's subject matter accessible to a broad spectrum of readers—essentially anyone with a business interest in making their website work better. After all, the concept of measuring success is a universal desire.

The content is not aimed at the complete web novice, nor is it aimed at engineers—I am not one myself. Installing, configuring, or using Google Analytics does not require an engineer! Rather, I hope that *Advanced Web Metrics with Google Analytics* will appeal to existing users of business data as well as readers new to the field of web measurement.

As the title implies, this book is intended for people who want to go beyond the basics of simply counting hits. These can be grouped into three user groups:

Marketers These are users who have experience with search-engine marketing (paid and organic search), email marketing, social search, PR, and affiliate management but have not yet managed to find a unified measurement tool to compare these side by side. For this group, most chapters focus on integrating your analytical skills with your marketing skills and require no coding ability.

Webmasters These are experienced website builders who have the skill set and authorization to modify a website. For this group of users, the book offers sections and exercises that require you to modify your web page content; after all, web analytics is all about instigating change using reliable metrics as your guide. Therefore, knowledge of HTML (the ability to read browser source code) and experience with JavaScript are required.

Senior managers These are decision makers who require guidance on preparing a data-driven strategy and action plan for their organization. I hope to supply these readers with an understanding of what can and cannot be achieved with web analytics and specifically provide information they need to plan the resources and timelines required for building an effective Google Analytics measurement team. My aim for this group is to provide you with the information necessary in order to make "informed decisions."

With a better understanding of your website visitors, you will be able to tailor page content and marketing budgets with laser-like precision for a better return on investment. I also discuss advanced configurations (Chapter 9, "Google Analytics Hacks"), which are not documented elsewhere. These provide you with an even greater understanding of your website visitors so that you can dive into the metrics that make sense for your organization. In as many areas as possible, I include real-world practical examples that are currently employed by advanced users.

You can use this book in several ways. The most straightforward (and demanding) is to start at the beginning and follow all the steps to completion, building your knowledge in a step-wise fashion. Alternatively, I have deliberately designed the book so that you can skip around and delve straight into a chapter as needed. To help with this approach, I frequently reference content within the book or other resources for further reading. However, I do recommend you put time aside to review the initial chapters (Chapters 1–3), as these introduce important approaches to web measurement, such as accuracy and privacy considerations. Web analytics is still a nascent industry and I am actively blogging about Google Analytics, the book's content and measurement issues in general at www.advanced-web-metrics.com. You can also follow my thoughts or what I am currently reading on Twitter (@brianclifton). You can download all presented code examples from the site using the referenced links within each chapter.

What You Will Learn

You will learn how to implement and *use* Google Analytics in a best-practice way. I deliberately emphasize the word *use* because this is the primary purpose of this book. That is, you will learn how to leverage Google Analytics to optimize your website—in terms of marketing, user experience, and ultimately conversions, all based on solid, reliable data.

What You Need

First and foremost, you need an inquisitive mind! This is not an engineering book, and you require no additional software or tools to apply the advice—just a good understanding of what your website is supposed to achieve, how your organization is marketing it, and an idea of the type of metrics that would help you judge its success.

That said, a couple of chapters do require you to have a good understanding of HTML and basic JavaScript skills. If that doesn't describe you, read this book in conjunction with a colleague who can help you. As you will learn, web analytics requires a multidisciplinary skill set, and collaboration is the key to success.

What Is Covered in This Book

Advanced Web Metrics with Google Analytics is organized to provide you with a clear step-wise progression of knowledge building.

Chapter 1: Why Understanding Your Web Traffic Is Important to Your Business introduces you to the world of web measurement, where it fits in, and what you can achieve.

Chapter 2: Available Methodologies and Their Accuracy provides the context of what can be measured via web analytics and its limitations.

Chapter 3: Google Analytics Features, Benefits, and Limitations focuses on what Google Analytics can do for you.

Chapter 4: Using the Google Analytics Interface walks you through the user interface, highlighting the key functionality.

Chapter 5: Reports Explained reviews in detail the top reports you need to understand.

Chapter 6: Getting Up and Running with Google Analytics gets you quickly up and running with the basic install.

Chapter 7: Advanced Implementation takes you beyond the basics to give you a more complete picture of your website's activity.

Chapter 8: Best-Practices Configuration Guide provides you with the knowledge to define success metrics (KPIs) and segment your data.

Chapter 9: Google Analytics Hacks gives you some lateral thinking for adding extra functionality to Google Analytics.

Chapter 10: Focusing on Key Performance Indicators is about how you focus on the metrics most important to you—KPIs and the process required to build them.

Chapter 11: Real-World Tasks jump-starts your analytical skills by showing you how to identify and optimize poorly performing pages, site search, and online and offline marketing. Website Optimizer is introduced as a method for testing a hypothesis.

Chapter 12: Integrating Google Analytics with Third-Party Applications shows you how to integrate data either by capturing cookies or using the new Google Analytics export API.

Appendix A: Regular Expression Overview gives you an introduction to understanding regular expressions.

Appendix B: Useful Tools describes some useful tools for helping you implement and use Google Analytics.

Appendix C: Recommended Further Reading gathers together books, blogs, and other web resources that can help you.

GA IQ Coupon

Democratizing web analytics data was a big part of the initial adoption strategy of Google Analytics. In 2007, while I was at Google, we really wanted to see such useful data being shared between sales, marketing, PR, senior management—anyone who had an interest in improving the company's website.

However, providing such large-scale access to data presented another problem: People didn't know how to interpret the data or what to do next. There was a serious dearth in web analytics education available to help people. I knew I could assist by writing this book, and another ambition was to establish an online learning center for Google Analytics.

It was therefore a logical step to produce an online version of our tiered internal training system so that any person, not just Googlers, could work through the online tutorials and then take the exam to demonstrate to their peers and potential employers their analytical and product-specific skills.

We started building the www.conversionuniversity.com online learning center in late 2007 and introduced the Google Analytics Individual Qualification (GA IQ) in November 2008. It was a huge achievement for the team and one that I am immensely proud of.

While there is nothing like a classroom workshop for a great learning environment—you not only learn the necessary skills but you also gain from the expertise of the trainer (as well as have time to pick their brains directly over a coffee!)—that's not always possible. Fortunately, this book, conversionuniversity.com, and the GA IQ help users learn Google Analytics and then have tangible proof of their proficiency. If you haven't taken the test, I encourage you to do so soon after reading this book. Use the coupon code on the last page to get 50 percent off the test while supplies last.

How to Contact the Author

I welcome feedback from you about this book or about anything related to website measurement and optimization. You can reach me via any of the following means:

- Website: www.advanced-web-metrics.com
- LinkedIn interactive group for readers of this book: http://www.linkedin.com/groupInvitation?groupID=66386
- Twitter: http://twitter.com/brianclifton
- LinkedIn profile: http://uk.linkedin.com/in/brianclifton
- Facebook profile: http://www.facebook.com/brianjclifton

Sybex strives to keep you supplied with the latest tools and information you need for your work. Please check their website at www.sybex.com, where we'll post additional content and updates that supplement this book if the need arises. Enter *advanced web metrics* in the Search box (or type the book's ISBN—9780470562314), and click Go to get to the book's update page.

Measuring Success

I

Lord Kelvin is often quoted as the reason why metrics are so important: "If you cannot measure it, you cannot improve it." That statement is ultimately the purpose of web analytics. By enabling you to identify what works and what doesn't from a visitor's point of view, web analytics is the foundation for running a successful website. Even if you get those decisions wrong, web analytics provides the feedback mechanism that enables you to identify mistakes quickly.

In Part I, you will learn the following:

Why Understanding Your Web Traffic Is Important to Your Business

Web analytics is a thermometer for your website—constantly checking and monitoring your online health. As a methodology, it is the study of online experience in order to improve it; without it, you are flying blind. How else would you determine whether your search engine marketing is effective at capturing your maximum potential audience or whether negative blog comments are hindering conversions? Is the user experience a good one, encouraging engagement and return visits, or are visitors bouncing off your website after viewing only a single page?

1

In Chapter 1, you will learn:

The kinds of information you can obtain from analyzing traffic on your site

The kinds of decisions that web analytics can help you make

The ROI of web analytics

How web analytics helps you understand your web traffic

Where web analytics fits into your organization

Website Measurement—Why Do This?

It's an obvious question and one that has an obvious answer —as provided by the 19th-century scientist Lord Kelvin, in my opening paragraph of Part I. But this question still comes up at initial meetings within an organization where website performance is being discussed. The idea of applying a measurement tool to assess a website's effectiveness is an easy sell—every business owner/executive understands the importance of measurement, but "why do we need another measurement tool in our business?"

The most common fear is data overload—collecting more information just because you can inevitably leads to more confusion, not clarity. This is particularly the case when your website is operating as a silo, that is, not integrated with the rest of your business—a common problem if yours is a nontransactional website. Therefore, an important early step when deciding on a website measurement strategy is to define the *value* that web measurement can bring to your business. You can achieve this whether yours is a transactional site or not (see "Monetizing a Non-E-Commerce Website," in Chapter 11, "Real-World Tasks"), though here I illustrate *value* using transactional examples because these are easier to grasp in the first instance.

Figure 1.1 shows the improvement a travel website gained by optimizing their online booking process—that is, the steps a visitor takes in order to book a chosen vacation. (In Google Analytics terminology, the booking process steps are referred to as a *funnel*—directly analogous to any sales funnel in your organization.)

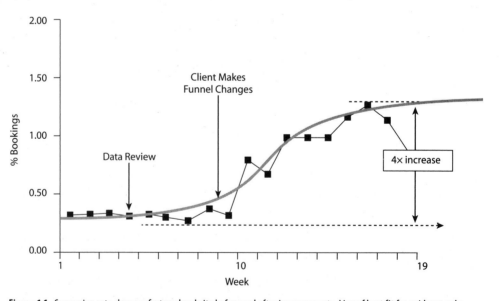

Figure 1.1 Conversion rate change of a travel website before and after improvements. Line of best fit for guidance only.

As you can see, the changes to the booking process took several weeks to implement (the client was not confident enough to take on board all the recommendations at once!), but the cumulative impact was dramatic—a 383 percent increase in their booking conversion rate. Put in monetary terms, this equated to an annualized increase in revenue of $7.5 million.

The second example of the *value* of web measurement is shown in Figure 1.2. In this case, a measurement tool was able to quickly identify problems following the launch of a new site redesign. Essentially, server redirects were incorrectly assigned in the new site, which resulted in a 48 percent loss of search engine traffic and a 21 percent loss in sales revenue. Following the identification of the problem, the client's visitor and revenue numbers were back to previous levels within four weeks.

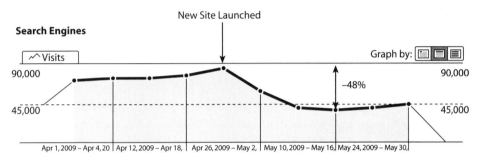

Figure 1.2 The loss of search engine traffic following the launch of a new design

If your website is an important part of your business strategy, then website measurement is also important to that strategy. The magnitudes of each are strongly correlated—that is, the more valuable your website is to you, the greater the significance of your web measurement tools. Such tools can be used to identify growth opportunities, measure efficiency improvements, and highlight things when they go wrong.

Glossary of Terms

At this stage it would be useful for you to be familiar with some of the terminology used in Google Analytics. The following is a short summary. For a more complete list, see `http://www.google.com/support/googleanalytics/bin/topic.py?topic=11285`.

Bounced visitor A visitor who views only a single page on your website and has no further actions. This is generally considered a bad experience.

Campaign The name of a paid campaign, for example, "book sales" (for a paid search campaign), "spring sale" (for a banner campaign), "January newsletter" (for an email shot).

Google Analytics Tracking Code (GATC) This snippet of code must be added to every page on your website to enable Google Analytics to collect and report on visit data. Also more generally referred to as the "page tag."

Continues

Glossary of Terms *(Continued)*

Goal conversion   Often abbreviated to just "goal" or "conversion," this is a desired action on your website that is defined as being more valuable than a standard pageview. For example, a "purchase confirmation" page (visitor becomes a customer), a "thank you for registering" page (visitor becomes a prospect), a download page, or an online presentation (visitor becomes engaged).

Funnel   A well-defined process (most usually pages) leading to a conversion goal, for example, a check-out system.

Landing page   The first page visitors arrive on when they visit your website. Also known as the "entrance page."

Medium   In the context of campaign tracking, *medium* indicates the means by which a visitor to your site received the link to you, for example, "organic" and "cost-per-click" for search engine links, "email" and "PDF" in the case of newsletters, "referral" for sites that link to you, and "direct" for a visitor who types your web address directly into their browser.

Referrer   The URL of an HTML page that refers visitors to a site, that is, the external page visitors click on to bring them to your website.

Return on investment (ROI)   Calculated as (revenue - cost) / cost and displayed as a percentage.

Session   Also referred to as a "visit" or "visitor session," this is the period of interaction a visitor has with your website. A session ends when a visitor either closes their browser or 30 minutes has elapsed without activity. The session timeout value can be adjusted (see Chapter 7, "Advanced Implementation"), though 30 minutes is the unwritten industry standard.

Site search   A website's *internal* site search facility (internal search engine), mostly used on sites with large volumes of content in order to improve the user experience, that is, find information faster.

Source   In the context of campaign tracking, the source is the origin of a referral, for example, google.com, yahoo.co.uk, the name of a newsletter, or the name of a referring website.

URL (Uniform Resource Locator)   A means of identifying an exact location on the Internet. It is how Google Analytics tracks and reports on pageview activity for your website, for example, `http://www.mysite.com/products/widget1.php`. URLs typically have four parts: protocol type (HTTP), host domain name (`http://www.mysite.com`), directory path (/products/), and filename (widget1.php).

Information Web Analytics Can Provide

In order to do business effectively on the Web, you need to continually refine and optimize your online marketing strategy, site navigation, and page content (as well as how your offline marketing, press releases, and communications interact with your website). A low-performing website will starve your return on investment (ROI) and can damage your brand. But you need to understand what is performing poorly—the targeting of your marketing campaigns, poor reviews of your products/services on the Web, or your website's ability to convert once a visitor arrives. Web analytics provides the tools for gathering this information and enables you to benchmark the effects.

Note that I have been deliberately using the word *tools* in its plural form. This is because the term *web analytics* covers many areas that require different methodologies or data-collection techniques. For example, *offsite tools* are used to measure the size of your potential audience (opportunity), your share of voice (visibility), and the buzz (comments/sentiment) that is happening on the Internet as a whole. These are relevant metrics regardless of your website's existence. Conversely, *onsite tools* measure the visitor's onsite journey, its drivers, and your website's performance. These are directly related to your website's existence.

Figure 1.3 schematically illustrates how onsite and offsite web analytics tools fit together. From a vendor perspective, the separation of methodologies is not as mutually exclusive as Figure 1.3 suggests. For example, Hitwise, comScore, and Nielsen//NetRatings also have onsite measurement tools, while Google, Yahoo, and Microsoft have the ability to provide offsite search query data to complement their onsite tools—see, for example, Microsoft Adlab resources (`http://adlab.microsoft.com/AdLab-Resources.aspx`) and Google Insights (`http://www.google.com/insights/search/`).

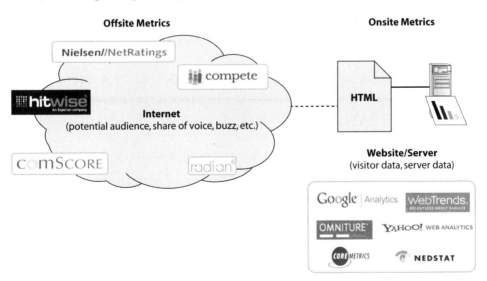

Figure 1.3 Onsite versus offsite web analytics

The differences in methodology between offsite and onsite web measurement tools are significant, and this leads to very different results. Even for basic website numbers, such as the number of visitors a website receives or the total number of pageviews, the values can vary dramatically. This is a constant and exasperating problem for site owners, media buyers, and marketers alike who attempt the futile task of reconciling the metrics. The truth is that metrics obtained with offsite methods cannot be reconciled with those from onsite tools—it's like comparing apples to oranges and often the differences are large, for example, +/-100 percent is not uncommon.

Whenever confronted with this problem from a client, I summarize the differences as follows: Offsite web analytics tools measure your potential website audience. They are the macro tools that allow you to see the bigger picture of how your website compares to others. Onsite web analytics tools measure the actual visitor traffic arriving on your website. They are capable of tracking the engagements and interactions your visitors have, for example, whether they convert to a customer or lead, how they got to that point, or where they dropped out of the process altogether. It is not logical to use one methodology to measure the impact of another. Offsite and onsite analytics should be used to complement each other—not compete against each other.

Google Analytics is an onsite visitor-reporting tool. From here on, when I use the general term *web analytics*, I am referring to onsite measurement tools.

Where to Start

If you have already experienced looking at metrics from pay-per-click advertising campaigns, Google Analytics is simply the widening of that report view to see all referrals and behavior of visitors. If you are new to any kind of web metrics reporting, then the amount of information available can feel overwhelming at first. However, bear with me—this book is intended to guide you through the important aspects of what you need to know in order to be up and running with Google Analytics quickly and efficiently.

If you are implementing web analytics for the first time, then you will want to gain an insight into the initial visitor metrics to ascertain your traffic levels and visitor distribution. Examples of first-level metrics include the following:

- How many daily visitors you receive.

- Your average conversion rate (sales, registration, download, and so on).

- Your top-visited pages.

- The average visit time on site and how often visitors come back.

- The average visit page depth and how this varies by referrer.

- The geographic distribution of visitors and what language setting they are using.

- How "sticky" your pages are: Do visitors stay or simply bounce off (single-page visits)?

If your website has an e-commerce facility, then you will also want to know the following:

- The revenue your site is generating
- Where your customers are coming from
- What your top-selling products are
- The average order value of your top-selling products

These metrics enable you to draw a line in the sand as the starting point from which you can increase your knowledge. Be warned, though, Google Analytics gives you statistics so readily that the habit of checking them can become obsessive! Hence, as you move deeper into your analysis, you will start to ask more complicated questions of your data, for example:

- What is the value of a visitor and how does this vary depending on where they came from?
- What is the value of a web page?
- How do existing customers use the site compared to new visitors?
- How do visits and conversions vary by referrer type or campaign source?
- How does bounce rate vary by page viewed or referring source?
- Is my site engaging with visitors?
- Is my internal site search helping or hindering conversions?
- How many visits and how much time does it take for a visitor to become a customer?

All of these questions can be answered with Google Analytics reports.

Consider Figure 1.4, a typical model that most websites fit. It illustrates that the vast majority of websites have single-figure conversion rates. Why is that, and can it be improved? I can say with certainty that in my 15 years of either developing websites or simply viewing web content for business or pleasure, there has always been room for improvement from a user-experience point of view—including on my own websites. Ultimately, assuming you have a good product or service to offer, the user experience of your visitors will determine the success of your website, and web analytics tools provide the means to investigate this.

Note: The average conversion rate reported by the e-tailing group corresponds closely with that of Forrester Research, July 2007, and the Fireclick Index (http://index.fireclick.com/fireindex.php?segment=0).

Amazon is often cited as the benchmark standard for optimizing the conversion of visitors to customers. Their conversion rate was reported as 17.2 percent in January 2009 (source: Nielsen Online via MarketingCharts.com).

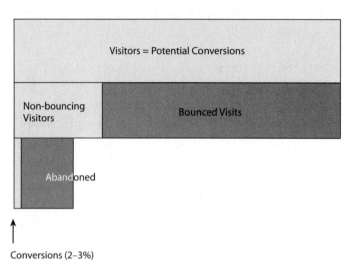

Figure 1.4 U.S. Conversion rates average 2–3 percent 2005–2007.

SOURCE: THE E-TAILING GROUP, APRIL 2007

Keep in mind that web analytics are tools—not ends in themselves. They cannot tell you why visitors behave the way they do or which improvements you should make. For that you need to invest in report analysis, and that means hiring expertise, training existing staff, using the services of an external consultant, or using a combination of all of these. Often, you may need to employ multiple tools to gain an insight as to "why." These include the use of voice-of-customer tools (surveys, customer ratings, and feedback) as well as offsite analytics measurement (blog comments, social network mentions, and sentiment).

Decisions Web Analytics Can Help You Make

Knowledge without action is meaningless. The purpose of web analytics is to give you the knowledge from which you can make informed decisions about changing your online strategy—for the better. So it's important to include change, that is, changing your website or its marketing, as part of your metrics strategy. That sounds easy in theory, though often for large organizations, getting all stakeholders aligned and implementing a change is a project in itself. Therefore, ensure you have that buy-in from an early stage; otherwise, you will rapidly become frustrated at your unrewarded efforts (the process is discussed in Chapter 10, "Focusing on Key Performance Indicators").

In terms of benchmarks, it is important that any organization spend time planning its *key performance indicators (KPIs)*. KPIs provide a distillation of the plethora of website visitor data available to you as clear, actionable information. Simply put, KPIs represent the key factors, specific to your organization, that measure success.

Google Analytics gives you the data from which KPIs are built and in some cases can provide a KPI directly. For example, saying "we had 10,000 visitors this week" is providing a piece of data. A KPI based on this could be "our visitor numbers are up 10 percent month on month"—that is an indicator saying things are looking good. Most KPIs are ratios or percentages that enable you to take action, and the job of an analyst is to build these specific to your organization. I discuss building KPIs in detail in Chapter 10.

Using KPIs, typical decisions you can make include those shown in Table 1.1.

While engaging in this process to improve your website's performance, consider the changes as part of a continuous process—not a one-hit fix. That is, think in terms of the AMAT acronym:

- Acquisition of visitors
- Measurement of performance
- Analysis of trends
- Testing to improve

▶ **Table 1.1** Typical decisions based on KPIs

Observation	Action
We have a new top-selling product that is delivering 20 percent more by revenue than any other.	Reward the web and marketing teams for a job well done!
The average visits per day from organic search has halved compared to last week.	Call the SEO team. Investigate any changes in content, redirection, or site architecture.
Our last banner campaign cost $5,000 and generated four sales worth $1,000.	Drop the banner campaign.
Online purchases increase by 50 percent if we send a follow-up email to new registered visitors within one week.	Ensure email marketing is an integral part of your business strategy and is tracked within your web analytics tool.
Internal site search is being actively used by 70 percent of visitors. However, most search results are zero, and those that are not generate little revenue.	Call the IT/Web team. Investigate changing your internal search engine to improve the user experience and boost sales.
Visits from an industry forum are driving goal conversions (brochure downloads), but the paid-search visitors are driving transactions.	Call the Marketing team. Acquire more forum visitors to drive branding, reach, and goal conversions. Acquire more paid-search visitors to provide further revenue growth.

The ROI of Web Analytics

Google Analytics is a free data collection and reporting tool. However, implementing, analyzing, interpreting, and making website changes all require a resource outlay at your end. The amount of investment you make in web analytics, therefore, depends on how significant your website is to your overall business.

How Much Should I Invest in This?

A great phrase often heard from Jim Sterne at his eMetrics conference series (http:// www.emetrics.org) is "What is the ROI of measuring your ROI?" In other words, how much time and effort should you spend on data measurement and analysis, considering that the vast majority of people performing this job role also have other responsibilities, such as webmaster, online marketer, offline marketer, content creator—even running a business. After all, you need to focus on delivering for your visitors and generating revenue or leads from your website.

I like to use the following analogy: analyzing your web analytics reports is similar to visiting the gym. Unless you go regularly, don't waste your time there, because you will only become frustrated at the little impact made from previous sessions. I recommend going to the gym (or performing your preferred form of exercise) at least three times per week. That way, your body/health improves because of the regularity of the exertion (I have spent a lot of time in gyms!). Similarly, regular website analysis is required to provide the insights needed to recommend change. Otherwise, all you have is a hit counter—you will never be able to improve your website because you don't have the insights to do so.

The key to calculating what your web analytics investment should be is understanding the value of your website in monetary terms—either directly as an e-commerce site or indirectly from lead generation or advertisement click-throughs. Marketers are smart, but they are not fortune-tellers. Purchasing clicks and doing nothing to measure their effectiveness is like scattering seeds in the air. Even highly paid experts can be wrong. Moreover, content that works today can become stale tomorrow. Using web analytics, you can ascertain the impact your work has and what that is worth to your organization.

Table 1.2 demonstrates a before-and-after example of what making use of web analytics data can achieve. In this theoretical case, the target was to grow the online conversion rate by 1 percent, using an understanding of visitor acquisition and onsite factors such as checkout funnel analysis, exit points, bounce rates, and engagement metrics. By achieving this increase, the values of total profit, P, and ROI, R, shown in the last two rows of the table, put the analysis into context—that is, profit will rise by $37,500 and return on investment will quadruple to 50 percent. Note that this is achieved solely by improving the conversion rate of the site—visitor acquisition costs remain the same.

▶ **Table 1.2** Economic effect of a 1 percent increase in conversion rate

	Symbol	Calculation	Before	After
Visitors	v		100,000	100,000
Cost per visit	c		$1.00	$1.00
Cost of all visits	c_T	$v \times c$	$100,000	$100,000
Conversion rate	r		3%	4%
Conversions	C	$r \times v$	3,000	4,000
Revenue per conversion	V		$75	$75
Total revenue	**T**	**$V \times C$**	**$225,000**	**$300,000**
Non-marketing profit margin	m		50%	50%
Non-marketing costs	n	$(1-m) \times T$	$112,500	$150,000
Marketing costs	c_T	$v \times c$	$100,000	$100,000
Total profit	**P**	**$T - (n + c_T)$**	**$12,500**	**$50,000**
Total marketing ROI	**R**	**P/c_T**	**13%**	**50%**

Note: The Excel spreadsheet of Table 1.2 is available at `http://www.advanced-web-metrics.com/chapter1`.

To calculate how much time you should spend on web analytics in your organization, try a similar calculation; then ask your boss (or yourself) how much time such an increase in revenue buys you. As a guide, I have worked with clients for whom the time from web analytics implementation, initial analysis, forming a hypothesis, testing, interpretation, and presenting the results—that is, the before and after—takes six months (that is unusually fast for an organization, though smaller businesses can be more agile). If you can achieve the same, allow six months' of your salary as your initial investment. Of course, the compounded impact of your work will last much longer, so the actual lifetime value of improvement is always higher than this calculation suggests.

How Web Analytics Helps You Understand Your Web Traffic

As discussed earlier, viewing the 100-plus reports in Google Analytics can at first appear overwhelming—there is simply too much data to consume in one go. Of course, all of this data is relevant, but some of it will be more relevant to you, depending on your business model. Therefore, once you have visitor data coming in and populating your reports, you will likely want to view a smaller subset—the key touch points with your potential customers. To help you distill visitor information, you can configure Google Analytics to report on goal conversions.

Identifying goals is probably the single most important step of building a website—it enables you to define success. Think of goal conversions as specific, measurable actions that you want your visitors to complete before they leave your website. For example, an obvious goal for an e-commerce site is the completion of a transaction—that is, buying something. However, not all visitors will complete a transaction on their first visit, so another useful e-commerce goal is quantifying the number of people who add an item to the shopping cart whether they complete the purchase or not—in other words, how many begin the shopping process.

Regardless of whether you have an e-commerce website or not, your website has goals. A *goal* is any action or engagement that builds a relationship with your visitors, such as the completion of a feedback form, a subscription request, leaving a comment on a blog post, downloading a PDF whitepaper, viewing a special offers page, or clicking a `mailto:` link. Think of a goal as something more valuable to you than a standard pageview. As you begin this exercise, you will probably realize that you actually have many website goals (defining goals is discussed in Chapter 8, "Best-Practices Configuration Guide").

With goals clearly defined, you simplify the viewing of your visitor data and the forming of a hypothesis. Your goal conversions become your at-a-glance key metrics. For example, knowing instantly how many, and what proportion, of your visitors convert enables you to promptly ascertain the performance of your website and whether you should do something about it or relax and let the computers continue to do the work for you.

Where Web Analytics Fits In

As you might expect, I consider web analytics to be at the center of the universe (well, the digital universe anyhow)—see Figure 1.5. The web is both your research tool and your feedback tool. For example, what are people looking for online and what do they think of your products/services—both before and after purchase? Whether you are actively engaged in digital marketing or not, it is highly likely that potential new customers will be looking online for a company just like yours to help them. Even your existing customers use the Web to find updates, your contact details, support information, or to submit valuable product suggestions. There are even job seekers and investors to consider.

Of course, I am preaching to the choir—why else would you be reading this book? The point I wish to make is that for a *switched-on* organization, your website touches all parts of your business. Hence, your web analytics tool is in a unique position to provide a unified measurement platform that all sides of your business can use—a common currency for measurement, so to speak.

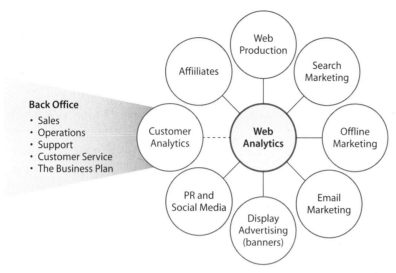

Figure 1.5 Where web analytics fits in an organization

That doesn't mean that you have to force all sides of your business to use only one measurement tool. That would be foolish to attempt. For example, customer analytics (data mining of CRM, or customer relationship management, systems) is a very different field from the almost completely anonymous world of web analytics, hence the dashed line connecting these two in Figure 1.5. Similarly, measuring the buzz and sentiment of your brand on social networks requires the use of offsite web analytics tools, which use very different techniques from onsite web analytics.

Nonetheless, it is still possible (and very desirable) to have a unified web analytics tool that can support all aspects of the business to a greater or lesser extent, while more specialist tools can be used to dig into finer detail if required.

Where to Get Help

Apart from reading this book to expand your knowledge, you can tap into Google itself for a number of self-help resources—in fact, it's the largest free resource of web analytics information available. However, with the huge adoption of Google Analytics (millions of accounts), there are also numerous self-help groups, forums, enthusiasts, and a global network of official Google Analytics Authorized Consultants.

Resources Provided by Google (Free)

- Google Analytics Help—an online searchable manual and reference guide: http://www.google.com/support/googleanalytics.

- Google Conversion University—structured learning enabling you to become qualified in Google Analytics. The Google Analytics Individual Qualification (IQ) is proof of implementation proficiency. A step-by-step curriculum is provided via YouTube video walk-throughs to help you prepare for the test: `http://www.conversionuniversity.com`.

- YouTube official Google Analytics channel—clear and concise video walk-throughs of features and real-world usage: `http://www.youtube.com/user/googleanalytics`.

- Official Google Analytics blog—news blog of the latest product announcements, what's new, events, Conversion University, Help Center, and more: `http://analytics.blogspot.com`.

Non-Google Resources (Free)

- Measuring Success—the official blog and companion site for this book: `http://www.advanced-web-metrics.com`.

- Google Analytics Help Forum—a threaded message-board system. Members are any Google Analytics users (and potential new users). Google Authorized Analytics consultants regularly participate as well the occasional Google support staff: `http://groups.google.com/group/analytics-help`.

- Numerous other helpful blogs and forums are listed in Appendix A.

Official Google Analytics Authorized Consultants (Paid)

The Google business model gives you a free product with the option to purchase a tailored professional services package directly from an authorized consultant in your region. If you are investing in web analytics yet cannot afford full-time resources in-house, a global network of third-party Google Analytics Authorized Consultants (GAAC) is available.

GAAC partners are independent of Google, are often experts with multiple vendor tools, have a proven track record in their field, and provide paid-for professional services such as strategic planning, custom installation, onsite or remote training, data analysis, and consultation. The full list of GAACs can be found at `http://www.google.com/analytics/support_partner_provided.html`.

Summary

In Chapter 1, you have learned the following:

The opportunities and benefits web analytics can bring your organization These include growing your business, improving efficiency, and reducing costs.

The kinds of information you can obtain from analyzing traffic on your site This includes visitor volumes, top referrers, time on site and depth on site to conversion rates, page stickiness, visitor latency, frequency, revenue, and geographic distribution, to name a few.

The kinds of decisions that web analytics can help you with For example, web analytics can help you determine whether blog visitors have a positive impact on your website's reach and conversions, which visitor acquisition channels work best and to what extent these should be increased or decreased, whether site search is worth the investment, or whether overseas visitors would be better served with more localized content.

The ROI of web analytics Knowing how much time and effort to invest in web analytics, without losing site of your objectives, will keep you focused on improving your organization's bottom line.

How web analytics helps you understand your web traffic By focusing metrics on goal-driven web design, you concentrate not only your own efforts but also those of your visitors on clear calls to action. This simplifies the process of forming a hypothesis from observed visitor patterns.

Where web analytics fits in Integrating web analytics into your entire organization helps keep everyone on the same page when it comes to measuring performance.

Where to get help The growth of web analytics adoption over recent years has led to a plethora of resources to turn to, should you wish to explore beyond this book.

Available Methodologies and Their Accuracy

Web analytics can be incredibly powerful and insightful—an astonishing amount of information is available when compared to any other forms of traditional marketing. The danger, however, is taking web analytics reports at face value, and this raises the issue of accuracy.

The key to successfully utilizing the volume of information collected is to get comfortable with your data—what it can tell you, what it can't, and the limitations therein. This requires an understanding of the data-collection methodologies. Essentially, there are two common techniques: page tags and server logfiles. Google Analytics is a page tag technique.

2

In Chapter 2, you will learn:

How web visitor data is collected

The relative advantages of page tags and logfiles

The role of cookies in web analytics

The accuracy limitations of web traffic information

How to think about web analytics in relation to user privacy concerns

Page Tags and Logfiles

Page tags collect data via the visitor's web browser and send information to remote data-collection servers. The analytics customer views reports from the remote server (see Figure 2.1). This information is usually captured by JavaScript code (known as *tags* or *beacons*) placed on each page of your site. Some vendors also add multiple custom tags to collect additional data. This technique is known as *client-side data collection* and is used mostly by outsourced, Software as a Service (SaaS) vendor solutions.

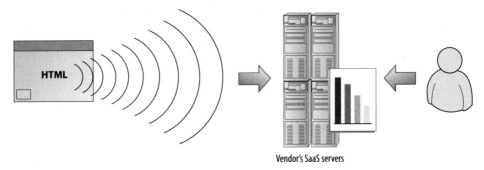

Vendor's SaaS servers

Figure 2.1 Schematic page tag methodology: Page tags broadcast information to remote data-collection servers, thus enabling the analytics customer to view reports.

 Note: Google Analytics is a SaaS page tag service.

Logfiles refer to data collected by your web server independently of a visitor's browser: The web server logs its activity to a text file that is usually local. The analytics customer views reports from the local server, as shown in Figure 2.2. This technique, known as *server-side data collection*, captures all requests made to your web server, including pages, images, and PDFs, and is most frequently used by stand-alone licensed software vendors.

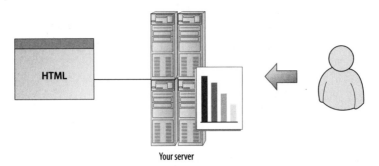

Your server

Figure 2.2 Schematic logfile methodology: The web server logs its activity to a text file locally, thereby enabling the analytics customer to view the reports on the local server.

In the past, the easy availability of web server logfiles made this technique the one most frequently adopted for understanding the behavior of visitors to your site. In fact, most Internet service providers (ISPs) supply a freeware log analyzer with their web-hosting accounts (Analog, Webalizer, and AWStats are some examples). Although this is probably the most common way people first come in contact with web analytics, such freeware tools are too basic when it comes to measuring visitor behavior and are not considered further in this book.

In recent years, page tags have become more popular as the method for collecting visitor data. Not only is the implementation of page tags easier from a technical point of view, but data-management requirements are significantly reduced because the data is collected and processed by external SaaS servers (your vendor), saving website owners the expense and maintenance of running licensed software to capture, store, and archive information.

Note that both techniques, when considered in isolation, have their limitations. Table 2.1 summarizes the differences. A common myth is that page tags are technically superior to other methods, but as Table 2.1 shows, that depends on what you are looking at. By combining both techniques, however, the advantages of one counter the disadvantages of the other. This is known as a *hybrid* method and some vendors can provide this.

Note: Google Analytics can be configured as a hybrid data collector—see "Backup: Keeping a Local Copy of Your Data," in Chapter 6, "Getting Up and Running with Google Analytics."

Other Data-Collection Methods

Although logfile analysis and page tagging are by far the most widely used methods for collecting web visitor data, they are not the only methods. Network data-collection devices (packet sniffers) gather web traffic data from routers into black-box appliances. Another technique is to use a web server application programming interface (API) or loadable module (also known as a plug-in, though this is not strictly correct terminology). These are programs that extend the capabilities of the web server—for example, enhancing or extending the fields that are logged. Typically, the collected data is then streamed to a reporting server in real time.

Methodology	Advantages	Disadvantages
Page tags	• Breaks through proxy and caching servers—provides more accurate session tracking. • Tracks client-side events—e.g., JavaScript, Flash, Web 2.0 (Ajax). • Captures client-side e-commerce data—server-side access can be problematic. • Collects and processes visitor data in nearly real time. • Allows the vendor to perform program updates for you. • Allows the vendor to perform data storage and archiving for you.	• Setup errors lead to data loss—if you make a mistake with your tags, data is lost and you cannot go back and reanalyze. • Firewalls can mangle or restrict tags. • Cannot track bandwidth or completed downloads—tags are set when the page or file is requested, not when the download is complete. • Cannot track search engine spiders—robots ignore page tags.
Logfile analysis software	• Historical data can be reprocessed easily. • No firewall issues to worry about. • Can track bandwidth and completed downloads—and can differentiate between completed and partial downloads. • Tracks search engine spiders and robots by default. • Tracks legacy mobile visitors by default.	• Proxy and caching inaccuracies—if a page is cached, no record is logged on your web server. • No event tracking—e.g., no JavaScript, Flash, Web 2.0 tracking (Ajax). • Requires your own team to perform program updates. • Requires your own team to perform data storage and archiving. • Robots multiply visit counts.

As you can see, the advantages of one data-collection method cancel out the disadvantages of the other. However, freeware tools aside, the SaaS page tagging technique is by far the most widely adopted method because of its ease of implementation and low IT overhead/support cost.

Cookies in Web Analytics

Page tag solutions track visitors by using cookies. *Cookies* are small text messages that a web server transmits to a web browser so that it can keep track of the user's activity on a specific website. The visitor's browser stores the cookie information on the local hard drive as name–value pairs. *Persistent cookies* are those that are still available when the browser is closed and later reopened. Conversely, *session cookies* last only for the duration of a visitor's session (visit) to your site.

For web analytics, the main purpose of cookies is to identify users for later use—most often with an anonymous visitor ID. Among many things, cookies can be used to determine how many first-time or repeat visitors a site has received, how many times a visitor returns each period, and how much time passes between visits. Web analytics aside, web servers can also use cookie information to present personalized web pages. A returning customer might see a different page than the one a first-time visitor would view, such as a "welcome back" message to give them a more individual experience or an auto-login for a returning subscriber.

The following are some cookie facts:

- Cookies are small text files (no larger than 4 KB), stored locally, that are associated with visited website domains.

- Cookie information can be viewed by users of your computer, using Notepad or a text editor application.

- There are two types of cookies: first party and third party.

  - A first-party cookie is one created by the website domain. A visitor requests it directly by typing the URL into their browser or by following a link.

  - A third-party cookie is one that operates in the background and is usually associated with advertisements or embedded content that is delivered by a third-party domain not directly requested by the visitor.

- For first-party cookies, only the website domain setting the cookie information can retrieve the data. This is a security feature built into all web browsers.

- For third-party cookies, the website domain setting the cookie can also list other domains allowed to view this information. The user is not involved in the transfer of third-party cookie information.

- Cookies are not malicious and can't harm your computer. They can be deleted by the user at any time.

- A maximum of 50 cookies are allowed per domain for the latest versions of IE8 and Firefox 3. Other browsers may vary (Opera 9 currently has a limit of 30; Safari and Google Chrome have no limit on the number of cookies per domain).

Note: Google Analytics uses first-party anonymous cookies only.

Understanding Web Analytics Data Accuracy

When it comes to benchmarking the performance of your website, web analytics is critical. However, this information is accurate only if you avoid common errors associated with collecting the data—especially comparing numbers from different sources. Unfortunately, too many businesses take web analytics reports at face value. After all, it isn't difficult to get the numbers. The harsh truth is that web analytics data can never be 100 percent accurate, and even measuring the error bars can be difficult.

So what's the point?

Despite the pitfalls, error bars remain relatively constant on a weekly, or even a monthly, basis. Even comparing year-by-year behavior can be safe as long as there are no dramatic changes in technology or end-user behavior. As long as you use the same yardstick, visitor number trends will be accurate. For example, web analytics data may reveal patterns like the following:

- Thirty percent of site traffic came from search engines.

- Fifteen percent of site revenue was generated by product page *x.html*.

- We increased subscription conversions from our email campaigns by 20 percent last week.

- Bounce rate decreased 10 percent for our category pages during March.

With these types of metrics, marketers and webmasters can determine the direct impact of specific marketing campaigns. The level of detail is critical. For example, you can determine if an increase in pay-per-click advertising spending—for a set of key-words on a single search engine—increased the return on investment during that time period. As long as you can minimize inaccuracies, web analytics tools are effective for measuring visitor traffic to your online business.

Conflicting Data Points Are Common

A UK survey of 800 organizations revealed that almost two-thirds (63 percent) of respondents say they experience conflicting information from different sources of online measurement data ("Online Measurement and Strategy Report 2009," Econsultancy.com, June 2009).

Next, I'll discuss in detail why such inaccuracies arise, so you can put this information into perspective. The aim is for you to arrive at an acceptable level of accuracy with respect to your analytics data. Recall from Table 2.1 that there are two main methods for collecting web visitor data—logfiles and page tags—and both have limitations.

Issues Affecting Visitor Data Accuracy for Logfiles

Logfile tracking is usually set up by default on web servers. Perhaps because of this, system administrators rarely consider any further implications when it comes to tracking.

Dynamically Assigned IP Addresses

Generally, a logfile solution tracks visitor sessions by attributing all hits from the same IP address and web browser signature to one person. This becomes a problem when ISPs assign different IP addresses throughout the session. A U.S.-based com-Score study (`http://www.comscore.com/Press_Events/Presentations_Whitepapers/2007/Cookie_Deletion_Whitepaper`) showed that a typical home PC averages 10.5 different IP addresses per month. Those visits will be counted as 10 unique visitors by a logfile analyzer. This issue is becoming more severe, because most web users have identical web browser signatures (currently Internet Explorer). As a result, visitor numbers are often vastly overcounted. This limitation can be overcome with the use of cookies.

Client-Side Cached Pages

Client-side caching means a previously visited page is stored on a visitor's computer. In this case, visiting the same page again results in that page being served locally from the visitor's computer, and therefore the visit is not recorded at the web server.

Server-side caching can come from any web accelerator technology that caches a copy of a website and serves it from their servers to speed up delivery. This means that all subsequent site requests come from the cache and not from the site itself, leading to a loss in tracking. Today, most of the Web is in some way cached to improve performance. For example, see Wikipedia's cache description at `http://en.wikipedia.org/wiki/Cache`.

Counting Robots

Robots, also known as spiders or web crawlers, are most often used by search engines to fetch and index pages. However, other robots exist that check server performance— uptime, download speed, and so on—as well as those used for page scraping, including price comparison, e-mail harvesters, competitive research, and so on. These affect web analytics because a logfile solution will also show all data for robot activity on your website, even though robots are not real visitors.

When counting visitor numbers, robots can make up a significant proportion of your pageview traffic. Unfortunately, these are difficult to filter out completely because thousands of homegrown and unnamed robots exist. For this reason, a logfile analyzer solution is likely to overcount visitor numbers, and in most cases this can be dramatic.

Issues Affecting Visitor Data from Page Tags

Deploying a page tag on every single page is a process that can be automated in many cases. However, for larger sites 100 percent correct deployment is rarely achieved. Perhaps it is because the page tag is hidden to the human eye or there is so much other data available that those errors often go unnoticed for long periods. Having a full deployment is crucial to the accuracy and validity of data collected by this method.

Setup Errors Causing Missed Tags

The most frequent error by far observed for page tagging solutions comes from its setup. Unlike web servers, which are configured to log everything delivered by default, a page tag solution requires the webmaster to add the tracking code to each page. Even with an automated content management system, pages can and do get missed.

In fact, evidence from analysts at MAXAMINE (`http://www.maxamine.com`)— now part of Accenture Marketing Sciences—who used their automatic page auditing tool has shown that some sites claiming that all pages are tagged can actually have as many as 20 percent of pages missing the page tag—something the webmaster was completely unaware of. In one case, a corporate business-to-business site was found to have 70 percent of its pages missing tags. Missing tags equals no data for those pageviews.

JavaScript Errors Halting Page Loading

Page tags work well, provided that JavaScript is enabled on the visitor's browser. Fortunately, only about 1 to 3 percent of Internet users have disabled JavaScript on their browsers, as shown in Figure 2.3. However, the inconsistent use of JavaScript code on web pages can cause a bigger problem: Any errors in other JavaScript on the page will immediately halt the browser scripting engine at that point, so a page tag placed below it will not execute.

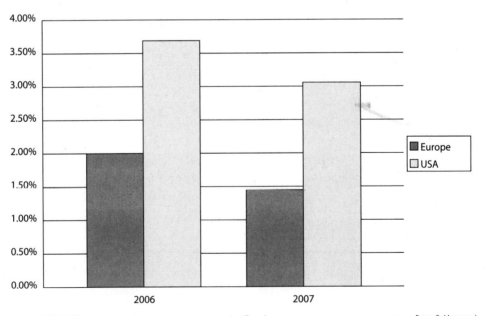

SOURCE: 1,000,000,000 VISITS ACROSS MULTIPLE INDUSTRY WEB PROPERTIES USING INDEXTOOLS (`http://www.visualrevenue.com/blog`—DENNIS R. MORTENSEN)

Figure 2.3 Percentage of Internet users with JavaScript-disabled browsers

Firewalls Blocking Page Tags

Corporate and personal firewalls can prevent page tag solutions from sending data to collecting servers. In addition, firewalls can also be set up to reject or delete cookies automatically. Once again, the effect on visitor data can be significant. Some web analytics vendors can revert to using the visitor's IP address for tracking in these instances, but mixing methods is not recommended. As discussed previously in "Issues Affecting Visitor Data Accuracy for Logfiles" (comScore report), using visitor IP addresses is far less accurate than simply not counting such visitors. It is therefore better to be consistent with the processing of data.

Page Tag Implementation Study

The following data is from over 10,000 websites whose page tags were validated. The page tags checked are from a variety of web analytics vendors. (Thanks to Stephen Kirby of MAXAMINE for this information.)

Summary

The more frequently a website's content changes, the more prone the site is to missing page tags. In the following image, website content was updated on January 14; by mistake, the updated pages did not include page tags.

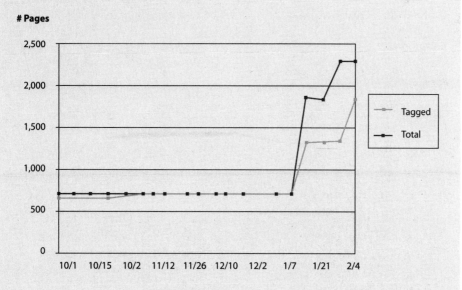

Continues

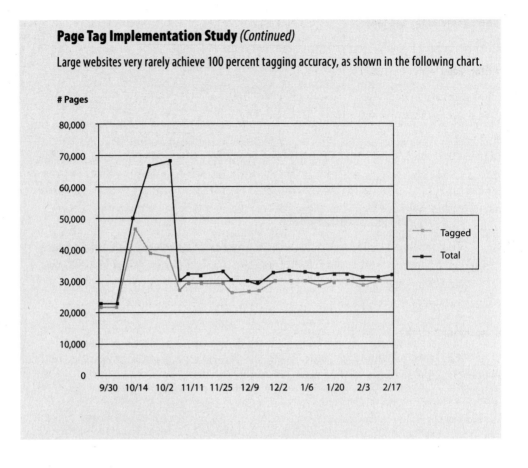

Page Tag Implementation Study *(Continued)*

Large websites very rarely achieve 100 percent tagging accuracy, as shown in the following chart.

Tracking Legacy Mobile Visitors

A mobile web audience study by comScore back in January 2007 (http://www.comscore.com/press/release.asp?press=1432) showed that in the United States, 30 million (or 19 percent) of the 159 million U.S. Internet users accessed the Internet from a mobile device. At that time, the vast majority of mobile phones did not understand JavaScript or cookies, and hence only logfile tools were able to track visitors who browsed using their mobile phones.

However, thanks mainly to the phenomenal success of the iPhone, mobile visitors on your website can now be tracked with page tag web analytics, because the browser software is very similar to that found on regular laptops and PCs, that is, where both JavaScript and cookies are used. Tracking mobile visitors is detailed in Chapter 8, "Best-Practices Configuration Guide."

Issues Affecting Visitor Data When Using Cookies

Cookies are a very simple, well-established way of tracking visitors. However, their simplicity and transparency (any user can remove them) presents issues in themselves.

The debate of using cookies or not remains a hot topic of conversation in web analytics circles.

Visitors Rejecting or Deleting Cookies

Cookie information is vital for web analytics because it identifies visitors, their referring source, and subsequent pageview data. The current best practice is for vendors to process first-party cookies only. This is because visitors often view third-party cookies as infringing on their privacy, opaquely transferring their information to third parties without explicit consent. Therefore, many antispyware programs and firewalls exist to block third-party cookies automatically. It is also easy to do this within the browser itself. By contrast, anecdotal evidence shows that first-party cookies are accepted by more than 95 percent of visitors.

Visitors are also becoming savvier and often delete cookies. Independent surveys conducted by Belden Associates (2004), JupiterResearch (2005), Nielsen//NetRatings (2005) and comScore (2007) concluded that cookies are deleted by at least 30 percent of Internet users in a month.

Users Owning and Sharing Multiple Computers

User behavior has a dramatic effect on the accuracy of information gathered through cookies. Consider the following scenarios:

Same user, multiple computers Today, people access the Internet in any number of ways—from work, home, mobile, or public places such as Internet cafes. One person working from three different machines still results in three cookie settings, and all current web analytics solutions will count each of these user sessions as unique.

Different users, same computer People share their computers all the time, particularly with their families, which means that cookies are shared too (unless you log off or switch off your computer each time it is used by a different person). In some instances, cookies are deleted deliberately. For example, Internet cafes are set up to do this automatically at the end of each session, so even if a visitor uses that cafe regularly and works from the same machine, the web analytics solution will consider that visitor a different and new visitor every time.

Correcting Data for Cookie Deletion and Rejection

Calculating a correction factor to account for your visitors either deleting or rejecting your web analytics cookies is quite straightforward. All you need is a website that requires a user login. That way you can count the number of unique login IDs and divide it by the number of unique users your web analytics tool reports. The result is a correction factor that can be applied to subsequent data (number of unique visitors, number of new visitors, or number of returning visitors).

Continues

Having a website that requires a user login is, thankfully in my view, quite rare, because people wish to access information freely and as easily as possible. So, although the correction-factor calculation is straightforward, you most probably don't have any login data to process. Fortunately, a small number of websites can calculate a correction factor to shed light on this issue. These include online banks and popular brands such as Amazon, FedEx, and social network sites, where there is a real user benefit to both having an account and (most importantly) using it when visiting the site.

A specific example is Sun Microsystems Forums (`http://forums.sun.com`), a global community of developers with nearly 1 million contributors. A 2009 study by Paul Strupp and Garrett Clark, published at `http://blogs.sun.com/pstrupp/`, reveals some interesting data.

When using third-party cookies:

- Seventy-eight percent is the correction factor for monthly unique users.
- Twenty percent of users delete (more correctly defined as *lose*) their measurement cookie at least once per month.
- Five percent of users block the third-party measurement cookie.

When using first-party cookies:

- The correction factor improves to 83 percent.
- Percentage of users who delete their measurement cookie at least once per month decreases to 14 percent.
- Percentage of users who block the first-party measurement cookie drops to less than 1 percent.

Note that this is a tech-savvy audience—those who can delete/block an individual cookie without a second thought.

An interesting observation from the study that Paul himself highlights is the relatively small value of the correction factor. That is, when using a first-party cookie, a more precise unique visitor count is 0.83 multiplied by the reported value. Putting this into context, as part of the analysis, 30 percent of users who used more than one computer in a month to visit the forum were removed from the data prior to analysis. This indicates that multiple-device access happens more frequently than cookie deletion.

It is tempting to think that this data can be used to correct your own unique visitor counts. However, the correction factor is a complicated function of cookie deletion, multiple computer use, and visitor return frequency. These factors will almost certainly be different for your specific website. Nonetheless, it is a useful rule-of-thumb guide.

Latency Leaving Room for Inaccuracy

The time it takes for a visitor to be converted into a customer (latency) can have a significant effect on accuracy. For example, most low-value items are either instant purchases or are purchased within seven days of the initial website visit. With such a short time period between visitor arrival and purchase, your web analytics solution has the best possible chance of capturing all the visitor pageview and behavior information and therefore reporting more accurate results.

Higher-value items usually mean a longer consideration time before the visitor commits to becoming a customer. For example, in the travel and finance industries, the consideration time between the initial visit and the purchase can be as long as 90 days. During this time, there's an increased risk of the user deleting cookies, reinstalling the browser, upgrading the operating system, buying a new computer, or dealing with a system crash. Any of these occurrences will result in users being seen as new visitors when they finally make their purchase. Offsite factors such as seasonality, adverse publicity, offline promotions, or published blog articles or comments can also affect latency.

Offline Visits Skewing Data Collection

It is important to factor in problems that are unrelated to the method used to measure visitor behavior but that still pose a threat to data accuracy. High-value purchases such as cars, loans, and mortgages are often first researched online and then purchased offline. Connecting offline purchases with online visitor behavior is a long-standing enigma for web analytics tools. Currently, the best-practice way to overcome this limitation is to use online voucher schemes that visitors can print and take with them to claim a free gift, upgrade, or discount at your store. If you would prefer to receive your orders online, consider providing similar incentives, such as web-only pricing, free delivery if ordered online, and the like.

Another issue to consider is how your offline marketing is tracked. Without taking this into account, visitors who result from your offline campaign efforts will be incorrectly assigned or grouped with other referral sources and therefore skew your data. How to measure offline marketing is discussed in detail in Chapter 11, "Real-World Tasks."

Comparing Data from Different Vendors

As shown earlier, it is virtually impossible to compare the results of one data-collection method with another. The association simply isn't valid. However, given two comparable data-collection methods—both page tags—can you achieve consistency? Unfortunately, even comparing vendors that employ page tags has its difficulties.

Factors that lead to differing vendor metrics are described in the following sections.

First-Party versus Third-Party Cookies

There is little correlation between the two because of the higher blocking rates of third-party cookies by users, firewalls, and antispyware software. For example, the latest versions of Microsoft Internet Explorer block third-party cookies by default if a site doesn't have a compact privacy policy (see http://www.w3.org/P3P).

Page Tags: Placement Considerations

Page-tag vendors often recommend that their page tags be placed just above the </body> tag of your HTML page to ensure that the page elements, such as text and images, load first. This means that any delays from the vendor's servers will not interfere with your page loading. The potential problem here is that repeat visitors, those more familiar with your website navigation, may navigate quickly, clicking onto another page before the page tag has loaded to collect data. Clearly, the longer the delay, the greater the discrepancy will be.

Tag placement was investigated in a 2009 whitepaper by TagMan.com. Their study of latency effects revealed that approximately 10 percent of reported traffic is lost for every extra second a page takes to load. In addition, moving the Google Analytics page tag from the bottom of a page to the top increased the reported traffic by 20 percent.

Stone Temple Consulting conducted a similar study in 2007. Their results showed that the difference between a tracking tag placed at the top or bottom of a page accounted for a 4.3 percent difference in unique visitor traffic. This was attributed to the 1.4 second difference in executing the page tag.

In addition, nonrelated JavaScript placed at the top of the page can interfere with JavaScript page tags that have been placed lower down. Most vendor page tags work independently of other JavaScript and can sit comfortably alongside other vendor page tags—as shown in the Stone Temple Consulting report in which pages were tagged for five different vendors. However, JavaScript errors on the same page will cause the browser scripting engine to stop at that point and prevent any JavaScript below it, including your page tag, from executing.

Did You Tag Everything?

Many analytics tools require links to files such as PDFs, Word documents, or executable downloads or outbound links to other websites to be modified in order to be tracked. This may be a manual process whereby the link to the file needs to be modified. The modification represents an event or action when it is clicked, which sometimes is referred to as a *virtual pageview*. Comparing different vendors requires this action to be carried out several times with their specific codes (usually with JavaScript). Take into consideration that whenever pages have to be coded, syntax errors are a possibility. If page updates occur frequently, consider regular website audits to validate your page tags.

Pageviews: A Visit or a Visitor?

Pageviews are quick and easy to track; and because they require only a call from the page to the tracking server, they are very similar among vendors. The challenge is differentiating a visit from a visitor; and because every vendor uses a different algorithm, no single algorithm results in the same value.

Cookie Timeouts

The allowed duration of timeouts—how long a web page is left inactive by a visitor—varies among vendors. Most page-tag vendors use a visitor-session cookie timeout of 30 minutes. This means that continuing to browse the same website after 30 minutes of inactivity is considered to be a new repeat visit. However, some vendors offer the option to change this setting. Doing so will alter any data alignment and therefore affect the analysis of reported visitors. Other cookies, such as the ones that store referrer details, will have different timeout values. For example, Google Analytics referrer cookies last six months. Differences in these timeouts between different web analytics vendors will obviously be reflected in the reported visitor numbers.

Page-Tag Code Hijacking

Depending on your vendor, your page tag code could be hijacked, copied, and executed on a different or unrelated website. This contamination results in a false pageview within your reports. By using filters, you can ensure that only data from your domains are reported.

Data Sampling

This is the practice of selecting a subset of data from your website traffic. Sampling is widely used in statistical analysis because analyzing a subset of data gives very similar results to analyzing all of the data, yet can provide significant speed benefits when processing large volumes of information. Different vendors may use different sampling techniques and criteria, resulting in data misalignment. Data sampling considerations for Google Analytics are discussed in "Understanding Data Sampling" in Chapter 5, "Reports Explained."

PDF Files: A Special Consideration

For page tag solutions, it is not the completed PDF download that is reported, but the fact that a visitor has clicked a PDF file link. This is an important distinction, because information on whether or not the visitor completes the download—for example a 50-page PDF file—is not available. Therefore, a click on a PDF link is reported as a single event or pageview.

Note: The situation is different for logfile solutions. When you view a PDF file within your web browser, Adobe Reader can download the file one page at a time, as opposed to a full download. This results in a slightly different entry in your web server logfile, showing an HTTP status code 206 (partial file download). Logfile solutions can treat each of the 206 status code entries as individual pageviews. When all the pages of a PDF file are downloaded, a completed download is registered in your logfile with a final HTTP status code of 200 (download completed). Therefore, a logfile solution can report a completed 50-page PDF file as 1 download and 50 pageviews.

E-commerce: Negative Transactions

All e-commerce organizations have to deal with product returns at some point, whether because of damaged or faulty goods, order mistakes, or other reasons. Accounting for these returns is often forgotten within web analytics reports. For some vendors, it requires the manual entry of an equivalent negative purchase transaction. Others require the reprocessing of e-commerce data files. Whichever method is required, aligning web visitor data with internal systems is never bulletproof. For example, the removal or crediting of a transaction usually takes place well after the original purchase and therefore in a different reporting period.

Filters and Settings: Potential Obstacles

Data can vary when a filter is set up in one vendor's solution but not in another. Some tools can't set up the exact same filter as another tool, or they apply filters in a different way or at a different point during data processing.

Consider, for example, a page-level filter to exclude all error pages from your reports. Visit metrics such as time on site and page depth may or may not be adjusted for the filter depending on the vendor. This is because some vendors treat page-level metrics separately from visitor-level metrics.

Time Differences

A predicament for any vendor when it comes to calculating the time on site or time on page for a visitor's session involves how to calculate for the last page viewed. For example, time spent on pageA is calculated by taking the difference between the visitor's timestamp for pageA and the subsequent timestamp for pageB, and so on. But what if there is no pageC; how can the time on page be calculated for pageB if there is no following timestamp?

Different vendors handle this in different ways. Some ignore the final pageview in the calculation; others use an onUnload event to add a timestamp should the visitor close their browser or go to a different website. Both are valid methods, although not every vendor uses the onUnload method. The reason some vendors prefer to ignore the last page is that it is considered the most inaccurate from a time point of view— perhaps the visitor was interrupted to run an errand or left their browser in its current state while working on something else. Many users behave in this way; that is, they complete their browsing task and simply leave their browser open on the last page while working in another application. A small number of pageviews of this type will disproportionately skew the time-on-site and time-on-page calculations; hence, most vendors avoid this issue.

> **Note:** Google Analytics ignores the last pageview of a visitor's session when calculating the time-on-site and time-on-page metrics.

Process Frequency

The frequency of processing is best illustrated by example: Google Analytics does its number crunching to produce reports hourly. However, because it takes time to collate all the logfiles from all of the data-collecting servers around the world, reports are three to four hours behind the current time. In most cases, it is usually a smooth process, but sometimes things go wrong. For example, if a logfile transfer is interrupted, then only a partial logfile is processed. Because of this, Google collects and reprocesses all data for a 24-hour period at the day's end. Other vendors may do the same, so it is important not to focus on discrepancies that arise on the current day.

> **Note:** This is the same reason why you should not panic if you note "missing" data from your reports—for example, no data showing for the period 10 a.m. to 11 a.m. This information should be picked up during the data reprocessing that takes place at the end of the day. If you have waited more than 24 hours and the data is still missing, contact the Google Analytics support team at `http://www.google.com/support/googleanalytics/bin/request.py`.

Goal Conversion versus Pageviews: Establishing Consistency

Using Figure 2.4 as an example, assume that five pages are part of your defined funnel (click-stream path), with the last step (page 5) being the goal conversion (purchase). During checkout, a visitor goes back up a page to check a delivery charge (step A) and then continues through to complete payment. The visitor is so happy with the simplicity of the entire process that she then purchases a second item using exactly the same path during the same visitor session (step B).

Depending on the vendor you use, this process can be counted in various ways, as follows:

- Twelve funnel page views, two conversions, two transactions
- Ten funnel page views (ignoring step A), two conversions, two transactions
- Five funnel page views, two conversions, two transactions
- Five funnel page views, one conversion (ignoring step B), two transactions

Most vendors, but not all, apply the last rationale to their reports. That is, the visitor has become a purchaser (one conversion); and this can happen only once in the session, so additional conversions (assuming the same goal) are ignored. For this to be valid, the same rationale must be applied to the funnel pages. In this way, the data becomes more visitor-centric.

 Note: In the example of Figure 2.4, the total number of pageviews equals 12 and would be reported as such in all pageview reports. It is the funnel and goal-conversion reports that will be different.

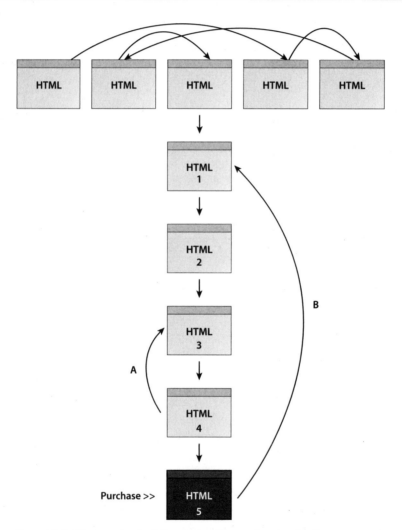

Figure 2.4 A visitor traversing a website, entering a five-page funnel, and making two transactions

Why PPC Vendor Numbers Do Not Match Web Analytics Reports

If you are using pay-per-click (PPC) networks, you will typically have access to the click-through reports provided by each network. Quite often, these numbers don't exactly align with those reported in your web analytics reports. This can happen for the reasons described in the following sections.

Tracking URLs Missing PPC Click-throughs

Tracking URLs are required in your PPC account setup in order to differentiate between a nonpaid search engine visitor click-through and a PPC click-through from the same referring domain—Google.com or Yahoo.com, for example. Tracking URLs are simple modifications to your landing page URLs within your PPC account and are of the form `http://www.mysite.com?source=adwords`. Tracking URLs forgotten during setup, or sometimes simply assigned incorrectly, can lead to such visits being incorrectly assigned to nonpaid visitors.

Slow Page Load Times

As previously discussed, the best practice location for web analytics data-collection tags is at the bottom of your pages—just above the </body> HTML tag. If your PPC landing pages are slow to download for whatever reason (server delays, page bloat, and so on), it is likely that visitors will click away, navigating to another page on your site or even to a different website, before the data-collection tag has had chance to load. The chance of this happening increases the longer the page load time is. The general rule of thumb for what constitutes a long page load is only two seconds (see `http://www.akamai.com/html/about/press/releases/2009/press_091409.html`).

Clicks and Visits: Understanding the Difference

Remember that PPC vendors, such as Google AdWords, measure clicks. Most web analytics tools measure visitors who can accept a cookie. Those are not always going to be the same thing when you consider the effects on your web analytics data of cookie blocking, JavaScript errors, and visitors who simply navigate away from your landing page quickly—before the page tag collects its data. Because of this, web analytics tools tend to slightly underreport visits from PPC networks.

PPC Account Adjustments

Google AdWords and other PPC vendors automatically monitor invalid and fraudulent clicks and adjust PPC metrics retroactively. For example, a visitor may click your ad several times (inadvertently or on purpose) within a short space of time. Google AdWords investigates this influx and removes the additional click-throughs and charges from your account. However, web analytics tools have no access to these systems and so record all PPC visitors. For further information on how Google treats invalid clicks, see `http://adwords.google.com/support/bin/topic.py?topic=35`.

Keyword Matching: Bid Term versus Search Term

The bid terms you select within your PPC account and the search terms used by visitors that result in your PPC ad being displayed can often be different: think "broad match." For example, you may have set up an ad group that targets the word *shoes* and solely relies on broad matching to match all search terms that contain the word *shoes*. This is your bid term. A visitor uses the search term *blue shoes* and clicks your ad. Web analytics vendors may report the search term, the bid term, or both.

Google AdWords Import Delay

Within your AdWords account, you will see data updated hourly. This is because advertisers want and need this data to control budgets. Google Analytics imports AdWords cost data once per day, and this is for the date range minus 48 to 24 hours from 23:59 of the previous day, so AdWords cost data is always at least 24 hours old.

Why the delay? Because it allows time for the AdWords invalid-click and fraud-protection algorithms to complete their work and finalize click-through numbers for your account. Therefore, from a reporting point of view, the recommendation is to not compare AdWords visitor numbers for the current day. This recommendation holds true for all web analytics solutions and all PPC advertising networks.

 Note: Although most of the AdWords invalid-click updates take place within 24 hours, they can take longer. For this reason, even if all other factors are eliminated, AdWords click-throughs within your PPC account and those reported in your web analytics reports may never match exactly.

Losing Tracking URLs through Third-Party Ad Tracking Redirects

Using third-party ad-tracking systems—such as Adform, Atlas Search, Blue Streak, DoubleClick, Efficient Frontier, and SEM Director—to track click-throughs to your website means your visitors are passed through redirection URLs. This results in the initial click being registered by your ad company, which then automatically redirects the visitor to your actual landing page. The purpose of this two-step hop is to allow the ad-tracking network to collect visitor statistics independently of your organization, typically for billing purposes. Because this process involves a short delay, it may prevent some visitors from landing on your page. The result can be a small loss of data and therefore failure to align data.

More important, and more common, redirection URLs may break the tracking parameters that are added onto the landing pages for your own web analytics solution. For example, your landing page URL may look like this:

```
http://www.mysite.com/?source=google&medium=ppc&campaign=Jan10
```

When added to a third-party tracking system for redirection, it could look like this:

```
http://www.redirect.com?http://www.mywebsite.com?source=google&medium=ppc↵
&campaign=Jan10
```

The problem occurs with the second question mark in the second link, because you can't have more than one in any valid URL. Some third-party ad-tracking systems will detect this error and remove the second question mark and the following tracking parameters, leading to a loss of campaign data.

Some third-party ad-tracking systems allow you to replace the second ? with a # so the URL can be processed correctly. If you are unsure of what to do, you can avoid the problem completely by using encoded landing-page URLs within your third-party ad-tracking system, as described at the following site:

```
http://www.w3schools.com/tags/ref_urlencode.asp
```

Note: From my experience, the most common reasons for discrepancies between PPC vendor reports and web analytics tools arise from the first, second, and last issues discussed in this section:

- Tracking URLs failing to distinguish paying and nonpaying visitors

- Slow page downloading

- Losing data via third-party ad-tracking redirects

Data Misinterpretation: Lies, Damn Lies, and Statistics

The following are not accuracy issues. However, the reference to Mark Twain in the title is simply to point out that data is not always so straightforward to interpret. Take the following two examples:

- New visitors plus repeat visitors does not equal total visitors.

  A common misconception is that the sum of new visitors plus repeat visitors should equal the total number of visitors. Why isn't this the case? Consider a visitor making his first visit on a given day and then returning on the same day. He is both a new and a repeat visitor for that day. Therefore, looking at a report for the given day, two visitor types will be shown, though the total number of visitors is one.

  It is therefore better to think of *visitors* in terms of *visit type*—that is, the number of first-time visits plus the number of repeat visits equals the total number of visits.

- Summing the number of unique visitors per day for a week does not equal the total number of unique visitors for that week.

  Consider the scenario in which you have 1,000 unique visitors to your website blog on a Monday. These are in fact the only unique visitors you receive for the entire week, so on Tuesday the same 1,000 visitors return to consume your next blog post. This pattern continues for Wednesday through Sunday.

If you were to look at the number of unique visitors for each day of the week in your reports, you would observe 1,000 unique visitors. However, you cannot say that you received 7,000 unique visitors for the entire week. For this example, the number of unique visitors for the week remains at 1,000.

Why Counting Uniques Is Meaningless

The term *uniques* is often used in web analytics as an abbreviation for unique web visitors, that is, how many unique people visited your site. The problem is that counting unique visitors is fraught with problems that are so fundamental, it renders the term *uniques* meaningless.

As discussed earlier in this chapter, cookies get lost, blocked, and deleted—nearly one-third of tracking cookies can be missing after a period of four weeks. The longer the time period, the greater the chance of this happening, which makes comparing year-on-year uniques invalid, for example. In addition, browsers make it very easy these days for cookies to be removed—see the new "incognito" features of the latest Firefox, Chrome, and Internet Explorer browsers.

However, the biggest issue for counting uniques is how many devices people use to access the Web. For example, consider the following scenario:

1. You and your spouse are considering your next vacation. Your spouse first checks out possible locations on your joint PC at home and saves a list of website links.

2. The next evening you use the same PC to review these links. Unable to decide that night, you email the list to your office, and the next day you continue your vacation checks during your lunch hour at work and also review these again on your mobile while commuting home on the train.

3. Day 3 of your search resumes at your friend's house, where you seek a second opinion. Finally, you go home and book online using your shared PC.

The above scenario is actually very common—particularly if the value of the purchase is significant, which implies a longer consideration period and the seeking of a second opinion from a spouse, friends, or work colleagues (the Sun Microsystems study discussed earlier in this chapter estimated the percentage of users using more than one computer in a month to visit the same website as 30 percent).

Simply put, there is not a web analytics solution in the world that can accurately track this scenario, that is, to tie the data together from multiple devices and where multiple people have been involved, nor is there likely to be one in the near future.

Combining these limitations leads to large error bars when it comes to tracking uniques. In fact, these errors are so large that the metric becomes meaningless and should be avoided where possible in favor of more accurate "visit" data. That said, if you must use unique visitors as a key metric, ensure the emphasis is on the trend, not the absolute number.

Improving the Accuracy of Web Analytics Data

Clearly, web analytics is not 100 percent accurate, and the number of possible inaccuracies can appear overwhelming at first. However, as the preceding sections demonstrated, you can get comfortable with your implementation and focus on measuring trends, rather than precise numbers. For example, web analytics can help you answer the following questions:

- Are visitor numbers increasing?
- By what rate are they increasing (or decreasing)?
- Have conversion rates gone up since beginning PPC advertising?
- How has the cart-abandon rate changed since the site redesign?

If the trend shows a 10.5 percent reduction, for example, this figure should be accurate, regardless of the web analytics tool that was used. These examples are all high-level metrics, though the same accuracy can also be maintained as you drill down and look at, for example, which specific referrals (search engines, affiliates, social networks), campaigns (paid search, email, banners), keywords, geographies, or devices (PC, Mac, mobile) are used.

When all the possibilities of inaccuracy that affect web analytics solutions are considered, it is apparent that it is ineffective to focus on absolute values or to merge numbers from different sources. If all web visitors were to have a login account in order to view your website, this issue could be overcome. In the real world, however, the vast majority of Internet users wish to remain anonymous, so this is not a viable solution.

As long as you use the same measurement for comparing data ranges, your results will be accurate. This is the universal truth of all web analytics.

Here are 10 recommendations for enhancing web analytics accuracy:

- Be sure to select a tool that uses first-party cookies for data collection.
- Don't confuse visitor identifiers. For example, if first-party cookies are deleted, do not resort to using IP address information. It is better simply to ignore that visitor.
- Remove or report separately all nonhuman activity from your data reports, such as robots and server-performance monitors.
- Track everything. Don't limit tracking to landing pages. Track your entire website's activity, including file downloads, internal search terms, and outbound links.
- Regularly audit your website for page tag completeness (at least monthly for large websites). Sometimes site content changes result in tags being corrupted, deleted, or simply forgotten.

- Display a clear and easy-to-read privacy policy (required by law in the European Union). This establishes trust with your visitors because they better understand how they're being tracked and are less likely to delete cookies.

- Avoid making judgments on data that is less than 24 hours old, because it's often the most inaccurate.

- Test redirection URLs to guarantee that they maintain tracking parameters.

- Ensure that all paid online campaigns use tracking URLs to differentiate from nonpaid sources.

- Use *visit* metrics in preference to *unique visitor* metrics because the latter are highly inaccurate.

These suggestions will help you appreciate the errors often made when collecting web analytics data. Understanding what these errors are, how they happen, and how to avoid them will enable you to benchmark the performance of your website. Achieving this means you're in a better position to then drive the performance of your online business.

Privacy Considerations for the Web Analytics Industry

With the huge proliferation of the Web, people are now more aware of privacy issues, concerns, and obligations. In my opinion, this is a step forward—the industry needs an informed debate about online privacy. So far, the discussion has been fairly basic, with people talking about online privacy as a single entity and using the example of the web analytics industry as proof of loss of privacy. For example, many people complain that tracking their visit to a website is an invasion of their privacy that they did not consent to. However, there are actually two privacy issues that web users and website owners should be aware of:

Non–Personally Identifiable Information (non-PII) This is anonymous aggregate data that cannot be used to identify or deduce demographic information. It is best illustrated by example. Suppose you wish to monitor vehicle traffic close to a school so that you can predict and improve the safety and efficiency of the surrounding road structure. You might stand on a street corner counting the number of vehicles, their type (car, van, truck, bus, and so on), time of day, and how long it takes for them to pass the school gates. This is an example of nonpersonal information—there is nothing in this aggregate data that identifies the individual driver or owner of each vehicle. Incidentally, you also cannot identify whether the same vehicle is repeatedly driving around the school in a circle.

As you can see, this is a great way to collect data to improve things for all people involved (school pupils, residents, shop owners, and drivers) without any interference of privacy. This example is directly analogous to using the Web. By far, the vast majority of Web users who are surveyed claim they are happy for their nonpersonal information to be collected and used to improve a website's effectiveness and ultimately their user experience.

Personally Identifiable Information (PII) Taking the previous non-PII example further, suppose the next day you started to collect vehicle license plate details, or stopped drivers to question them on their driving habits, or followed them home to determine whether they were local residents. These are all examples of collecting personal data—both asked-for data such as their name, age, and address, as well as non-volunteered information that can be discovered, such as gender and license plate details.

Collecting personally identifiable information clearly has huge privacy implications and is regulated by law in most democratic countries. Collecting data in this way would mean that all drivers would need to be explicitly informed that data collection was occurring and offered the choice of not driving down the street. They could then make an informed decision as to whether they wish to take part in the study or not. Again, this is analogous to using the Web—asking the visitor to opt in to sharing their personal information.

> **Note:** On the Internet, IP addresses are generally classed as Personally Identifiable Information.

The current issue with regard to privacy on the Web is that many users are confused as to what form of tracking, if any, is taking place when they visit a website. This is reflected in the fact that on large, high-traffic websites for which I have worked (1 million–50 million visitors per month), the number of pageviews for the privacy policy statement were consistently and considerably less than 0.01 percent of the total.

Even when viewing privacy statements, the public is cynical. Often, these statements tend to be written in a legal language that is difficult to understand, they change without notice, and they primarily appear to be there to protect the website owner rather than the privacy of the visitor.

Regardless of the public's confusion or apathy about website privacy, it is your responsibility as a website owner to inform visitors about what data-collection practices are occurring when a visitor views your website. In fact, within the European Union, law requires it. Chapter 3, "Google Analytics Features, Benefits, and Limitations," contains a best-practice example of a clear privacy statement when using Google Analytics.

Summary

In Chapter 2, "Available Methodologies and Their Accuracy," you have learned the following:

Page tags versus logfiles We discussed how web visitor data is collected, the relative advantages of page tags and logfile tools, as well as why page tagging has become the de facto standard.

The perils of cookies You learned about the role of cookies in web analytics, what they contain, and why they exist, including the differences between first-party and third-party cookies.

Difficulties of interpreting traffic data We explored the accuracy limitations of web traffic information in terms of collecting web visitor data, its interpretation, and comparing numbers from different vendors.

Visitors' privacy issues You learned how to think about web analytics in relation to end-user privacy concerns and your responsibilities as a website owner to respect your visitors' privacy.

Google Analytics Features, Benefits, and Limitations

Understanding how Google Analytics data collection works is a great way to recognize what you can achieve with web analytics reporting. Don't worry—this is not an engineering book, so technicalities are kept to a minimum. However, it is important to know what can and cannot be accomplished, because this knowledge will help you spot erroneous data that may show up in your reports.

As well as a discussion of the key features and capabilities of Google Analytics, included in this chapter is a description of Urchin Software—a separate web analytics tool from Google.

3

In Chapter 3, you will learn:

The key features and capabilities of Google Analytics

How Google Analytics works

What Google Analytics cannot do

The Google Analytics approach to user privacy

What Urchin software is

The differences between Google Analytics and Urchin Software

Key Features and Capabilities of Google Analytics

I started my career running my own business of web professionals, so I understand the analytic needs of a small company. Now, having worked at Google for a number of years, I am familiar with the other end of the spectrum—working with some of the largest organizations in the world. What still amazes me is just how similar both large and small companies are in their analytics requirements—from understanding what is happening on their website and how to interpret the data to what action to take to improve matters, small and large organizations face the same challenges.

Both types of users express an understanding of the need for measurement, yet they also fear data overload when combined with other aspects of the business and their job. Both also expect the collection and reporting of data to be at the smaller end of their investment budget, with professional services the key to unlocking their online business potential.

This feature list is not intended to be exhaustive, though it does highlight the more important ones you can find in Google Analytics. I group these into two categories, standard and advanced features. Screenshots of most of these features in use are shown in the next two chapters.

Standard Features

I describe standard features as those that you would expect to find in any commercial-strength web analytics tool. The tool includes the "must have" basic metrics you need in order to get an initial understanding of your website performance. However, these are not basic reports. You can quickly extract rich detail with a couple of mouse clicks, for example, cross-referencing e-commerce revenue by referral source or search engine keyword.

Full Campaign Reporting—Not Just AdWords

Google Analytics enables you to track and compare all your visitors—from nonpaid organic search, paid ads (pay per click, banners), referrals, email newsletters, affiliate campaigns, links from within digital collateral such as PDF files, and any other search engine or medium that forwards a visitor to your website. You can even get a handle on your offline marketing campaigns—discussed in Chapter 11, "Real-World Tasks."

Advertising ROI—Integration with AdWords and AdSense

If you manage a pay-per-click campaign, you know what a chore tagging your landing page URLs can be—each one has to have at least one campaign variable appended to differentiate visitors who click through from nonpaid search results. In addition, you will want to import your AdWords cost and impression data. As you might expect, Google has simplified the integration process as much as possible, in fact to just two check boxes. As a result, all your AdWords landing page URLs are tagged, and cost data is imported automatically each day.

Similarly for publishers who display AdWords on their site, that is, use AdSense, the integration is straightforward. The result is reports showing you which content drives the most revenue alongside the import of AdSense page impressions and the number of AdSense ads clicked on.

E-commerce Reporting

You can trace transactions to campaigns and keywords, get loyalty and latency metrics, and identify your revenue sources. Similarly, you can drill down to this information on a per-product or per-category basis.

Goal Conversions (Key Performance Indicators)

A *goal conversion* is a key pageview that brings you closer to your otherwise anonymous visitors. Think of these as your more valuable pageviews. An obvious goal conversion is an e-commerce purchase-confirmation page. However, other nontransactional goals exist, for example, completing a registration or feedback form, downloading a file, watching a movie (how-to guides, product demonstrations), commenting on blogs, submitting surveys, or clicking an outbound link.

In addition to defining pageviews as goal conversions, you can also set thresholds. For example, time on site greater than 30 seconds or pages per visit greater than 2.5. In total, you can define up to 20 separate goals, which can be grouped into four categories (termed *goal types*).

Funnel Visualization

Funnels are set paths visitors take before achieving a goal conversion. An obvious funnel is an e-commerce checkout process. However, just as for goal conversions, other nontransactional funnels exist—for example, a multiform subscription process where each completed form is a funnel step. It is also possible to define funnel steps as the completion of individual form fields, such as name or product selection, so that partial form completion can be visualized.

By visualizing the visitor path (the funnel), you can discover which pages result in lost conversions and where your would-be customers go. Each funnel can contain up to 10 steps.

Customized Dashboards

The *dashboard* is the first section you see when viewing your reports. The dashboard is a selection of abridged reports from the main sections of Google Analytics. Here you place and organize your key data selections for an at-a-glance comparison. Up to 12 reports can be added, changed, and reordered within the dashboard at any time. Dashboards are on a per-user basis; that is, different user logins have different dashboards.

Site Overlay Report

Site overlay is a graphical way of looking at the popularity of links on your pages. You view your key metrics overlaid on your web page links. It's an easy-to-view snapshot of which links are working for you.

Map Overlay Reports

Similar to site overlay, *map overlay* is a graphical way of presenting data that reflects where visitors are connecting from around the world when viewing your website. Based on IP address location databases, they show your key metrics overlaid on a world, regional, or country map, depending on your zoom level. This provides a clear representation of which parts of the world visitors are connecting from, down to city level. In my view, this report sets the industry standard for visualizing where visitors come from to your site.

Geo-IP information has improved dramatically in recent years—mainly driven by the security industry, that is, improvements in online credit card fraud detection. The database used in Google Analytics is the same as that used for geotargeting ads in your AdWords campaigns. Data can be as accurate as a 25-mile (40-km) radius. However, sometimes location details are not available, and this is reported as "(not set)" in your reports.

Map Overlay Accuracy

MaxMind is one company that provides geo-IP database information to third parties such as banks and web analytics vendors, though not Google Analytics. The MaxMind accuracy table presented at www.maxmind.com/app/city_accuracy is typical for this industry. As an example, for the U.S., their databases are 99.8 percent accurate on a country level, 90 percent accurate on a state level, and 83 percent accurate at city level within a 25-mile (40-km) radius.

Cross Segmenting Drill-Down

Cross segmenting is the terminology used for cross-referencing, or correlating, one set of data against another. An example of cross segmentation might be displaying the geolocation report for California and then cross segmenting to display which search engines these visitors are coming from. As another example, suppose you want to determine, for U.K. visitors, the most frequently used keywords to find your site. That would be a cross-reference of U.K. visitors against keywords. Similarly, for new visitors, what landing pages they arrived at—a cross-reference of visitor type against landing page.

There are many other examples, and cross segmentation is available within nearly every Google Analytics report. It's a powerful feature that allows you to drill into table data to isolate particular visit types.

Data Export and Scheduling

Report data can be manually exported in a variety of formats, including CSV (best for Excel), TSV, PDF (best for printing), or the open-source XML (best for importing into another system). You can also schedule any report to be emailed to you and your colleagues automatically, for up to 10 email addresses. For example, you may want to email your e-commerce manager the list of top-selling products each week, your marketing manager the list of campaign performance, or your web designer the list of error pages generated.

The key to remember with exporting is What-You-See-Is-What-You-Get (WYSIWYG). That means by default Google Analytics displays 10 rows of data, and so an export of a default report view will be for those 10 rows. If you want a greater sample size, you must expand the report view to, say, 100 rows and then export. Similarly, you can cross segment and drill into report data and then export that specific view.

Tip: If you have more than 10 people who would like an email copy of a report, you can create a mailing list on your server, for example, marketing@mysite.com, and use this for your Google Analytics export list. That way you can independently manage your mailing list members.

Date Range Slider

A problem all web analysts face when attempting to establish overall website performance, that is, not viewing a specific campaign, is what date range to consider. Unless you regimentally log in to Google Analytics at the same frequency, it is possible to miss important peaks and troughs in your data, simply because they are just beyond the boundaries of the date window you are looking at. The default date window in Google Analytics is the last 30 days, but what if something really important happened 31 days ago that you are not yet aware of?

Google's approach to this is to use its timeline window. In addition to showing side-by-side date range comparisons within the same browser window, the timeline window allows you to select date ranges while also viewing the trends beyond the boundaries. For example, you can select a date range that shows a visitor spike you were previously unaware of. It's a difficult feature to describe, and so it is illustrated in Chapter 4, "Using the Google Analytics Interface."

Site Search Reporting

For complex websites (those with a large number of pages), internal site search is an important part of the site-navigation system and in many cases is critical for providing a positive user experience. A dedicated report section enables you to assess the value of your internal site search engine, comparing it with those visitors who do not search. In addition, you can discover which pages result in visitors performing a search, the search phrases used, post-search destination pages, and the conversion goals or products purchased as a result of a search.

Multiple Language Interfaces and Support

Google Analytics currently can display reports in 25 languages, and this number is continually growing. Languages include Czech, Chinese, Danish, Dutch, English (US), English (UK), Filipino, Finnish, French, German, Hungarian, Italian, Indonesian, Japanese, Korean, Malaysian, Norwegian, Polish, Portuguese (Brazil), Portuguese (Portugal), Russian, Spanish, Swedish, Taiwanese, and Turkish.

In addition to the display of reports in multiple languages, all documentation is internationalized and each language is directly supported by Google staff.

High Scalability

The Google Analytics target audience can be compared to that of online advertising—just about everyone with a website. Only five years ago, the number of clients using a professional web analytics tool could be counted in the tens of thousands. Now, following the launch of Google Analytics as a free service, the number of accounts is measured in the millions (free is obviously a strong incentive!). And it's a broad spectrum of organizations. Clients range from those with a few pageviews per day to some of the best-known brands and most highly trafficked sites on the Web—that is, sites receiving more than 1 billion pageviews per day.

Multiline Graphing

Being able to plot multiple data points on the same graph allows for faster analysis. For example, you can show the number of visitors to your site alongside the average time on site, bounce rate, or percentage of new visitors.

Administrator and Individual Access Controls

There are two levels of access to Google Analytics reports—administrators and report viewers. Administrators have access to all account functionality, including all data reports, creating profiles, defining filters, funnel steps, and conversion goals. They are also the gatekeepers for creating other user access. A Google Analytics report viewer has access to report data only, though each user can customize their user interface, such as their dashboard, advanced filters, custom reports, and chart annotations.

There are no limits on the number of administrators or report viewers who can be set up with access.

Market Share of Google Analytics

Measuring market share of web analytics tools turns out to be quite straightforward. Page-tag tools, the ones used by the vast majority of commercial websites (estimated at over 90 percent by this author), leave their telltale "marks" on a website—either in the form of JavaScript text that can be read by viewing a page's HTML source code or as cookie name-value pairs that vendor tools set. Both of these can be detected by viewing a page in your browser (see Appendix B). Of course, there is also good old-fashioned survey data.

A 2009 study by Forrester Research Inc. of 210,810 websites, using the cookie-detection method, showed that of those sites that had a visible web analytics tool in place, that is, one that sets a recognizable cookie name, Google Analytics has a 70 percent market share (*US Web Analytics Forecast, 2008 To 2014*, Forrester Research Inc., May 2009).

In a separate study using cookie detection, 27 percent of global corporate websites (organizations sampled from the Financial Times Global 500 Index) used Google Analytics as their web analytics tool (Search & Analytics Adoption study of Global Corporates, Advanced-Web-Metrics.com, 2010).

A UK survey of 800 organizations revealed that 80 percent of companies are now using Google for analytics compared to 66 percent in 2008 ("Online Measurement and Strategy Report 2009," Econsultancy.com, June 2009).

The Internet Retailer 500 are the top 500 U.S. retailing sites as shown at www.internetretailer.com/top500/list.asp. A page scan (using cookie detection) revealed that 37 percent of the websites were using Google Analytics (http://blog.vkistudios.com, February 2008).

"Google Analytics has been deployed in some form by around 60% of the companies in the Fortune 1000" (Eric Peterson, "Measurement, Analytics and Optimisation Briefing," eConsultancy.com, March 2008).

You can find an updated snapshot of major brands using Google Analytics at www.advanced-web-metrics.com/who-uses-google-analytics.

Advanced Features

I describe advanced features as those that are unique to Google or are for advanced users wishing for greater metrics insight, for example, intelligent alert system, Flash (event) tracking, animated motion charts, and pivot views. In some cases when viewing your reports, you may see these labeled as beta features. As you may be aware, Google has a history of running long beta test programs!

Advanced Segmentation and Advanced Table Filtering

Advanced segmentation allows you to isolate and analyze subsets of visitor traffic side by side with other segments. For example, you can view "Paid Traffic" visits alongside "Visits with Conversions" or view "Visits lasting longer than 1 minute" next to "Visits between 10-60 seconds." There are predefined segments as well as a custom segment builder. Custom segments are built on a per-user basis and can be shared with other users—both within your organization and external if you wish.

Closely related to advanced segmentation is *advanced table filtering*. While you're within a specific report, advanced filtering enables you to isolate specific table row data.

Secondary Cross-Segmenting Drill Down

This is an extension to the cross-segmenting drill-down feature mentioned previously. The difference with a secondary cross-segmenting drill down is that the data appears side by side in the *same* table. For example, cross segmenting "landing page URL" against "source" results in a data table that lists each landing page URL alongside each of its referrers.

Motion Charts

"Data in five dimensions" is this feature's headline. Motion Charts add sophisticated multidimensional analysis to most Google Analytics reports. You can select metrics for the x-axis, y-axis, bubble size, and bubble color and view how these metrics interact over time.

Motion charts are animated statistics to aid with data visualization (the result of a Google acquisition for Trendalyzer software in 2007). It's one of the first charts I look at to gain a big-picture overview of site performance prior to focusing on specific metrics. It allows you to expose data relationships that would be difficult to see in tra-ditional "static" reports.

API and Developer Platform

The Google Analytics application programming interface (API) allows programmers to extend Google Analytics in new and creative ways. Developers can integrate Google Analytics data into existing products or create standalone applications that can be built on (with no Google contact required). For example, users could see snapshots of their analytics data in developer-created dashboards and gadgets; have automatically updated Key Performance Indicators (KPIs) in Excel, PowerPoint, or Word documents; and view web visitor data integrated within CRM and CMS platforms.

Analytics Intelligence

Analytics Intelligence provides automatic alerts for significant changes in data patterns from your website. Instead of you having to monitor reports and comb through data, Analytics Intelligence alerts you to the most significant information to pay attention to. In addition, you can also create custom alerts and have an email sent to you when this is triggered. For example, Intelligence can automatically highlight a 200 percent surge in visits from Twitter last Monday or let you know bounce rates of visitors from the U.S. dropped by 70 percent yesterday.

Mobile Reporting

Google Analytics can track mobile websites and mobile applications on all web-enabled devices—whether or not the device runs JavaScript. This is possible by using a server-side code snippet on your mobile website. Google Analytics currently supports PHP, Perl, JSP and ASPX sites. This is separate from tracking visits to your regular website from Smartphone devices (JavaScript and cookie-enabled phones).

Pivot Views

If you are familiar with Excel, then pivot views (also known as pivot tables) will be familiar to you. Pivot views are powerful when it can be difficult to get summarized information from a flat table. Essentially, a pivot table helps you quickly gain insight, giving a table depth. Two pivot fields are available in Google Analytics reports.

Custom Reports

As the name suggests, custom reports allow you to create, save, and edit reports that present the information you want to see, organized in the way you want to see it. A drag-and-drop interface lets you select the metrics you want and define multiple levels of subreports. Custom reports are built on a per-user basis and can be shared with other users—both within your organization and externally, if you wish.

Benchmarking Reports

By anonymously sharing your website visitor data with Google, you gain access to valuable benchmarking data. Benchmarking is a service from Google that lets you see how your website's statistics compare against aggregated industry verticals, that is, other Google Analytics users. It allows you to put your key metrics into a broader context.

Each user can select the comparison benchmark category, and Google compares that data with sites of a similar size. It's important to note that your site's identity and visitor data are always anonymous and reported in aggregate form within the benchmarking reports. You can opt in or out of the service at any time, though past data is not removed should you later opt out.

Event Tracking

Events are defined as in-page actions that do not generate a pageview. For example, if your website incorporates Flash elements, widgets, Ajax, or embedded video, you will want to see how users interact with these separately from your pageview reports, such as clicks on Play, Pause, Select, or Watch To Completion. Any Flash element, Ajax content, file download, and even load times can be reported on in this way. The Event Tracking section is a dedicated collection of reports that show your events displayed separately from pageviews. Events can be grouped into categories and even monetized.

Did You Know...?

You should be aware of a number of broader points when using Google Analytics that are sometimes lost when reviewing the plethora of features:

The ability to distinguish visitors from any source You can track any search engine, any pay-per-click advertising network (such as AdWords, Yahoo Search Marketing, Microsoft adCenter, or Miva), email campaigns, banner ads, and affiliates and attribute them to the correct source.

More than just pageview tracking In addition to tracking standard pageviews, Google Analytics can track error pages, file downloads, clicks on mail-to links, partial form completion, outbound links, error pages, Flash, and Ajax interactions (event tracking). See Chapter 7, "Advanced Implementation," for further details.

More readable reports (virtual pageviews) Unreadable dynamic URLs can be converted into human-readable form. For example

    www.mysite.com/home/product?rid=191045&scid=184282

can be converted to

    www.mysite.com/products/menswear/shirts/white button down

These are known as virtual pageviews. See Chapter 7 for further details.

Data retention for 25 months (or longer) Google has committed to retaining your data for at least 25 months, so you can go back and perform year-by-year comparisons. Note that Google has made no attempt to remove older data; see Figure 3.1.

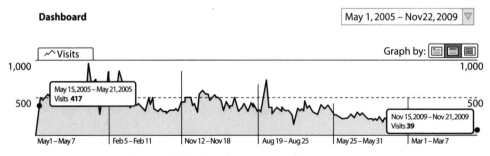

Figure 3.1 Example Google Analytics data held for four-plus years

Conversion attribution In building a relationship with your organization, a visitor may use multiple referrers to your website before converting. In this way, all referrers are tracked within Google Analytics. However, for a conversion only the last referrer is attributed the credit.

For example, consider the following scenario: A visitor first views a banner ad on the Web and clicks through to your site. The visitor does not convert on that first visit but returns later that day after performing a keyword query on a search engine. Still not convinced that they are ready to purchase (or convert into a lead), the visitor leaves your website. Later in the week, a friend of the visitor recommends via email a review article published on a blog. Happy with the review, the same visitor clicks the link from the blog article directly to your website. On this third visit, a purchase is made. For this scenario, Google Analytics will show all three referrers and attribute the conversion to the blog website, and its URL will be listed in your reports.

However, there is one exception to this rule: when the last referrer is "direct." A direct visit means the visitor typed your website address directly into their browser or used a bookmark to arrive on your website. In that case, the penultimate referrer is given credit. For example, using the preceding scenario, if the purchaser bookmarks your website and then later returns to make a repeat purchase by selecting the bookmark, credit for that conversion will still be given to the referring blog. Modifying the attribution model is discussed in Chapter 9, "Google Analytics Hacks."

Note: The use of "direct" can be ambiguous when analyzing your referral data. Out of the box, Google Analytics will not track email campaigns, links within files (such as PDF, DOC, XLS, PPT etc.), RSS referrers, or even your email signature for you—you need to make changes to those in order to track them. If you don't do this, such visitors will be classified as "direct."

Multiple accounts and roll-up reporting You can track visitor data into multiple Google Analytics accounts, for example, tracking at a regional or country level as well as having an aggregate account for all visits. See Chapter 6, "Getting Up and Running with Google Analytics," for details.

Regular expressions You can use a regular expression (regex) to filter report data into visitor segments. Maximum regex length is 255 characters. See Chapter 7 for details.

Customizing the recognized list of search engines You can change or append the recognized search engines list. For example, by default all Google search engine properties are grouped under a single search engine referrer—"google." However, you may wish to split out google.co.uk, google.fr, google.de, and others from google.com. You can achieve this by a simple modification of the Google Analytics tracking code. See Chapter 9 for details.

Running multiple tracking tools together If you have an existing web analytics solution, you can run Google Analytics alongside without any interference. Append the Google Analytics tracking code in the usual way. This allows you to evaluate Google Analytics or even enhance existing data.

Storing data locally as a backup You can have the same data that Google Analytics receives stored locally in your web server logfiles. That can be useful if you wish to store data for very long periods (longer than Google's commitment of 25 months) or for reprocessing locally with Urchin Software. Urchin Software is discussed later in this chapter. Configuring a backup copy of your data is discussed in Chapter 6.

As you can see from this section, Google Analytics is both a broad brush and a scalpel when it comes to tracking and reporting on your website visitor data. In addition, because of it implementation simplicity, it is also incredibly flexible. To comprehend the simplicity, ensure that you understand the principles of how Google Analytics works, as discussed next.

How Google Analytics Works

From Chapter 2, "Available Methodologies and Their Accuracy," you gained an understanding of data-collection techniques and the role that cookies play in web analytics. Google Analytics is a page-tag solution that employs first-party cookies. By this method, all data collection, processing, maintenance, and program upgrades are managed by Google as a hosted service—also referred to as SaaS (Software as a Service). But what are the process and data flow that make this work? These are best illustrated with the three-step schematic shown in Figure 3.2.

1. Nothing happens until a visitor arrives at your website. This can be via many different routes, including search engines, email marketing, referral links, and so forth. Whatever the route, when the visitor views one of your pages with the Google Analytics Tracking Code (GATC), an automatic request is made for the file at http://www.google-analytics.com/ga.js. This is the Google Analytics master file—an 18Kb JavaScript file that is downloaded only once during a visitor session. Further requests for it will be retrieved from the visitor's browser cache.

   With the ga.js file in place, referrer information plus other visitor data (for example, page URL, timestamp, unique ID, screen resolution, color depth) are collected, and a set of first-party cookies is created to identify the visitor—or updated if the visitor is a returning one.

2. For each pageview, the GATC sends this information to Google data collection servers via a call of a transparent, 1 × 1-pixel GIF image at google-analytics. com. In-page visitor actions can also be tracked in this way, for example, clicking to start a Flash animation. The entire transmission of data takes a fraction of a second.

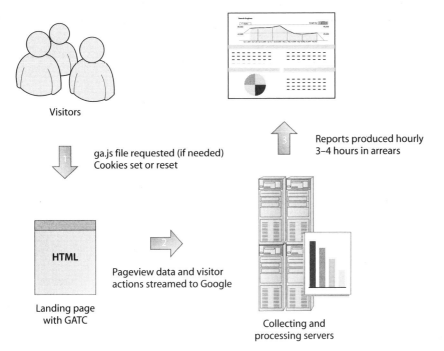

Visitors

ga.js file requested (if needed)
Cookies set or reset

HTML

Landing page
with GATC

Pageview data and visitor
actions streamed to Google

Collecting and
processing servers

Reports produced hourly
3–4 hours in arrears

Figure 3.2 Schematic diagram of how Google Analytics works

3.   Each hour, Google processes the collected data and updates your Google
Analytics reports. However, because of the methodology and the huge quantity
of data involved, reports are typically displayed 3–4 hours in arrears, and this
may sometimes be longer, though not more than 24 hours.

> **Note:** In most cases, collating data from the multitude of data-collection servers is a smooth process, but
> sometimes things can go wrong, for example, if a logfile transfer is interrupted. Because of this, Google collects
> and reprocesses all data for a 24-hour period at the day's end. Therefore, don't panic if you have missing data for
> the current day. Should this persist for longer than 24 hours, contact the Google Analytics support team: `http://`
> `www.google.com/support/googleanalytics/bin/request.py`.

> **Note:** Although Google Analytics processes visit data hourly, data imports take place at different frequen-
> cies. For example, the import of AdWords and AdSense data (if applicable to you) takes place once per day and is
> 24 hours behind. This is to allow for Google's click-fraud algorithms to complete their work. Potential discrepancies
> because of AdWords data import are discussed in Chapter 2.

By design, Google Analytics uses the same `ga.js` tracking snippet for all visitors
and for all website owners. This means that it is cached by a very large proportion of

web users—the advantage of having an adoption base of millions of websites including some very popular web properties. That's good news, because it means that if a visitor to your website has previously visited another website that also runs Google Analytics, the ga.js file does not need to be downloaded at all—it will already be cached. The result is that Google Analytics has a minimal impact on your page-loading times. Typical file caching lasts for seven days, though this value can be adjusted in your browser configuration.

As you have probably realized from the description of Figure 3.2, if a visitor blocks the execution of JavaScript or blocks the setting of first-party cookies, or if you forgot to add the GATC to your page, or your web server does not allow the GATC to execute (that is, it's behind a firewall), Google Analytics will not function and no data will be collected. Once data is lost, you cannot go back and reprocess it, so regular audits of your GATC deployment should be part of your implementation plan.

Note: There are presently two versions of the Google Analytics Tracking Code (GATC) in existence: the original legacy code called urchin.js, which is no longer updated but still functioning, and the current ga.js code, which is what you require in order to benefit from the latest Google Analytics features, such as event tracking.

The current ga.js was launched at the end of 2007. Although Google has not set a date to deprecate urchin.js, if you are still using this you should plan on replacing it in the not-too-distant future. To do this, log into your Google Analytics account as an administrator and click the Check Status link within each of your profile settings. Your new tracking code will be displayed.

Note that if you are also using urchin.js legacy functions, for example, capturing virtual pageviews, these will also need to be updated to the new format.

What Google Analytics Cannot Do

As you might expect, I consider Google Analytics a great tool that has helped many organizations optimize and improve their websites. In some cases this had led to conversion improvements of tens of millions of dollars. However, the truth is that no one web analytics tool can achieve absolutely everything for an organization; there are just too many possibilities. Therefore, I'll summarize some of the things Google Analytics cannot do and describe why that is and its significance.

Data Reprocessing

As shown in the schematic of Figure 3.2, the data flow of your web visitors and the processing by Google Analytics means that reports are always appending information to a previous report. So if there is an error in your implementation (for example, pages on your site missing the GATC or an incorrectly set up filter), that error is carried through into the reports. The data will be missing or incorrect as the report timeline moves forward. Even when you correct this error, Google Analytics cannot go back in time and reprocess the data.

The reason for this is simple: The dataset of Google Analytics for all users is enormous and, prior to processing, is stored in aggregate form, that is, mixed with other Google Analytics accounts. At present it is not possible for Google to isolate and reprocess a single Google Analytics account.

Lack of data reprocessing is a genuine limitation that can be frustrating for any implementer. To mitigate this, you should always have a test profile that you can use to experiment with new filters and configuration settings before applying them to your main report profile; this will be discussed in Chapter 8, "Best-Practices Configuration Guide."

Note: To give you an idea of the volume of data that Google Analytics must process each hour, 24 hours per day, consider the following:

- A typical website receives 100 visits per hour.

- Each visit generates 10 pageviews on average, or 1,000 pieces of data per hour.

- There are several million active Google Analytics accounts.

Therefore, Google Analytics processes several billion lines of visit data each hour. Reprocessing a subset of this is therefore not a simple task. However, it may be possible in the future.

Bid Management

Wouldn't it be great after viewing the performance of your AdWords visitors within your Google Analytics reports (for example, time in site, bounce rate, and e-commerce value), you could update bid strategy, pricing, and ad creatives all from within the same interface? That is not possible at present; you need to log into your AdWords account to make changes. However, I would expect Google to crack this nut in the not-too-distant future. After all, Google makes 97 percent of its $20-plus-billion-per-year revenue from its pay-per-click advertising network.

Non-Real-Time Reporting

As previously discussed, reports are typically three to four hours in arrears. Therefore, viewing a report at midday will typically show data up to 9 A.M. that morning. Providing real-time reporting is extremely expensive (resource intensive) for any web analytics vendor, but is this expense worth it? I have yet to meet a user who is able to take action based on report data in real time. Typically, even for very proactive (constantly changing) websites, report users and management review and approve potential website changes on a weekly basis. Therefore, in my opinion, real-time reporting is not worth the expense. That said, the more up to date your reports are the better. Urchin, discussed later in this chapter, has the capability to produce reports hourly at a time you define.

Importing Third-Party Cost Data

At present, only cost data from AdWords and AdSense is imported, allowing ROI to be reported. That means visitor acquisition costs from, for example, other pay-per-click networks, banner advertising, email marketing, Search Engine Optimization, and the like cannot be taken into account, and so these referrers have no associated ROI data within your reports—meaning a manual calculation for you.

However, with the recent release of the Google Analytics export API, importing third-party cost data should not be too far away from reality (this is speculation on my part). Urchin software, discussed later in this chapter, already has this capability.

Per-Visitor Tracking (against Google Policies)

In 2005, following the acquisition of the company and technology known as Urchin Software Inc., Google took the very deliberate decision not to track individuals (a feature that was in beta development at that time). That is, all website visitor data is reported within Google Analytics in an aggregate and anonymous form.

While it is attractive for advertisers to identify visitors from their previous visit behavior, from Google's point of view, it is a step too far—invading the right of the end-user's privacy (that of the general public) by using Google Analytics.

Of course, if you have a special arrangement with your visitors whereby they do not mind such individual tracking, Urchin software is an alternative tool.

Google Analytics and Privacy

Those of you who have read my blog or heard me speak know that I am a strong advocate of end-user privacy, that is, the right of the end user (general public) not to be tracked in any identifiable way while using the Web.

To be clear, providing the end user with the right not to be identified does not mean giving the user the option of *opting out* of such tracking by reading verbose, jargon-filled terms and conditions (as an example, the MySpace.com privacy policy currently stands at 2,752 words and is noticeably written by a legal professional, rather than from an end-user's point of view). Instead, the default position should be to track visitors only in an anonymous and aggregate way, unless they give their express permission by *opting in*. That's a best-practice approach and will ensure you have the trust and loyalty of your visitors and customers—something that is always good for business.

As discussed in the previous section, all Google Analytics reports contain aggregate non–Personally Identifiable Information. That has been a deliberate policy of Google toward its products. From my own experience, it is a vision and commitment that comes from the very top of the organization and played a key role in my decision to work for Google.

With that in mind, three parties are involved in the Google Analytics tracking scenario: Google, an independent website, and a visitor to that website. Google has designed its privacy practices to address each of these participants by requiring each website that uses Google Analytics to abide by the privacy provisions in the terms of service, specifically section 7 (see www.google.com/analytics/tos.html):

> *You will not (and will not allow any third party to) use the Service to track or collect personally identifiable information of Internet users, nor will You (or will You allow any third party to) associate any data gathered from Your website(s) (or such third parties' website(s)) with any personally identifying information from any source as part of Your use (or such third parties' use) of the Service. You will have and abide by an appropriate privacy policy and will comply with all applicable laws relating to the collection of information from visitors to Your websites. You must post a privacy policy and that policy must provide notice of your use of a cookie that collects anonymous traffic data.*

Note: The content of section 7 of tos.html may vary depending on which country you operate in. Ensure you view the most relevant Terms of Service by selecting from the drop-down menu at the top of the page.

The Google Analytics cookies collect standard Internet log data and visitor behavior information in an anonymous form. They do not collect any personal information such as addresses, names, or credit card numbers. The logs include standard log information such as IP address, time and date stamp, browser type, and operating system. The behavior information includes generic surfing information, such as the number of pages viewed, language setting, and screen resolution settings in the browser, and can include information about whether or not a goal was completed by the visitor to the website. The website can define the goal to mean different things, such as whether a visitor downloaded a PDF file, completed an e-commerce transaction, visited more than one page, and so on. Note that Google Analytics does not track a user across multiple unrelated sites, and it uses different cookies for each website.

Google Analytics prepares anonymous and statistical reports for the websites that use it. As you will see in the next chapter, such reports include different information views and show data such as geographic location (based on generic IP-based geolocation codes), time of visit, and so on. These reports are anonymous and statistical. They do not include any information that could identify an individual visitor; for example, they do not include IP addresses.

Common Privacy Questions

Typical questions asked by potential Google Analytics clients include the following:

- What does Google do with the data it collects?

- Who at Google sees the analytics data?

- How securely is data kept?

- As a website owner, what is my obligation to data privacy?

I answer these questions from my own perspective, having worked at Google for a number of years.

- What does Google do with the data it collects?

  Google Analytics is a tool specifically targeted at advertisers (and potential advertisers) who want to gain a better understanding of their website traffic. In fact, it is one of many tools that make up what I refer to as an advertiser's tool-kit. Others include Google Trends, Google Insights, Webmaster Central, Product Search (formally Froogle), Google Maps, Website Optimizer, Google Base, and Checkout. Google Analytics provides advertisers with the transparency and accountability they need in order to have confidence in the pay-per-click, online auction model. Essentially, a happy advertiser is good for business.

  Keep in mind that the Google AdWords auction model prevents anyone from interfering with the pricing of ads. The system is completely transparent, so it would be ludicrous for Google to artificially adjust bids—destroying a business overnight. On the Web, the competition is always only one click away, and Microsoft and Yahoo are serious competitors in this space.

- Who at Google sees the analytics data?

  Google Analytics data, as with all data at Google, is accessed on a strict need-to-know basis, for example, by support staff and maintenance engineers. If, as a client, you want Google staff to look at your reports, for example, to provide help with managing an AdWords campaign, then you must request this from your Google account manager or via the Google Analytics Help Center (www .google.com/support/googleanalytics/). All internal Google access to your reports is monitored for auditing purposes.

- How secure is the analytics data?

  Data security and integrity are paramount for continued end-user confidence in all Google services. Therefore, Google Analytics data is subject to the same rigorous security checks and audits as all other Google products. Of course, one can never be 100 percent certain of security in any organization, but Google employs some of the best industry professionals in the world to ensure that its systems remain secure.

- As a website owner, what is my obligation to data privacy?

  In addition to Google's commitment to data privacy and integrity, owners of websites that use Google Analytics also have an obligation to visitor privacy.

In fact, this is true for any analytics solution. For Google Analytics, the terms of service state that you will not associate any data gathered from your website with any Personally Identifiable Information. You will, of course, also need to comply with all applicable data protection and privacy laws relating to your use of Google Analytics and have in place (in a prominent position on your website) an appropriate privacy policy.

These are commonsense best-practice approaches to owning a website and collecting visitor information about its usage. However, I recommend that you view your obligations as a website owner from the Terms of Service link at the bottom of any page on the Google Analytics website (www.google.com/analytics). To ensure that you read the most relevant terms for your location, select the region that most closely matches your own from the country drop-down menu at the top of the page.

Best-Practice Privacy Statement When Using Google Analytics

The following is a best-practice example of a clear privacy statement when using Google Analytics—modified from the Information Commissioner's Office, the U.K. independent authority to protect personal information (www.ico.gov.uk) and a Google Analytics user.

Our Policy for Protecting Your Online Privacy

This website uses Google Analytics to help analyze how users use the site. The tool uses "cookies," which are text files placed on your computer, to collect standard Internet log information and visitor behavior information in an anonymous form. The information generated by the cookie about your use of the website (including your IP address) is transmitted to Google. This information is then used to evaluate visitors' use of the website and to compile statistical reports on website activity for Your_Company_Name.

We will never (and will not allow any third party to) use the statistical analytics tool to track or to collect any Personally Identifiable Information of visitors to our site. Google will not associate your IP address with any other data held by Google. Neither we nor Google will link, or seek to link, an IP address with the identity of a computer user. We will not associate any data gathered from this site with any Personally Identifiable Information from any source, unless you explicitly submit that information via a fill-in form on our website.

Further Information about Cookies

The Interactive Advertising Bureau (IAB) is an industry body that develops standards and guidelines to support online business processes. It has produced a series of web pages that explain how cookies work and how they can be managed.

If you have questions concerning our privacy policy, please use our contact details to discuss them.

How Is Google Analytics Different?

On November 11, 2005, Google Analytics was launched, and a major part of the announcement was that the product was free. This was a tipping point in the industry. Overnight Google rewrote the entire industry business model—giving away a deep-dive web analytics tool while everyone else charged based on volume of traffic.

The impact of that decision was dramatic. An industry that once counted its customers in the tens of thousands now exploded. In fact, so dramatic was the uptake of the service that it had to close to new subscribers for 10 months while new machines were allocated to the number-crunching tasks at Google's data centers. However, once we reopened, the user base of Google Analytics rapidly expanded and went beyond a million in a matter of months.

There is a common, old-economy saying, "There's no such thing as a free lunch." However, providing free products has been a key driver for the growth of the Internet over the past 15 years. Pioneered in the early days by products such as Linux, Apache, and Hotmail, and further extended by Google, Mozilla (Firefox), Facebook, YouTube, Twitter, and many others, the business ethos has been rewritten—offering items for free in order to make gains elsewhere.

For Google Analytics, the "gains elsewhere" are Google's advertising products—AdWords and AdSense. By providing a tool that helps website owners, in particular digital marketers, understand the performance of their website, Google hopes you will have the confidence to spend more money with its web advertising products. Google Analytics therefore provides transparency and accountability for these revenue-generating products (Google dominates online advertising globally with its $20-billion-a-year turnover).

 Note: Many books discuss the free and open-source business ethos of companies such as Google and its peers. I recommend those written by Chris Andersson, John Battelle, and Seth Godin as great examples.

Although the data collection and reporting from Google are free, an investment is required from your organization in order to have Google Analytics implemented correctly, staff trained, and insights gleaned. However, the use of Google Analytics remains free, whether you are an advertiser or not. The only caveat is that if you receive more than 5 million pageviews per month, you need to open an AdWords account, as described in the Google Analytics Terms of Service. Consider it a gentle reminder to experiment with AdWords. Spending $1 per day is sufficient to allow you to have an unlimited pageview volume collected and reported on.

Targeting Digital Marketers Rather Than IT Departments

Historically, and still to a great extent today, web analytics vendors target IT departments to sell their products. Hence the focus is on features, technology, complexity, and the big budgets required to utilize these. To illustrate this, Figure 3.3 is taken from a 2008 survey of companies that have implemented web analytics within their organization. Although it's a U.K.-focused survey, the results are typical for other markets—that is, the majority of web analytics expenditure is spent on the tool itself (data collection and reporting), rather than on those things that drive improvement, such as staff training and consultancy.

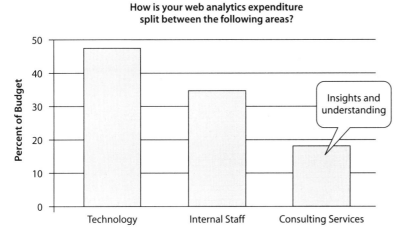

Figure 3.3 Typical breakdown of web analytics expenditure for an organization

Google's approach to analytics is opposite of the industry trend (another key reason I joined the company!). Targeting marketing departments by simplifying the implementation, minimizing complexity, and removing the barrier to adoption, that is, providing the product for free, has proved to be an extraordinary success. Figure 3.4 is a schematic example of the alternative approach Google Analytics espouses.

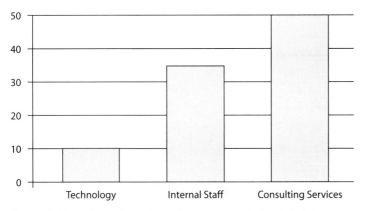

Figure 3.4 Schematic breakdown of expenditure as espoused by Google Analytics

The Google Analytics philosophy, therefore, is for you to focus your budget on insights rather than reporting. That way, you are much more likely to invest online with products such as AdWords and AdSense.

 Tip: For more on the approach and vision of Google Analytics, read Occam's Razor (kaushik.net/avinash), the popular blog from Avinash Kaushik, official Google Analytics evangelist, author, and all-round nice guy.

What Is Urchin?

Although this book's focus concerns Google Analytics, it is worth mentioning that Google has two web analytics products: Google Analytics and Urchin Software.

Urchin Software Inc. is the company and technology that Google acquired in April 2005, which then went on to become Google Analytics—a free web analytics service that uses the resources at Google. Urchin software is a downloadable web analytics program that runs on a local server (Unix or Windows). Typically, this is the same machine as your web server. The Urchin Software creates reports by processing web server logfiles (including hybrid ones) and is commonly referred to as *server-side web analytics*. This approach was discussed in Chapter 2. Example screenshots of Urchin Software (version 6) are shown in Figure 3.5 and Figure 3.6.

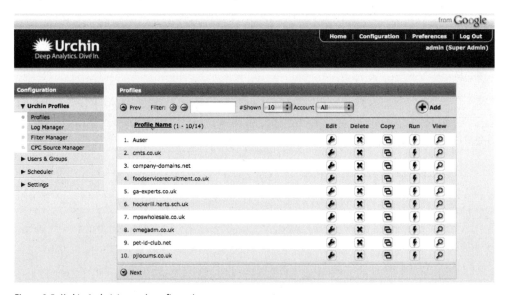

Figure 3.5 Urchin 6 administrator's configuration screen

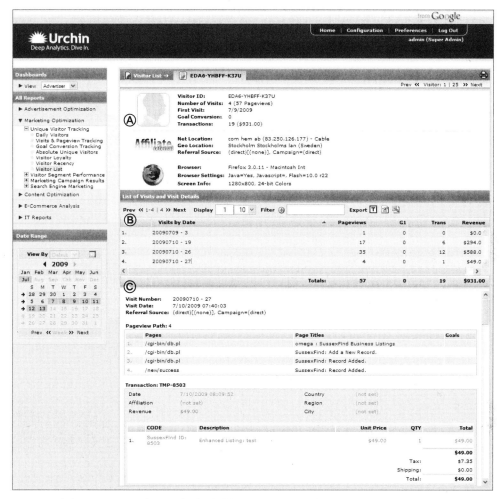

Figure 3.6 Urchin 6 visitor report showing A) individual (anonymous) visitor information, B) visits by date, and C) path and resultant transaction information for a particular visit

Urchin is essentially the same technology as Google Analytics—the difference when using Urchin is that your organization needs to provide the resources for log storage and data processing. As Table 2.1 in Chapter 2 shows, logfile tools can report on information that page-tag solutions alone cannot provide. Therefore, Urchin Software provides complementary reports that Google Analytics currently does not (or cannot because of its methodology). Let's look at some examples:

Visitor history report Tracking individual visitors enables you to view the path a visitor takes through your website as well as their referral information. As discussed earlier in this chapter, for privacy reasons Google has deliberately taken the decision not to track individuals with Google Analytics. However, with the data collection and processing under your control, you have the freedom to do this with Urchin. Each visitor is tracked anonymously.

Error page and status code reports More than just reporting completed page views (as is the case for Google Analytics), Urchin can report partial downloads and any error code.

Bandwidth reports Reporting on bandwidth allows you to view how "heavy" your pages are and how this impacts the visitor's experience.

Login reports If your website has a login area, you can report on this access by username. This supports standard Apache (.htaccess) or any authentication that logs usernames in the logfile.

 Note: As discussed in Chapter 9, it is possible to configure your website to report error pages within Google Analytics. However, Urchin software reports on errors out of the box because your web server tracks these by default.

Differences between Google Analytics and Urchin

With two analytics products from Google to choose from, how do you determine which one of these is right for your organization? As you may have guessed from the title of this book, Google Analytics is perfect for most organizations, for two very simple reasons:

- Google Analytics is a free service. This is generally considered a major benefit for small and medium-size organizations where budgets for analysis are tight. Urchin Software is a licensed product and therefore must be purchased (currently $2,995 per installation).

- Google Analytics handles a large part of the IT overhead. That is, Google conducts the data collection, storage, program maintenance, and upgrades for you. This is generally considered a major benefit for large organizations where web analytics is a priority for the Marketing department and less so for the IT department. If your organization is using Urchin Software, it is responsible for the IT overhead. Hence, good interdepartmental communication (IT and Marketing) is required.

The second point is not trivial. In fact, in my experience, the IT overhead of implementing tools was the main reason why web analytics remained a niche industry for such a large part of its existence. Maintaining your own logfiles has an overhead, mainly because web server logfiles get very large, very quickly. As a guide, every 1,000 visits produce approximately 4 MB of log info. Therefore, 10,000 visits per month are approximately 500 MB per year. If you have 100,000 visits per month, that's 5 GB per year, and so on. Those are just estimates—for your own site, these could easily double. At the end of the day, managing large logfiles isn't something your IT department gets excited about.

Urchin also requires disk space for its processed data (stored in a proprietary database). Though this will always be a smaller size than the raw collected numbers, storing and archiving all this information is an important task because if you run out of disk space, you risk file or database corruption from disk-write errors. This kind of file corruption is almost impossible to recover from.

As an aside, if you maintain your own visitor data logfiles, the security and privacy of collected information (your visitors) also become your responsibility.

Why, then, might you consider Urchin Software at all? Urchin Software does have some real advantages over Google Analytics. For example, data is recorded and stored by your web server, rather than streamed to Google, which means the following:

Data processing and reprocessing Urchin can process data as and when you wish, for example, on the hour, every hour. You can also reprocess data—to apply a filter retroactively or to correct a filter error. Google Analytics reports are three to four hours in arrears and cannot reprocess data retroactively (in my opinion, the benefit of reprocessing data is the strongest advantage of Urchin).

Unlimited data storage Urchin can keep and view data for as long as you wish. Google Analytics currently commits to keeping data for a maximum of 25 months, though to date, Google has made no attempt to remove data older than this—see Figure 3.1.

Third-party auditing Urchin allows your data to be audited by an independent third party. This is usually important for publishers who sell advertising space on their site, where auditing is required to verify visitor numbers and provide credibility for advertisers (trust in their rate card). Google Analytics does not pass data to third parties.

Intranets and firewalls Urchin works behind the firewall; that is, it's suitable for intranets. Google Analytics page tags cannot run behind a closed firewall.

Database access Urchin stores data locally in a proprietary database and includes tools that can be used to access the raw data outside a web browser, allowing you to run ad hoc queries. Google Analytics stores data in remote locations within Google datacenters around the world in proprietary databases and does not provide direct access to the raw data for ad hoc queries. That said, the Google Analytics API does allow you to query your processed data.

Note: Urchin is sold and supported exclusively through a network of Urchin Software Authorized Consultants. For a full list of USACs, see www.google.com/urchin/usac.html.

Criteria for Choosing between Google Analytics and Urchin

There are a few crucial issues to consider when choosing one of the Google analytic services, detailed in the following list. Generally speaking, apart from intranets, Urchin is used mostly by web-hosting providers where deployment scalability for large numbers of websites is important. Google Analytics, apart from being a free service, is used by organizations that wish to have greater control of their *individual* web analytics implementation.

When Google Analytics is the best fit Select Google Analytics if you are measuring the success (or not) of your website, its ability to convert, and the effectiveness of online marketing. Google Analytics is much easier to implement, has stronger AdWords integration, and by comparison is maintenance free.

When Urchin is the best fit Select Urchin if:

- You have an intranet site behind a firewall that blocks Internet activity. Google Analytics is a hosted solution that needs access to the Internet in order to work.

- You are unable to tag your pages.

- You are a hosting provider wishing to offer visitor reports to thousands of customers. Urchin has a command-line interface that can be scripted to create and modify multiple website reports at once. That is, Urchin has greater flexibility when it comes to large-scale, multiuser deployments.

When you need both Select both if you need the flexibility of maintaining your own visitor data, for example, for third-party auditing purposes. Combining Google Analytics with Urchin software gives you the best of both worlds—the advanced features of Google Analytics (free) and the flexibility of Urchin (data control). Chapter 6 discusses how you can configure your page tags to stream data to Google Analytics and Urchin simultaneously.

Note: Some third-party hardware solutions can automatically insert Google Analytics page tags for you on the fly, that is, as the page is requested from your web server. They achieve this by using proxy servers that sit within your network (in front of your web server) and insert the code for you. See, for example, www.click-stream.com/googleanalytics.

My personal view is to use Google Analytics wherever possible. It is easier to implement, has a slicker user interface (with best-in-class geomap overlay reports), and is primarily aimed at digital marketers. Urchin Software should be used where there is a specific technical need that Google Analytics cannot fulfill. Urchin lacks site overlay and internal site-search reports, though it can track individual visitors anonymously. If you can, use both tools.

Summary

In Chapter 3, you have learned the following:

Key features You explored the key features and capabilities of Google Analytics, which will enable you to ascertain what it can do for you and whether it is suitable for the analytics needs of your organization.

The principles of how it all works You learned how Google Analytics works from a nontechnical perspective, so that you can understand how Google collects and processes data.

Google's position on data integrity and privacy Google Analytics takes its responsibility for visitor data seriously, in terms of Google Analytics users and website visitors.

The uniqueness of the Google approach You saw how Google Analytics is different from other approaches and what drives its business model.

Considerations for server-side analytics You learned what Urchin Software is, how it compares with Google Analytics, and what criteria you should consider when selecting an analytics product from Google.

Using Google Analytics Reports

Part II is intended as a familiarization jump start, aimed to get you up to speed with using the Google Analytics report interface as quickly and efficiently as possible. Consider it your user guide, walking you through the important aspects in order for you to understand website visitor behavior. Rather than describe every report, I've highlighted the key areas as well as how to find your way around the information presented. I've deliberately focused on the most important and interesting aspects you need to know first in order for you to enjoy the process of discovering more of its capabilities and going deeper into the data in your own time.

In Part II, you will learn about the following:

II

Using the Google Analytics Interface

The Google Analytics user interface makes use of the latest developments in Web 2.0 technology to construct report data in a highly accessible, industry-leading format. For example, rather than use a side menu to navigate through different reports (though that is available), the user is encouraged to drill into the data itself.

In this chapter we review the Google Analytics interface, particularly in relation to discovering information. By understanding the report layout, you will quickly become accustomed to drilling down into the data, investigating whether a number or trend is good, bad, or indifferent for your organization.

In this chapter, you will learn:
Discoverability and the context of data
The difference between dimensions and metrics
How to navigate your way around the plethora of information
How to manipulate data tables and charts
How to schedule exports of data
The value of segmentation and pivot views
How to annotate charts to highlight key events

Discoverability and Initial Report Access

A common complaint from users of other web analytics tools is that the vast quantity of data generated is often overwhelming and difficult to find. The result is that report users get lost and frustrated—unable to decipher the information—and the web metrics project can stall at this point. Such feedback enabled Google to build an intuitive Google Analytics report interface focused on the user, usually a marketer, as opposed to the data. The revised user interface design (the team responsible came from MeasureMap, a Google acquisition of 2006) has proved so successful in user-experience studies that the format is being adopted throughout Google—notice the similarly styled graphs you now see in AdWords, AdSense, FeedBurner, and the geo-map overlay of Google Insights, for example.

In addition to data being very accessible, the user interface enhances *discover-ability*. By this I mean how easy it is for you to ascertain whether the report you are looking at is good news, bad news, or indifferent to your organization. In other words, Google Analytics simplifies the process of turning raw data into useful information so that you can take appropriate action, such as reward your team, fix something, or change your benchmarks.

The Google Analytics drill-down interface differs from other web analytics tools that have a menu-driven style of navigation. You can select menu-driven navigation if you prefer it, but the Google Analytics interface makes it much easier to explore your data in context—that is, within the data, so that you do not waste your time navigating back and forth between reports to answer your questions. In addition, links within the reports suggest related information, and fast, interactive segmentation enables you to reorganize data on the fly. Short narratives, scorecards, and *sparklines* summarize your data at every level. Moreover, to help you understand, interpret, and act on data relationships, context-sensitive Help and Conversion University articles are available in every report.

Note: A sparkline is a mini-image (thumbnail) of graphical data that enables you to put numbers in a temporal context without the need to display full charts. For example, the following screen shot shows an array of numbers that on their own would be meaningless. However, the sparkline graphics show these in context by illustrating the trends over the time period selected. It's a neat and condensed way of conveying a lot of information.

Assuming you already have a Google Analytics account (or have access to one), Figure 4.1 schematically illustrates the report-access process. As with all Google products, access to your Google Analytics account is via your *Google Account*—a Google-registered email address that can be any email address you control, such as `me@my-organization.com`. Your Google Account is your centralized access point. From it, you may have access to multiple Google Analytics accounts, each one with multiple profiles (report sets).

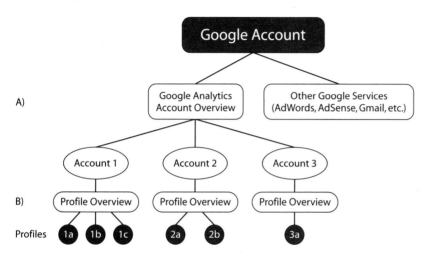

Figure 4.1 Schematic access process for Google Analytics reports

When you first log in to your Google Analytics account, you will be presented with one of two possible overview screens. In most situations you will have access to a single Google Analytics account, in which case you will see the Profile Overview screen, as shown in Figure 4.2. However, in an agency environment you may have access to many Google Analytics accounts and hence you will see the Account Overview screen, as shown in Figure 4.3. These points of access are hierarchical and are labeled as B) and A) respectively in Figure 4.1. If you are an agency, clicking on the first name in the Name column in Figure 4.3, for example, Site 1, takes you to that account's Profile Overview report.

At this stage, consider a profile to be defined as a *report set*, that is, a set of Google Analytics reports dedicated for a particular purpose, such as U.K. visitors only, U.S. visitors only, and so forth. The use of profiles is discussed in the section titled "Using Accounts and Profiles" in Chapter 6, "Getting Up and Running with Google Analytics."

Note: Considerations for agencies are discussed in Chapter 6 in the section "Agencies and Hosting Providers: Setting Up Client Accounts."

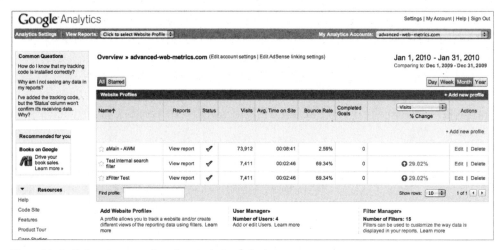

Figure 4.2 Profile Overview report shown for a single Google Analytics account

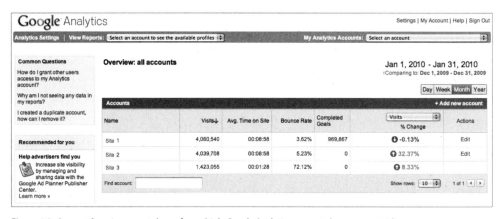

Figure 4.3 Account Overview report shown for multiple Google Analytics accounts (agency scenario)

Both Overview reports allow you to quickly view and compare your performance with high-level metrics displayed for the past month by default—that is, assuming today is day *x* of the month, the default date range for reports is from day *x* of the previous month to day *x*-1 of the current month. The current day is not included by default, because this is the least accurate day to view data—see Chapter 2, "Available Methodologies and Their Accuracy," for a detailed discussion of web analytics accuracy considerations.

To highlight data changes, the penultimate column of Figure 4.2 and Figure 4.3 displays the % Change for the same time window prior to the current reporting period, that is, the previous month. By default the metrics displayed are for visits. However, Average Time On Site, Bounce Rate, or Completed Goals can also be selected. Using the buttons above the data table, you can change the comparison interval for these metrics to Day, Week, or Year.

If you set up your Google Analytics account or have been granted administrator access, you have complete control over the account, and Figures 4.2 and 4.3 will show an additional column containing an Edit or Delete link. The alternative access level is Report Viewer, which has no administrative access. If you are a Report Viewer, the last column is blank and no edit or delete facility is available to you. Administering a Google Analytics account is discussed in Chapter 8, "Best-Practices Configuration Guide."

Warning: Do not place too much emphasis on small percentage changes when comparing month-on-month or year-on-year data in the Overview reports. For example, months may have a different number of days—April (30) compared with March (31). If the number of visits and goal completions per day for March and April is identical, you would expect the total for April to be 3.3 percent lower than in March, simply because April contains one less calendar day. This difference could be greater depending on the number of weekend days in each month, such as in the case when comparing January with February.

Navigating Your Way Around: Report Layout

As with all web-based software applications, the best way to get to know its capabilities is to see it in action. With the Google Analytics report interface, you can do this quickly—one of its key strengths. You can see an initial preview of some of its capabilities at `http://www.google.com/analytics/tour.html`. The walkthrough is in English, with other languages shown as subtitles.

Note: With the exception of Figure 4.15, all screenshots are taken from the Traffic Sources > All Traffic Sources report, as shown in the menu.

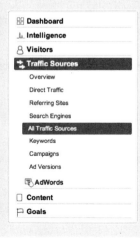

An example of a typical report is shown in Figure 4.4. We'll use this as our guide for introducing the features of the Google Analytics user interface. If you have access to a Google Analytics account, view a similar report by going to the Traffic Sources > All Traffic Sources report. I recommend having this at hand while reading this chapter in order to become familiar with the points discussed.

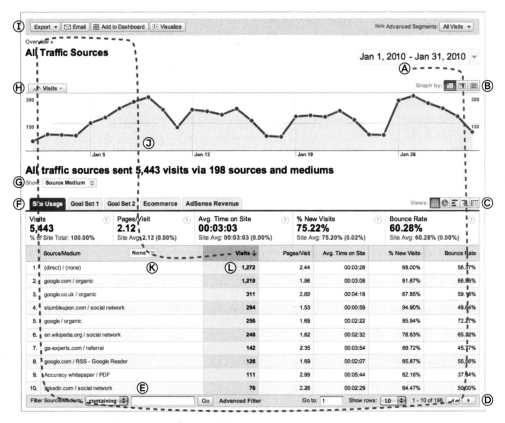

Figure 4.4 A typical Google Analytics report with guideline path

Normally when I examine a report such as Figure 4.4 for the first time, my eyes travel in a clockwise fashion—starting from the date selector at the top-right corner, down through the data table, past the footer option, around to the report tab menu, up to the data chart, to the export features, and then back to the center of the report table. The dotted path in Figure 4.4 illustrates this route with the most significant elements highlighted along the way. The following sections describe each of these in detail. However, before looking at these we first need to clarify the terminology of dimensions and metrics.

Dimensions and Metrics

Two types of data are represented in Google Analytics reports, dimensions and metrics:

- *Dimensions* are text strings that describe an item. Think of them as names, such as page URL, page title, hostname, browser type, connection speed, transaction ID, product name, and so on.

- *Metrics* are numbers, for example, time on page, time on site, number of pageviews per visit, bounce rate, purchase total, and so forth.

Figure 4.5 illustrates the differences when viewing a report table.

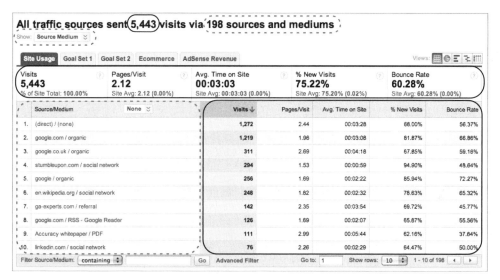

Figure 4.5 The difference between dimensions and metrics: dotted lines = dimensions; solid lines = metrics.

> **Note:** The labels referred to in the following sections correspond to those shown in Figure 4.4.

Date Range Selector

Label A: At first glance this is very straightforward. However, there are some subtleties here that go unnoticed by many users, so I recommend getting familiar with all the date range options.

By default, when you view reports, you view the last month of activity. As discussed earlier in this chapter, for account and profile overview reports this means, assuming today is day x of the month, the default date range for reports is from day x of the previous month to day x-1 of the current month. By default, the current day is not included, because this skews calculated averages.

Clicking the date area within the report allows you to make changes. This is shown in Figure 4.6. For example, perhaps you wish to focus on only a single day's activities. In that case, select only that day by clicking it on the calendar. You can also enter the date manually by using the fill-in fields provided. In this respect, the date range selector works like any other calendar tool.

- To select an entire calendar month, click the month name.
- To select an entire week (Sunday–Saturday), click the rounded end of a particular week.

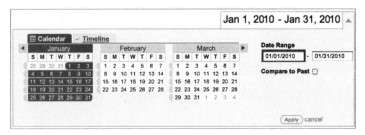

Figure 4.6 Selecting a date range

To compare the current date range data with any other date range, check the "Compare to Past" box. By default, Google Analytics will select a date range to compare. For example, if your first date range is the current day, the previous day will be automatically selected as the comparison. If your first date range is the last 30 days of data, the previous 30 days will be selected by default, and so forth. You can overwrite the second date range as required.

All comparison data is shown within the same browser window. Positive data changes—that is, an increase over the previous period—are shown in green, whereas negative changes are shown in red, as shown in Figure 4.7. The exception to this is when viewing bounce rates. In this case, a decrease in bounce rate would be green and an increase would be red, to reflect that a decrease in bounce rate is desirable.

Note: Take care when viewing chart data for different date ranges. By default, Google Analytics will select a suitable second date range for you—the previous 30 days, for example. However, this usually does not align with the first date range—for example, Mondays may not align with Mondays. When comparing date ranges, always attempt to align days of the week. For example, compare Monday–Friday of this week with Monday–Friday of the previous week.

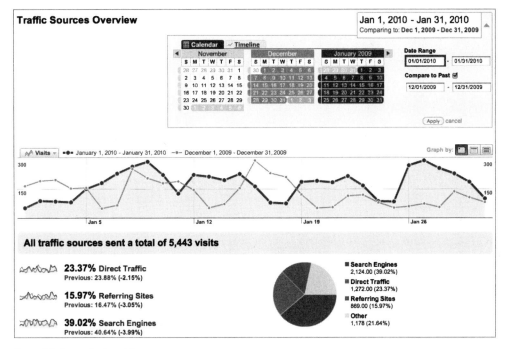

Figure 4.7 Comparing two date ranges

An alternative way to select your date range that I strongly recommend when initially viewing a profile is to use the *timeline sliders*, as shown in Figure 4.8. The Timeline view enables you to make informed decisions regarding what date range to select because you can see the visitor totals *before* selecting it, that is, beyond the date boundaries. Therefore, if you notice a large peak or trough just prior to the default date range window, then you are much more likely to select it for comparison. Without that information, you may select a different range and miss a key event on your website. The timeline slider bars enable you to make this comparison—you drag the data window to the area you wish to investigate and expand or contract the window boundaries as desired.

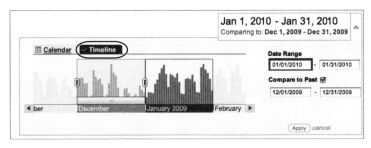

Figure 4.8 Timeline selection

Changing Graph Intervals

Label B: The default report graph interval is daily. That is, you see an aggregate point on the data-over-time graph for each day. That works well when viewing data from 1 to 60 days. However, for longer time periods such as a quarter or a year, daily data points often appear as noise, obscuring information contained in the signal. To improve this, and to reveal longer-term trends, change the graphing interval to weekly or monthly. Figure 4.9 compares the effect of viewing long-term trends when using daily and weekly graphing intervals. Although Figure 4.9a does hint at a growing trend, 4.9b shows it more clearly and is an easier-to-read format.

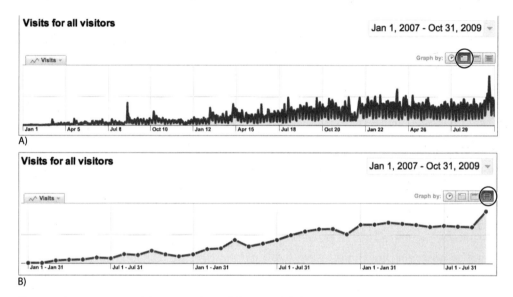

Figure 4.9 Data-over-time graph for a 34-month period showing a) daily data points, b) monthly data points

Some reports also have the ability to change the graphing interval to hourly. These are labeled as "Trending" reports within the navigation menu and show the time of day visitors come to your site. An example of an hourly trending graph is shown in Figure 4.10.

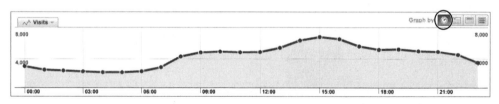

Figure 4.10 Hourly trending graph

The report in Figure 4.10 enables you to track at what times of the day visitor traffic arrives on your site—midnight to midnight. Knowing what times of the day are most productive for you provides powerful insight for scheduling campaigns or downtime—for example, starting and stopping ads, changing your keyword buys, viral marketing events, and the best time to perform web server maintenance.

You should take care when interpreting the report of Figure 4.10 if you are receiving significant visitors from different time zones—for example, U.S. versus European time zones. If this is your situation, consider segmenting your visitors using a geographical filter before interpreting these reports. See Chapter 8 for more information.

Changing Table Views

Label C: If you would rather see data in a pie chart than a table, the data view option available in most reports enables you to select a different view to display your data: table (default), pie chart, bar chart, delta (comparison), and pivot view. My most common selection when initially viewing data is the bar chart view. For me it gives the clearest perspective of overall performance of each data row—highlighting the major influences before I investigate further.

The delta view compares the displayed metric to the site average or the second date range if selected. For example, when used with the Compare To Past date feature, the delta view adds a time context to an otherwise static snapshot of data. Figure 4.11 illustrates this, showing that compared to the previous time period (last month), email visits have been the major changer, with a 200 percent increase in traffic from this medium.

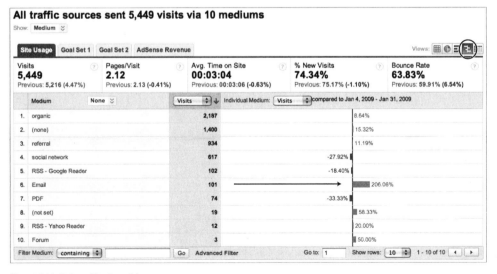

Figure 4.11 Delta table view of data

The pivot view acts in an analogous way to pivot tables in spreadsheet programs such as Excel (though a little more simplified than Excel because this is via your web browser!). The resulting data view can appear complex at first glance, so it is worth spending some time understanding what the pivot view of Figure 4.12 is showing.

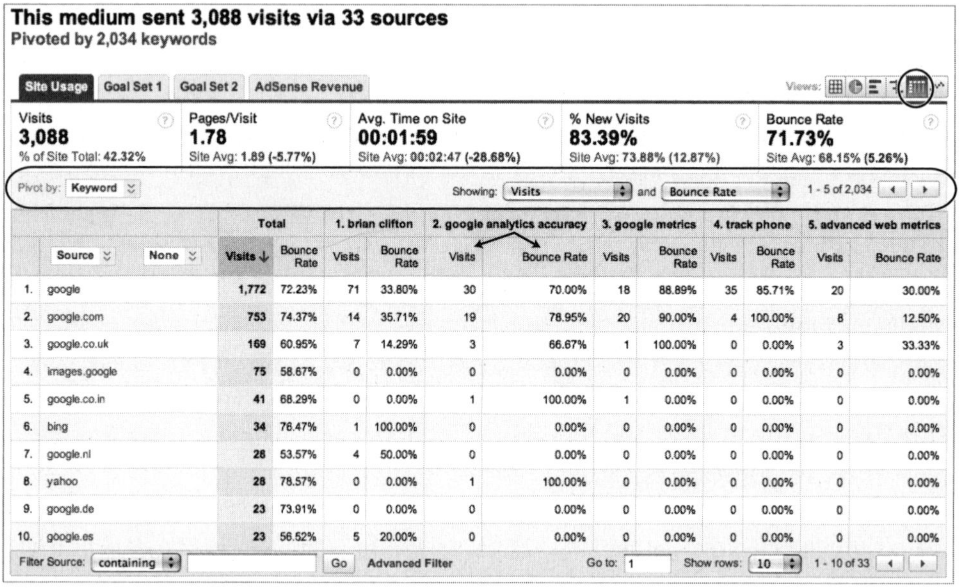

This medium sent 3,088 visits via 33 sources
Pivoted by 2,034 keywords

Site Usage	Goal Set 1	Goal Set 2	AdSense Revenue			Views:

Visits	Pages/Visit	Avg. Time on Site	% New Visits	Bounce Rate
3,088	**1.78**	**00:01:59**	**83.39%**	**71.73%**
% of Site Total: 42.32%	Site Avg: 1.89 (-5.77%)	Site Avg: 00:02:47 (-28.68%)	Site Avg: 73.88% (12.87%)	Site Avg: 68.15% (5.26%)

Pivot by: Keyword   Showing: Visits and Bounce Rate   1 - 5 of 2,034

			Total		1. brian clifton		2. google analytics accuracy		3. google metrics		4. track phone		5. advanced web metrics	
	Source	None	Visits ↓	Bounce Rate	Visits	Bounce Rate	Visits	Bounce Rate	Visits	Bounce Rate	Visits	Bounce Rate	Visits	Bounce Rate
1.	google		1,772	72.23%	71	33.80%	30	70.00%	18	88.89%	35	85.71%	20	30.00%
2.	google.com		753	74.37%	14	35.71%	19	78.95%	20	90.00%	4	100.00%	8	12.50%
3.	google.co.uk		169	60.95%	7	14.29%	3	66.67%	1	100.00%	0	0.00%	3	33.33%
4.	images.google		75	58.67%	0	0.00%	0	0.00%	0	0.00%	0	0.00%	0	0.00%
5.	google.co.in		41	68.29%	0	0.00%	1	100.00%	1	0.00%	0	0.00%	0	0.00%
6.	bing		34	76.47%	1	100.00%	0	0.00%	0	0.00%	0	0.00%	0	0.00%
7.	google.nl		28	53.57%	4	50.00%	0	0.00%	0	0.00%	0	0.00%	0	0.00%
8.	yahoo		28	78.57%	0	0.00%	1	100.00%	0	0.00%	0	0.00%	0	0.00%
9.	google.de		23	73.91%	0	0.00%	0	0.00%	0	0.00%	0	0.00%	0	0.00%
10.	google.es		23	56.52%	5	20.00%	0	0.00%	0	0.00%	0	0.00%	0	0.00%

Filter Source: containing   Go   Advanced Filter   Go to: 1   Show rows: 10   1 - 10 of 33

Figure 4.12 Pivot view of data

In order to obtain the screenshot of Figure 4.12, first drill down into the "medium = organic" data set. This results in the first dimension column displaying the referral source for this medium—in this example, organic search engines. Then, selecting the pivot view, choose to pivot by Keyword, showing Visits and Bounce Rate.

The result is a table that lists the top five keywords along the top, each one further split to show Visits and Bounce Rate on a per–organic search engine basis. The pivot table view is therefore a powerful way to view multiple data points simultaneously, without the need to navigate back and forth between different reports.

Moving through the Data

Label D: As you may have noticed from Figure 4.4, the default table view is to show the top 10 rows of data, ordered by number of visits (highest first). The control options displayed in the bottom footer row allow you to change this. First, note that in Figure 4.4 there are 198 rows of data. Paginated in rows of 10, that requires 20 table, or "window," views to see all of the data for this report.

To scroll through the data tables, move the position of your "window" by using the forward and backward arrows at the bottom of the page. You can adjust the size of the window, that is, the number of rows displayed, by expanding the drop-down menu next to the arrow buttons. Lastly, you can also set the point from which you wish to start your view of the data. For example, you can start from row 25 onward. Note that the maximum number of report rows that can be displayed in the user interface is 500. To view more than this, export the data as described in the section "Export and Email Features" later in this chapter.

Table Filters

Label E: Websites can receive a lot of data. Even a small, moderately active blog can generate thousands of visits per month and therefore tens of thousands of data points to go with it. As shown in Figure 4.4, the total number of rows for the Source Medium report is 198—see the footer row at the bottom of the table. Although expanding and changing the data window, as described in the previous section, can be of help, visually browsing through each table row is clearly not going to be something you wish to do regularly (or fun!).

To avoid such a laborious task, you can quickly get to a data row (or group of rows) by using the table filter. This comes in two parts—a simple format of containing or excluding a pattern match and an advanced filter.

A simple filter acts on the first dimension column only (the second table column after row numbering) and is applied to all data, not just the visible rows. In Figure 4.13 this is the Source/Medium dimension, with the filter set to *exclude* any data row where the source/medium matches "google" or "direct." The term "direct" is used to describe any visitor who has typed your web address directly into their browser or used a previously saved bookmark. The filter can also be reversed, that is, set to *include* "google" and "direct" visits or other pattern match. When this field is blank, no filter is applied.

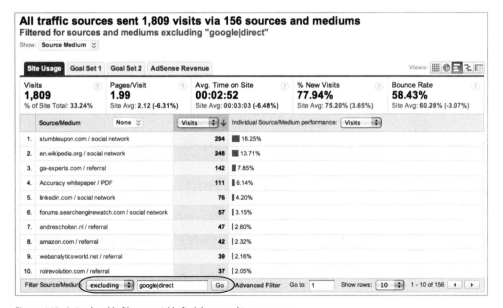

Figure 4.13 A simple table filter to quickly find data matching a pattern

The advanced filter of Figure 4.14 is an extension of the previous standard filter. That is, multiple filter criteria are specified. In this case, a Time on Site of 5 minutes or greater AND a Goal Conversion Rate of greater than 10 percent are specified. Note that at the time of writing only the AND logic operator is available for advanced filters. Therefore, the data shown in the table of Figure 4.14 matches all of these conditions.

Figure 4.14 An advanced table filter for complex table filtering

Using table filters is a powerful way of drilling down into large volumes of table data by specifying either simple or complex filter criteria. Try different examples and combinations to become familiar with these.

 Note: Figures 4.13 and 4.14 make use of a simple regular expression for pattern matching. Appendix A contains an overview of using regular expressions. You can also specify partial matches as filter criteria—for example, "whitepaper" will match "Accuracy Whitepaper," "Whitepaper for SEO," and so forth. The filter criteria are not case sensitive.

Tabbed Report Menus

Label F: Above the report table is a set of tabbed menus. You can think of tab menus as extensions of the table width—that is, rather than having an overly wide table containing all visit metrics, we can have more manageable, shorter tables separated into tabs. Effectively, a tab is used to hide the extended table from view.

You will notice that the Site Usage tab is always present for this report (and many others). The report provides headline metrics of Visits, Pages Per Visit, Average Time on Site, Percent New Visits, and Bounce Rate. Whether you see additional tabs will depend on your configuration. For example, if you have configured your goals (up to 20 split into five sets), use e-commerce transaction tracking, or use AdWords or AdSense, then metrics for all of these may be displayed in their own separate tabs. If you have not configured these, the tabs will not show.

In effect, moving between tab menus is analogous to moving across a large data table. If you find an interesting data point in your Site Usage report, at the very least you will want to see if this is replicated in your goal conversion and e-commerce tabs. For example, does a large influx of visitors from Twitter lead to a concomitant increase in goal conversions or revenue from that source?

> **Tip:** Ideally you will want to see all data viewable in one long, continuous row. However, that would never fit into your browser so neatly! If you do wish to achieve this, export your data into CSV format (or XML or TSV), and view this using Excel or a similar spreadsheet application. The export contains the data from all menu tabs.

Segmentation View

Label G: As you will discover from reading this book and experimenting with reports yourself, there are many ways to segment data in Google Analytics. One of the simplest is the segmentation view. Using this drop-down menu enables you to compare one set of data against another.

To best illustrate this feature, I use the Visitors > Map Overlay report shown in Figure 4.15. The following statement interprets the example presented: Show only California visitors who used an organic (non-paid) search engine to reach my website—that is, cross-segment visitors by geography and referral source.

Segmenting your data is a powerful way for you to understand your visitor personas—both geographics and demographics. As shown in the drop-down menu of Figure 4.15, there are a large number of segmentation dimensions to select from. Segmentation is discussed in greater detail in Chapter 8.

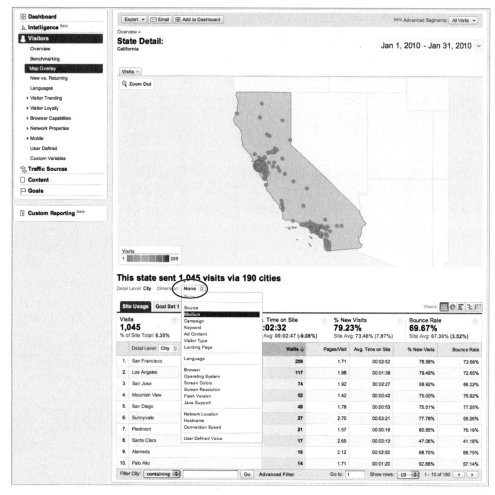

Figure 4.15 Example of the segmentation view

Chart Options

Label H: By clicking on the drop-down menu above the data-over-time graph, you can select which metrics you wish to see plotted. The default is always Visits, though the list can be extensive. In addition to changing the graphed metric, you can simultaneously compare two metrics against one other. Each metric is presented in a different color and is scaled by either the left or right y-axis—see Figure 4.16.

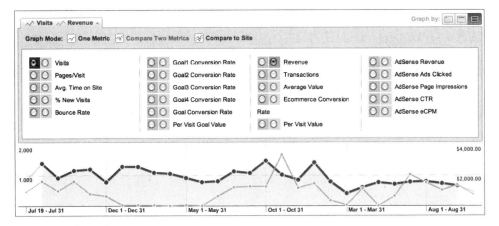

Figure 4.16 Different chart options

A further chart option is Compare to Site. For a single graphed metric, this adds a plot for the site-wide average. Compare to Site makes sense when you drill down into your reports. For example, when viewing data from the Google search engine only, selecting Compare to Site plots Google visits relative to the site-wide data. This is illustrated in Figure 4.17, where you can see that Google contributes to the majority of visits to this site. Without the Compare to Site option, this information, particularly how the correlation varies over time, would not be so obvious.

Note: Unless you drill down into your reports, the Compare to Site option will overlay its chart data directly on top of your current data. This is because report data is not segmented by default.

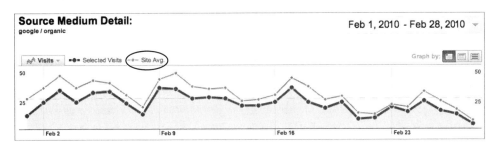

Figure 4.17 Comparing the segment google / organic with the site average

Export and Email Features

Label I: Data export is available in four industry-standard formats: PDF, XML, CSV, and TSV. Select Export from the top of each report to have your data exported in PDF (for printable reports), CSV or TSV (to import into Excel or a similar spreadsheet application), or XML (the open-source standard for importing into third-party applications).

> **Note:** The additional CSV for Excel format is there to better handle the UTF-8 encoding used by Google Analytics reports. UTF-8 encoding is a way to ensure non-ASCII characters sets are handled correctly in web pages. Google Analytics requires this because reports need to be available in 25 languages. However, an import of UTF-8 encoded data into Excel does not go smoothly—hence the slightly modified format for this purpose.

Manually exporting data is great for manipulating it further or for creating one-off reports to present to your team. Once you have chosen which reports are important to your stakeholders, you will probably wish to have these sent to them via email—either ad hoc or scheduled on a regular basis. To do this, choose the Email link next to the Export link. You can schedule reports to be sent daily, weekly, monthly, or quarterly, as per Figure 4.18.

Figure 4.18 Scheduling a report for email export

If you wish to group a set of reports into an existing email schedule, use the Add to Existing link, as shown in Figure 4.19.

Set Up Email: All Traffic Sources
Back to report

| ✉ Send Now | ⏱ Schedule | ▣ **Add to Existing** |

○ **PDF downloads** (sent monthly)
  Reports: Top Content
  Recipients: brian@omegadm.co.uk
  Attachment: pdf

○ **Wiki referrals** (sent monthly)
  Reports: Medium Detail: referral
  Recipients: brian@omegadm.co.uk
  Attachment: pdf

Add Report

Figure 4.19 Adding a report to an existing email schedule

Email Scheduling Settings

Settings are saved on a per-user and profile combination. Therefore, two different users viewing the same profile can set their own e-mail schedules.

When scheduled, all times are local to Mountain View, California (Google headquarters). Although the exact time is not specified, a daily report sent in the morning will actually be sometime in the afternoon for European customers.

Exporting data is an effective feature of Google Analytics that provides you with the flexibility of manipulating your web visitor data. If exporting data is a key requirement for your website analysis, consider also the automatic export options the Google Analytics export API can provide—discussed in Chapter 12, "Integrating Google Analytics Data with Third-Party Applications."

Exporting More Than the Maximum Number of Rows Displayed

The maximum number of report rows that can be displayed in the user interface is 500. The data export functions of Google Analytics also have the same maximum. To increase the number and avoid this limitation, use the following tip:

Append &limit=5000 (or however many rows you need) to the URL displayed in your browser address bar. Press Enter to reload the report. For example:

```
https://www.google.com/analytics/reporting/all_sources?id=2097117&
seg0=-1&pdr=20090101-20090131&cdr=20081201-20081231&cmp=average&gdfmt=
nth_day#lts=1258641047453&limit=5000
```

This does not change the display in the user interface, but it does allow you to export the data with more table rows. Select the Export tab (label I), and select CSV or TSV format (not CSV for Excel). The current export limit is 20,000 rows. If you require more than this, export the first 20,000 rows then view the 20,000th line (via Label D of Figure 4.4), and export again.

The other options shown around label I, namely Add To Dashboard and Visualize, are discussed in Chapter 5, "Reports Explained."

Chart Display and Annotation

Label J: If you mouse over any of the data points within the data-over-time graph, you will notice that each point displays its date and value, alongside the equivalent comparison data point if Compare To Past is selected. In addition, at the bottom of the chart (along the x-axis), you can click to add a chart annotation. That is, you can add a note to highlight your thoughts or mark a key event relevant to your website.

An example set of annotations is shown in Figure 4.20. Looking at the data-over-time chart, you can see that there was a catastrophic drop in visitor numbers on July 8—from 20,000-plus visits down to zero. An investigation revealed that the Google Analytics Tracking Code (GATC) was left off by mistake during a systemwide update. At the time all those involved in the metrics collection and analysis team were made aware of the issue, but looking back months or even years later, the incident will be forgotten.

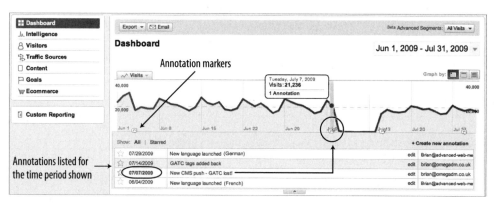

Figure 4.20 Viewing a chart annotation

The use of chart annotations allows you to log events such as this directly on the data charts and therefore avoid wasting time reinvestigating the issue later. Similarly, large peaks can be labeled. Website updates, new campaign launches, system maintenance, public holidays, dates of blog posts, tweets, product launches, PR pushes, unseasonal weather conditions, world news—whatever events you consider would significantly influence your traffic—should be recorded.

Annotations are added on a per-day basis, and any day can have multiple associated annotations. To create a new one, select a data point on *any* data-over-time chart and click Create New Annotation. This reveals the creation window just below the chart, as shown in Figure 4.21. Alternatively, if a data point has an existing annotation, the creation window will be revealed when you select it (as per Figure 4.20). You can then create a new annotation from within the window.

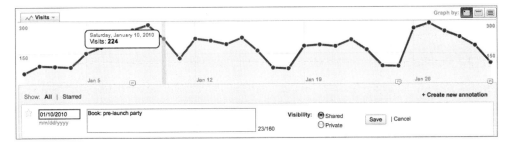

Figure 4.21 Adding a new chart annotation

Within the creation window shown in Figure 4.21, use the default displayed date or edit it accordingly. Then add your event note in the box provided—up to 160 characters. Annotations are applied on a per-user basis. Therefore, you can choose your notes to be private—only viewable by yourself—or public—viewable by all report users. Once set, annotations are displayed on *all* data-over-time charts within the same profile. Owners can edit or delete these at any time.

For those events that are more important than others, you can highlight your annotations by adding a star (this is a highlighting technique familiar to any Gmail user). Highlighted annotations are set on a per-user basis. That is, another user viewing the same profile will not see your starred annotations.

Secondary Dimensions

Label K: So far, only one dimension has been displayed in the example reports presented here—from Figure 4.4, this is the Source / Medium referral combination for a visit. It is also possible to display a secondary dimension within the same table. The secondary dimension employs a drop-down menu—containing the same items as used in Figure 4.15 for the segmentation view—to add an extra layer of information, as shown in Figure 4.22.

The example in Figure 4.22 shows the top referral Source / Medium and Landing Page combinations. This allows you to ascertain which combinations perform best while within the *same* report, that is, quickly and efficiently. Without the secondary dimension, you would need to view two separate reports to gather this information.

Table Sorting

Label L: For any particular report you may be viewing, you will initially see the Site Usage chart with concomitant table report. By default, tables are sorted by the third column entry in descending order; usually this is the number of *visits*. To reverse the sort order, click the Visits column header entry. Alternatively, to sort on another column, click the desired column header.

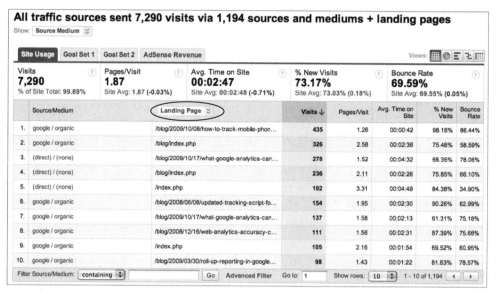

All traffic sources sent 7,290 visits via 1,194 sources and mediums + landing pages

Show: Source Medium ⌄

Site Usage	Goal Set 1	Goal Set 2	AdSense Revenue					Views:

Visits	Pages/Visit	Avg. Time on Site	% New Visits	Bounce Rate
7,290	**1.87**	**00:02:47**	**73.17%**	**69.59%**
% of Site Total: 99.89%	Site Avg: 1.87 (-0.03%)	Site Avg: 00:02:48 (-0.71%)	Site Avg: 73.03% (0.18%)	Site Avg: 69.55% (0.05%)

	Source/Medium	Landing Page ⌄	Visits ↓	Pages/Visit	Avg. Time on Site	% New Visits	Bounce Rate
1.	google / organic	/blog/2009/10/08/how-to-track-mobile-phon...	435	1.26	00:00:42	98.16%	86.44%
2.	google / organic	/blog/index.php	326	2.58	00:02:36	75.46%	58.59%
3.	(direct) / (none)	/blog/2009/10/17/what-google-analytics-can...	278	1.52	00:04:32	68.35%	78.06%
4.	(direct) / (none)	/blog/index.php	236	2.11	00:02:26	75.85%	66.10%
5.	(direct) / (none)	/index.php	192	3.31	00:04:49	84.38%	34.90%
6.	google / organic	/blog/2008/06/08/updated-tracking-script-fo...	154	1.95	00:02:30	90.26%	62.99%
7.	google / organic	/blog/2009/10/17/what-google-analytics-can...	137	1.58	00:02:13	61.31%	75.18%
8.	google / organic	/blog/2008/12/16/web-analytics-accuracy-c...	111	1.56	00:02:31	87.39%	75.68%
9.	google / organic	/index.php	105	2.16	00:01:54	69.52%	60.95%
10.	google / organic	/blog/2009/03/30/roll-up-reporting-in-google...	98	1.43	00:01:22	81.63%	78.57%

Filter Source/Medium: [containing ⌄] [_____] [Go] [Advanced Filter]   Go to: 1   Show rows: [10 ⌄]   1 - 10 of 1,194 ◄ ►

Figure 4.22 Viewing a secondary dimension

Note: The other items viewable in Figure 4.4, namely, Add to Dashboard, Visualize, and Advanced Segments, are discussed in more detail in Chapters 5 and 8.

Summary

In Chapter 4, you have learned the following:

Viewing data You now understand metrics and dimensions and the different ways you can view data with chart options, data views, and table sorting.

Comparing date ranges You have learned the different ways you can select and compare date ranges and how to make use of the timeline feature to select periods of interest, such as data peaks or troughs.

Drilling down into data You have seen the role of table filters and the use of regular expressions to refine displayed data to a specific page or group of pages.

Looking at visitor segments You know how to focus on particular visitor segments using the tabbed layout and cross-segmentation drop-down menu.

Exporting and scheduling of reports You have learned how to export and schedule the emailing of reports in different file formats.

Annotating charts You now understand how to annotate charts so that important events or changes are logged for further reference.

Reports Explained

At my last count, Google Analytics had over 100 default reports—and when you take into consideration segmentation options, pivot views, intelligent alerts, and custom reporting, the number grows exponentially. Clearly, no one person is going to look at all those reports on a regular basis—nor should you try. Going through all of the types of reports would be tedious and laborious. Hence, I attempt to whet your appetite to investigate further.

In this chapter, I focus on the important first-level reports—the ones I consider to be the top reports (areas of interest) in Google Analytics— that can give you that initial understanding.

Of course, my report selection may not reflect the information most important to you—every website is different in some way. Once you understand the drivers or blocking points for your visitors, you can focus on more detail and build your own list of top reports.

In this chapter, you will learn:

The Dashboard overview

The top reports

To understand page values

To understand data sampling

The Dashboard Overview

Before delving into specific reports, I want to discuss the Dashboard view—as this is not really a report in itself. The Google Analytics Dashboard is the first screen displayed when you log in to view your reports; see Figure 5.1. This is the overview area where you can place a summary chart or table copied from the main body of the Google Analytics reports. From here, if you notice a significant change, you can click through to go to the detailed report section.

Figure 5.1 The Dashboard summary report

You can also change the selection of reports shown on your Dashboard at any time, with a maximum of 12. To add to the Dashboard, navigate to a report and click the Add To Dashboard link at the top of the page, as highlighted by label I in Figure 4.4 in the previous chapter. When viewing the Dashboard, you can move the summary report's placement by dragging and dropping it into another desired position.

Try the following exercise as an example. Suppose a key market for you is California, and at the current time, being able to log in to Google Analytics and immediately view the summary data from California visitors is a key requirement.

1. From the Visitors menu, select Map Overlay.

2. From the displayed map, drill into the area of the map as required, and then click Add to Dashboard.

3. Select the Dashboard item from the side menu. Your map overlay for California will be displayed as the last item on the Dashboard page.

4. Drag and drop the map overlay into the top position (or any desired position).

From now on, each time you log in to Google Analytics and view your reports, the first item displayed in your Dashboard will be the map overlay summary of visitors from California, with just one click to access more detail.

Once you have your key reports set on your Dashboard, consider scheduling an email export of this to yourself and senior management. Click the Email button at the top of the Dashboard report and set it accordingly. I recommend you schedule this weekly at most, although monthly may be the optimal frequency in order for you to maintain interest—a key factor when disseminating information to people not directly involved with the performance of your website. You'll learn more about this in Chapter 10, "Focusing on Key Performance Indicators."

A key point to emphasize is that a Dashboard is configured on a per-user basis. That is, the contents are specific to your login and cannot be adjusted by others.

The Top Reports

This section is not intended as a definitive list of the only reports you should look at. Rather, these are suggestions to take you beyond the initial visitor volume numbers that you will see. Reviewing these reports for your organization will give you an understanding of visitor behavior before mapping your organization's stakeholders and determining what key performance indicators to use for benchmarking your website.

The reports in this chapter are not listed in any particular order, except for the first one, which is a clever piece of technology (released October 2009) that deserves special attention. Before reading this chapter, review Chapter 3, "Google Analytics Features, Benefits, and Limitations," to understand how to use the Google Analytics user interface.

Intelligence Report

The Intelligence report can dramatically impact your day-to-day analysis of web traffic data—for the better. It is a *key* report (deliberate emphasis) to greatly help you spot important changes in traffic patterns. This not only saves you the trouble of having to drill down into reports to find important changes yourself but also actually finds the important changes for you in the first place. By that, I mean the Google Analytics Intelligence engine is able to spot and highlight changes in metrics that often go unnoticed, buried beneath a plethora of other metrics—hence the name for this report set.

Intelligence Overview

Intelligence works by performing statistical analysis on your previous data patterns. Assuming you have reasonable levels of visits to your site each day (more than 100 visits per day) and have enough historical data for the algorithms to work with (at least a month), Google Analytics can *predict* with reasonable accuracy what traffic levels are expected for the current day, week, and month. Comparing predicted values with the level of traffic you actually receive allows Google Analytics to highlight significant changes and optionally send you email alerts about them.

 Note: Regardless of your traffic levels, Google Analytics will still generate Intelligence reports for you. However, because all statistical methods require good sample sizes (hundreds of data points) to become valid, low traffic volumes can yield odd results. The larger your traffic volumes, the more accurate predicted statistics are.

Figure 5.2 shows an example Intelligence report with four areas highlighted—the two types of alerts (Custom and Automatic), an alert triggered on November 14, the Sensitivity slider, and the Significance bar.

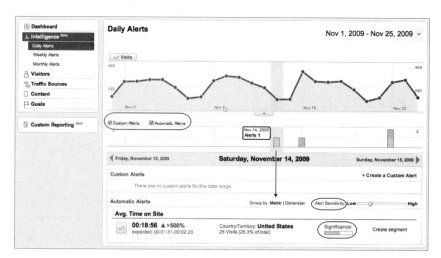

Figure 5.2 The Intelligence report

A mouseover of an alert brings up the mini display showing the date and number of alerts for that period. Clicking an alert bar reveals the metrics that triggered the alert. Alongside each alert is a Significance bar. Significance is the probability that a result is not due to chance. The grayer the Significance bar appears, the more likely the result is real and not simply by coincidence.

By default, daily alerts are displayed when this report is first loaded. That is, Google Analytics compares metrics for one day against the previous day and determines if this meets expectations. If not, an alert is highlighted. From the menu navigation you can change the comparison frequency to weekly or monthly. For example, you can compare the aggregate metrics for one week (or month) against the previous week (or month).

Automatic Alerts

Automatic alerts, color-coded green on the alert chart (for example, the alert of November 14), are those Google Analytics determines by its algorithmic method. Each day, the Intelligence engine checks for significant changes in the following 12 dimensions:

- All Traffic
- Visitor Type (new or returning visitor)
- City
- Region
- Country/Territory
- Campaign
- Keyword
- Source
- Medium
- Referral Path
- Landing Page
- Exit Page

Any metric for these dimensions that falls outside the computed expected range is flagged on the report as a green bar—underneath the corresponding date of the main data-over-time graph. From Figure 5.2, the automatic alert generated on the November 14 is due to U.S. visitors spending an average of greater than 500 percent more time on site compared to what Google Analytics expects it to be for that day. The alert also shows what the expected range is for the triggered metric—in this case, between 1:31 and 2:20 minutes.

Knowing that on a particular day, U.S. visitors spent on average six times longer on your website than normal could be a valuable piece of information that your marketing or sales department can act on. Without the Intelligence alert, this information could go unnoticed as just another data point on the Visitors overview chart.

What Constitutes a Significant Change?

The Google Analytics definition of a significant change, or what triggers an alert, is when a metric varies by a magnitude of X-sigma or greater from its expected value—where X-sigma is a multiple of the metric's standard deviation. To understand this, let's look at some standard statistical theory.

A normal (Gaussian) distribution is defined by two parameters: the mean value mu (μ) and its standard deviation sigma (σ). Sigma is a measure of the average difference a value is from the mean. The universal properties of a normal distribution are such that differing from the mean by +/− one standard deviation will account for 68 percent of all measured values. Differing by two standard deviations will account for 95 percent of all values. Differing by +/− six standard deviations will represent 99.9999998 percent of all values—in order words, as close to all measured values of the distribution as possible without being pedantic.

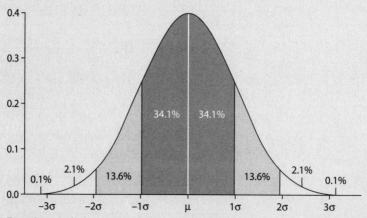

This graphic is taken from http://en.wikipedia.org/wiki/File:Standard_deviation_diagram.svg and is used with permission.

The sensitivity of an alert, that is, how easy it is to trigger an alert, is determined by the Sensitivity slider bar—highlighted in Figure 5.2. Although not labeled, the slider bar scales from 7-sigma (least sensitive) to 1-sigma (highest sensitivity). For example, at the highest sensitivity, if a metric is more than one standard deviation away from the predicted mean, an alert will be triggered. Conversely, at the lowest sensitivity value, a metric must be seven standard deviations away from the mean to trigger an alert. Hence, the sensitivity slider is a balance between highlighting significant changes and alert overload. My preference is to set this just to the left of halfway—approximately 3-sigma, 99.7 percent away from the mean value.

What Constitutes a Significant Change?

Related to the Sensitivity setting is the Significance bar shown for each alerted metric. This is a complex calculation that determines whether the alert is real, not the result of a random fluctuation. However, in Google's traditional way, the complexity of this calculation (confidence intervals and p-values) is hidden from the user and replaced with the very simple gray bar graphic that represents a scale of 0 to 9. The darker gray the bar appears, the more "real" the result. Essentially, alerts with a low Sensitivity setting that produce significant results should be prioritized for further investigation.

For more information on the statistics of normal distributions, see http://en.wikipedia .org/wiki/Normal_distribution.

Custom Alerts

Custom alerts are color-coded blue on the alert chart and displayed in a same way as automatic alerts along the alert timeline. If for a given period you have both automatic and custom alerts, then a stacked bar of both blue and green alerts is displayed (as per the alert on November 22).

To create a custom alert, follow the + Create a Custom Alert link, as shown in Figure 5.2. The same 12 dimensions used for automatic alerts are available for custom alerts. In addition, you can select from 16 metrics to trigger your alert:

- Visits
- Visitors
- Pageviews
- Bounce Rate
- Average Time on Site
- Percent New Visits
- Goal Conversion Rate
- Goal 1-4 Conversion Rate
- Goal 1-4 Value
- Per Visit Goal Value
- Revenue
- Average Order Quantity

An example custom alert is shown in Figure 5.3. This is set up in advance of an online campaign (Jan10 sale) with the purpose of emailing the account user when the campaign starts to generate revenue.

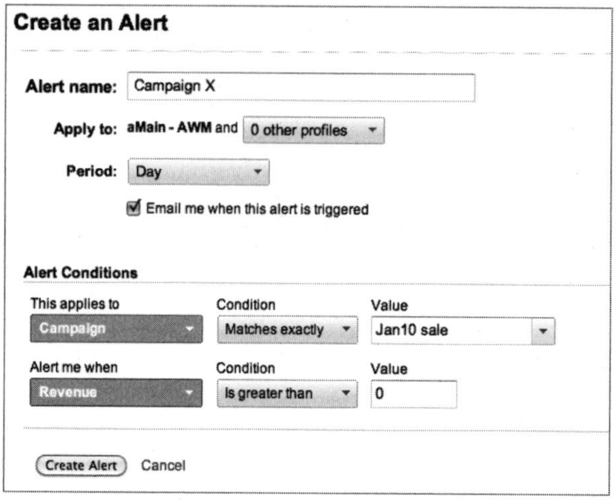

Create an Alert

Alert name: Campaign X

Apply to: aMain - AWM and [0 other profiles ▾]

Period: [Day ▾]

☑ Email me when this alert is triggered

Alert Conditions

This applies to
[Campaign ▾]

Condition
[Matches exactly ▾]

Value
[Jan10 sale ▾]

Alert me when
[Revenue ▾]

Condition
[Is greater than ▾]

Value
[0]

(Create Alert) Cancel

Figure 5.3 Example custom alert

 Note: Emailing of alerts is currently available for custom alerts only.

Visitors: Map Overlay

First shown in Figure 4.15, Map Overlay shows you where your visitors come from, enabling you to identify your most lucrative geographic markets. Visually stunning, the Map Overlay report is also an extremely powerful report—it gets across the information you need to know at a glance. The displayed maps are color-coded by density—the darker the color, the higher the reported metric, such as more visits or revenue. A density key is shown in the bottom-left corner, and you can mouse over the regions, countries, or cities to view top-level metrics.

Geographic information is extremely powerful for targeting your online marketing activities. For online marketing, Google AdWords (and other pay-per-click networks) enable you to geo-target your advertisements. In this respect, the Map Overlay report of Google Analytics can be used in two ways: to identify new locations for potential online campaigns and to measure the effectiveness of existing geo-targeted campaigns.

To illustrate its ability, consider the two charts in Figure 5.4—shown for the same profile and date range. Figure 5.4a shows the visitor information, whereas Figure 5.4b shows the e-commerce conversion rate data from the same visitors. As you can see, the map densities are quite different.

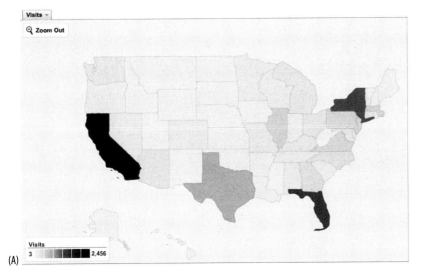

(A)

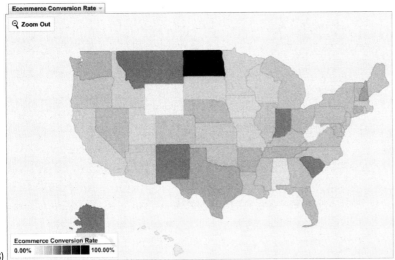

(B)

Figure 5.4 a) Geographic density of visits, b) geographic density of e-commerce conversions for the same data set

Within the map, you can zoom in from world view to continent, regional, and country view and along the way examine visitor statistics from that part of the world—right down to city level. Below the displayed map is the tabulated data for the selected region. For each location, you can cross-segment your visitors against other metrics, such as referral source, medium, language, and so on, as shown in Figure 4.15. For example, once you have found your location of interest, you can cross-segment to view which search engines are popular with your visitors there.

Ecommerce: Overview Report

Even if you do not have an e-commerce facility, you can still monetize your website by adding goal values. Either way, the e-commerce reports of Google Analytics enable you to identify revenue sources and trace transactions back to specific campaigns—right down to the keyword level. Individual product data can be viewed and grouped (shown as categories), as can loyalty and latency metrics.

 Note: Monetizing a non-e-commerce website is discussed in detail in Chapter 11, "Real-World Tasks."

From the initial Ecommerce Overview report (see Figure 5.5), a wealth of information is provided for you to feast on. From here, any click-through takes you to a more detailed report. For example, click one of the top-performing products to view its individual report, and then cross-segment against other fields, such as referral source, campaign name, keywords, and so on. These details are driving visitor transactions. Such information is critical for a successful product-by-product search-engine marketing initiative.

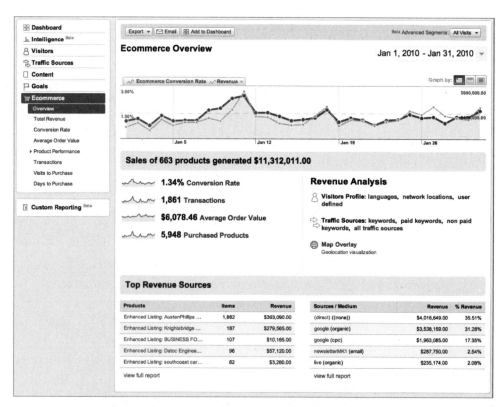

Figure 5.5 A typical e-commerce report

Motion Charts

Simply put, motion charts are a great aid for data visualization. They turn static, dry, two-dimensional data tables into something that is interesting and even exciting to look at—a rare phenomenon in the world of data analysis! Most important, motion charts animate data against time, so that you can see how multiple metrics evolve. A static version is shown in Figure 5.6.

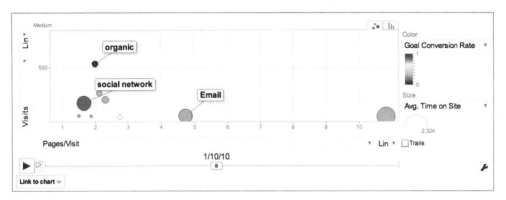

Figure 5.6 Motion chart for the Traffic Sources Medium report

A motion chart is not a report in itself. Rather, it's an animated view of an existing report. Hence, you can access motion charts from most Google Analytics reports by selecting the Visualize button at the top of the screen (refer to Figure 4.4, label I). When a report is animated, five dimensions are plotted: x-axis, y-axis, data point size, data point color, and time. Because of the difficulty in describing how all of these interact on paper, I strongly encourage you to view the official YouTube demonstration on the Google Analytics channel at www.youtube.com/watch?v=D4QePIt_TTs.

> **Note:** The voice behind many Google Analytics demonstrations on YouTube is Alden DeSoto. You can view one of his many talents (and other Google Analytics team members) by searching for "Motion Charts Anthem" at youtube.com.

In the example of Figure 5.6, the five dimensions for each data point are as follows:

- Visits—shown on the y-axis
- Pages Per Visit—shown on the x-axis
- Goal Conversion Rate—color
- Average Time on Site—bubble size
- Time—displayed as a time slider (paused on January 10)

The signals for success in this motion chart are data points that are up and to the right, have a large bubble size, and appear hot (red in color). This informs me of any mediums that are driving high volumes of traffic, with strong engagement (in terms of pages per visit and time on site), and convert. Knowing if and when that happens, how long such a situation lasts, and how each medium compares over time are key pieces of information that are practically impossible to ascertain from a static set of data tables.

There are many more features of motion charts that you should explore. For example, you can plot x- and y-axis on a log scale (used when the range of displayed values is very broad), adjust the speed of an animation, plot trails for each data point, zoom in on a particular chart area, alter the opacity of data points to highlight those of most importance, or even change the presentation from a bubble chart to a bar chart—though I have always preferred the bubble chart format.

At first, the motion of multiple metrics moving across the screen can make your eyes glaze over; it can even be mesmeric. "It's pretty, but what's it telling me?" is often the initial response from users. However, once you get familiar with following the different metrics, you'll learn how to spot unusual events that require further investigation.

The key to getting the most from this report is selecting long time periods (greater than a month) and repeatedly viewing the animation in slow motion. After three or four run-throughs you should notice any activity of interest. Select Trails and adjust the opacity to focus on certain data points accordingly. Remember that motion charts are a visualization tool—that is, the precursor for further analysis.

Tip: Ensure you use all five dimensions of the motion chart available to you—even if fewer are required. For instance, I often use the color and bubble dimensions as duplicates to highlight a significant change. In the example of Figure 5.6, if the Average Time on Site is not a metric of interest, I would also use the bubble size for the Goal Conversion Rate. That way, higher conversion-rate data points are double highlighted with a large bubble and warmer color. The more you can make important data stand out, the better.

Benchmarking Report

Benchmarking is actually not a report that I refer to often—more likely once a quarter or even once per year. However, I include it here because it can contain interesting information, particularly in the initial phases of assessing your website's performance.

One of the issues that faces all website owners is how to quantify success. For example, is capturing 10,000 visits a day good or bad compared to similar-sized websites? Is an average bounce rate of 34 percent high or low compared to that of your peers? Those can be difficult questions to answer because most people, particularly your competitors, wish to keep such information confidential. However, Google Analytics does have a solution to this if you choose to share your web data anonymously with Google.

Figure 5.7 shows how six high-level metrics compared with other sites of a similar size that are Google Analytics users. You can be more specific in your comparison by selecting an industry from the Open Category List link. The selected category is user specific. That is, each Google Analytics user can choose an industry category for comparison, though you cannot narrow this down by geography. You can change the selection at any point with results updated in real time.

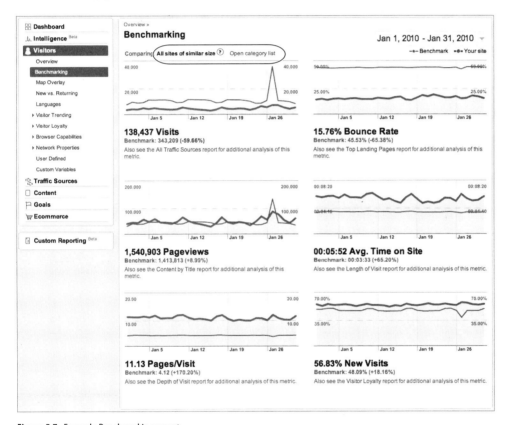

Figure 5.7 Example Benchmarking report

New industry categories are added automatically to the list when the number of Google Analytics users in them passes a critical number. This is to ensure the sample size is large enough to make comparisons valid and to protect the identity of participants (small sample sizes may enable you to deduce identities). The emphasis here is that all shared data is anonymous—you are unable to know which websites are in the comparison report, and no revenue or conversion information is revealed.

Goal and Funnel Reports

As discussed throughout this book, goal reporting (conversions) is an important measurement for your organization. Regardless of whether you have an online retail facility or not, measuring goal conversions is the de facto way to ascertain whether your website is engaging to your visitors.

In addition to measuring your goal-conversion rate, the Goal Verification report enables you to view the specific URLs that trigger the reporting of a goal. This is particularly useful when a wildcard is used to define the goal, for example, *.pdf. In this case, the Goal Verification report will list all the PDF downloads that trigger the reporting of that defined conversion.

Also within this section, the Reverse Goal Path report considers the last three steps (pages) visitors took before reaching a goal. This is an excellent place to look for visitor paths that could be considered for *funnel analysis*.

What Is a Conversion?

It is important to clarify that a goal is synonymous with conversion in this context. Say, for example, one of your website goals is *.pdf—that is, the download of any PDF file. A visitor arrives on your website and downloads five PDF files. Google Analytics will count this as one goal conversion (not five, as you might expect). The rationale for this is that visitors can convert only once during their session, which makes sense.

To view the total number of PDF downloads and which files they were, you can either view the Goals > Goal Verification report or, if you wish to cross-segment the data, go to the Content > Top Content report and use the table filter to display only .pdf files, as shown in the following graphic:

Funnel analysis (sometimes referred to as *path analysis*) is a subsection of the Goals report. Some goals have clearly defined paths that a visitor takes to reach the goal. An obvious example is an e-commerce checkout process; others include newsletter sign-ups, registration subscriptions, reservation systems, and brochure requests. Not all goals have a defined path, but if yours do, then it is useful to visualize how your visitors traverse them (or not) to reach the goal. The Funnel Visualization report does just that, and an example is shown in Figure 5.8.

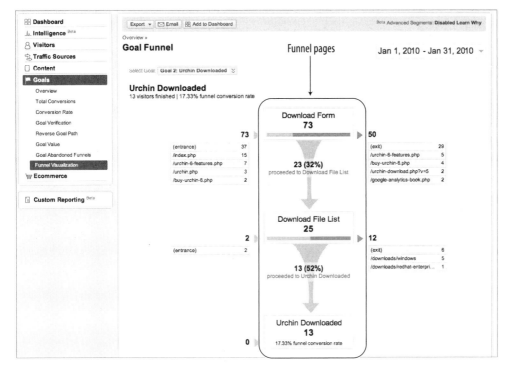

Figure 5.8 A three-step Funnel Visualization report

The pages of a funnel a visitor is expected to pass through (as defined by your configuration) to reach the goal are in the central section highlighted in Figure 5.8—in this example, to download software. The tables to the left are entrance pages into the funnel. The tables to the right are exit pages out of the funnel steps—that is, where visitors go when they leave the funnel page. The exit pages listed can be other pages within your website or show the visitor leaving the site completely. A well-defined funnel should have the vast majority of visitors passing downward into a minimum number of funnel steps.

Funnel visualization enables you to assess how good your funnel pages are at persuasion—that is, how good are they at getting visitors to proceed to the next step, getting closer to approaching conversion. A funnel with pages optimized for persuasion and conversion should have a minimal number of exit points (pages to the right of the funnel), thereby leading to a high conversion rate. A detailed funnel analysis is considered in the section "Funnel Visualization Case Study" in Chapter 11.

Traffic Sources: AdWords

As you might expect from a product by Google, Google Analytics integrates tightly with AdWords, and this has recently been extended and enhanced (March 2010). Other integrations include AdSense and FeedBurner. Undoubtedly in the future there will be further integrations with other Google products. In fact, I see this as Google's main challenge moving forward—integrating Google Analytics within all Google products to provide a unified measurement platform for each.

AdWords, being a key component of any digital marketer's armory these days, has a dedicated subsection within the Traffic Sources report section, as shown in Figure 5.9. Assuming you have an AdWords account and this is linked to your Google Analytics account, your AdWords impression, cost, position, and click-through data are imported into this report section once per day.

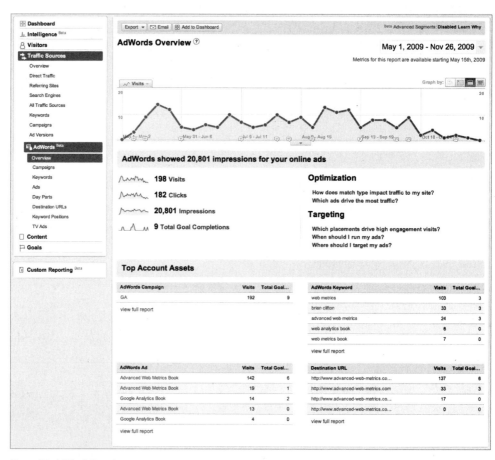

Figure 5.9 AdWords Overview report

The power of combining your AdWords account data with Google Analytics is illustrated in Figure 5.10—that is, when you wish to drill down into the data. For example, clicking the Ads menu takes you to the ads level of data with the same column headings and report tabs as for any other visitor type. That is, for each specific ad you are running, you can view its performance in terms of site usage, goal conversions, and e-commerce performance. You can achieve the same at the Campaigns and Keywords levels by selecting these reports from the side menu.

Figure 5.10 AdWords performance report at the Ad Group level

The data-over-time graph shown in Figure 5.10 reveals how AdWords visitor traffic has decreased (left-hand scale), while at the same time the average ad position has increased (right-hand scale). Perhaps there is a correlation between click-through rates and ad position. Experience tells us there is such a correlation, but maybe the cause is due to reduced ad budgets (your ad showing for only parts of the day) or some other effect. Whatever the cause, you can investigate this further by graphing other AdWords metrics—for example, impressions, click-through rates, cost per click, and the like. In order to view your ads, place your mouse cursor over one of the ad names. This reveals the ad itself as a pop-over.

Note: When viewing your ads within the AdWords report section, bear in mind that if changes have been made over time, only the current version is displayed when you mouse over the ad name.

A unique menu tab for AdWords reports is Clicks, shown in Figure 5.11. With the exception of the Revenue and ROI columns, the data in the Clicks report is imported directly from your AdWords account. Revenue is obtained by summing your website's monetized goals and e-commerce revenue generated by AdWords visitors.

In addition to tracking your AdWords cost data, you should keep a close eye on your ROI (Return on Investment). Chapter 11 looks at interpreting this data in more detail.

Figure 5.11 AdWords Campaigns report showing the Clicks detail

 Note: As per other Google Analytics reports, the data shown in the AdWords reports is based on visitors with cookies. Therefore, the numbers may not match the totals viewed in your AdWords account reports, because AdWords can only track clicks. For a more detailed explanation of discrepancies between AdWords and Google Analytics reports, see Chapter 2, "Available Methodologies and Their Accuracy."

Traffic Sources: AdWords Keyword Report

For managing an AdWords account, digital marketers create ads for groups of related search terms. For example, to target visitors to this book's website, I might select the following search terms:

- Web metrics
- Advanced web metrics
- Advanced web metrics first edition
- Advanced web metrics second edition
- Advanced web metrics *any* edition

Assuming the same landing-page URL is suitable for each search term, I would create a single ad for all four-plus search terms—there is no need to create separate ads for each term. Within AdWords you achieve this by setting the match type equal to *phrase* for the term "web metrics." In this way, any search query with this phrase will result in my ad being displayed to the user. Incidentally, I could also add negative search terms, so that "web metrics with Yahoo Analytics" does not display my advertisement!

In this case, a single ad targeting multiple search terms, "web metrics" is the *bid term*, whereas the visitor's actual search term that triggers the ad is called the *search term*. You can view the correlation between bid terms and search terms in the Traffic Sources > AdWords > Keywords report, as shown in Figure 5.12. Note that Google Analytics uses the terminology "AdWords Keyword" and "Matched Search Query" for the bid term and search term, respectively.

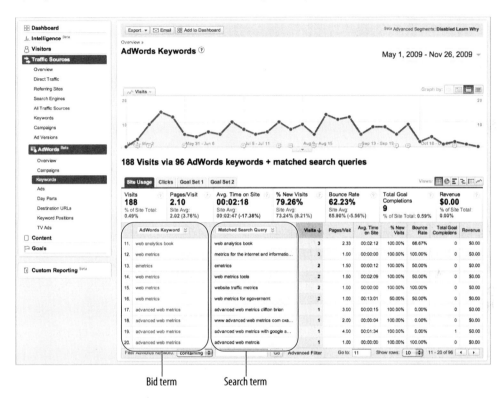

Bid term   Search term

Figure 5.12 AdWords Keywords report showing the bid term and corresponding search terms used

Digital marketers also have the option of displaying ads on either the Google search network (google.com, ask.com, aol.com, and so on), the content network, or both of these. The Google content network comprises websites, news pages, and blogs that partner with Google to display targeted AdWords ads. The partner uses AdSense to manage this and shares in some of the click-through revenue.

If you have opted in to displaying your ads on the Google content network, then the AdWords Keyword column will display the domain of the site where your ad appeared. This is shown in Figure 5.13, where the secondary dimension is set to show the Ad Distribution Network the visitor came from. As you can see, when the Ad Distribution Network is equal to Content, the AdWords Keyword (bid term) displayed is the referring domain displaying your ad. At this time it is not possible to view the actual keyword matching that AdSense has performed.

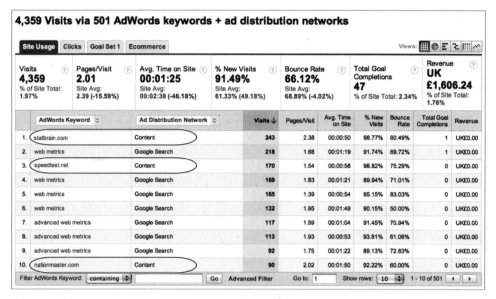

Figure 5.13 AdWords Keywords report showing the referring domain for content network visitors

Note: You can find further information on AdSense and the content network at www.google.com/
adsense and http://adwords.google.com/select/afc.html.

Traffic Sources: AdWords Keyword Positions Report

This is a unique report, not found in any other web analytics tool, and an extremely powerful report it is too. The AdWords Keyword Positions report tells you what position your AdWords ad was in when the visitor clicked it. In addition, you can drill down and view how your ad conversion rate, bounce rate, per-visit goal value, number of transactions, revenue, and other metrics vary by position, using the Position Breakdown drop-down menu.

In Figure 5.14, the left side of the report table lists the AdWords keywords you have bid on during the specified time frame. Selecting one of these options changes the view on the right to a schematic screen shot of the Google search engine, with the positions your ad was shown at and the number of visits received while in that position. This emulates what the positions would look like on the Google search engine results page.

You might expect that the higher your position in the AdWords auction model, the more visitors you receive. Figure 5.15 illustrates the data showing just that—an expected long-tail chart (this figure was created by exporting the report data into a spreadsheet).

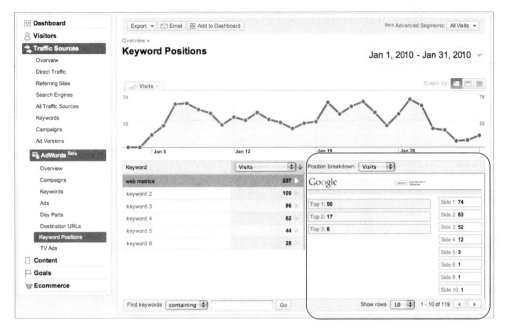

Figure 5.14 AdWords Keyword Positions report

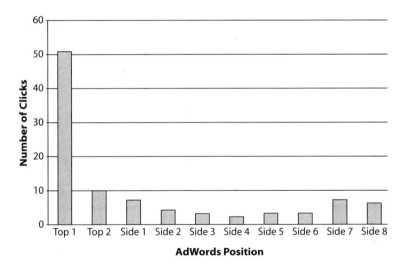

Figure 5.15 Number of clicks by AdWords position—export 1

However, long-tail charts are not always the case. Figure 5.16 shows a different keyword selected from the same report. As you can see, positions 3, 5, and 9 are more popular. With this information you may consider the use of the Position Preference feature in your AdWords account. Position Preference is an AdWords option that enables you to set where you would like your ad to rank among all ads shown on a given search engine results page. For instance, from Figure 5.16, you may prefer your ads to appear only when they rank between positions 3 and 9. By enabling Position Preference in your AdWords account, the AdWords system will attempt to make your ad appear in the positions you set—though no position is guaranteed. For more information on Position Preference in AdWords, see `http://adwords.google.com/support/bin/answer.py?hl=en&answer=31788`.

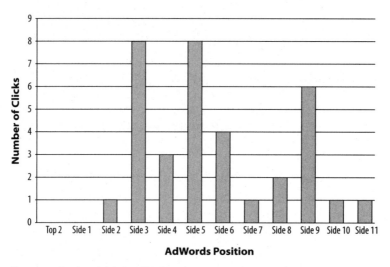

Figure 5.16 Number of clicks by AdWords position—export 2

The data shown in Figures 5.15 and 5.16 reflects only visits. However, you can select and compare any of the other segments listed in the Position Breakdown menu. Chapter 11 looks at how you can optimize your AdWords advertising by using the Keyword Positions report.

Content: Top Content Report

Knowing which pages are popular on your site is an obvious first step when assessing your website's performance. In addition to common per-page metrics such as pageviews, time on site, bounce rate (single-page visits), and percentage of visits that leave from this page (% Exit), an additional column is labeled $ Index. This is a measure of the value of a page, and it is computed from goal and e-commerce values. The higher the $ Index value, the higher the importance of that page in generating conversions. The calculation of $ Index is discussed later in this chapter.

The Top Content report is much more than just a hit counter for successful page views. It can provide valuable insight into visitor behavior. Consider the report shown in Figure 5.17. Notice in this example I have used the table filter to exclude visits to blog pages. Why? Because it was suspected for this site that blog visitors would exhibit very different behavior from those visitors likely to complete the goal conversions defined.

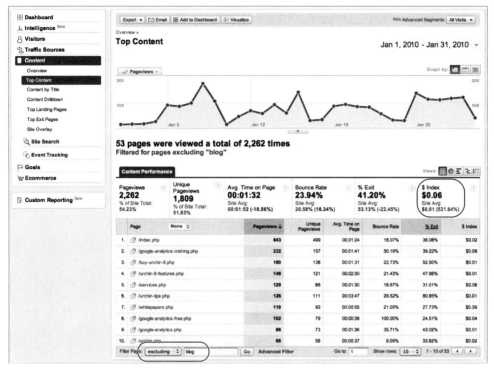

Figure 5.17 Top Content report, with blog pages excluded

This hypothesis is confirmed by the report. That is, pages viewed outside the blog section are more than six times (+521.64%) more valuable than the average for the site as a whole. That, of course, does not mean that the blog is not valuable. However, its purpose is clearly different, and therefore different marketing strategies and different success metrics should be employed for the blog section of the site.

> **Note:** Because the differences in page value ($ Index) for blog and non-blog pages are so great, it would make sense to segment other reports by this criterion. Segmenting visitors is discussed in Chapter 8.

You can drill down and investigate page properties in greater detail by clicking the page name links. This enables you to perform navigational analysis and cross-segmentation against other metrics. For example, Figure 5.18 shows the navigational analysis of the page /index.php (the website home page). This shows how visitors arrived on that page and where they went next.

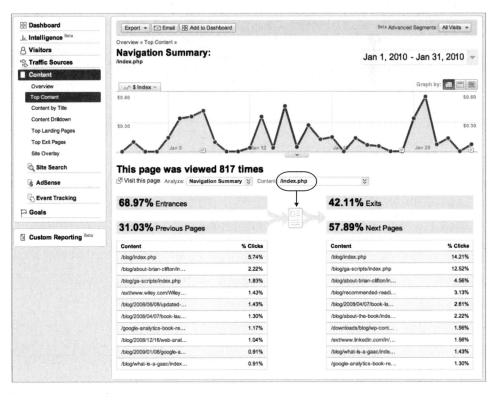

Figure 5.18 Navigation Summary report

Content: Site Overlay Report

The Site Overlay report loads a page from your website and then overlays it with the key metrics for each link on that page. It's an excellent visual way to see which links on your website drive traffic, conversions, transactions, and revenue (see Figure 5.19). The default view is to display the number of clicks received for each link on a page using a small bar chart under the link—mouse over the bar chart to see the corresponding pop-up metrics. You can easily change the metrics displayed using the Displaying dropdown menu at the top of the report.

Figure 5.19 shows Goal Value metrics overlaid on this book's home page. The pop-up metrics shown are for the link Hacks & Downloads. As you can see, the goal value for this link is $108, which is 11 percent of the page total. However, another link (Site Blog) is driving even more goal revenue—22 percent of the page total. The Site Overlay report is a working HTML preview of your website. Hence, you can click any of your links to navigate to that page and view its site overlay statistics.

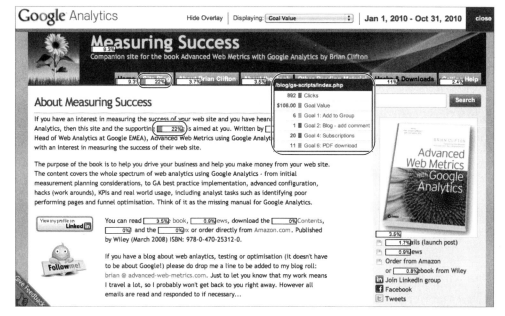

Figure 5.19 Site Overlay report

As you may have noticed in Figure 5.19, some metrics are duplicated. For example, beneath the Site Blog link is another link that also contributes 22 percent of the goal revenue from this page. In fact, these two metrics are duplicates because each link points to exactly the same page. Chapter 9, "Google Analytics Hacks," describes how you can customize your links so that the Site Overlay report can be used to differentiate links that point to the same URL.

Current Limitations of Site Overlay

In order for site overlay to work correctly, the page referenced by each link must exist as an HREF element on the page being viewed. That is, if you use the function `trackPageView()` for generating virtual pageviews (as described in Chapter 7, "Advanced Implementation"), the Site Overlay report will not work. Nor will site overlay work for pages containing Flash content.

Another example is the submission of forms. A submit button or form tag does not contain an HREF element. Therefore, if you have a goal conversion configured as a form submission, the Site Overlay report will not show this as part of the metrics.

Site Search: Usage Report

The Site Search reports contained in the Content section of Google Analytics are dedicated to understanding the usage of your internal search engine (if you have one). For large, complex websites with thousands, and in some cases hundreds of thousands, of product pages, having an internal site search engine is critical for a successful visitor experience—no navigational system can perform as well as a good internal search engine in these cases.

At the very least, Site Search reports are a form of market research—every time visitors enter a keyword into your search box, they are telling you exactly what they want to find on your website. Marketers can use this information to better target campaigns. Content creators can use this to improve page titles and descriptions. Product managers can use this as a feedback mechanism for designing new features or adding new products. Hence, a report on the search terms used by visitors on your website is clearly powerful information for your organization.

In addition, understanding where on your website a visitor uses your search box, what page they go to following a search, how long they stay on your site after conducting a search, whether they perform further search refinements, whether they are more likely to make a conversion, and whether their average order value is higher are also vital clues that can help you optimize the visitor experience.

The answers to all these questions can be found in the Content > Site Search section, as shown in Figure 5.20.

Figure 5.20 Site Search report showing which destination pages are visited following a search

Understanding Page Value

$ Index is an incredibly useful per-page metric that you will see throughout the Content reports section. As described earlier in this chapter, $ index is a measure of the value of a page and is defined as follows:

$$\text{\$ Index} = \frac{(\text{goal value} + \text{e-commerce revenue})}{\text{unique pageviews}}$$

$ Index goes beyond a simple measurement of popularity by indicating how valuable a specific page is to you in monetary terms. Essentially, it is a way for you to prioritize the importance of pages on your website. For example, when you are optimizing your website content for user experience—that is, to improve conversion rates—you probably want to start by first looking at the pages with the highest $ Index, because these have been shown to have the greatest impact.

To understand its significance, consider the following page paths that four different visitors take on a website. In these examples, the goal page is set as page D, and its goal value when reached is $10 (assuming no e-commerce revenue):

Page path 1: B > C > B > D

Page path 2: B > E > B > D

Page path 3: A > B > C > B > C > E > F > D > G

Page path 4: B > C > B > F

To calculate $ Index for these pages (A–G), Google Analytics sets each unique page in a path that precedes the goal page (D) to have the same goal value ($10). That is, goal values are attributed only to the pages leading up to and including the goal page, not after. These goal values are assigned to a page only once per path. This may sound complicated as written, but actually the calculation is quite simple, as illustrated by Table 5.1.

Unique pageviews are used for the calculation to show how many times a page in a session contributes to the goal.

▶ **Table 5.1** Calculating $ Index

Page	(Goal Value + Revenue) / Unique Pageviews	$ Index
A	10/1	10
B	30/4	7.5
C	20/3	6.7
D	30/3	10
E	20/2	10
F	10/2	5
G	0/1	0

As you can see from Table 5.1, the highest-value pages over all visitor sessions (highest $ Index) are pages A, D, and E—whenever these pages are in a path, a goal conversion occurs. Second highest is Page C—its value is 7.5, because it occurs in most paths that contain a goal conversion. Page G never appears before a goal, so there is no goal value for it.

The order of $ Index values for pages on this example website is as follows (where pages A, D, and E are the same value):

(A, D, E) B C F G

With this in mind, if you were to perform page optimization testing, it would make sense to first work on pages A and E (page D is the goal page, and in this case it is the thank-you page, so optimization is not required). You may also question the value of keeping page G—it appears to add no value to this website, as indicated by its zero $ Index value. That's a good question for investigation.

Because $ Index is so powerful at highlighting key pages that contribute a monetary value for your website, I recommend you always sort your Content reports by $ Index to see how they factor into your success (see Figure 5.21).

Figure 5.21 Listing $ Index page values

The list of $ Index values shown in Figure 5.21 could be considered your prioritization list for optimizing pages, and the power of this is illustrated by example: Notice row 3 of the table. The page /SecureTrading/purchase-failure.php is the failure page displayed when a purchaser incorrectly completes their payment details. It obviously has a high relevance to a successful order (high $ Index) and shows a significant number of pageviews compared to /SecureTrading/purchase-success.php—the page displayed when payment is completed successfully.

The data clearly indicates that the owner of this website should investigate the payment form (/SecureTrading/purchase-form.php) to identify whether elements on that page are causing visitor confusion. For example, maybe date values are expected in U.S. format, which is not clear to a European visitor. Whatever the reason, the use of $ Index has highlighted an opportunity to improve the efficiency of a page that provides significant revenue to the organization.

You can plot the trend of $ Index over time for a specific page by clicking its page link and selecting the appropriate chart to display.

Note: $ Index is independent of path route and path length. Using the preceding example, $ Index for page B = 10 for paths 1, 2, and 3.

Understanding Data Sampling

This may seem like an odd chapter in which to be discussing the intricacies of data sampling. Nonetheless, I include it here because it may affect how you view your reports. Hopefully this section will allow you to mitigate those circumstances when numbers appear to not look right.

Google Analytics collects *all* visitor data regardless of the volume of traffic your website receives. For example, I am aware of websites using Google Analytics that have in excess of one billion pageviews per day! However, because most Google Analytics reports are built on the fly, in real time as you query your data, Google may automatically sample your data as the report is being generated. The purpose is to optimize the data query and minimize any delays in the building of your report.

Whether your data is automatically sampled or not is determined on a per-report basis. Ultimately this comes down to the volume of data to be processed by your report request—determined by the date range and report type you select in the user interface. At present, sampling occurs when you use the Dimension drop-down menu within a report and the resulting data for that segment contains more than 500,000 visits for that selected date range.

To illustrate this, suppose you are viewing the report of a single page that received 10,000 pageviews. The data shown will be calculated from a sampled data set if the total number of visits to your website profile for the same date range exceeds 500,000.

As shown in Figure 5.22, Google Analytics indicates that a report is sampled with a yellow notification box at the top of the screen and a confidence interval by the side of each sampled metric—for example, +/-5%. The confidence interval indicates the range of values that is likely to include the correct statistic. Keep in mind that the larger the data set being sampled, the more reliable the estimate and therefore the smaller the confidence interval—and vice versa.

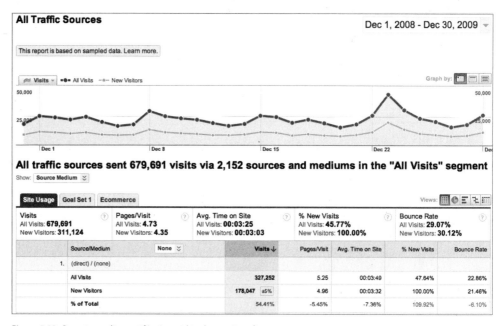

Figure 5.22 Report sampling notification within the user interface

Report sampling takes place at the profile level. If you wish to avoid automatic sampling, you can use profile filters to separate visitors into smaller profiles, for example, U.S. visitors only, UK visitors only, and so on—see Chapter 8 for further details. An alternative is to view your reports over a smaller time frame, such as weekly rather than monthly, to reduce the number of unique table row entries.

 Note: You can control how much data is collected and sent to Google servers from your website. This is discussed in Chapter 7, in the section "Customizing the GATC."

Summary

In Chapter 5, you have learned the following:

How to effectively use the Dashboard The Dashboard is an ideal place to save and organize your most important reports and key metrics.

How to identify the most useful reports You have learned about the top reports that can help you understand visitor behavior and provide a starting point for further investigation and optimization.

How to assess web pages with page values You saw how page values can be used to evaluate the importance of a web page.

How to understand data sampling You have learned how data sampling may impact the numbers you see in your reports and how to mitigate these.

Implementing Google Analytics

Part III provides a detailed description of everything you need to do in order to collect visitor data—from creating an account to installing the tracking code in a best-practice manner.

Following this, we look at the configuration of goals, funnels, filters, and visitor segmentation. Finally, "Google Analytics Hacks" is a workaround chapter for when you have bespoke requirements.

If you are a webmaster or web developer, this section is for you. However, in keeping with this book's philosophy, the content is not aimed at programmers, so we keep technicalities to a minimum. You should, though, at least be familiar with HTML and JavaScript.

In Part III, you will learn to do the following:

III

Getting Up and Running with Google Analytics

This chapter is all about getting the basics right—creating an account in the right place (stand-alone or linked to AdWords), tagging your pages, becoming familiar with the concept of multiple profiles, and ensuring that you track AdWords visitors and import the concomitant impression and cost data for such visitors. If you are an agency or hosting provider, you need to consider a couple of additional points, which are described in this chapter.

In Chapter 6, you will learn:

To create your Google Analytics account

To tag your pages with the tracking code

To create a backup of your web traffic data to a local server

To use profiles in conjunction with accounts

To roll up reporting and collecting data into multiple accounts

To set up agency client accounts

To link Google Analytics with Google AdWords

To link Google Analytics with Google AdSense

To answer common implementation questions

Creating Your Google Analytics Account

Opening a Google Analytics account and performing a base setup is straightforward. An initial setup enables you to receive data that you can use to begin to understand your website traffic. The time required to do this varies depending on your expertise and familiarity with HTML, your website architecture, and the level of access you have to your web pages. Setting up one website can take as little as an hour or as long as a full working day.

However, it is important to manage your expectations. The initial collection of data is only the first step in understanding your visitor traffic. Configuring your Google Analytics account to your specific needs (see Chapters 7–9) is what will give you the most insight. Nonetheless, collecting the base data first will give you the initial information with which you can fine-tune your setup, so let's get the foundations right.

You can open a Google Analytics account in one of two ways. If you have an AdWords account, it makes sense to do it there, so that your campaigns can automatically be tracked and cost and impression data imported. Click the Analytics tab at the top of your AdWords account area, as shown in Figure 6.1a.

If you do not have an AdWords account, visit the stand-alone version at `www.google.com/analytics/sign_up.html`, as shown in Figure 6.1b. These versions are identical, though the stand-alone version is limited to a maximum of five million pageviews per month—approximately three thousand visitors per day. Obviously, Google wishes to encourage you to try their online advertising solutions! If you really do not wish to use AdWords, open an account and limit your spend to $1 per day.

If you use the stand-alone version, note that the e-mail address you use to create the account is a Google login. A Google login account is a registered e-mail address for a single sign-on for any Google-hosted service. It gives you access to Google Analytics and other Google services such as AdWords, Gmail, Google Groups, personalized search, your personalized home page, and more. If you've used any of these services before, you already have a Google login.

 Note: You can register and use any e-mail address, such as your company e-mail address, as your single sign-on Google login. It does not have to be a Gmail account. In fact, it is preferable to use your company email address so that users and administrators are easily identified and managed. The only requirement is that the email must belong to an individual and not a mailing list. Further information is available at `www.google.com/accounts`.

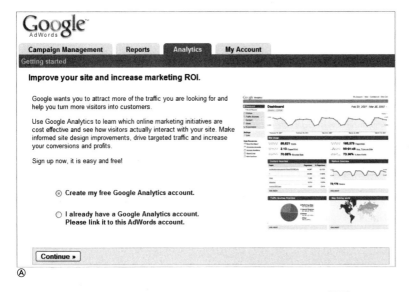

Figure 6.1 Creating a Google Analytics account from (a) within AdWords or (b) via the stand-alone interface

Once you have your Google account, follow the instructions during the sign-up process. If you are using the stand-alone version and you have multiple Google accounts, choose the one you most frequently use. That way you will be automatically logged into Google Analytics if you have previously logged in to another Google service. In addition, ensure that you select the correct region (the one closest to you) from the drop-down menu at the top-right corner of the sign-up page. This sets the language for the sign-up process and ensures that you are shown the correct Terms of Service that you agree to on completion of the account-creation process.

AdWords Users—a Special Case

If you have a Google AdWords account, it is important to create your Google Analytics account from within the AdWords interface. This enables you to quickly and easily link the two—that is, automatically import your AdWords cost data and be able to log into Google Analytics via your AdWords account interface. You will also be able to log in via the stand-alone interface if you wish.

If you have created a stand-alone Google Analytics account first and then wish to link to your AdWords account, ensure that your AdWords administrator e-mail address is also a Google Analytics administrator. Then when you click the Analytics tab within AdWords, you will be given the option to link your two accounts.

Tagging Your Pages

The most important part of the sign-up process is the penultimate setup screen, which identifies your unique tag to be placed on all your pages. This is referred to as the Google Analytics Tracking Code (GATC). It is the use of this single tag to collect visitor data—the exact same tag for every page—that makes Google Analytics so easy to install.

Note: As of December 2009, Google Analytics has an alternative version of its GATC in beta, known as "asynchronous GATC," or "async" for short. This modified GATC is loaded in *parallel* with your page. By using this method load times may be improved and latency reduced. The asynchronous GATC is aimed at content heavy websites with rich media applications. This book describes the standard GATC only, which is applicable to the vast majority of websites. For further information on async, see: `http://code.google.com/apis/analytics/docs/tracking/asyncTracking.html`.

Understanding the Google Analytics Tracking Code

The GATC is a snippet of JavaScript that is pasted into your pages. The code is hidden and acts as a beacon for gathering visitor information and sending it to Google Analytics data-collection servers. An example is given in Figure 6.2.

Note: If your Google Analytics account is already set up, you can access the settings shown in Figure 6.2 from the Profile Settings area. Click on the "Check Status" link.

The purpose of the GATC was schematically described in Figure 3.2 in Chapter 3, "Google Analytics Features, Benefits, and Limitations." Here we discuss the code in a little more detail. Essentially, there are three parts:

(1) The call of a master JavaScript file from Google servers The master file, ga.js, contains the necessary code to conduct data collection. This file is approximately 18KB in size,

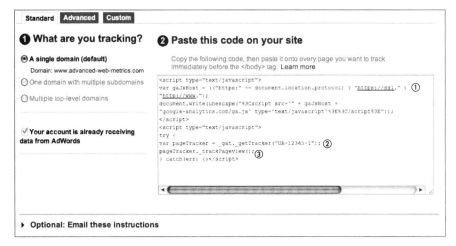

Figure 6.2 Typical GATC to add to your pages

although once it is called it is cached by the visitor's browser and available for all subsequent pageviews. It is the exact same file for all Google Analytics accounts. Therefore, if your visitor has recently visited another website that also has Google Analytics installed (highly likely), the ga.js file may not be requested at all.

Although this section of the GATC looks verbose, it is simply detecting whether to load ga.js via a standard HTTP web request or via the HTTPS (encrypted) protocol. This autodetection means you do not have to change anything should your visitors access secure areas of your website, for example, to enter credit card details.

(2) Your unique account ID, in the form UA-*XXXX*-*YY* This is unique for each Google Analytics account and must be used exactly as quoted or your data will be sent to another account. This can happen accidentally (an implementation typo) or deliberately (people wishing to "spoil" your data by using your account ID elsewhere). You can use a filter to prevent the latter, and we discuss this in Chapter 8, "Best-Practices Configuration Guide."

(3) The call of the JavaScript routine _trackPageview() This is the workhorse of Google Analytics. Essentially, the line pageTracker._trackPageview() collects the URL of the pageview a visitor loads in their browser, including associated parameters such as browser type, language setting, referrer, and timestamp. Cookies are then read and set, and this information is passed back to Google data-collecting servers.

As you can see in Figure 6.2 sections 2 and 3 are embedded in a try-catch code block. This is a neat little JavaScript trick to handle errors—preventing unnecessary error messages from being shown to the visitor. For example, if a visitor has an ad blocker installed (such as AdBlock Plus for Firefox) that prevents the ga.js file from loading, an error will be produced when _trackPageview()attempts to communicate with it. Using the try-catch code, the error is captured (not displayed) and no visitor tracking takes place. This is considered better than showing an irrelevant message to the visitor.

Also noticeable in Figure 6.2 are alternatives to the GATC depending on your requirements: These are shown in the top tabbed menu as Standard, Advanced, and Custom. Essentially, if you have a single domain name that requires tracking, for example, www.mysite.com, the Standard GATC is what you need. The other variations are for when you have a site where visitors can pass between subdomains, for example, www.mysite .com to helpdesk.mysite.com, or third-party domains, for example, www.mysite.com to www.payment-gateway.com. We cover the Advanced and Custom variations in "Customizing the GATC" in Chapter 7, "Advanced Implementation."

Migrating from urchin.js to ga.js

Prior to December 2007, the file referenced by the GATC was called urchin.js and contained different code from that of ga.js. If you are still using urchin.js, you should migrate to the newer ga.js code. To get your new tracking code, you'll need to have administrator access to the Google Analytics account. Follow these steps:

1. Log in to your Google Analytics account.

2. For each profile, click Edit.

3. Click the Check Status link.

4. Follow the onscreen instructions for adding the new tracking code (ga.js).

Deploying the GATC

Next, all that is required is for you to place the GATC on your pages. If you have a relatively small website in terms of number of pages, you can copy and paste the GATC into your HTML. Alternatively, if you have built your website using a template or content management system (CMS), simply add the GATC to your master template or footer file. The recommended placement is just above the </body> tag at the bottom of the page. This will minimize any delay in page loading, because the ga.js file will be loaded last.

Once your pages are tagged, you should start to see data in your account within 4 hours. However, for new accounts, it can take up to 24 hours, so be patient at this stage!

An important aspect of the deployment of your GATC is that it must be pasted onto *all* of your pages. As described in Chapter 2, "Available Methodologies and Their Accuracy," missing page tags is a common issue that casts doubt over the validity of your data. Apart from incorrect visitor and pageview counting, you may see your own website listed as a referrer, missing referrer information altogether (usually overwritten), having overly long or short time onsite and time-on-page metrics, showing unusual values for bounce rates, and many other peculiarities.

The greater the percentage of missing page tags, the greater the inaccuracy. As a guide, I aim for a minimum of 98 percent deployment of the GATC. That is, 98 percent of all your pages should have the GATC present for you to have confidence in your reports. Less than this requires investigation. If you have less than 90 percent deployment, then don't even bother looking at your reports—fix the problem first. Table 6.1 lists available tools that can help you troubleshoot the deployment of your GATC. Other troubleshooting tools are listed in Appendix B.

▶ **Table 6.1** Tools to help troubleshoot your GATC deployment

Tool Name	Comment
SiteScan by EpikOne	Free and paid Software as a Service (SaaS) vendor. Performs a text search and regular expression match for the GATC: www.sitescanga.com.
WASP (Web Analytics Solution Profiler)	A Firefox plug-in that detects the setting of the GATC cookies plus 100 other vendor tools. Works on a page-by-page (free) or site-scanning (paid) basis: www.webanalyticssolutionprofiler.com.
Joost de Valk's statistics detector	Free Greasemonkey script for Firefox. Performs a text search and regular expression match for the GATC plus 34 other vendor tools. Works on a page-by-page basis only: http://yoast.com/tools/seo/greasemonkey/statistics-detector/.
ObservePoint	Paid Software as a Service (SaaS) vendor. Detects the setting of the GATC cookies plus Omniture's. Works as a site-scanning and monitoring/alert tool: www.observepoint.com.
Accenture Digital Diagnostics (formerly Maxamine)	Paid Software as a Service (SaaS) vendor. High-end site diagnostic tool: www.accenture.com/Global/Consulting/Marketing_and_Sales_Effectiveness/Digital/Transformation_Suite/AMSDiagnostics.htm.

Although having a CMS is a more reliable way to insert your GATC, you still need to ensure this includes all newly created pages—not always taken into account by default—and any pages that do not use your standard template. If you do not have a content management system, there are alternatives for automatically tagging your pages. Two of these are Apache mod_layout and PHP auto_append_file.

Mod_layout is a loadable module (similar in principal to a plug-in) for the Apache web server. It can be used to tag your pages as visitors request them. If you use Apache, ask your development team or hosting provider to install the mod_layout loadable module from http://tangent.org. Once implemented, the Apache web server will automatically insert your GATC on every page it serves. Note that this means exactly that, *every* page served, so you should add exclusions to those files where the GATC is not required, such as robots.txt, cgi-bin files, and so forth.

A full description of mod_layout is beyond the scope of this book, but an example configuration for your httpd.conf file is given in the following snippet. In this example, two file types are ignored (*.cgi and *.txt) and the file contents of utm_GA.html (the

GATC content—as per Figure 6.2) are inserted just above the </body> tag of the HTML page being served:

```
#mod_layout directives
LayoutMergeBeginTag </body>
LayoutIgnoreURI *.cgi
LayoutIgnoreURI *.txt
LayoutHeader /var/www/html/mysite.com/utm_GA.html
LayoutMerge On
```

 Warning: If your pages use the CAPTCHA method (http://en.wikipedia.org/wiki/CAPTCHA) of generating security images to protect your site from automated form submission, test that your security image still loads. If not, you may need to exclude the embedded file that calls the security image from mod_layout.

If your pages are PHP generated (filenames ending in .php), then you can use the auto_append_file directive. This specifies the name of a file that is automatically parsed after the main file. The file is included as if it was called with the PHP require() function. The directive can be included in your php.ini configuration file (therefore applied to *all* files and hosts on your server), or more specifically in an .htaccess file in your website root directory, as follows:

```
<IfModule mod_php5.c>
    php_value include_path ".:/usr/local/lib/php"
    php_value auto_append_file "/home/www/utm_GA.html"
</IfModule>
```

In this way, the file utm_GA.html, the file containing your GATC, is automatically appended to the bottom of all your PHP web pages—after the HTML </head> tag. Note that the full path is used to define the utm_GA.html location. In this way, all subdirectories also receive the GATC without further modification. If you wish to avoid this, define a relative path.

 Note: Because auto_append_file is applicable only to PHP files, you do not have to exclude non-PHP files such as robots.txt. If other file types do require the GATC, you will need to do this manually. You also do not need to worry about other included PHP files receiving a double page tag. For example if you use <? include("/includes/navigation.php"); ?> within your pages to build your navigation menu, these will not be tagged.

If you are a Wordpress user, there are several plugins available to help you automatically insert your GATC onto your pages. See: http://wordpress.org/extend/plugins/search.php?q=google+analytics.

Back Up: Keeping a Local Copy of Your Data

Keeping a local copy of your Google Analytics data can be very useful for your organization. For example, Google currently commits to keeping data for up to 25 months, enabling you to compare annual reports. That is adequate for most users, but what if you wish to retain your data longer? Also, because Google will not pass raw data to third parties, you will need an alternative if your web visitor data must be audited. Publishing sites often require this.

The technique is to modify the GATC so that it simultaneously sends your visitor data to your web server logfiles as well as to Google Analytics data-collection servers. This is a one-line modification of the GATC as highlighted:

```
<script type="text/javascript">
    var gaJsHost = (("https:" == document.location.protocol) ? "https://ssl."
: "http://www.");
    document.write(unescape("%3Cscript src='" + gaJsHost + "google-analytics.
com/ga.js' type='text/javascript'%3E%3C/script%3E"));
</script>
<script type="text/javascript">
try {
    var pageTracker = _gat._getTracker("UA-12345-1");
    pageTracker._setLocalRemoteServerMode();
    pageTracker._trackPageview();
} catch(err) {}</script>
```

The consequence of this modification is an additional request for a file named __utm.gif from your web server when your GATC is loaded. This is a 1 × 1-pixel transparent image that Google Analytics uses to append its information into your web server logfiles. Create the file for yourself and upload it into your document root, that is, where your home page resides.

Because all web servers log their activity by default, usually in plaintext format, you should see the presence of additional __utm.gif entries in your logfile almost immediately after making this change. These correspond to the visit data as seen by Google Analytics. Also, your web server must log cookie information. If you do not see cookie values in your logfiles, check the specified log format of your web server. A correctly working Apache logfile line entry should appear as follows:

```
79.79.125.174 advanced-web-metrics.com - [03/Jan/2010:00:17:01 +0000] "GET
/images/book-cover.jpg HTTP/1.1" 200 27905 "http://www.advanced-web-
metrics.com/blog/2008/02/16/accuracy-whitepaper/" "Mozilla/5.0 (Windows; U;
Windows
 NT 6.0; en-GB; rv:1.9.0.15) Gecko/2009101601 Firefox/3.0.15 (.NET CLR
3.5.30729)"
```

```
"__utma=202414657.217961957.1257207415.1257207415.1257207415.1;
__utmb=202414657.1.10.1257207415; __utmc=202414657;
__utmz=202414657.1257207415.1.1.utmcsr=google.co.uk|utmccn=(referral)|utmcmd
=referral|utmcct=/imgres; session_start_time=1257207419839"
```

Note that this is a single line in your logfile, beginning with the visitor's IP address and ending with the GATC cookie values.

For Microsoft IIS, the format can be as follows:

```
2010-01-01 01:56:56 68.222.73.77--- GET /__utm.gif
utmn=1395285084&utmsr=1280x1024&utmsa=1280x960 &utmsc=32-
bit&utmbs=1280x809&utmul=en-us&utmje=1&utmce=1&utmtz=-
0500&utmjv=1.3&utmcn=1&utmr
=http://www.yoursite.com/s/s.dll?spage=search%2Fresultshome
1.htm&startdate=01%2F01%2F2010&man=1&num=10&SearchType=web&string=looking+fo
r+mysite
.com&imageField.x=12&imageField.y=6&utmp=/ 200 878 853 93 - -
Mozilla/4.0+(compatible;+MSIE+6.0;+Windows+NT+5.1;+SV1;+ .NET+CLR+1.0.3705;
+Media+Center+PC+3.1;+.NET+CLR+1.1.4322) - http://www.yoursite.com/
```

In this example, the log entry starts with the visitor's timestamp and ends with the website hostname.

In both examples, the augmented information applied by the GATC is the addition of utmX name–value pairs. This is known as a *hybrid data-collection method* and is discussed in Chapter 2.

Note that there are overhead considerations to keeping a local copy of visitor data, and we discussed these in Chapter 3, "Google Analytics Features, Benefits, and Limitations." Because web server logfiles can get very large very quickly and swamp hard disk space, I generally do not recommend keeping a local copy of your data unless you have a specific reason for doing so. That said, maintaining a local copy of your Google Analytics data does provide you with the option to do the following:

• Maintain greater control over your data—for auditing purposes, for example

- Troubleshoot Google Analytics implementation issues
- Process historical data as far back as you wish—using Urchin Software
- Reprocess data when you wish—using Urchin Software

Let's look at these benefits in detail:

Maintain greater control over your data Some organizations feel more comfortable having their data sitting physically within their premises and are prepared to invest in the IT resources to do so. You cannot run this data through an alternative web analytics vendor because the GATC page tag information will be meaningless to anyone else. However, you do have the option of passing your data to a third-party auditing service. Some website owners use third-party audit companies to verify their visitor numbers—useful for content and publishing sites that sell advertising and therefore need to validate their rate cards.

> **Warning:** Be aware that when you pass data to a third party, protecting end-user privacy (your visitors') is your responsibility, and you should be transparent about this in your privacy policy.

Troubleshoot Google Analytics implementation issues A local copy of Google Analytics visit data is very useful for troubleshooting complex Google Analytics installations. This is possible because your logfile entries show each pageview captured in real time. Therefore, you can trace whether you have implemented tracking correctly—particularly nonstandard tracking such as PDF, EXE, and other download files types and outbound exit links. See Appendix B for more troubleshooting tools.

Process historical data as far back as you wish—using Urchin Software As mentioned previously, Google Analytics currently stores reports for up to 25 months (though Google has so far made no attempt to remove older data—refer back to Figure 3.1). If you want to keep your reports longer, you could purchase Urchin Software and process your local data as far back as you wish. The downloadable software version runs on a local server and processes web server logfiles, including hybrids. Urchin also provides complementary reports to Google Analytics, as described in Chapter 3.

> **Warning:** Reports from Urchin Software will not align 100 percent with reports from Google Analytics, because these are two different data-collection techniques. For example, a logfile solution tracks whether a download completes, whereas a page-tag solution tracks only the onclick event—and these are not always going to be the same thing. Data alignment and accuracy issues are discussed in Chapter 2.

Reprocess data when you wish—using Urchin Software With data and the web analytics tools under your control, you can apply filters and process data retroactively. For example, say you wish to create a separate profile just to report on blog visitors. This is typically done by applying a page-level filter—that is, including all pageview data from the /blog directory. For Google Analytics, reports are populated as soon as that profile filter is applied—that is, from that point forward. For Urchin Software, you can also reprocess older data to view the blog reports historically.

 Note: Urchin, discussed in Chapter 3, is sold and supported exclusively through a network of Urchin Software Authorized Consultants. For a full list of USACs, see www.google.com/urchin/usac.html.

Using Accounts and Profiles

A Google Analytics profile is a set of configuration parameters that define a report. You need at least one profile in order to view your visitor data. Figure 6.2 showed the penultimate step of creating a new Google Analytics account. The last step, following the click of the Continue button, automatically creates your first profile, and this is all you need to get started viewing reports.

However, one website may have numerous separate reports. For example, perhaps you want a dedicated profile that reports on U.S. visitors only and a separate profile just for U.K. visitors. That would be one Google Analytics account with two profiles (configurations), which generates two report sets. This is best explained using the diagram shown in Figure 6.3a.

Another scenario occurs when you have multiple websites, as shown in Figure 6.3b. For example, if you have two product websites, then you could have reports for each within the same Google Analytics account with the same or different filters applied to each.

Typically you create additional profiles for your organization when you have different functions or divisions within your business. Having multiple websites is an obvious choice for generating additional profiles. For example, content targeted at different markets (mysite.com, mysite.co.uk, mysite.cn, and so on) will often have a separate team responsible for marketing. Therefore it makes sense for them to have a set of dedicated reports just for their needs. You may also wish to manage separate businesses (separate websites) within a single Google Analytics account. However, be sure you have the authority to do this—see "Agencies and Hosting Providers: Setting Up Client Accounts."

Another scenario for which having additional profiles can be beneficial is a single website with split responsibilities, for example, for customer support as well as product marketing. Customer support usually has a very different objective for the user experience compared to the rest of the website. For example, they wish to minimize the time on site (customers finding answers they are looking for quickly) and reduce goal conversions (less contact with the expensive call center). Hence providing a separate profile for this area of your website can be beneficial.

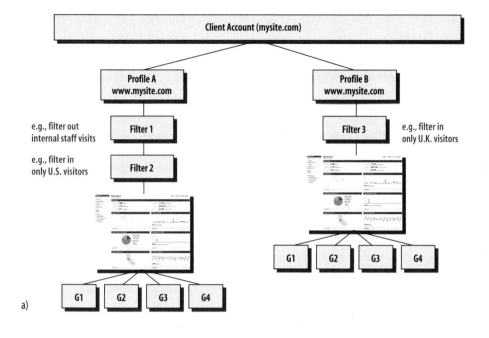

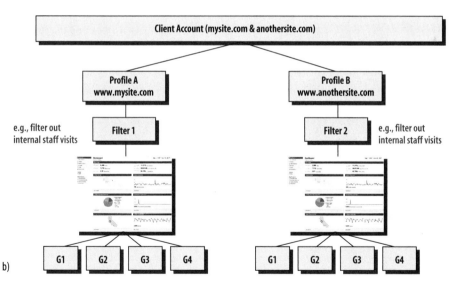

Figure 6.3 (a) Multiple profiles (reports) for the same website within one account; (b) multiple profiles for different websites within the same account

In order to create an additional profile, go to the initial Administrator login screen (refer to Figure 4.2), and select "Add new profile" from the right side of the screen. This takes you to Figure 6.4. From here, you can select to create a profile for a new domain or an existing one. Creating a profile for a new domain generates a completely new GATC. Apply this to the pages of the new domain you wish to track. Alternatively, creating a profile for an existing domain does not change your GATC— that is, you do not need to change anything on your pages. Instead it creates a separate container for existing visit data that you can then apply filters to.

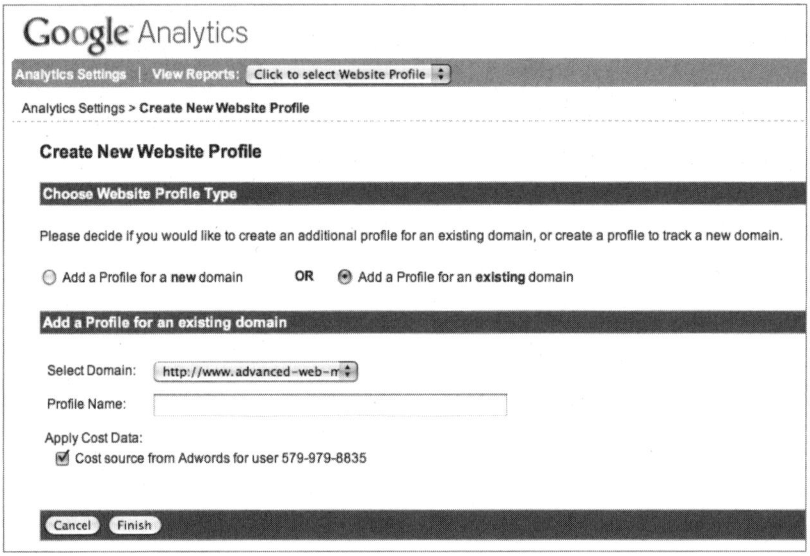

Figure 6.4 Creating additional profiles

Whether creating a profile for a new or existing domain, you have the option of applying cost data from any linked AdWords account—see "Getting AdWords Data: Linking to Your AdWords Account" later in this chapter. Creating profiles by applying filters is described in detail in Chapter 8.

Note: The maximum number of profiles for a Google Analytics account is currently 50.

An Important Note on Profile Aggregation

Once you have defined your profiles, you cannot produce an aggregate report at a later date— that is, you cannot roll up the individual reports. The strategy, therefore, is to produce an aggregate report first and then use filters to generate the separate reports, or you can add an extra GATC and collect the data into a separate Google Analytics account, as described next under "Roll-up Reporting."

Roll-up Reporting

Roll-up reporting is not a standard feature in Google Analytics. However, with a little extra coding, you can have stand-alone reports for specific (product-dedicated) websites and a roll-up report to provide a global overview.

Consider the following scenario; you have semi-autonomous country offices that have brand- or product-specific websites suitable for their particular market needs. Because of these specific needs, it makes sense to have separate, stand-alone Google Analytics accounts for each website. That way, segmentation, referral analysis, and e-commerce revenue (or lead generation) can be analyzed in detail.

However, global HQ also needs a high-level overview of *all* web visitor activity. You can achieve this by having a single "catch-all" Google Analytics account with all data from all websites aggregated together—a roll-up report. So long as the GATC deployment is managed centrally for consistency, this solution provides both autonomy for your country- or product-specific websites and a big-picture reporting view on all website activity for HQ. Each can manage their own reporting needs without impacting the other.

The principle of roll-up reporting is straightforward—you create additional Google Analytics accounts and add multiple GATCs to your web pages. One specifies the individual account, and the other is for the roll-up account. Schematically this is shown here for two websites:

```
<script>
    Call the master JavaScript file
</script>
<script>
    1. Track the siteA pageview into the individual account
    2. Track the siteA pageview into the roll-up account
</script>
```

Although I describe this technique as adding multiple GATCs, a full additional GATC is not added to your pages, just a second tracker object. An actual GATC, with the second tracker object highlighted, is as follows:

```
<script type="text/javascript">
    var gaJsHost = (("https:" == document.location.protocol) ? "https://ssl." :
"http://www.");
    document.write(unescape("%3Cscript src='" + gaJsHost + "google-
analytics.com/ga.js' type='text/javascript'%3E%3C/script%3E"));
</script>
<script type="text/javascript">
try {
    var firstTracker = _gat._getTracker("UA-12345-1");
    firstTracker._trackPageview();
```

```
var secondTracker = _gat.getTracker("UA-67890-1");
secondTracker._trackPageview();
} catch(err) {}</script>
```

Note that I have renamed pageTracker from the original GATC to firstTracker and secondTracker in order to differentiate the two instances. These can be any names you choose, though it pays to be as clear as possible. For each stand-alone website (siteA, siteB, and so on), modify the var firstTracker line to use your specific UA account number for that website. The roll-up account information, var secondTracker, remains the same for each site—in this case UA-67890-1, though of course that needs to be changed to your roll-up account number.

In this way, the marketing department at global HQ can log into Google Analytics account UA-67890-1 for their roll-up report and filter, segment, or configure as required. Country- or product-specific offices can log into UA-12345-1 and modify as they wish without impacting the global roll-up report.

 Note: For a full implementation, you also need to consider e-commerce tracking as well as the impact of numerous caveats that this approach has. This is discussed in more detail in Chapter 9, "Google Analytics Hacks."

Choosing between Roll-up Reporting and Multiple Profiles

As you will have noticed from the previous sections, roll-up reporting and multiple account profiles have very similar sets of criteria for deciding their use. So which is better?

For the vast majority of implementations, profiles will be the most appropriate choice. For example, if you have one website, use a single AdWords account and transact in a single currency and time zone. You would like to segment visitors—perhaps by location, language, or website area visited—and for this you need to ensure any associated e-commerce or AdWords data is shown consistently across all profile reports. Creating profiles by applying filters will enable you to do this efficiently, without any modification of your GATC. By default, all e-commerce and AdWords data is applied to all profiles in your account.

Roll-up reporting answers a very specific requirement of enterprise clients. Use this if you have antonymous offices or departments that wish to manage their own reporting needs, while you maintain control over data integrity, that is, the GATC deployment across the enterprise, so that all offices can compare apples with apples. Having a stand-alone Google Analytics account gives each department control over who has account access (such as web and marketing agencies) and provides a set of reports and configurations without the obfuscation of other departments. For example, if you transact in different time zones and currencies, you will want to keep these separate. You also overcome the limit of 50 profiles per account. Note that roll-up reporting of accounts is a nonstandard feature of Google Analytics that requires modification of the GATC. This is discussed in more detail in Chapter 9.

Agencies and Hosting Providers: Setting Up Client Accounts

It is tempting to think that Figure 6.3b is an excellent route for agencies and hosting providers to take on behalf of their clients—that is, have all client reports in one Google Analytics account. However, in accordance with the Google Analytics Terms of Service (found on www.google.com/analytics), any party setting up Google Analytics on behalf of clients must set up a separate Google Analytics account for each business entity. This is the same way AdWords operates and should therefore be familiar to existing AdWords agencies.

Other limitations include the constraint of 50 profiles per Google Analytics account. Also, if you import AdWords data, by default it is applied to *all* profiles in your account; if you have an e-commerce setup, by default e-commerce data is applied to *all* profiles in your account. Clearly, these are undesirable effects. Even with filters in place to counter these, there is always a real possibility that one client's data will end up in another client's report. At best, this muddies the metrics; at worst, it's a breach of your client's data confidentiality.

For agencies (or hosting providers) to move efficiently between different client accounts, Google Analytics has a similar feature to the My Client Center of AdWords. As long as you use the same Google login for each Google Analytics account you create or manage, you will see a drop-down menu on the right side of your report interface. This lists all the accounts to which you have access, as shown in Figure 6.5. You can also create new accounts from this area.

> **Note:** More information on the My Client Center feature of AdWords can be found here: http://adwords.google.com/support/bin/answer.py?answer=7725.

You can create a maximum of 25 accounts using the Create New Account option on the drop-down menu. However, there's no limit on the number of Google Analytics accounts that can be associated with your Google login. That is, any number of clients can add your Google login e-mail address as their administrator or report viewer, and these will appear in your My Analytics Accounts drop-down menu.

If you need to create more than 25 Google Analytics accounts, set up a secondary Google login for yourself and use this for creating further Google Analytics accounts. Once they're created, you can then add your primary Google login as an administrator and have the account appended to your My Analytics Accounts drop-down list.

Figure 6.5 The My Analytics Accounts area is the equivalent of the My Client Center feature for AdWords.

Getting AdWords Data: Linking to Your AdWords Account

If you're an online advertiser, chances are good that you are using Google AdWords as part of your marketing mix. AdWords is a way of targeting text ads to visitors using the Google search engine by the keywords they use. That way, your advertisement is displayed to people who are actually looking for something related to your product. AdWords are also shown in a similar way on Google partner sites such as Ask.com, AOL.com, and the AdSense network. Importing your AdSense data is discussed in the next section for the benefit of AdSense users.

Google AdWords is an extremely effective and efficient way of marketing online, because the auction system used is based on how many visitors click on your ad rather than just its display. Hence, this method of advertising is referred to as pay-per-click (PPC) or cost-per-click (CPC). Yahoo! Search Marketing, Microsoft adCenter, Miva, and Mirago operate similar advertising networks. Google Analytics can track visits and conversions from all of these.

As you might expect, Google Analytics, being a part of Google, offers enormous benefits when it comes to integrating data from its AdWords pay-per-click network. In a manner unique for a web analytics tool, getting your AdWords data in is simply a matter of ticking two check boxes—one in your AdWords account, the other in your Google Analytics account. From within your AdWords account, follow these steps:

1. Go to the My Account > Account Preferences area.
2. Click the Edit link next to Tracking (see Figure 6.6a).
3. Select the box that says Destination URL Auto-tagging and then click Save Changes.
4. Click the Analytics tab and choose Analytics Settings > Profile Settings > Edit Profile Information.
5. Place a check in the check box under Apply Cost Data, and select Save Changes (see Figure 6.6b).

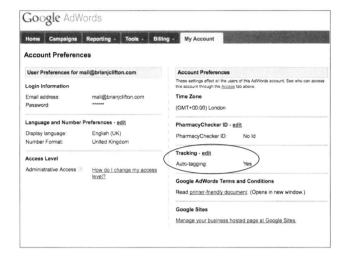

Figure 6.6 (a) Setting auto-tagging within your AdWords account; (b) applying AdWords cost data

That's it! All your AdWords data (impressions, clicks, cost) will automatically be imported into your account. The import takes place once per day (usually in the middle of the night Pacific time) and is for the period minus 48 to 24 hours in arrears from 23:59 the previous day. The reason for this delay is to allow time for the AdWords fraud-detection algorithms to work through your account. This is the same situation for any web analytics tool that imports your AdWords data.

Data import discrepancies are discussed in Chapter 2 in the section "Why PPC Vendor Numbers Do Not Match Web Analytics Reports."

Importing Cost Data from Multiple AdWords Accounts

You may wish to import cost data from multiple AdWords accounts—for example, if you are running campaigns in the United States and the United Kingdom, or you have two separate agencies managing two separate campaigns. Should you wish to do this, you need to submit a support ticket to Google from within your Google Analytics account.

Note that the terminology here is important for this; *importing* multiple cost data sources is not the same as *linking* accounts. Linking, that is, the ability to log into Google Analytics from your AdWords account, can happen only on a one-to-one basis—one AdWords account can be linked to only one Google Analytics account. That is part of the data security and integrity method used by Google. However, it is possible to have multiple cost data *imported* into a single Google Analytics account, that is, on a one-to-many basis.

Bear in mind that when importing multiple cost sources into one Google Analytics account, the data needs to be aligned. That is, all time zone and currency settings will be aligned with the one AdWords account to which your Google Analytics account is linked—the one you log into via the AdWords interface. This may not be desirable. An alternative is to add multiple GATCs to your pages as described previously in the section "Roll-up Reporting."

With auto-tagging enabled, you will notice an additional parameter showing in the landing page URLs of your AdWords ads, should you click through to them. For example:

```
www.mysite.com/?gclid=COvQgK7JrY8CFSUWEAodKEEyuA
```

The gclid parameter is a keyword-specific parameter unique to your account. AdWords appends this for Google Analytics tracking, and this must remain in place when visitors arrive on your website in order for them to be detected as AdWords visitors. If the gclid parameter is missing or corrupted, then the visitor will be incorrectly assigned as "google (organic)" as opposed to "google (cpc)."

Testing after Enabling Auto-tagging

As discussed in "Why PPC Vendor Numbers Do Not Match Web Analytics Reports" in Chapter 2, third-party ad-tracking systems can inadvertently corrupt or remove the gclid parameter required by Google Analytics AdWords tracking. For example, systems such as Adform, Atlas Search, Bluestreak, DoubleClick, and Efficient Frontier use redirection URLs to collect visitor statistics independently of your organization. These may inadvertently break the AdWords gclid. Therefore, after enabling auto-tagging, always test a sample of your AdWords ads by clicking through from a Google search results page.

If the test fails, then contact your third-party ad-tracking provider, because there may be a simple fix. For example, your AdWords auto-tagged landing page URL may look like this:

```
http://www.mysite.com/?gclid=COvQgK7JrY8CFSUWEAodKEEyuA
```

If a third-party tracking system is used for redirection, it could end up as this:

```
http://www.redirect.com?http://www.mysite.com/?gclid=COvQgK7JrY8CFSUWEAodKEEyuA
```

Notice the two ?—this is invalid because you cannot have two question marks in a URL. Some systems may allow you to replace the second ? with a # so the URL can be processed correctly. This has to be done within the third-party ad tracking system, not within AdWords. Another workaround is to append an encoded dummy variable to your landing page URL, as shown here:

```
http://www.mysite.com/%3Fdum=1
```

AdWords auto-tagging will then append the `gclid` as

```
http://www.mysite.com/%3Fdum=1&gclid=COvQgK7JrY8CFSUWEAodKEEyuA
```

so that when you use your third-party ad-tracking system the URL becomes the following:

```
http://www.redirect.com?http://www.mysite.com/%3Fdum=1&gclid= ↵
COvQgK7JrY8CFSUWEAodKEEyuA
```

This will work. That is, the URL will retain the `gclid` parameter for Google Analytics tracking in the correct format. You can then exclude the tracking of the dummy variable in the Google Analytics configuration settings (see "Initial Configuration" in Chapter 8).

> **Note:** If you already have parameters in your landing page URLs, you do not need to add a dummy parameter. However, you will need to change your ? to its encoded equivalent, %3F.

Getting AdSense Data: Linking to Your AdSense Account

If you're an online publisher, you may be using Google's AdSense product. AdSense is the tool that allows you to display Google ads on your own website—thereby sharing in the click-through revenue. The clever part of AdSense is that the ads displayed on your site are targeted to your content, that is, contextual advertising. By this method, the ads shown are more suited to your audience's interests. The result is that you focus on building engaging high-quality content, while Google takes care of the technology for displaying relevant advertisements to your readers. For more information about AdSense see `http://adsense.google.com`.

Similar to importing your spend and impression data from AdWords as described in the previous section, you can also import your AdSense earnings, impression, and content performance data. Within your AdSense account, go to the Reports section and select the link Integrate Your AdSense Account With Google Analytics, as shown in Figure 6.7.

Figure 6.7 Integrating AdSense with Google Analytics

The following screen allows you to either create a Google Analytics account or select an existing one. If you choose the latter, ensure that the AdSense account you are using is also listed as an administrator within your Google Analytics account before proceeding. If you have done this, AdSense then connects to your Google Analytics account and displays its profiles—see Figure 6.8.

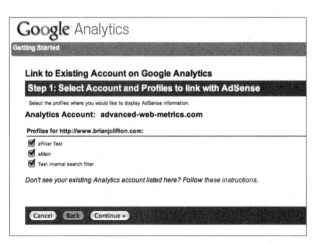

Figure 6.8 Selecting Google Analytics profiles to receive AdSense data

Assuming you are managing only a single website domain in your Google Analytics account, select the profiles you wish to import your AdSense data into. Generally, this will be for all your profiles, and so no changes are required to your GATC. However, it may be that you manage multiple domains, with AdSense displaying ads across your entire network of sites. If this describes your situation, you will need to decide which domain is the primary domain for your data import; see Figure 6.9. The primary domain does not require any changes to its GATC, but secondary domains will require changes. Therefore, you should choose the most complex GATC profile as your primary domain so that you minimize changes. See also the Help Center article at www.google.com/support/analytics/bin/answer.py?answer=92625.

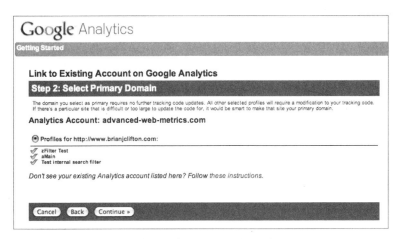

Figure 6.9 Selecting Google Analytics profiles to receive AdSense data

If you are required to select a primary domain, the following screen will display the code snippets to update your GATC—see Figure 6.10. Finally, click Continue to complete the linking process. Doing so immediately creates a new section in your Google Analytics reports in the Content > AdSense section. AdSense data (impressions, clicks, revenue) will automatically be imported into your account.

Bear in mind that just as for AdWords, the import takes place once per day (usually in the middle of the night Pacific time) and is for the period minus 48 to 24 hours in arrears from 23:59 the previous day. The reason for this delay is to allow time for the AdWords fraud-detection algorithms to work through your account. You should also be aware of data import discrepancies, as discussed in Chapter 2 in the section "Why PPC Vendor Numbers Do Not Match Web Analytics Reports."

Note: It is currently not possible to import multiple AdSense account data into a single Google Analytics account.

Figure 6.10 Final configuration of the AdSense import screen

Common Pre-implementation Questions

Installing Google Analytics, as with any other web analytics tool, requires a commitment from you as a website owner—be it the hiring of expertise to achieve a best-practice implementation or the use of your own time in reading this book and doing it yourself. Clearly you will want to know if the Google Analytics tool is right for you before investing in such a process.

Assuming you have already had an initial demonstration of the user interface, the following are answers to common questions I regularly receive from people about to decide on their Google Analytics commitment.

Can we use an existing tracking tool with Google Analytics? Yes. Google Analytics will happily sit alongside any other page-tagging, logfile, or web analytics solution. As long as there are no JavaScript errors on your web pages, Google Analytics will collect visitor information independently. Similarly, for tracking paid campaigns, Google Analytics variables are simply appended to your existing landing page URLs—regardless of whether another vendor also has tracking variables.

Can we track visitors across different websites? Yes. You can track whether a visitor traverses many website domains owned or managed by you—for example, a visitor passing from www.mysiteA.com to www.mysiteB.com. Typically this happens if you process credit card information with a third-party payment gateway such as WorldPay, PayPal, SecureTrading, NETBANX, or something similar. Tracking across the two sites is achieved by ensuring that the links to the subsequent domains are modified to include a JavaScript function call to either _link (when using an href link) or _linkByPost (when using a form). This is discussed in detail in "Tracking E-Commerce Transactions" in Chapter 7.

Can we track transactions on a third-party payment gateway? Yes, provided you are able to add your GATC to your template pages hosted on the third-party site. Ensure that you use either _link (when using an `href` link) or _linkByPost (when using a form) when linking to the third-party payment gateway website. This is discussed in detail in "Tracking E-Commerce Transactions" in Chapter 7.

Do we have to modify the GATC in order to cross-segment data? No. Cross-segmentation is built into the Google Analytics product by drilling down into data when clicking links within the various reports. In addition, cross-segment drop-down menus exist in most reports.

Does Google Analytics use first-party cookies, and what happens if the visitor disables these? All Google Analytics data is collected via first-party cookies only. The GATC loads JavaScript into your site from `google-analytics.com`. Because it is your site that executes the JavaScript, all cookies are first party. You can view these in your browser privacy settings.

If cookies are disabled or blocked by a visitor, their data will not be collected.

Is the AdWords `gclid` auto-tagging parameter bespoke? Yes, the `gclid` parameter is unique for each keyword in your AdWords account.

Can Google reprocess my historical data? Google cannot currently reprocess historical data, so it is important to always have a default catch-all profile with no filters applied in case you introduce an error in your filters and lose data. Filters are discussed in Chapter 8.

Can we customize the reports? Yes. Custom reporting allows you to design one-of-a-kind reports to fit your specific needs. For example, perhaps you would like to see total goal completions by day of the month or view how affiliate sales are going. These are not standard reports in Google Analytics, but you can build them using the drag-and-drop interface. This lets you select the metrics you want and define multiple levels of subreports. Customizing reports is discussed in Chapter 11, "Real-World Tasks."

Can I schedule a report to be e-mailed to me or a colleague regularly? Yes, each report has an Email link. The feature includes a scheduler to automate future e-mailings.

Can I import cost data from Yahoo! Search Marketing or Microsoft adCenter? At present, this is not possible. Yahoo! Search Marketing visitors (or those to any other pay-per-click network) can be tracked in the same way other paid visitors can be tracked—using campaign variables appended to the landing page URLs. However, cost and impression data cannot be imported.

How many goals can I track? By default, you can track up to 20 goals in Google Analytics and group these into categories; by creating more profiles, you could also track additional goals. However, if you have numerous goals—for example, you have a PDF library you wish to track—it is better to have a pseudo e-commerce configuration. That is, you trigger a virtual transaction for each goal completed. That way, each goal is considered a product, and the entire e-commerce reporting section of Google Analytics is available to you. See "Monetizing a Non-E-Commerce Website" in Chapter 11, for further details.

Can I monetize goals? Yes. You can assign a goal value within the goal configuration section of the Admin area of your Google Analytics account. In fact, this is strongly encouraged, particularly for non-e-commerce sites, so that you may see the intrinsic value of your website. Also see "Monetizing a Non-E-Commerce Website," in Chapter 11.

Is there a relationship between the Google Analytics map overlay and the geotargeting options available in AdWords? Yes, the geo-IP database used for both services is the same, so you can use the map overlay information presented in Google Analytics to measure existing AdWords geotargeted campaigns or to help target new markets.

Does Flash break Google Analytics? No, Flash actions can be tracked, but it requires your input—that is, you need to implement event tracking within your FLA file. Chapter 7 discusses this in detail.

Will tagging my pages with the GATC slow them down? The GATC calls the ga.js file, which is approximately 18KB in size, from Google servers. The ga.js file is the same for every page you tag on your site. Therefore, once a visitor has downloaded the file from their initial pageview, it will be cached on their machine—so no further requests for the file are required. In addition, the ga.js file is the same for all users of Google Analytics. If a visitor to your website has previously visited another website running Google Analytics tracking, then the ga.js file will already be cached on their machine or Internet service provider's caching server. The result is an industry-leading minimal download time for tagging your pages.

Note that to avoid any latency when no caching is present, the recommended placement for the GATC is just above your HTML </body> tag

Are gclids still valid if accounts are not linked? No, this was a change made in April 2009 as part of security updates. If your Google Analytics account is not linked to your AdWords account, AdWords visitors will not be tracked correctly. Therefore, if you use AdWords, you need to link your accounts in order to track visitors correctly.

Will using Google Analytics directly affect the ranking of my natural search results, ad quality score, or ad placement? No. There are a great number of myths, conspiracy theories, and—to be frank—rubbish written about this on various forums and blogs. As a search marketer, Xoogler (ex-Googler), and now web consultant, I have seen both sides of the "Google fence," and that has been fascinating. I know from my experience as a senior manager at Google that individual website data, from Google Analytics or any other product, is not used to affect your natural search results, ad quality score, or ad placement. Of course, Google wants to improve its products for you—both as a website owner and as a general web user. To that end, aggregate data from multiple sources and across many web properties is used to improve them.

Can Google Analytics track search engine robots? No, not unless the robot can execute JavaScript and set cookies. Most search engine robots cannot do either of these. In particular Googlebot does not do these and cannot execute the GATC. Similar to the previous question, there are many myths and rumors about Googlebot being able to execute JavaScript. However, as of the time of writing, this is not the case. If you wish to track robot activity, you can use Urchin software, as described in Chapter 3, or for Googlebot specifically, use Google's Webmaster Central (www.google.com/webmasters). Note that apart from being aware that a robot has visited your website, there is little further information to be gained from analyzing search engine robot activity than what Google's Webmaster Central cannot already provide.

Summary

In Chapter 6, you have learned the following:

How to get started You learned how to create your Google Analytics account either as part of your AdWords account or via the stand-alone version.

How to deploy the tracking code We explained the functions of the GATC code and how to deploy it; we also showed the help that server-side-delivered page tags can offer in simplifying the process.

How to back up and store data locally You learned how to back up traffic data in your local web server logfiles to give you greater flexibility, and we discussed the options for Google Analytics troubleshooting, auditing, and reprocessing.

The difference between accounts and profiles We showed you how to use accounts, profiles, and roll-up reports and what to consider if you are setting up accounts on behalf of clients as an agency or hosting provider.

How to import AdWords data We demonstrated how to link Google Analytics with your Google AdWords account and the importance of testing the auto-tag feature, especially when using AdWords in conjunction with a third-party tracking tool that employs redirects.

How to import AdSense data You learned how to link Google Analytics with your Google AdSense account.

How to manage expectations We presented answers to common implementation questions.

Advanced Implementation

Now that you understand the basics of getting your web visitor data into Google Analytics, this chapter looks at the more advanced setup considerations you may require. We discuss capturing e-commerce transactions, tagging your marketing campaigns, and tracking events (those actions on your website that are not a standard pageview).

In addition, you'll learn how to customize the Google Analytics Tracking Code (GATC) for your specific needs. For example, do you want to convert dynamic URLs into something more readable? Do you use multiple domains or subdomains? Do you have nonstandard requirements such as changing timeout settings, controlling keyword preferences, or setting sampling rates? All these scenarios and more are covered here.

7

In Chapter 7, you will learn:

To use the `_trackPageview()` function to create virtual pageviews

To capture e-commerce transactions

To track online campaigns in addition to AdWords

To track events such as Flash interactions

To customize the GATC for your specific needs

_trackPageview(): the Google Analytics Workhorse

As discussed in Chapter 6, "Getting Up and Running with Google Analytics," the final part of the GATC is a call to the JavaScript routine _trackPageview(). This is the main function for tracking a page within Google Analytics. _trackPageview() sets up all the required cookies for the session and submits the data to the Google servers. Table 7.1 lists the cookies that Google Analytics sets. You can view these values by using the preferences settings of your browser—typically located in your privacy setup.

▶ **Table 7.1** The five cookie names and types Google Analytics uses

Cookie Name	Time to Live, Type	Purpose
__utma	24 months, first-party	Stores domain and visitor identifiers, for example, unique ID, timestamp of initial visit, number of sessions to date.
__utmb	Session, first-party	Stores session identifiers. Changes to identify each unique session.
__utmc	Session, first-party	Stores session identifiers. Expires after 30 minutes of inactivity.
__utmv	24 months, first-party	Stores custom labels, for example, customer, subscriber, registered user.
__utmz	6 months, first-party	Stores campaign variables, for example, referrer, keyword (if search engine), medium type (CPC, organic, banner, email).

When viewing your Google Analytics cookies, you will notice that all values are preceded by a hash of the host.domain name that the GATC is located on. The hash value is a fixed-length numerical value that represents your website. For example, a hash of www.mysite.com might be 202414657, and hence a value of the _utmv cookie could be 202414657.test%20user. Similarly for www.yoursite.com the hash could be 195485746, with a _utmv cookie of 1954857467.another%20test. Notice that the hash values are both nine digits in length, despite the domain length being different. This is the purpose of the hash. The domain-hashing functionality in Google Analytics uses this number to check cookie integrity for visitors.

 Tip: If you are interested in the workings of the Google Analytics hash algorithm, see http://www .google.com/support/forum/p/Google+Analytics/thread?tid=626b0e277aaedc3c&hl=en.

If you have multiple subdomains, such as www.mysite.com and support.mysite.com, and you want to track users who pass across both of these subdomains, you need to turn off domain hashing so that the cookie integrity check will not reject a user cookie coming from one domain to another. Similarly, you also need to make changes if you pass visitors to other third-party domains that you control, such as from www.mysite.com to www.mysite.co.uk. These special cases are discussed later in this chapter in "Customizing the GATC."

With an understanding of how _trackPageview() works, you can leverage it to track virtual pageviews and file downloads, as discussed next.

Tracking Unreadable URLs with Virtual Pageviews

If you have a site that includes a shopping cart or has more than a few dozen pages of content, chances are good that you are using dynamic URLs. In this context, these are pages generated on the fly—that is, the visitor requests them by clicking page links, as opposed to prebuilt static HTML content. This is how a content management system operates.

Dynamic URLs work by using a server-side scripting language, such as CGI-PERL, PHP, ASP, or Python, that pulls nonformatted information into a common design template. Usually, URL parameters define the page content. You can tell if you are using dynamic URLs by your page names. Static URLs have page filenames ending in .htm or .html. Dynamic ones end in .cgi, .pl, .php, .asp, or .py. That does not mean all page names ending in .php are generated dynamically. However, if your website URLs also include a query (?) symbol followed by parameters such as name/value pairs, they are most likely dynamic URLs, as shown in the following three examples:

Example 1—a static URL:

`http://www.mysite.com/catalogue/product101.html`

Example 2—a dynamic URL with one parameter:

`http://www.mysite.com/catalogue/product.php?sku=123`

Example 3—a dynamic URL with three parameters:

`http://www.mysite.com/catalogue/product.php?sku=148&`
`lang=en&sect=suede`

In the dynamic examples, the query parameters sku, lang, and sect define the content of the page within a design template.

Note: Some web servers may use an alternative to ?, such as #, to define dynamic URL parameters.

For the purposes of Google Analytics, a URL structure is shown in Figure 7.1.

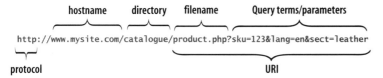

Figure 7.1 Parts of a URL

The following URL is broken down into its constituent parts:

- Protocol: `http://`
- Hostname: `www.mysite.com`
- Directory: `/catalogue`
- Filename: `product.php`
- Query parameters: `sku=123&lang=en&sect=leather`
- URI: `/product.php?sku=123&lang=en&sect=leather`

For this scenario, the query terms used in the vast majority of cases are completely meaningless to the human reader; they are present in order to communicate with your database. To help report users, it is therefore preferable to have reader-friendly URLs. Google Analytics can achieve this by rewriting query terms as product names or descriptions and displaying these in your reports as virtual URLs, that is, virtual pageviews.

By default, Google Analytics tracks your viewed pages by calling the JavaScript routine `_trackPageview()` in the GATC. As described in Chapter 6, the standard GATC calls `_trackPageview()` without an argument (without a value in the parentheses). With the parentheses empty, Google Analytics records the URI directly from your browser address bar and displays this in the reports as the pageview. You can override this behavior by modifying the `_trackPageview()` call to create virtual pageviews. For example, using Figure 7.1 these could be:

```
pageTracker._trackPageview('/catalogue/products/english/leather/↵
blue tassel shoe');
pageTracker._trackPageview('/catalogue/products/english/suede/↵
high heeled boot');
```

The parentheses contain the virtual pageview and path. This overrides the URI value. By using virtual pageviews, reports become much easier to read and interpret. As long as the argument begins with a forward slash, virtual pageview names may be organized into any virtual directory style structure you wish. However, this does not mean all query terms should be rewritten, only those that are important in identifying specific pages, because some may be required for reporting on other information such as internal site search.

You can manually modify the argument for `_trackPageview()` on each page, or you can use the variables present within your web environment, such as your shopping cart or content management system, to build a more meaningful virtual URL. A good webmaster or web developer will be able to set this up quickly. At the very least, simply using what is already available in the example of Figure 7.1, you could have the following:

```
pageTracker._trackPageview ('/catalogue/products/eng/leather/↵
prod code 123');
```

Clearly, this is not the finished article, but it is a lot more readable to your report users than the original. As stated previously, you should use this technique only to rewrite dynamic URLs that are necessary to you. In addition, you should discuss the full consequences with your webmaster. For example, it is not necessary or desirable to rewrite the following:

```
http://www.mysite.com/search?q=shoes
```

In this example, the URI relates to an onsite search query that you will want to view in your Site Search reports. Rewriting this will break those reports. Taking this further, if your URL contains a mix of variables, some of which you want to overwrite and some you do not, then you can achieve this by including the variables in the virtual pageview. For example, consider the following dynamic URL that contains a Site Search query term plus other dynamic variables:

```
http://www.mysite.com/search?q=shoes&lang=en
&sect=leather
```

As a virtual URL, this could be written as:

```
pageTracker._trackPageview('/products/eng/leather/?q=shoes');
```

Here, the original q=shoes query is written back into the virtual pageview, enabling you to view Site Search reports as normal. As with all URLs, if you wish to write query variables in your virtual pageviews, then use the standard convention—a question mark (?) to begin the variable definition and an ampersand (&) to separate multiple name/value pairs.

> **Note:** A consequence of using virtual pageviews is that they will break the Site Overlay reports as well as the Visit This Page link in the Content reports because the page doesn't exist in the real world. If these features are important to you, then don't rewrite your URLs. However, you'll likely find that the greater clarity virtual pageviews bring to the reporting of complex URLs far outweighs the loss of these features.

Avoiding Pageview Inflation

The function `_trackPageview()` contains a self-check variable to keep it from executing twice when there is no argument (virtual pageview) defined. This prevents pageview overcounting when a GATC has been mistakenly added to the same page multiple times. However, if you use virtual pageviews, `_trackPageview()` will execute each time it is called—even if identical virtual pageviews are defined. If you wish to track data in multiple Google Analytics accounts, use the roll-up reporting method described in Chapter 6.

Tracking File Downloads with Virtual Pageviews

By default, Google Analytics will not track your file downloads (for example, PDF, EXE, DOC, XLS, ZIP), because these pages cannot be tagged with the GATC. However, it is easy to track these by modifying the download link on your web pages using the virtual pageview technique just described.

In the following example, the link itself within your web page is modified, not the GATC. Here is the original HTML link that cannot be tracked:

```
<a href="mydoc.pdf">Download a PDF</a>
```

This new link is tracked in the virtual /downloads directory:

```
<a href="mydoc.pdf"
onclick="pageTracker._trackPageview('/downloads/mydoc.pdf');">
Download a PDF</a>
```

Tracking Partially Completed Forms with Virtual Pageviews

Virtual pageviews can also be used to track the partial completion of forms. This is particularly useful if you have a long (more than 10 fields) or multipage form, such as a registration form or a feedback survey. Using virtual pageviews in this way enables you to see where visitors bail out before getting to the Submit button. This is achieved using the Funnel Visualization report, as discussed in the section "Goal And Funnel Reports" in Chapter 5, "Reports Explained."

In order to accomplish this, use the onBlur event handler to modify your HTML form fields as follows:

```
<form action="cgi-bin/formhandler.pl" method="post" name="theForm">
<input type="text" name="firstname" onBlur="↵
if(document.theForm.firstname.value != '');pageTracker._trackPageview↵
('/forms/signup/firstname')">

<input type="text" name="lastname" onBlur="↵
if(document.theForm.lastname.value != '');pageTracker._trackPageview↵
('/forms/signup/lastname')">

<input type="text" name="dob" onBlur="↵
if(document.theForm.dob.value != '');pageTracker._trackPageview↵
('/forms/signup/dob') ">

<input type="text" name="address1" onBlur="↵
if(document.theForm.address1.value != '');pageTracker._trackPageview↵
('/forms/signup/address1') ">
```

```
          .
          .
          .

</form>
```

The `if() != ''` statement is included to confirm that each form field has content before creating the event. Of course, not all form fields will be compulsory to the visitor, so use the `if` statement appropriately.

> **Warning:** The virtual pageviews tracked in this example are labels that enable you to confirm whether a field has been completed—they are not personal information submitted by the visitor. It is against the Google Analytics Terms of Service to track personally identifiable information. For more information see `www.google.com/analytics/tos.html`.

Virtual Pageviews versus Event Tracking

Using virtual pageviews to track file downloads, or partial form completion, inflates your pageview count, because obviously these are not real pageviews. Therefore consider carefully your use of these.

If the action you are tracking can be considered as analogous to a pageview, then the virtual pageview technique is valid. In my opinion, this is the case for readable file downloads (PDF, DOC, XLS, PPT, and the like) and partial form completion. My hypothesis is that these are just as valid as other pageviews tracked for payment confirmation receipts, form submission thank-you pages, subscription confirmation pages, and so on—that is, pages that confirm a user has viewed content but are not content pages themselves.

The alternative approach is to use Event Tracking, as discussed later in this chapter. However, if you are to track file downloads as events, consider also that payment confirmation receipts, form submission thank-you pages, subscription confirmation pages, and so on should also be tracked as events in order to be consistent.

My recommendation is therefore to use Event Tracking only where the action being tracked is in no way related to a pageview. See the "Event Tracking" section later in this chapter for examples.

Tracking E-commerce Transactions

Before describing how to capture e-commerce data, consider the salient points to take into account when collecting visitor transactional data:

Using one Google Analytics account for each localized website Within Google Analytics, the transaction and item values are currency agnostic—that is, although you can specify the currency symbol used in your configuration (see Chapter 8, "Best-Practices

Configuration Guide"), this is simply a report label. If you are running multiple web-sites with localized currency values, then these will not be converted into USD by Google Analytics (or whatever currency label you configure).

Of course, you can perform an exchange rate calculation on each of your websites to unify the currency and then forward this to Google Analytics, but that is likely to confuse your regional marketing departments, who will need to back out exchange rate fluctuations in order to ascertain whether a campaign is successful or not.

Best practice is therefore to use one Google Analytics account for each localized website. This makes sense when you consider that each localized website is also likely to be running in its own time zone and its own AdWords campaigns, where the cost data is also localized.

If you want an aggregate report of all local websites, add a second GATC to your pages. Chapter 6 discusses this scenario in more detail in "Roll-up Reporting."

Measuring your success in terms of revenue derived from online channels Use Google Analytics E-commerce reports to measure the effectiveness of your website and its marketing campaigns at deriving revenue from online channels. Thus, it should not be used as a substitute for your back office or customer relationship management system, because there will always be discrepancies between these data sources.

For example, JavaScript-disabled browsers, cookies blocked or deleted, visitor multiple clicks, Internet connection blips, returned orders, mistakes, and so on all add errors bars when it comes to aligning web visitor data with order fulfillment systems. Accuracy considerations for this scenario are discussed in Chapter 2, "Available Methodologies and Their Accuracy," in the section "Comparing Data from Different Vendors."

Importing cookie data into your CRM system Google Analytics does not collect any personally identifiable information, and it is against the Terms of Service to attempt to collect such information. However, it is possible to pass Google Analytics cookie data, along with the transaction detail, to your CRM system, for example. This is discussed in Chapter 12, "Extracting Google Analytics Information."

With these points in mind, the first step is to get your visitor transactional data into Google Analytics, and we discuss this process next.

Capturing Secure E-commerce Transactions

Google Analytics supports a client-side data-collection technique for capturing e-commerce transactions. With some straightforward additions to the GATC on your purchase receipt page, you can configure Google Analytics to record transaction and product information. The following is an example GATC to do this:

```
<script type="text/javascript">
    var gaJsHost = (("https:" == document.location.protocol) ? "https://ssl." : ↵
"http://www.");
```

```
        document.write(unescape("%3Cscript src='" + gaJsHost + "google-↵
analytics.com/ga.js' type='text/javascript'%3E%3C/script%3E"));
</script>
<script type="text/javascript">
try {
    var pageTracker = _gat._getTracker("UA-12345-1");
    pageTracker._trackPageview();

    pageTracker._addTrans(
      "1234",                        // order ID - required
      "Mountain View Book Store",    // affiliation or store name
      "89.97",                       // total - required
      "6.30",                        // tax
      "5",                           // shipping
      "San Jose",                    // city
      "California",                  // state or province
      "USA"                          // country
    );
    pageTracker._addItem(
      "1234",                        // order ID - required
      "DD44-BJC",                    // SKU code (stock keeping unit)
      "Advanced Web Metrics",        // product name
      "Web, Technical",              // category or variation
      "29.99",                       // unit price - required
      "3"                            // quantity - required
    );
    pageTracker._trackTrans();
} catch(err) {}</script>
```

For this example, three additional lines have been added within the GATC:

- The transaction line, as defined by _addTrans(), which is a list of comma-separated values, delimited by quotation marks
- The product item line, as defined by _addItem(), which is an list of comma-separated values, delimited by quotation marks
- A call to the JavaScript function _trackTrans(), which sends the transaction and item information to Google Analytics

The order of these lines within your GATC is important, so maintain the order shown here on your receipt page.

As shown in the examples, both _addTrans() and _addItem() can be written on multiple lines for clarity. Conversely, they can also be written on a single line, which may be an easier format for you to use with transactions containing multiple items, for example:

```
pageTracker._addTrans("1234","Mountain View Book Store",↵
"89.97","6.30","5","San Jose","California","USA");
pageTracker._addItem("1234","ISBN-9780470253120",↵
"Advanced Web Metrics","Web","29.99","2");
pageTracker._addItem("1234","ISBN-9780321344755",↵
"Don't Make me Think","Web","29.99","1");
```

For each transaction, there should be only one _addTrans() entry. This line specifies the total amount for the transaction and the purchaser's city, state, and country. For each item purchased, there must be an _addItem() line. That is, two purchased items require two _addItem() lines, and so forth. Item lines contain the product names, codes, unit prices, and quantities. The variable values required are shown in Table 7.2. You obtain these from your e-commerce shopping system.

▶ **Table 7.2** E-commerce parameter reference guide

Variable	Description
Transaction Line Variables	
order-id	Your internal, unique order ID number
affiliation	Optional affiliation or store name
total	Total value of the transaction
tax	Tax amount of the transaction
shipping	The shipping amount of the transaction
city	Purchaser's city address to correlate the transaction with
state	Purchaser's state or province address to correlate the transaction with
country	Purchaser's country address to correlate the transaction with
Item Line Variables	
order-id	Your internal, unique order ID (must match the transaction line)
sku-code	Product stock-keeping unit code
product-name	Product name or description
category	Category name of the product
price	Unit price of the product
quantity	Quantity ordered

If you don't have data for a certain variable, leave the quotation marks for the variable empty (with no spaces). For example, if you have no affiliate network, shipping is included in the purchase price, and you do not use categories, you would use the following:

```
pageTracker._addTrans("1234","",↵
"89.97 ","6.30 ","","San Jose","California","USA");
```

```
pageTracker._addItem("1234","ISBN-9780470253120",↵
"Advanced Web Metrics","","29.99","2");
pageTracker._addItem("1234","ISBN-9780321344755",↵
"Don't Make me Think","","29.99","1");
```

Note: In the preceding example there are no spaces between the double quotes (""). Also note the deliberate spaces at the end of the total transaction and tax amounts. I emphasize these to illustrate that they do not affect the reporting because they are removed by Google Analytics during processing. Spaces between words in variable values are not trimmed. For example, "San Jose" remains as defined.

The Importance of Unique Order IDs

It is important to use unique order IDs (consisting of numbers or text or a mixture of both) for each transaction. Otherwise, separate transactions that have the same order ID will be compounded, rendering the data meaningless. This can happen to you if customers inadvertently multiple-click the final purchase button. For best practice, prevent this behavior. Following is a JavaScript example:

```
<script>
var firsttime;
function validator(){
  if (firsttime == "Y"){
    alert("Please wait, your payment is being processed.");
    return (false);
  }
  firsttime = "Y";
  return (true);
}
</script>
```

Paste the above code into the <head> area of your HTML page that contains the final e-commerce checkout link or button. Then within your HTML of the same page, modify your submission form as follows:

```
<FORM METHOD="POST" ACTION="authorize.cgi" onSubmit="return validator()">
```

The onSubmit event handler will prevent multiple submissions of the form, thus preventing Google Analytics from capturing any duplicate transaction IDs.

If your purchase form already has an onSubmit event handler, append the validator call as follows:

```
<FORM METHOD="POST" ACTION="authorize.cgi" onSubmit="return checkEmail;↵
return validator()">
```

Using a Third-Party Payment Gateway

If your website initiates a purchase checkout process on a separate store site (for example, if you send customers from www.mysite.com to a payment gateway, such as www.secure-site.com), you need to make additional changes to your web pages. This is because Google Analytics uses first-party cookies for best-practice purposes. As discussed in Chapter 2, using first-party cookies means only the domain that sets the cookies can read or modify them—a security feature built into all web browsers by default. You can overcome this and pass your Google Analytics first-party cookies to your third-party domain with the following method.

First, modify the GATC on all your pages—on both your primary site and all store site pages. Two of these pages require further modification of the GATC: the last page of the checkout process that occurs on www.mysite.com and the entry page visitors use to complete their checkout on www.secure-site.com. However, rather than having two slightly different versions of your GATC, I recommend *all* pages be modified to the same GATC format as follows:

```
<script type="text/javascript">
    var gaJsHost = (("https:" == document.location.protocol) ? "https://ssl." :↵
 "http://www.");
    document.write(unescape("%3Cscript src='" + gaJsHost + "google-↵
analytics.com/ga.js' type='text/javascript'%3E%3C/script%3E"));
</script>
<script type="text/javascript">
try {
    var pageTracker = _gat._getTracker("UA-12345-1");
    pageTracker._setDomainName("none");
    pageTracker._setAllowLinker(true);
    pageTracker._trackPageview();
} catch(err) {}</script>
```

Strictly speaking, pageTracker._setAllowLinker(true); is required on only two pages—the ones that pass over and receive the first-party cookies. However, by using the same GATC throughout your website, you minimize any potential errors—particularly if you later add further crossover links to your pages, that is, additional ways for visitors to checkout via the third-party payment gateway. By defining only one GATC, you provide a simple level of proofing your tracking requirements in the future.

The modified GATC does two things: _setDomainName("none") forces the domain hash of the Google Analytics cookies to be set to "1", which makes the cookies generic enough to be associated with another domain and sets the cookie's host to be whatever the current URL's host is. In this way, cookies can be "pushed" from one domain to the next. To achieve this "push," you must also set _setAllowLinker(true).

Then modify the web page on www.mysite.com that calls the third-party gateway site, in one of two ways:

Link method If your website uses a link to pass visitors to the third-party site, modify it to look like this:

```
<a href=https://www.secure-site.com/?store=parameters
onclick="javascript:pageTracker._link(this.href); return false; ">
Continue to Purchase</a>
```

With this method, the Google Analytics cookies are passed to the receiving domain by appending them to the URL string. If you see __utma, __utmb, and __utmc parameters in your third-party landing page URL, then this has worked.

> **Note:** Note the use of return false; here. This ensures that for visitor browsers that have JavaScript disabled, the href link will be followed without error. Of course, if JavaScript is disabled, Google Analytics tracking won't occur. However, the modified link will still work.

Form method If your website uses a form to pass visitors to the third-party site, then modify the form as follows:

```
<form method="post" action="http://www.secure-site.com/process.cgi"
onSubmit="pageTracker._linkByPost(this)">
```

With this method, the Google Analytics cookies are passed to the receiving domain via the HTTP headers. This will work even for forms where method="GET". You can verify that this has worked by viewing the HTTP headers sent in Firefox using the add-on LiveHTTPheaders (http://livehttpheaders.mozdev.org).

I recommend using the first _link method to test to see whether your setup is correct, that is, you can see your cookie values in your third-party landing page URL. Then switch to the _linkByPost method if required.

What to Do When a Third-Party Gateway Does Not Allow Tracking

If your third-party payment gateway does not allow you to modify their payment pages—that is, add your GATC—you cannot directly capture completed transactions. However, there two workarounds, as detailed in the following sections.

Using onClick or onSubmit

Use an onClick or onSubmit event handler at the point where visitors are just about to click away to the payment gateway. Using one of these methods, call the _trackTrans() function and capture the transaction details. The addTrans and addItem arrays also must be configured on the same page.

Continues

What to Do When a Third-Party Gateway Does Not Allow Tracking *(Continued)*

An example call via a link would be as follows:

```
<a href=https://www.secure-site.com/?store=parameters onclick="↵
javascript:pageTracker._trackTrans(); return false; ">
Continue to Purchase</a>
```

For a form it would be:

```
<form action="http://www.secure-site.com/process.cgi"
onSubmit="pageTracker._trackTrans()">
```

The caveat with this method is that you are tracking not completed transactions but merely the intent to complete. Perhaps the visitor's credit card details are declined, or they change their mind at the last minute before completing payment. Whatever the reason, your Google Analytics E-commerce reports will only be a guide to transaction activity and are unlikely to exactly align with reports provided by your third-party gateway company.

Using a Page Callback

A better method, if available, is to use a page callback to your website from the third-party gateway site. The callback is a page the visitor is returned to on your site when the transaction completes successfully. Many payment gateways offer this feature.

Provided this page is unavailable to visitors other than via a callback, you can place your e-commerce variables on the same page. That is, they are under your control because the call-back page is hosted within your website. E-commerce data will then align much better with that of your third-party gateway company. Similarly, you can track transaction failures with a callback method.

Tracking Negative Transactions

All e-commerce organizations have to deal with product returns at some point, whether because of damaged or faulty goods, order mistakes, or other reasons. It is possible to account for these within your Google Analytics reports by processing a *negative transaction*. However, I don't recommend this for two reasons:

Aligning web visitor data with internal systems does not yield perfect results. A negative transaction usually takes place well after the original purchase, therefore in a different reporting period. This is generally more confusing than simply leaving the returned transaction in your reports.

Consider carefully the purpose of including a negative transaction. If I search for "running shoes" and then make a purchase from your website, that is a perfectly good transaction—one that reflects the effectiveness of your website and your marketing campaigns.

If subsequently I decide I don't like the shoes and return them, this would be because of the product, perhaps a quality issue. That is separate from the effectiveness of your marketing; just because I return my running shoes does not mean that no further marketing investment should be made for that product.

For completeness, I include how to process a negative transaction here.

First, create an internal-only version of your completed purchase form that can be edited for the negative details. The form should be edited in a text editor and *not* loaded in a browser at this stage; otherwise it will trigger the code. To remove an order, edit as follows:

For the _addTrans line:

- Use the same *order-id* for the transaction as the one used for the original purchase.
- Ensure that the *total* variable is negative.
- Ensure that the *tax* and *shipping* variables are negative.

For the _addItem line:

- Use the same *order-id* for the transaction as the one used for the original purchase.
- Ensure that the *price* is positive.
- Ensure that the *quantity* is negative.

Process the form details by loading the modified copy of your order receipt page into your browser. This will call the pagetracker._trackTrans function as if it were a regular purchase.

By this method, you will still be able to see the actual transaction and the duplicate negative transaction when you select the days on which each of these transactions was recorded. However, when you select a date range that includes both the original and the negative transaction, the transaction will not be included in the total revenue reported.

Campaign Tracking

For any web analytics tool, being able to track online campaigns depends on the use of landing page URLs. A *landing page* is the destination page on which you want visitors to enter your website, following a click-through on a referring website. In most cases, you can control what destination page your visitors arrive at (land on) by specifying the URL. For example, if you have a link on a product portal directory that specializes in all things widget, then you may decide to point your link URL to a specific product landing page such as www.mysite.com/widgets.htm, as opposed to your generic home page. That way, you improve the experience for visitors who click through, by showing them a specific page relevant to their interests.

For the product portal directory example, nothing more is required. You will see how many visitors and conversions are received from that website in your Google Analytics Traffic Sources > Referring Sites report. However, if the referrer has a mixture of paid and nonpaid links to your website, you will need to differentiate these links; otherwise, they appear as a single source. The way to differentiate them is to tag your landing page URLs. This is a common requirement for pay-per-click advertising.

Another use of campaign tracking is to track a visitor who does not click a web page to reach your website. For example, the visitor reaches your site using a link within an email or a document such as DOC, PPT, or PDF. Because these documents cannot receive a GATC, the only way to track such visitors is to tag your landing page URLs.

Tagging Your Landing Page URLs

Tagging your landing page URLs to differentiate paid versus nonpaid links from the same referrer is the most common use of this technique. The principle and process are straightforward—you append additional Google Analytics parameters to the end of your URLs.

The following are two examples (which will be discussed in more detail) of tagging landing pages for use in paid campaigns on the Yahoo! Search Marketing network:

Tagging a static landing page Original landing page URL:

```
http://www.mysite.com/widgets.htm
```

Tagged landing page URL:

```
http://www.mysite.com/widgets.htm?↵
utm_source=yahoo&utm_medium=ppc&utm_term=widgets
```

Tagging a dynamic landing page Original landing page URL:

```
http://www.mysite.com/widgets.php?prod=101
```

Tagged landing page URL:

```
http://www.mysite.com/widgets.php?prod=101&↵
utm_source=yahoo&utm_medium=ppc&utm_term=widgets
```

 Note: You need not manually tag your landing page URLs for AdWords campaigns. This is done for you automatically (see "Getting AdWords Data: Linking to Your AdWords Account," in Chapter 6).

Whether you wish to track pay-per-click networks, banners, links within documents, or email, the same variables are applied in this straightforward way. Here is a two-step process to get you started:

Step 1: Tag Only What You Need

Generally speaking (AdWords being the exception), you need to tag all of your paid keyword links, such as Microsoft adCenter, Yahoo! Search Marketing, banners, and any other form of online advertising. You should also tag the links inside email messages—even your signature and embedded links within digital collateral such as DOC, XLS, and PDF files.

If you don't tag these, visitor click-throughs are still being tracked. However, the referrer information is not known, and so it becomes aggregated with other sources. For example, a nontagged paid link from Yahoo! Search Marketing will show as an organic link from Yahoo! Search—that is, it will show in your reports as "yahoo (organic)" for both visits. Similarly, nontagged links in email messages and digital collateral will show as "direct" visits—that is, grouped with those visitors who either type your web address directly into their browser or click a previously saved bookmark or favorite. Clearly, marketers wish to differentiate these visit referrals.

You don't need to tag certain links. For instance, you should not tag organic (nonpaid) links from search engines, and it isn't necessary to tag links that come from referral sites where your link listing is free, such as web portals. In addition, you should not attempt URL tagging for internal links (links within your website). Doing so will overwrite existing referrer campaign variables, which will result in data misalignment.

Do Not Use Campaign Tracking for SEO Purposes

For Search Engine Optimization (SEO) purposes, it is important not to use campaign tracking for links that are visible to search engine robots. You do not want to have such URLs indexed by the search engines because such links are viewed as different URLs to the same content and therefore appear as duplicates to the search engines—a technique that is considered search engine spam.

Apart from the hazard of your page rankings being penalized as spam, it also is not necessary to do this. Any web page that contains a link to your website will be tracked via Google Analytics by default and the referrer information reported. If you have a special case, you can customize a particular referrer using a rewrite filter. Creating filters is discussed in Chapter 8.

Step 2: Use Google's URL Builder (tinyurl.com/urlbuilder)

As previously shown, campaign links consist of a URL address followed by a ? (or & if you have existing parameters), followed by two or more of your campaign variables, as described in Table 7.3.

▶ **Table 7.3** Landing page campaign variables

Tag Variables	Condition	Description
utm_source	Required	Used to identify a particular search engine, newsletter, or other referral source
utm_medium	Required	Used to identify a medium, for example, CPC, PPC, banner, email, PDF, DOC, or XLS, etc.
utm_term	Optional	Used for paid search to note the keywords being targeted for a particular ad
utm_content	Optional	Used for ad-version testing to distinguish different ads that link to the same landing page
utm_campaign	Recommended	Used to identify different strategic campaigns from the same source–medium combination, for example, for an email newsletter using "spring promotion" or "summer promotion"

Appending these additional variables to your landing page URLs enables Google Analytics to differentiate visitors—for example, between an organic visitor from Yahoo! and a pay-per-click visitor from Yahoo!, or a direct visitor from one who clicked an email link.

Because up to five variables are allowed, the URLs can appear complicated. To avoid worrying about syntax, use the URL Builder tool at www.google.com/support/googleanalytics/bin/answer.py?answer=55578, though an easier-to-remember address is tinyurl.com/urlbuilder.

The URL Builder tool creates the tagged links for you—you simply copy and paste the resultant URL as your ad landing page URL. Once you understand the structure of the tagged URLs, you may want to switch to using a spreadsheet of these for bulk upload into your pay-per-click account or other management system.

Note: If you are using a third-party ad-tracking system to track click-throughs to your website, your visitors will be passed through redirection URLs. If this describes your scenario, be sure to test your tagged landing page URLs, because redirection may break them. You can test by clicking the resultant combined link (ad-tracking link plus campaign-tagged link). See "Test after Enabling Auto-tagging" in Chapter 6 for further details.

The examples in the following section demonstrate the best ways to tag the four most common kinds of online campaigns: banner ads, email campaigns, paid keywords (pay-per-click campaigns), and digital collateral. Note that a landing page URL is specific to the campaign you create it for—do not use it anywhere else!

Tagging Banner Ad URLs

Consider the following hypothetical marketing scenario on the AOL.com website: You have a graphical banner for branding purposes and an organic listing from the non-paid listings. AOL has informed you that the banner will display only when a visitor searches for the term *shoes*; in this case the banner campaign is about *Sprint shoes*. These are two different campaigns, from the same domain name (reported as aol.com), that can refer a visitor to your website.

Using the URL Builder tool, shown in Figure 7.2, you can differentiate visitors from banner click-throughs by supplying the resultant tagged landing page URL to the person or agency setting up your AOL banner. It is not necessary (or possible) to tag your AOL organic listing, because this will be detected automatically.

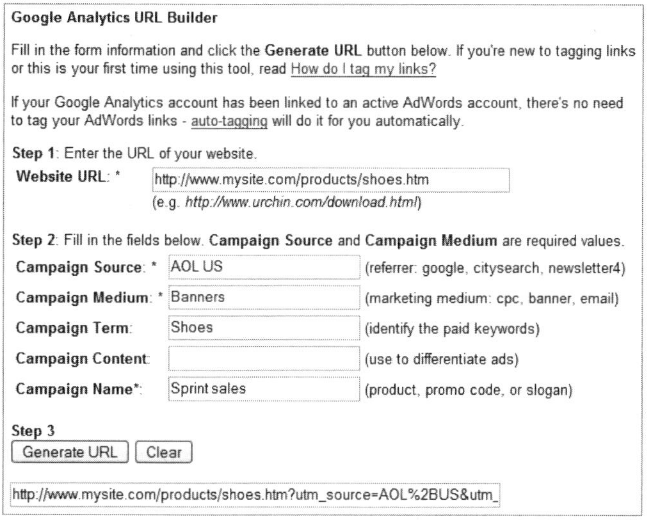

Figure 7.2 Tagging banner ad URLs

Tagging Email Marketing Campaigns

Continuing with the previous example, suppose you also plan to run a monthly email newsletter that begins in July 2010. The newsletter is for the shoe department and concerns a summer promotion. You want to ensure that all click-throughs from the email campaign are tracked in your Google Analytics reports.

To add to the mix, your marketing department also wants to compare the effectiveness of sending plain-text emails versus HTML format, which includes rich-text formatting and images. They would like to know whether visits and conversions vary depending on the format of the sent email (this is the basis of A/B split testing).

You can track these two email campaigns by using the example landing page URLs shown in Figure 7.3. In both cases, the Campaign Content field is used to differentiate the email formatting. You then supply the resultant tagged landing page URL to the person setting up your email marketing.

You may have numerous links within the same email message that point to different landing pages on your website. Therefore, you'll need to adjust each landing page URL accordingly. For example, shoes.htm may become boots.htm. However, the tracking parameters will remain the same.

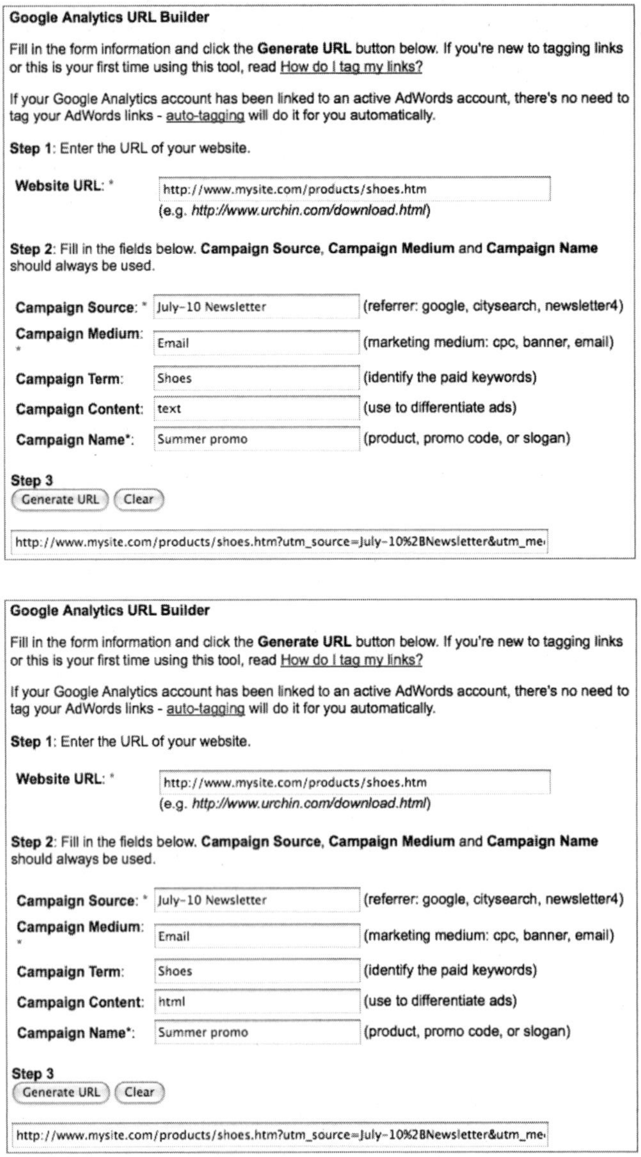

Google Analytics URL Builder

Fill in the form information and click the **Generate URL** button below. If you're new to tagging links or this is your first time using this tool, read How do I tag my links?

If your Google Analytics account has been linked to an active AdWords account, there's no need to tag your AdWords links - auto-tagging will do it for you automatically.

Step 1: Enter the URL of your website.

Website URL: *   http://www.mysite.com/products/shoes.htm
(e.g. *http://www.urchin.com/download.html*)

Step 2: Fill in the fields below. **Campaign Source**, **Campaign Medium** and **Campaign Name** should always be used.

Campaign Source: *	July–10 Newsletter	(referrer: google, citysearch, newsletter4)
Campaign Medium: *	Email	(marketing medium: cpc, banner, email)
Campaign Term:	Shoes	(identify the paid keywords)
Campaign Content:	text	(use to differentiate ads)
Campaign Name*:	Summer promo	(product, promo code, or slogan)

Step 3
(Generate URL) (Clear)

http://www.mysite.com/products/shoes.htm?utm_source=July–10%2BNewsletter&utm_me·

Google Analytics URL Builder

Fill in the form information and click the **Generate URL** button below. If you're new to tagging links or this is your first time using this tool, read How do I tag my links?

If your Google Analytics account has been linked to an active AdWords account, there's no need to tag your AdWords links - auto-tagging will do it for you automatically.

Step 1: Enter the URL of your website.

Website URL: *   http://www.mysite.com/products/shoes.htm
(e.g. *http://www.urchin.com/download.html*)

Step 2: Fill in the fields below. **Campaign Source**, **Campaign Medium** and **Campaign Name** should always be used.

Campaign Source: *	July–10 Newsletter	(referrer: google, citysearch, newsletter4)
Campaign Medium: *	Email	(marketing medium: cpc, banner, email)
Campaign Term:	Shoes	(identify the paid keywords)
Campaign Content:	html	(use to differentiate ads)
Campaign Name*:	Summer promo	(product, promo code, or slogan)

Step 3
(Generate URL) (Clear)

http://www.mysite.com/products/shoes.htm?utm_source=July–10%2BNewsletter&utm_me·

Figure 7.3 Tagging email campaigns as (a) text format, (b) HTML format

> **Plain Text versus HTML Email**
>
> HTML-formatted email is very popular and widespread these days. However, as the format was emerging, research was conducted to ascertain its impact.
>
> A 2006 study showed that recipients were more likely to click links in HTML emails than plain text (MailerMailer Email Metrics Report, Jan–Jun 2006).
>
> According to E-consultancy's Online Marketing Benchmarks 2004 for the UK, HTML generally generates 20–40 percent more response than an equivalent plaintext version. The caveat is that this is very dependent on the target market and products/services in question.

Tagging Paid Keywords

As discussed earlier in this section, Google automatically tags your paid keywords from AdWords campaigns. However, campaigns running on other paid networks do require tagging. Otherwise, a paid visitor will be reported as an organic (nonpaid) visitor. Figure 7.4 shows an example URL Builder to differentiate Yahoo! organic visitors from pay-per-click Yahoo! Search Marketing visitors, that is, paid versus nonpaid visitors from Yahoo!.

You supply the resultant tagged landing page URL to the person setting up your pay-per-click campaigns. You should use a similar approach for other pay-per-click accounts that you run—for example, Microsoft adCenter. The only difference is that the Campaign Source would be set as "adCenter" (or any phrase you wish to use to identify such visitors).

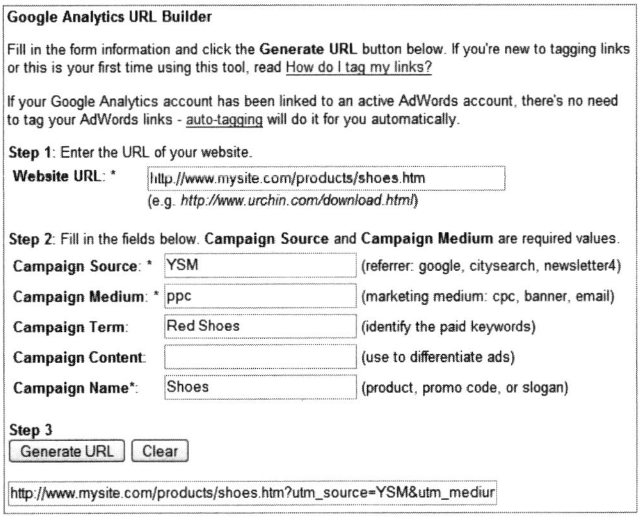

Figure 7.4 Tagging paid keywords

> **Note:** Google AdWords auto-tagging always labels AdWords visitors as `medium = cpc` (cost-per-click). You may wish to continue this labeling convention for Yahoo! Search Marketing, Microsoft adCenter, and other pay-per-click networks, so they are reported together when viewing "medium" reports. However, because AdWords is currently so prevalent for online advertising, I have found it useful to group all other pay-per-click networks as `medium = ppc` (or any other alternative label) and treat them as if they were a separate medium. This enables them to be compared against AdWords as a whole.

Tagging Embedded Links within Digital Collateral

If you host non-HTML content on your website, such as `catalogue.pdf`, `spec-sheet.doc`, or `price-matrix.xls`, you probably have links within those documents that point back to your website. By tagging these links, you can track visits that result from those documents, which in turn will enable you to monetize your digital collateral. Without tagging, visitors from your digital collateral are labeled as direct—that is, they are grouped together with visitors who typed the URL directly into their browser or bookmarked your site from a previous visit.

Using the method shown in Figure 7.5 ensures that links from your digital collateral are given credit for referring visitors to your website. Supply the resultant tagged landing page URL to the people who create such documents. Alternatively, coach your content creators to use the URL Builder tool themselves. That way, they will be tracking links as an integral part of their content creation and design process.

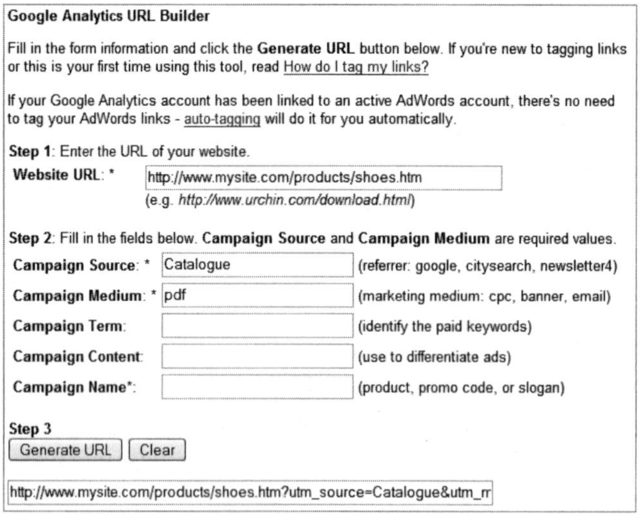
Google Analytics URL Builder

Fill in the form information and click the **Generate URL** button below. If you're new to tagging links or this is your first time using this tool, read How do I tag my links?

If your Google Analytics account has been linked to an active AdWords account, there's no need to tag your AdWords links - auto-tagging will do it for you automatically.

Step 1: Enter the URL of your website.

Website URL: * http://www.mysite.com/products/shoes.htm
(e.g. *http://www.urchin.com/download.html*)

Step 2: Fill in the fields below. **Campaign Source** and **Campaign Medium** are required values.

Campaign Source: * Catalogue (referrer: google, citysearch, newsletter4)
Campaign Medium: * pdf (marketing medium: cpc, banner, email)
Campaign Term: (identify the paid keywords)
Campaign Content: (use to differentiate ads)
Campaign Name*: (product, promo code, or slogan)

Step 3
Generate URL | Clear

http://www.mysite.com/products/shoes.htm?utm_source=Catalogue&utm_m

Figure 7.5 Tagging embedded links within digital collateral

Creating Custom Campaign Fields

If you have been using another tracking methodology or tool, you have probably already manually tagged your landing page URLs for paid campaigns, banners, email, and digital collateral. Rather than disregard these or append the additional Google Analytics variables, it is possible to configure Google Analytics to recognize your existing tags. As stressed previously, this is not required for AdWords tracking.

Add the following highlighted code to your GATC, replacing *orig_name* with the variable name that you are currently using. If no original value exists, then omit that line from your GATC.

```
<script type="text/javascript">
   var gaJsHost = (("https: " == document.location.protocol) ? "https://ssl.↵
 " : "http://www. ");
   document.write(unescape("%3Cscript src='" + gaJsHost + "google-↵
analytics.com/ga.js' type='text/javascript'%3E%3C/script%3E"));
</script>
<script type="text/javascript">
try{

   var pageTracker = _gat._getTracker("UA-12345-1");
   pageTracker._setCampNameKey("orig_campaign");       // default: utm_campaign
   pageTracker._setCampMediumKey("orig_medium");       // default: utm_medium
   pageTracker._setCampSourceKey("orig_source");       // default: utm_source
   pageTracker._setCampTermKey("orig_term");           // default: utm_term
   pageTracker._setCampContentKey("orig_content");     // default: utm_content
   pageTracker._trackPageview();
}catch(err) {}</script>
```

At a minimum, `orig_source` and `orig_medium` are required. If these are not present in your current landing page URLs, you need to include the Google Analytics equivalents.

Event Tracking

Google Analytics is capable of tracking any browser-based event, including Flash and JavaScript events. Think of these as *in-page* actions from visitors that do not generate a pageview. However, when considering Event Tracking, also bear in mind the possibility of virtual pageviews, as discussed earlier in this chapter.

Event activity is reported separately from your pageview activity. Example in-page events include the following:

- Any Flash-driven element, such as a Flash website or a Flash movie player
- Embedded Ajax page elements, such as onClick, onSubmit, onReset, onMouseOver, onMouseOut, onMouseMove, onSelect, onFocus, onBlur, onKeyPress, onChange, etc.
- Page gadgets
- File downloads
- Load times

An important consideration when tracking events is the impact on page bounce rates. With no events being tracked, a bounce is a single page visit. This is generally considered a bad experience for the visitor—they came, viewed one page, and left. The theory is that if your site content is good and relevant to the visitor, then surely they will want to read more than one page from you! Hence, pages with high bounce rates are a strong indicator that something is wrong with that process.

Now consider a visitor arriving on a page to view or interact with your Ajax widget or Flash movie. While viewing only a single HTML page, it is entirely possible that a visitor can have a great user experience. Event Tracking allows you to measure this, because a single page with any triggered event is no longer considered a bounce. You then use other metrics to ascertain if the experience is a good one or not, such as the number and type of events per visit. Of course, if the bounce rate for that page remains high, then you know your widget/Flash movie is not a good match for your visitors.

Bounce rates are popular key performance indicators used for optimizing websites. These are discussed in the section entitled "Content Creator KPI Examples," in Chapter 10, "Focusing on Key Performance Indicators," and in the section entitled "Identifying and Optimizing Poor Performing Pages" in Chapter 11, "Real-World Tasks."

 Note: Currently, tracked events cannot be used to define a conversion goal or funnel step in Google Analytics.

Setting Up Event Tracking

Event Tracking reports are available by default in the Content section of Google Analytics. Therefore no configuration changes to your account are necessary. However, you are required to modify your page or application in order to collect event-driven data and populate the reports. To do this, follow these two steps:

1. Define your event reporting structure.
2. For each event, call the _trackEvent() function in your web page or application source code.

In order understand how to define your events, I describe these steps in reverse order.

The _trackEvent Function

Event Tracking uses standard JavaScript method calls and provides a hierarchy data model of categories, actions, labels, and values. These parameters (Table 7.4) map directly to elements in the Analytics Reports interface.

▶ **Table 7.4** _trackEvent parameters

Parameter	Condition	Description
category	Required	The name you supply for the group of objects you want to track.
action	Required	A string that is uniquely paired with each category and commonly used to define the type of user interaction for the web object, such as a visitor's mouse click.
optional_label	Optional	A string to provide additional dimensions to the event data. Note that any spaces used in the label parameter must be encoded as %20.
optional_value	Optional	An integer that you can use to provide numerical data about the user event, such as time or a dollar amount.

The following example illustrates how you might use the Event Tracking method to record a user interaction with a video play link on your page.

```
<a href="#" onClick="pageTracker._trackEvent('Category-name',↵
'Action-name', 'Label-name', 'Value-integer');">Play video</a>
```

Any text-string value can be used for the event parameters, though if optional_value is used, this must be an integer. In practice, the values could be:

```
<a href="#" onClick="pageTracker._trackEvent('Video', 'Play',↵
'Birthday Party');">Play</a>
```

In this scenario, the report for Events would display *Video* as the category, *Play* as the action, and *Birthday Party* as the label (there is no value in this example). An example Event Tracking report is shown in Figure 7.6.

Because events can rapidly accumulate for a visitor's session (imagine tracking every mouse movement!), there is a limit to the number of events that can be tracked per visit. At the time of writing the maximum is 500 combined GATC requests—both events and page views. Therefore, consider the following caveats:

- Avoid scripting a video to send an event for every second played and other highly repetitive event triggers.
- Avoid excessive mouse movement tracking.
- Avoid time-lapse mechanisms that generate high event counts.

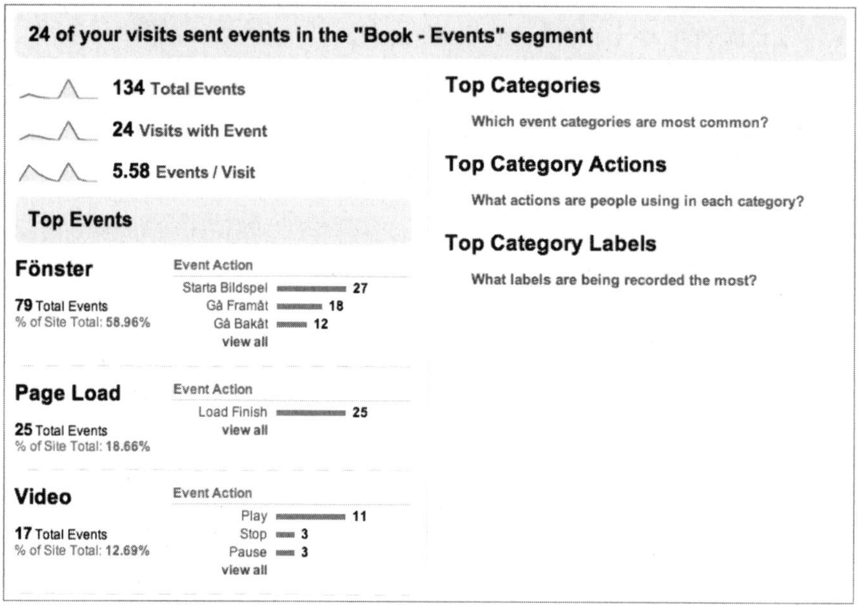

Figure 7.6 Event Tracking overview report showing three event categories—Fönster, Page Load, and Video

Tracking Flash Video from YouTube

If you create your own Flash video files and have access to the FLA file, you can track user interactions with Event Tracking. However, a common use of video on the Web is via YouTube.

YouTube allows you to upload your own video content and host your files at Google as a free service. In additional to sharing content with other YouTube visitors as a potential viral marketing medium, organizations can take advantage of Google's video hosting by embedding the YouTube video files back into their own websites. However, you cannot modify the YouTube FLA player.

Instead, YouTube provides a player API that allows a site owner to control how videos look and are controlled when embedded on their website. The JavaScript API exposes Play and Pause buttons and the like as external calls that you can attach events to. Although these cannot be extended to track video interactions on youtube.com, all interactions with the video embedded within your site can be tracked. See http://code.google.com/apis/youtube/getting_started.html#player_apis for more details.

> **A Note of Caution for Using the Examples Provided**
>
> For all Event Tracking examples, I have assumed a standard GATC implementation. That is, the `pageTracker` object is defined, for example, as follows:
>
> ```
> var pageTracker = _gat._getTracker("UA-12345-1");
> ```
>
> If you have a different Tracker object defined, for example, `firstTracker`, you will need to adjust these examples accordingly.

Defining Your Event-Reporting Structure

Because of the setup flexibility for Event Tracking, it is important to first plan your desired reporting structure and then test it before implementing it. As mentioned earlier, this is really your first step once you understand the structure of the Event Tracking implementation.

Defining Categories

A category represents the root level of the hierarchical structure of Event Tracking, and you can use this structure in any way to suit your needs. Typically, you will use the same category name multiple times in order to group metrics under a given category. For example, you might track user interaction on two separate controls, Play and Pause, on a single video interface using the following:

```
pageTracker._trackEvent('Video', 'Play', 'Birthday Party');
pageTracker._trackEvent('Video', 'Pause', 'Birthday Party');
```

You can also track events for different video files in the same category:

```
pageTracker._trackEvent('Video', 'Play', 'Xmas 2009');
pageTracker._trackEvent('Video', 'Play', 'Xmas 2010');
```

This allows you to see aggregate data for the category Video as well being able to drill down into action and label details, as schematically shown in Figure 7.7.

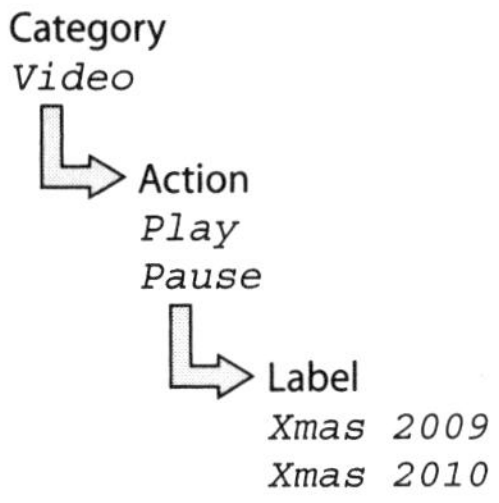

Figure 7.7 Schematic hierarchical structure of Event Tracking

Perhaps you would like to categorize your videos in a different way:

```
pageTracker._trackEvent('Videos 2009', 'Play', 'Xmas');
pageTracker._trackEvent('Videos 2010', 'Play', 'Birthday');
pageTracker._trackEvent('Downloads', 'Click', 'Birthday 2010');
```

In this scenario you can view the total combined event count for all three categories. The Total Events metric counts all categories supplied in your implementation. However, you will not be able to view combined metrics for all Videos separately from Downloads, because detailed event metrics are combined under their respective categories.

Syntax for Event-Tracking Parameters

Be aware of the following syntax requirements that apply to all event text parameters (category, action, play):

- If you plan to use the same parameter name in multiple locations on your site, be careful to correctly reference it. For example, if you call your video tracking category "Video" and later use the plural "Videos," you will have two separate categories for video tracking.

- If you decide to change the parameter name of an object that has already been tracked under a different name, for example, the historical data for the original name will not be reprocessed, and you will have metrics for the same event listed under two categories.

- The text-string values you define for your event parameters are case sensitive. That is, the category "Video" will be reported separately from "video," the action "Play" will be reported separately from "play," and so forth.

Tip: If you manage an e-commerce site with events related to your shopping categories (for example, an introduction Flash animation for each of your store sections), consider matching your event categories to your store categories. This way you will be able to compare the performance of your events on a per-shopping-section basis—a common requirement for e-commerce managers.

Defining Actions

Typically, the action parameter defines the interaction or event that you wish to capture from a visitor. Using the video example, these would be:

- Play—button clicks
- Stop—button clicks
- Pause—button clicks

Additional event actions could be:

- Time—how much of the video is watched, how much of the game is played, how long it takes to add to cart, and so on
- Click—click-through on a download link
- Click—click-through on a banner advertisement

Usually, defining the action parameter for Event Tracking is straightforward, because in most cases it is the physical action of the visitor's interaction. The exception in the previous examples is Time.

Importantly, action names can be used to either aggregate or differentiate user interaction. Consider the last two examples that have an action named Click for both the Downloads category and the Banners category. The Top Actions report will contain *all* interactions with that same name, that is, no differentiation of clicks for Banners or Downloads. You can view a detailed breakdown of the Click action by category in the next report level. However, the point is, if you use the action Click indiscriminately across your Event Tracking implementation, the usefulness of that segment will be diminished in the reports.

As you probably have realized, the action value of Click, although useful for aggregation reports, is not particularly meaningful. An alternative approach is to differentiate the two types of click actions. For the download link, you could use the document file type as the action parameter. In this way, your reports for the Downloads category would be broken out by file types (PDF, DOC, XLS, and so on), with the filename detail as the label. See Figure 7.8a.

Similarly, for the Banners category, you could use the banner type or version to differentiate the same ad in different formats. In this way you can compare overall banner events with other events, as well as distinguish different creative formats, animated versus static, for example. See Figure 7.8b.

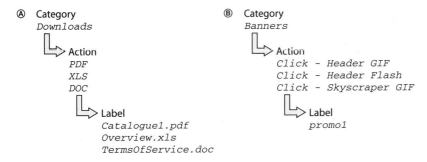

Figure 7.8 Schematic Event Tracking report structure for (a) file downloads, (b) banner click-throughs

Both aggregating and differentiating action names have their advantages, and it's a matter of personal choice which method you use. Generally, it usually comes down to how your business is structured. If you have a video directory, download catalogue, or much library-type content, you will probably wish to differentiate actions—by video genre or file type, for example. If you have a small collection of disparate actions (two Flash demos, one how-to video guide, three download files), then it makes sense to aggregate the actions so that each event performance can be compared against the other.

Unique Events Are Incremented by Unique Actions

Any time a visitor interacts with an object tagged with a particular action name, the initial interaction is logged as one unique event for that action name. Any additional interaction with the same action name for that user's visit will not contribute to the unique event calculation for that particular action. This is the case even if the visitor leaves that object and begins to interact with another object tagged via the same action name.

This has two significant consequences in the reports. First, suppose a user interacts with the Play action from two unique video players tagged with separate categories. The Top Actions reports for Play will list one unique event even though the user engaged with two unique players. Second, each category's Action report will list one unique action, since there is indeed one unique event per category/action pair.

Defining Labels—Optional

With labels, you can provide additional information for events that you want to track, such as the movie title in the previous video examples or the name of a file when tracking downloads. If you have multiple events with the same category and action names, use the label parameter to differentiate.

Defining Values—Optional

This parameter differs from the others in that it is an integer used to assign a numerical value for a tracked event (all other parameters are text strings). For example, you could use it to provide the Play Time—how much of a video has been watched in seconds, minutes, or a percentage; Load Time—how long a page takes to download; or Revenue—a monitory value assigned to a triggered event. Examples of these are discussed in upcoming sections.

Tracking Flash Events

Unless you have built your entire website content in Flash (why?), most Flash-user interactions can be considered as events rather than virtual pageviews. However, this is not a hard or fast rule. Consider the benefits, or not, of both prior to implementing. Here I explain only how to track Flash-user interactions as Google Analytics events. The use of virtual pageviews is discussed earlier in this chapter.

The technique you choose to track Flash events will be determined by two factors:

- What software you use to generate the Flash FLA file, more specifically, the version of ActionScript you use

- The type of Flash development you perform, that is, occasional Flash development as part of a larger website project or as a dedicated Flash professional

Different Versions of ActionScript

The method for tracking Flash events differs depending on whether you are coding in the legacy ActionScript 2 or the latest ActionScript 3. ActionScript was first included in Flash Player 5, with version 3 introduced in 2006 as part of Flash Player 9 and upward. If you are developing your Flash applications in Flash CS3 or higher, you are using ActionScript 3.

I recommend you use ActionScript 3 wherever possible because it is better designed to handle Flash-browser communications and is therefore more robust for Event Tracking.

Using Legacy ActionScript 2

For this example, I assume that you have the standard GATC on your HTML page and that you are embedding a Flash SWF movie file with a Play button. You wish to track clicks on the Play button as an event with category name Video, action name Play, and label name Ratatouille.

Within your Flash application, call the `trackEvent` object with `getURL` and pass the associated category, action, and label parameters to be displayed in the reports:

```
on (release) {
    getURL ("javascript:(function(){pageTracker._trackEvent('Video', 'Play',↵
'Ratatouille');})()");
}
```

That's all there is to it! Other Flash buttons can have their events defined in a similar way, such as Stop and Pause. Multiple videos can be tracked by passing different labels. Thus, to track three movies, your video Flash object might be reported schematically as per Figure 7.9.

```
Category
Video
  ↳ Action
      Play
      Pause
      Stop
        ↳ Label
            Ratatouille
            The Incredibles
            Ice Age 3
```

Figure 7.9 Schematic event reporting example

Extending the Flash example further, when the video is placed on the web page, you can use the FlashVars parameter (Flash MX or newer) to provide individual *label* and *value* input values. FlashVars is the Flash counterpart to a URL query string. That is, it's a way to pass variables from HTML to a Flash movie. Variables passed via FlashVars are placed into the _root level of the Flash movie, as shown in the following example:

```
<object classid="clsid:D27CDB6E-AE6D-11cf-96B8-444553540000" -- ↵
codebase="http://download.macromedia.com/pub/shockwave/↵
cabs/flash/swflash.cab#version=7,0,19,0" width="300" height="400">
    <param name="FlashVars" value="label=The%20Incredibles&value=9" />
    <param name="movie" value="movie1.swf" />
    <param name="quality" value="high" />
    <embed src="movie1.swf" -- FlashVars="label=The%20Incredibles&value=9"↵
quality="high" -- pluginspage="http://www.macromedia.com/go/getflashplayer" ↵
type="application/x-shockwave-flash" width="300"-- height="400"></embed>
</object>
```

This makes your ActionScript code within the player generic and reusable—you reuse the same code for each movie with the necessary parameters picked up from FlashVars. This is a particularly useful technique if, for example, you have hundreds (or thousands) of video files that you don't wish to create individual SWF files for.

Within your Flash application, call the _trackEvent object as follows:

```
on (release) {
    getURL ("javascript:(function(){pageTracker._trackEvent('Video', 'Play', "↵
+label+ ", " +value+ ");})()");
}
```

For the same three movies, your video Flash object might be reported schematically as per Figure 7.10.

Category
Video

↳ Action
  Play
  Pause
  Stop

  ↳ Label
    Ratatouille
    The Incredibles
    Ice Age 3

    ↳ Value
      8
      9
      10

Figure 7.10 Schematic event reporting example generated by using FlashVars

Using ActionScript 3

A little more coding is required when using ActionScript 3, though the principle is the same. As for the last example, I assume you have the standard GATC on your HTML page and that you are embedding a Flash SWF movie file with a Play button. You wish to track clicks on Play as an event with category name of Video, action name of Play, and label name of Ratatouille. Essentially there are three steps to follow:

1. Add an external class reference within your FLA file. This is a one-time call:

```
import flash.external.ExternalInterface
```

2. Modify the button or link within your FLA file and pass the associated category, action, label, and value parameters to be displayed in the reports:

```
myBtn.addEventListener(
MouseEvent.CLICK, ExternalInterface.call('pageTracker._trackEvent', ↵
'Video', 'Play', 'Ratatouille', '9'));
```

3. Modify the HTML where the SWF file is embedded:

```
<object ...
    <param name="allowScriptAccess" value="always" />
    <!-- {...REMAINING OBJECT CONTENT...}   -->
    <embed ...
      allowScriptAccess="always"
```

```
<!-- {...REMAINING EMBED CONTENT...}    -->
    </embed>
</object>
```

As described for using ActionScript 2, you can also use FlashVars parameters to provide *label* and *value* input values for your SWF file, making it generic and easy to reuse. Within your HTML document, the use of FlashVars is exactly the same as previously described for ActionScript 2:

```
<param name="FlashVars" value="label=The%20Incredibles&value=9" />
```

However, for ActionScript 3, incoming FlashVars variables are no longer available as a loose collection in the main timeline. Instead, such variables are stored in the parameters property of the LoaderInfo class associated with the DisplayObject. To utilize these values in your FLA file, use the following format:

```
myBtn.addEventListener(
MouseEvent.CLICK, ExternalInterface.call('pageTracker._trackEvent', ↵
'Video', 'Play', root.loaderInfo.parameters.label, ↵
root.loaderInfo.parameters.value));
```

Event Tracking for Flash Professionals

The previous examples allow you to track Flash actions as events on a per-event basis when the need arises. Typically, you use these techniques when you are embedding your SWF file into a page that already contains the GATC. It is the simplest method if you are a webmaster and want to communicate Google Analytics tracking requirements to a third-party Flash designer.

However, if you develop Flash applications full-time yourself, the previous methods of constantly coding each action can become laborious. Therefore, you can use the gaforflash software component available at: http://code.google.com/p/gaforflash/. This is an ActionScript 3 API for Google Analytics data collection, developed under an open source initiative with Adobe Systems Inc. It can simplify the tracking of your Flash content in a number ways, such as these:

- When you have a large number of embedded Flash files on HTML pages
- When you are creating a standalone Flex application or Flash-only site hosted on an HTML page
- When you are distributing your Flex/Flash application where you have no control over where the file will be placed

 Note: Currently, Flash tracking is available for any Flash content embedded in a web page. Tracking of data sent from Adobe Air, Shockwave, or via the Flash IDE is not supported at this time.

To get started, download and install gaforflash from http://code.google.com/p/gaforflash/. The installation is as straightforward as copying, or importing, the class files (SWC) into the relevant directory where your Flash or Flex installation can read them. Then you will have two ways of tracking your Flash events—Bridge Mode or AS3 Mode.

Bridge Mode is the most common method because it is utilized when a GATC is already embedded within the HTML. It provides a simple wrapper to all the ga.js functions using the ExternalInterface class, as previously described. Everything else is managed from within Flash itself. In Bridge Mode, gaforflash will call ExternalInterface (or getUrl if ExternalInterface is blocked for some reason) in the background. The following code is an example of Bridge Mode in use:

```
import com.google.analytics.AnalyticsTracker;
import com.google.analytics.GATracker;
var tracker:AnalyticsTracker = new GATracker(this, "window.pageTracker",↵
"Bridge", false);
tracker.trackPageview("/Movies");              // track a virtual pageview
tracker.trackEvent("Video", "Play", "Ice Age 3", 9);     // track an event
```

AS3 Mode provides a method of bypassing any Flash-JavaScript communication issues. This is particularly relevant if your SWF file is to be deployed on different domains, that is, sites using third-party content, because often such sites do not allow the ExternalInterface method. In AS3 Mode, you do not require a GATC to be present within your HTML—it is an implementation of Google Analytics tracking written entirely in ActionScript. As a result, all Google Analytics interactions are generated from within the Flash object. The following code is an example of AS3 Mode use:

```
import com.google.analytics.AnalyticsTracker;
import com.google.analytics.GATracker;
var tracker:AnalyticsTracker = new GATracker(this, "UA-12345-1", "AS3",↵
false);
tracker.trackPageview("/Movies");              // track a virtual pageview
tracker.trackEvent("Video", "Play", "Ice Age 3", 9);     // track an event
```

Unless you are developing the same Flash content for deployment on multiple domains, you will most likely use gaforflash in Bridge Mode.

There is a great deal more to gaforflash that is beyond the realm of this book. I hope by scratching the surface I have whet your appetite for its capabilities. If you are a Flash developer, check out http://code.google.com/apis/analytics/docs/tracking/eventTrackerOverview.html for the latest developments.

Flash Cookies and Privacy Considerations

In AS3 Mode, Google Analytics cookies are stored with other Flash cookies. However, these are not controlled within a user's browser but are part of the Flash Player install on your machine, known as Shared Objects. A fuller description is provided at Wikipedia: `http://en.wikipedia.org/wiki/Local_Shared_Object`.

Because a user's browser does not control Shared Objects, there are important privacy implications of using this method. Chapters 2 and 3, "Google Analytics Features, Benefits, and Limitations," discuss the privacy issues of web analytics and Google Analytics, respectively. The key to a best-practice implementation of your tracking methodology is to be transparent in how you handle visitor privacy and provide visitors with clear instructions of how to opt out of such tracking.

From a user's perspective, Flash Shared Objects can be managed using the Adobe Flash Player Settings Manager at `http://www.macromedia.com/support/documentation/en/flashplayer/help/settings_manager.html`. A number of Firefox add-ons can provide similar functionality, such as BetterPrivacy.

Tracking Load-Time Events

By default, Google Analytics cannot track page download times, because a pageview request is tracked as a single instance at the point at which the GATC is embedded in your HTML. The recommended placement of the GATC is at the bottom of each page. Therefore, Google Analytics tracks a pageview at the point close to the completed page download.

Event Tracking provides a method to track your page download times. In this example I use a generic time-tracking script from Google to track page download times. This is achieved by creating a timestamp at the top of an HTML page using the JavaScript Date() method and another timestamp when the page has fully downloaded using the JavaScript window.onload method. The difference between the two timestamps is passed to Google Analytics as an event value.

First, download a copy of the time-tracker.js file from www.advanced-web-metrics.com/chapter7. Then modify the HTML <head> section of the page you wish measure the download time for, as follows:

```
<head>
<script type="text/javascript" src="/scripts/time-tracker.js"></script>
<script type="text/javascript">
    var timeTracker = new TimeTracker();
```

```
    timeTracker._recordStartTime();

    function getPageLoad(){
        timeTracker._recordEndTime();
        timeTracker._track(pageTracker, 'Page load time', document.location. ↵
        pathname);
    }
    window.onload = getPageLoad;
</script>
    [ ... REMAINING HTML HEAD CONTENT ... ]


</head>
```

The `time-tracker.js` script groups each event value (the calculated download time) into buckets for easy comparison. An example report is shown in Figure 7.11. Note that computers report time in milliseconds. Rather than convert into minutes and seconds, this is maintained in the script so that the event value remains an integer—required for Event Tracking values.

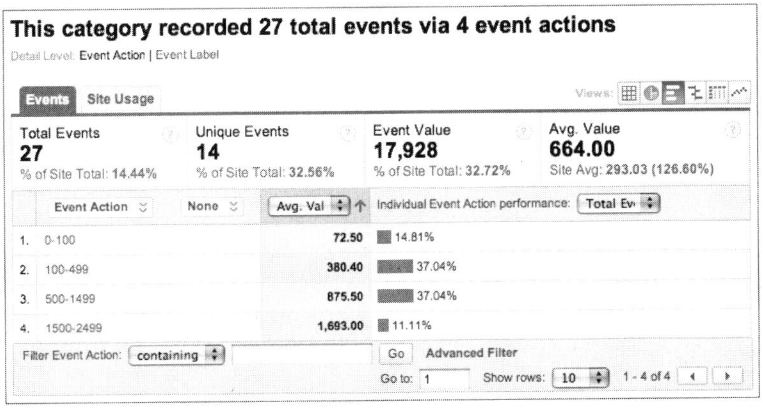

Figure 7.11 Page download times grouped and tracked as events; times reported in milliseconds

From your Event Tracking reports, you can determine the distribution of load times for individual pages, the average page load time, and if implemented sitewide, the average time for page loads across your entire site.

The implementation as shown will work for the vast majority of users. However, it may be necessary for you to modify the contents of the `timeTracker._track` line. The call to the event track routine of Google Analytics is constructed as follows:

```
timeTracker._track(tracker_object_name, event_category, event_label)
```

If you're using a standard GATC, as shown previously in Figure 6.2, your tracker_object_name will be pageTracker. Therefore no change is required. If you have a custom GATC, change the value in your <head> code to match. For example:

```
timeTracker._track(firstTracker, 'Page load time', document.location.pathname);
```

Your event_category and event_label can be any value text label you wish to use.

Note: The page load-time example is a modification of the one available at the Google Code site at http://code.google.com/apis/analytics/docs/tracking/eventTrackerWrappers.html, which at the time of writing contained a number of deprecated functions (for example, _createEventTracker). The Google code is incredibly flexible in its usage and can be employed to time user interactions, such as the time it takes for a visitor to click Next, complete a form registration, or watch a video file. View the Google Code site for more detailed documentation.

Tracking Banners and Other Outgoing Links as Events

If you publish advertising banners or links on your site that refer visitors to other websites, you have two options for tracking: track the click-through as a virtual pageview or track the click-through as an event. Both options allow you to monetize the click action; the merits of each are discussed earlier in this chapter in "Virtual Pageviews versus Event Tracking." In this section I consider only Event Tracking with the category defined as Exit Points.

For an animated GIF or other non-Flash banner ad, modify the outgoing link as follows:

```
<a href="http://www.advertiser-site.com" onClick=↵
"pageTracker._trackEvent('ExitPoints', 'Click', 'advertisername – Ad ↵
version A', 4) "><img src="bannerA.gif"></a>
```

Note that a value of 4 has been assigned to this event, which is a click-through. The equivalent code used within a Flash banner, assigned with a higher monetary value, is as follows:

```
myBtn.addEventListener(
MouseEvent.CLICK, ExternalInterface.call('pageTracker._trackEvent', ↵
'Exit Points', 'Click', 'advertisername – Ad version B', 5));
```

For both examples, it is possible to view and segment the event reports both by the advertiser's name and the ad version, for example, header banner versus skyscraper.

Note: ActionScript 3.0 is used for the Flash examples from now on. In addition to the code shown, you will also need to set import flash.external.ExternalInterface in your FLA file and allowScriptAccess in your HTML—as described previously in "Tracking Flash Events."

However, I prefer to use action names to distinguish object elements. For example, rather than aggregate the event action Click for all outbound link types, go one step further and differentiate between click-throughs on Flash and GIF banners, as follows:

GIF banner event tracking:

```
<a href="http://www.advertiser-site.com" ↵
onClick="pageTracker._trackEvent('Exit Points', 'Click - GIF banner', ↵
'advertisername - Ad version A', 4)"><img src="bannerA.gif"></a>
```

Flash banner event tracking:

```
myBtn.addEventListener(
MouseEvent.CLICK, ExternalInterface.call('pageTracker._trackEvent', ↵
'Exit Points', 'Click - FLASH banner', 'advertisername - Ad ↵
version A', 5));
```

To wrap up this series of outbound click tracking, for an outbound link, use link event tracking:

```
<a href="http://www.advertiser-site.com"
onClick="pageTracker._trackEvent('Exit Points', 'Click - link', ↵
'linkURL', 1) ">View our Partner</a>
```

Tracking Mailto: Clicks as Events

The mailto: link is another outgoing link that can be tracked in exactly the same way as described previously. I discuss it here separately simply to emphasize the importance of tracking mailto: clicks—particularly for non-e-commerce websites, where any action that can bring a visitor closer to lead generation for you has an intrinsic value. As your sales department follows up on these contacts, you will be able to assess the conversion rate and average order value of such leads and therefore monetize the mailto: onClick event. Modify your mailto: links as follows:

```
<a href="mailto:mail@mysite.co.uk"
onClick="pageTracker._trackEvent('Exit Points', 'Click - email', ↵
'mail@mysite.co.uk') ">mail@mysite.co.uk</a>
```

Add a monetary value to this event as desired.

Customizing the GATC

As discussed in Chapter 6, in "Understanding the Google Analytics Tracking Code," for the majority of websites, you will not need to make any customizations to your GATC—you will use the example code presented in the Standard tab of Figure 6.2, accessed from the Profile Settings area of your account (click on the "Check Status" link). However, should the need arise, the following sections describe some of the available options you can use.

Subdomain Tracking

This is a simple one-line change to your GATC. As such, you can automate the change required by selecting "One domain with multiple subdomains" from your profile "Check Status" area, as shown in Figure 7.12. The following is a description of why the change is required and what it achieves. You should also consider the filter to differentiate your different subdomains (discussed in Chapter 8).

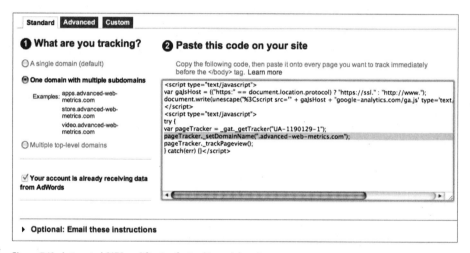

Figure 7.12 Automated GATC modification for tracking subdomains

Google Analytics uses first-party cookies, which means collected information is associated with your fully qualified host name—for example, www.mysite.com. Only your fully qualified host name can read or set its first-party cookies. This is a built-in security feature of all web browsers.

A *subdomain* is one that is a part of the parent domain. In this example, the parent domain is mysite.com, so www is actually a subdomain of mysite.com. Other example subdomains include secure.mysite.com, ww2.mysite.com, en.mysite.com, and so on.

The default behavior when you set up Google Analytics is that subdomains are tracked in separate profiles. That is, you enter the subdomain name in the URL field of

the Add A Profile For A New Domain section—as described in Chapter 6 in the section "Using Accounts and Profiles." This will generate a unique tracking code for each subdomain, so ensure that you add the correct code to your pages.

As a consequence, by default Google Analytics tracks visitors that traverse your different subdomains as referrers. For example, www.mysite.com becomes a referrer of secure.mysite.com. That can be valuable information in itself, but the original referrer (for example, a keyword search on google.com), which is captured and reported on for www.mysite.com, cannot be transferred into your reports for secure.mysite.com. If this was for a transaction, you would know how your visitors found you but would have no information on how your customers found you.

Fortunately, modifying this behavior for your own domains is straightforward. You can achieve this by combining all your subdomain data under the one parent domain. To accomplish this, set your parent domain in the GATC so that the Google Analytics first-party cookies can be shared across your subdomains, as highlighted here:

```
<script type="text/javascript">
    var gaJsHost = (("https: " == document.location.protocol) ? "https://↵
ssl." : "http://www. ");
    document.write(unescape("%3Cscript src='" + gaJsHost + "google-↵
analytics.com/ga.js' type='text/javascript'%3E%3C/script%3E"));
</script>
<script type="text/javascript">
try{
    var pageTracker = _gat._getTracker("UA-12345-1");
    pageTracker._setDomainName(".mysite.com");
    pageTracker._trackPageview();
} catch(err) {}</script>
```

This way all subdomains of .mysite.com can read, write, or edit the _utm cookies that Google Analytics uses. No further GATC modifications are required. However, as you may have realized, both subdomains are now aggregated, meaning that visits to www.mysite.com/index.html and secure.mysite.com/index.html will show in your reports as the same page—that is, both /index.html. In addition, you will not know how many visits your www site referred to your secure site. Correct these by applying the filter, as shown in Figure 7.13.

Note: The filter shown in Figure 7.13 will make site overlay inoperable and may require you to modify your goal settings accordingly. However, I find the loss of the Site Overlay report is more than compensated by the greater insight that applying this filter provides.

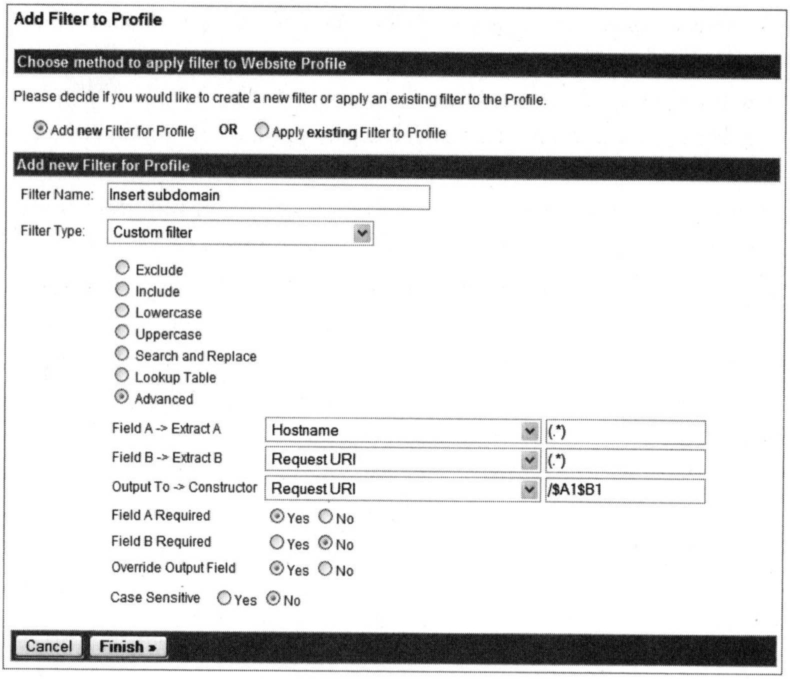

Add Filter to Profile

Choose method to apply filter to Website Profile

Please decide if you would like to create a new filter or apply an existing filter to the Profile.

◉ Add **new** Filter for Profile   **OR**   ○ Apply **existing** Filter to Profile

Add new Filter for Profile

Filter Name: Insert subdomain

Filter Type: Custom filter ▾

○ Exclude
○ Include
○ Lowercase
○ Uppercase
○ Search and Replace
○ Lookup Table
◉ Advanced

Field A -> Extract A	Hostname ▾	(.*)
Field B -> Extract B	Request URI ▾	(.*)
Output To -> Constructor	Request URI ▾	/$A1$B1

Field A Required   ◉ Yes ○ No
Field B Required   ○ Yes ◉ No
Override Output Field ◉ Yes ○ No
Case Sensitive   ○ Yes ◉ No

[Cancel] [Finish ▸]

Figure 7.13 Filter to differentiate identical subdomain page names

By using this filter, page names will include your subdomains, allowing you to differentiate accordingly. For example, in the Content > Top Content reports will be www.mysite.com/index.html and secure.mysite.com/index.html, respectively.

The use of filters is discussed in detail in Chapter 8.

Multiple Domain Tracking

As discussed in the previous section, web browsers have built-in security features that prevent the sharing of first-party cookies with other domains. If your website passes a visitor to different parent domains, then this needs special consideration.

Consider the following example: Your main website is www.mysite.com and you host regional variations (language, currency, and so on) on different parent domains such as www.mysite.co.uk. Both sites are tagged with your GATC. A visitor arrives on www.mysite.com by clicking a link from a search results page on www.google.com, for example. Next, they click the option to select your regional version at www.mysite.co.uk. A conversion is then made on this site.

Note: Google Analytics cannot track visitors traversing the Web to unrelated domains. It can only track visitors across domains that you own or control and to which you can add your GATC.

By default, the visitor converting at www.mysite.co.uk will be reported as a refer-ral visitor from www.mysite.com. The original referral information (search at www.google.com and associated search keywords) is lost because the cookie information cannot fol-low the visitor to the third-party domain. This is analogous to the situation described earlier for subdomain tracking.

If you maintain separate Google Analytics profiles for these two websites, then all page metrics (time on site, page depth, bounce rate, and so on) will be counted separately—in this example, a one-page visit for www.mysite.com and *x-1* page visits for www.mysite.co.uk. On the other hand, if you have configured data for both websites to be collected into a single profile (that is, you used the same GATC on both domains), then your page metrics will be skewed with overinflated numbers of single-page visits for www.mysite.com. Clearly, this is not the outcome you want.

The solution for tracking visitors across multiple sites is to maintain the ses-sion by transferring cookies across the multiple domains. There are two methods of achieving this, depending on how you forward visitors to your other domains—either by a link or via a form submission. These are the same as those discussed earlier (see "E-commerce Tracking—Using a Third-Party Payment Gateway"), because in both cases first-party cookies need to be handed over to a third-party domain.

Regardless of which method you use, you will need to modify your GATC on the pages where a visitor leaves one domain and enters another. In the example given, this would be the home pages of www.mysite.com and www.mysite.co.uk, respectively. However, for this scenario it is common to have multiple pages where this can happen. Therefore, I recommend you make the GATC modification to *all* pages for *all* your domains to ensure consistency of your visitor tracking. The modification required is shown in the following highlighted code:

```
<script type="text/javascript">
    var gaJsHost = (("https: " == document.location.protocol) ? "https://ssl.↵
" : "http://www. ");
    document.write(unescape("%3Cscript src='" + gaJsHost + "google-↵
analytics.com/ga.js' type='text/javascript'%3E%3C/script%3E"));
</script>
<script type="text/javascript">
try {
    var pageTracker = _gat._getTracker("UA-12345-1");
    pageTracker._setDomainName("none");
    pageTracker._setAllowLinker(true);
    pageTracker._trackPageview();
} catch(err) {}</script>
```

The use of pageTracker._setDomainName("none") forces the domain hash of the _utm cookies to be set to "1", making them generic enough to be associated with any domain, and sets the cookies' host to be whatever the current URL host is. The next line, pageTracker._setAllowLinker(true), allows the cookie name/value pairs to be either transferred or received.

As for subdomain tracking, these detailed GATC changes can be automated by selecting "Multiple top-level domains" from your profile "Check Status" area, as shown in Figure 7.14.

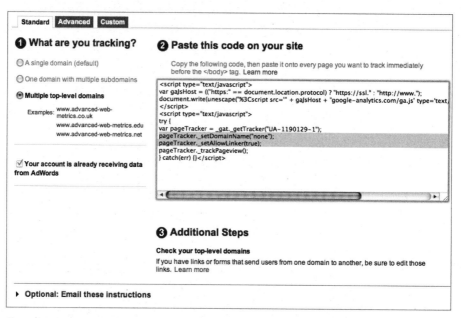

Figure 7.14 Automated GATC modification for tracking across multiple domains

With your pages modified, you then amend the link, or form, your visitors use to navigate between the domains, as described next.

Method 1: Track a Visitor across Domains When Using a Link

Use this method when you are passing visitors to another domain using a standard hyperlink. Within your web pages, modify all links to your other domains as follows:

```
<a href="http://www.mysite.co.uk" onclick="pageTracker._link('http://↵
www.mysite.co.uk/');return false; ">
Go to our UK web site</a>
```

With this method, the Google Analytics cookies are "pushed" to the receiving domain by appending them to the URL string (HTTP GET). If you see _utma, _utmb, and _utmc parameters in the URL of the landing page, then this has worked.

Method 2: Track a Visitor across Domains When Using a Form

Use this method when you are passing visitors to another domain using a form. Within your web pages, modify all form references to your other domains as follows:

```
<form method="post" onsubmit="pageTracker._linkByPost(this)">
...
</form>
```

If you already have an `onSubmit` validation routine, you append the cross-domain modification to your existing function call as follows:

```
<form method="post"
onsubmit="validate_routine(this);pageTracker._linkByPost(this) ">
...
</form>
```

With this method, the Google Analytics cookies are "pushed" to the receiving domain via the HTTP headers (HTTP POST). This will work even for forms where `method="GET"`. You can verify if this has worked by viewing the HTTP headers sent in Firefox using the add-on LiveHTTPheaders (`http://livehttpheaders.mozdev.org`).

The GATC Setup Wizard

The changes illustrated in Figures 7.12 and 7.14 are examples of using the GATC setup wizard. That is, changes required to your tracking code that Google Analytics can automatically provide for you—without the need for you to manually edit page code.

In this section, how to track visitors that traverse subdomains or multiple domains, the required changes are all contained within the "Standard" tab menu of the GATC setup wizard. As you will have noticed, there is also an "Advanced" and "Custom" menu tab.

The Advanced menu provides additional instructions that affect your GATC. For example, how to import data from AdWords, how to track paid campaigns for non-AdWords pay-per-click accounts, how to use Urchin in conjunction with Google Analytics, and so forth. These are discussed in the relevant sections of this book. Neither the Standard nor Advanced GATC code can be edited within the wizard.

The Custom menu is an area where you can manually edit the GATC within the wizard and save it for later reference. For all menu tabs, you can distribute the required code via email. The text supplied for you to do this is obtained by selecting "Optional: Email these instructions."

Tracking Visitors across Subdomains and Multiple Domains

This is a special scenario where you have visitors traversing subdomains *and* third-party domains within their visit. Consider the following example:

- A visitor goes to www.mysite.com.

- Next the visitor clicks a link to blog.mysite.com.

- Then the visitor decides to purchase a product and so clicks the shopping cart link, which sends them off to www.shoppingcart.com/widgets.

Tracking this correctly requires two different GATCs—one for your "main" site containing the subdomains, the other for your third-party site. On your main site, use the as following modified GATC:

```
<script type="text/javascript">
    var gaJsHost = (("https:" == document.location.protocol) ? "https://ssl.↵
" : "http://www. ");
    document.write(unescape("%3Cscript src='" + gaJsHost + "google-↵
analytics.com/ga.js' type='text/javascript'%3E%3C/script%3E"));
</script>
<script type="text/javascript">
try {
    var pageTracker = _gat._getTracker("UA-12345-1");
    pageTracker._setDomainName(".mysite.com");
    pageTracker._setAllowLinker(true);
    pageTracker._setAllowHash(false);
    pageTracker._trackPageview();
} catch(err) {}</script>
```

Note the use of _setAllowHash(false) in order to make the cookies generic for this scenario.

On the third-party site, www.shopppingcart.com/widgets, modify the GATC just as you would for tracking across multiple domains. This was shown previously and is reproduced here for consistency:

```
<script type="text/javascript">
    var gaJsHost = (("https:" == document.location.protocol) ? "https://ssl." :↵
"http://www. ");
    document.write(unescape("%3Cscript src='" + gaJsHost + "google-↵
analytics.com/ga.js' type='text/javascript'%3E%3C/script%3E"));
</script>
<script type="text/javascript">
try {
    var pageTracker = _gat._getTracker("UA-12345-1");
```

```
    pageTracker._setDomainName("none");
    pageTracker._setAllowLinker(true);
    pageTracker._trackPageview();
} catch(err) {}</script>
```

Restricting Cookie Data to a Subdirectory

By default, any page on your domain can view Google Analytics first-party cookies. If
you want to restrict the use of cookies to a subdirectory—for example, in cases where
you own only a subdirectory of the parent domain—you can set the preferred cookie
path in your GATC using the _setCookiePath() function:

```
<script type="text/javascript">
    var gaJsHost = (("https:" == document.location.protocol) ? "https://ssl.↵
" : "http://www. ");
    document.write(unescape("%3Cscript src='" + gaJsHost + "google-↵
analytics.com/ga.js' type='text/javascript'%3E%3C/script%3E"));
</script>
<script type="text/javascript">
try {
    var pageTracker = _gat._getTracker("UA-12345-1");
    pageTracker._setCookiePath("/path/of/cookie/");
pageTracker._trackPageview();
} catch(err) {}</script>
```

To copy existing cookies from other subdirectories on your domain, use the
function _cookiePathCopy(), as follows:

```
<script type="text/javascript">
    var gaJsHost = (("https:" == document.location.protocol) ? "https://ssl."↵
: "http://www. ");
    document.write(unescape("%3Cscript src='" + gaJsHost + "google-↵
analytics.com/ga.js' type='text/javascript'%3E%3C/script%3E"));
</script>
<script type="text/javascript">
try {
    var pageTracker = _gat._getTracker("UA-12345-1");
    pageTracker._trackPageview();
    pageTracker._cookiePathCopy("/new/path/for/cookies/");
} catch(err) {}</script>
```

Controlling Timeouts

You can control two cookie timeouts from within your GATC: the session timeout and
the campaign conversion timeout.

By default, a visitor's session (visit) times out after 30 minutes of inactivity, so if a visitor continues browsing your website after 31 minutes of inactivity, that visitor is counted as a returning visitor. The original referral information is maintained as long as a new referral source was not used to continue their session.

The 30-minute rule is the unwritten standard across the web analytics industry. However, there may be instances when you wish to change this. Typical examples include when your visitors are engaging with music or video or reading lengthy documents during their visit. The latter is a less-likely scenario, because visitors usually print large documents and read them offline. However, music and video sites are common examples in which visitors set and forget their actions, only to return and complete another action on your site when the content has finished playing.

If inactivity is likely to last longer than 30 minutes for a continuous visit, then consider increasing the default session timeout as follows:

```
<script type="text/javascript">
    var gaJsHost = (("https:" == document.location.protocol) ? "https://ssl."↵
    : "http://www. ");
    document.write(unescape("%3Cscript src='" + gaJsHost + "google-↵
analytics.com/ga.js' type='text/javascript'%3E%3C/script%3E"));
</script>
<script type="text/javascript">
try {
    var pageTracker = _gat._getTracker("UA-12345-1");
    pageTracker._setSessionCookieTimeout("3600000");
    // increased to 1 hour
    pageTracker._trackPageview();
} catch(err) {}</script>
```

Note: In Google Analytics, time is measured in seconds. Therefore, 30 minutes = 1,800 seconds, 1 hour = 3,600 seconds, and so forth.

Another timeout that you can adjust is the length of time for which Google Analytics credits a conversion referral. By default, the campaign conversion timeout is six months (15,768,000 seconds), after which the referral cookie (__utmz) expires. For example, you may wish to reduce this value when you are paying a commission to affiliates. You can achieve this as follows:

```
<script type="text/javascript">
```

```
    var gaJsHost = (("https:" == document.location.protocol) ? "https://ssl."↵
  : "http://www. ");
    document.write(unescape("%3Cscript src='" + gaJsHost + "google-↵
analytics.com/ga.js' type='text/javascript'%3E%3C/script%3E"));
</script>
<script type="text/javascript">
try {
    var pageTracker = _gat._getTracker("UA-12345-1");
    pageTracker._setCampaignCookieTimeout("2592000000");
    // decreased to 30 days
    pageTracker._trackPageview();
} catch(err) {}</script>
```

The value of the campaign conversion timeout can also be increased. However, it doesn't make much sense to go beyond six months, due to the increased risk that the original cookie information is likely to be lost, making your conversion referral data less reliable. See "Issues Affecting Visitor Data When Using Cookies," in Chapter 2.

Note: There is a third timeout value you can control: the visitor cookie. By default, the visitor cookie is set to expire after two years. If you prefer, you can change the expiration date using the following setting within your GATC: pageTracker._setVisitorCookieTimeout(63072000000); //number of milliseconds in 2 years. However, I do not see any value in changing this and so do not recommend using it.

Setting Keyword Ignore Preferences

You can configure Google Analytics to treat certain keywords as direct traffic (that is, not as a referral)—for example, visitors who type your domain (www.mysite.com) into a search engine.

Use _addIgnoredOrganic() to treat a keyword as a referral or _addIgnoredRef() to treat a referral as direct, as shown here:

```
<script type="text/javascript">
    var gaJsHost = (("https:" == document.location.protocol) ? "https://ssl."
  : "http://www. ");
    document.write(unescape("%3Cscript src='" + gaJsHost + "google-↵
analytics.com/ga.js' type='text/javascript'%3E%3C/script%3E"));
</script>
<script type="text/javascript">
try {
```

```
    var pageTracker = _gat._getTracker("UA-12345-1");
    pageTracker._addIgnoredOrganic("mysite.com");
    pageTracker._addIgnoredRef("sistersite.com");
    pageTracker._trackPageview();
} catch(err) {}</script>
```

Although these variables are available for you to adjust, I recommend that you do not use them. Discovering that your brand is being used in the search engines as a keyword is an important piece of information that you can use to evaluate your brand effectiveness.

In terms of treating a particular referral as direct, if you have multiple domain names, then you probably want to see the interaction between them. If not, then consider using 301 redirect codes on your web server (or .htaccess file) to ensure that all visitors and search engine robots are forwarded to your main domain.

 Note: You can find further information on redirection for the Apache web server at `http://httpd.apache.org/docs/1.3/mod/mod_alias.html#redirect`.

Controlling the Collection Sampling Rate

By default, Google Analytics collects pageview data for every visitor. For very-high-traffic sites, the amount of data can be overwhelming, leading to large parts of the "long tail" of information being missing from your reports, simply because they are too far down in the report tables. You can diminish this issue by creating separate profiles of visitor segments—for example, /blog, /forum, /support, and so on. However, another option is to *sample* your visitors.

Sampling occurs at the visitor level and is specified as a percentage of the total to sample using the _setSampleRate() function, as shown here:

```
<script type="text/javascript">
    var gaJsHost = (("https: " == document.location.protocol) ? "https://↵
ssl." : "http://www. ");
    document.write(unescape("%3Cscript src='" + gaJsHost + "google-↵
analytics.com/ga.js' type='text/javascript'%3E%3C/script%3E"));
</script>
<script type="text/javascript">
try {
    var pageTracker = _gat._getTracker("UA-12345-1");
    pageTracker._setSampleRate(25);
    // set sample rate to 25%
    pageTracker._trackPageview();
} catch(err) {}</script>
```

A sample rate of 25 percent means that every fourth visitor is counted for Google Analytics tracking. Unless you receive more than one million visitors per day, it is unlikely you will need to use the _setSampleRate() function.

> **Note:** The automatic sampling of data for report building is discussed in Chapter 5 in the section "Understanding Data Sampling."

Summary

In Chapter 7, you have learned the following:

Leveraging tagging and tracking Having read this far, you will have now

- tagged all of your website pages with the GATC,
- tagged your landing page URLs,
- adjusted your setup for tracking file downloads and event tracking
- modified your checkout completion page for the capture of e-commerce transactions, if you have such a facility on your site.

With all that in place, your installation is complete. Take an initial look at some of your reports and get comfortable with using them, as described in Part II.

Using the _trackPageview() **function to create virtual pageviews** You have learned how to modify the Google Analytics workhorse function to report more meaningful URL names as well as track those not captured by default.

Capturing e-commerce transactions We discussed how to capture transactional information both on your site and if you are using a third-party payment gateway.

Tracking online campaigns in addition to AdWords You learned how to using campaign variables to identify and differentiate online campaigns.

Tracking in-page visitor interactions as events You can now use the Google Analytics Event Tracking feature to capture actions separately from pageviews, including Flash movie interaction.

Customizing the GATC for your specific needs You learned to modify the default behavior of Google Analytics when your needs are more specialized.

Best-Practices
Configuration Guide

Having read the first seven chapters of this book, you should now have your Google Analytics account set up and collecting quality data. To help you gain a better understanding of visitor behavior and get the most out of your data, this chapter will assist you with your configuration.

By following the recommended steps, you will gain real insight into the performance of your online presence. If you don't follow the steps, reread this chapter. Seriously, this information is too important to skip over without implementing the suggested configurations—particularly goals and funnels.

No modifications of the Google Analytics Tracking Code (GATC) or your pages are required here. However, you will need administrator access to your Google Analytics account to use this chapter.

In Chapter 8, you will learn:

Best practices for configuring Google Analytics

The importance of defining goals and funnels

The importance of visitor segmentation

How to use filters and advanced segments

Initial Configuration

It is important that the marketer and webmaster work together to understand each other's needs. The marketer will be building the marketing strategy, and that requires working in conjunction with the webmaster to implement the necessary configuration changes. If you are a part of a large organization, then it is you as the analyst who manages and oversees this part of the project. Unless you are performing all three roles yourself, collaboration is the key to success here.

Once you have established your first Google Analytics profile—created as part of your initial account-creation process—there are a couple of options you should configure in the first instance, as shown in Figure 8.1. To access this area from your initial login area, click the Edit link next to your profile name.

Figure 8.1 Initial profile setup options

Note: In the top-right corner of Figure 8.1, Receiving Data will show a green tick once you have added your GATC to your home page. This is a quick verification that Google Analytics can see your GATC. For a new profile allow 24 hours for this to be detected. Note that Google Analytics will check only your home page for the presence of a correctly formatted GATC—not other web pages on your site. If you include the GATC as part of another loaded JavaScript file, this verification method will not work. See Appendix B for a list of alternative troubleshooting tools.

Apart from the time zone and localization of currency options, you should enter your default page and any URL query parameters for which reports are not required. Click the Edit link in the top-right corner to do this, which takes you to the screen shown in Figure 8.2.

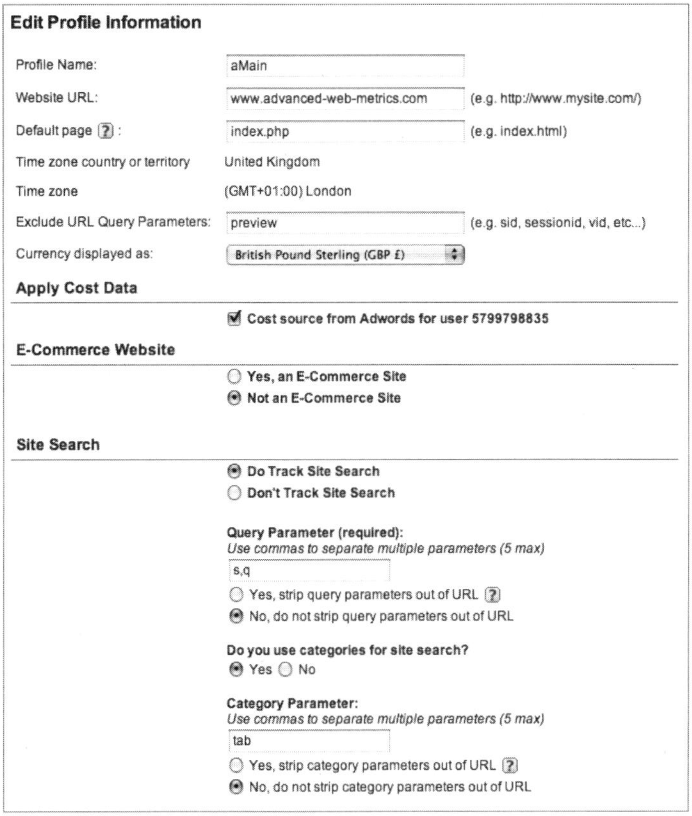

Figure 8.2 Editing profile information

Setting the Default Page

Your Google Analytics settings, shown in Figure 8.2, contain a field where you can specify your default page. The default page is the web page your server defaults to when no page is specified—that is, the filename of your home page. This is usually `index.html`, `index.htm`, `index.php`, or `default.asp`, but it can be anything your web-hosting company or webmaster has specified. Once you enter your default page, Google Analytics is able to combine visits to `www.mysite.com` and `www.mysite.com/index.html`, which are in fact the same page. If the default page is not specified, then these are reported as two separate pages, which is not desirable.

Excluding Unnecessary Parameters

If your site uses unique session IDs or displays other query parameters in your URLs that are of no interest to you, then you can exclude these parameters by entering them in the Exclude URL Query Parameters field (see Figure 8.2). In fact, it is best practice to do this, because it reduces the amount of superfluous data collected, making reports faster loading and easier to read. Enter the variable name that you wish to exclude as it appears in your URLs. Variable name/value pairs follow a query symbol (?) in your URL and are separated by ampersands (&). Enter the name part you wish to exclude here—the part before the equals sign (=).

Enabling E-commerce Reporting

If your site has an e-commerce facility, you will want to see this data in your reports so that you can follow the complete visitor journey from referral source and pages viewed to checkout and payment confirmation. Selecting "Yes, An E-Commerce Site," as shown in Figure 8.2, enables this reporting; you will see it as a separate menu item on the left side of the reports and as an additional tab within most report tables. If you have an e-commerce website, select your currency label and its placement, as well as the number of decimal places. Otherwise, keep the default selection of "Not An E-Commerce Site."

Enabling e-commerce provides additional reports within your account. Selecting this feature does not collect the e-commerce data for you. To do this, you need to apply additional tags to the receipt page of your checkout system—see "E-commerce Tracking," in Chapter 7, "Advanced Implementation."

Enabling Site Search

If your site has an internal search engine to help visitors locate content, you will want to see how this facility affects your visitors' experience. Capturing internal search terms is an important asset when tuning your website. For example, it can reveal misspellings, synonyms, partial matches, or just plain different descriptions.

To do this, first select "Do Track Site Search," as shown in Figure 8.2. This enables an additional Google Analytics report menu that can be found in the Content > Site Search section.

With this feature enabled, you need to define which query parameter in your URLs contains the visitor's site search term. You can usually discover this quickly by performing a site search yourself and looking for your search term in the result page URL. This is typically of the form ?q=mykeyword or &search=mykeyword. For these examples, the query parameter names are q and search, respectively. Google Analytics uses these values to determine that a visitor has made a search and which search terms were used.

Notice also that there is an option to strip your defined site search query parameters from the URL after site search processing has been completed. This can be helpful if those query parameters are of no further use to you for the purpose of Google Analytics reporting. However, those parameters may be important for defining your goals, your funnel steps, or your filters (see the next two sections). Site search query parameters could also be important if you are using virtual pageviews to aid in the reading of your reports (discussed under "trackPageview(): the Google Analytics

Workhorse," in Chapter 7). Therefore, you should strip query parameters only if absolutely necessary.

Google Analytics Site Search also provides the option to define categories. Use this if your site search facility allows visitors to select a category for their search. For example, a retail site may have categories such as Menswear, Ladies Wear, and so on. A real estate website may have categories such as Apartments, Condos, Houses, and so forth. Categories help visitors find information easier by focusing their search. Understanding how categories compare is often the initial step when assessing the performance of your internal site search engine.

As with defining the site search query parameter, category parameters are obtained from the results page URL—for example, ?cat=menswear or &sect=condo. For these examples, the category parameter names are cat and sect, respectively. As with your defined query parameter, you can also strip your defined category parameters from the URL after site search processing has been completed. However, for the same reasons, strip query parameters only if absolutely necessary.

What if My URLs Don't Contain Site Search Parameters?

For this situation you can employ virtual pageviews to insert the parameters for you. If your site search results page contains the visitor's query term as an environment variable, for example, *%searchterm*, then you can use this as a virtual pageview. The following example is a modified GATC to achieve this:

```
<script type="text/javascript">
   var gaJsHost = (("https:" == document.location.protocol) ? "https://
ssl. " : "http://www. ");
   document.write(unescape("%3Cscript src='" + gaJsHost +
   "google-analytics.com/ga.js' type='text/javascript'%3E%3C/
script%3E"));
</script>
<script type="text/javascript">
try {
   var pageTracker = _gat._getTracker("UA-12345-1");
   pageTracker._trackPageview('/site search/?q=%searchterm');
}catch(err) {}</script>
```

In this example I have created a virtual pageview with a query parameter of q and its value set as the environment variable *%searchterm*. You can then use q as your site search query parameter as if this were the physical URL. The use of virtual pageviews is discussed in the section "trackPageview(): the Google Analytics Workhorse," in Chapter 7.

Note: Site search processing takes place before filter processing. Although it is possible to apply filters that modify the site search query or category parameters (perhaps making them more reader-friendly), these will not show in your site search reports.

Tracking Zero Results for Site Search

A common requirement when assessing the effectiveness and performance of a site search facility is the ability to track which search terms generate zero results. Returning zero results is a particularly bad user experience that often leads to an automatic dismissal—the visitor moves on to another website.

That reaction is fair enough if you do not have the products or services the visitor is looking for. However, I regularly find that this is not the case. On the contrary, for some reason internal site search is frequently added to a site as an afterthought with little attention given to the quality of its performance, despite the obvious fact that web users rely heavily on search when using the Web. Hence, many visitors leave a website with the mistaken belief that it cannot cater to their need.

Capturing zero results allows you to distinguish between good and bad user experiences. To achieve this, use a category parameter labeled zero in your search result URL when this happens, for example:

```
www.mysite.com?q=widget&tab=zero
```

Ensure that you have added the category parameter tab (or other name) to your configuration, as per Figure 8.2. Then when you view your Site Search reports, you will have a dedicated category just for analyzing zero search results.

Note: Using Key Performance Indicators for site search is discussed in Chapter 10, "Focusing on Key Performance Indicators." Measuring the success of site search is described in Chapter 11, "Real-World Tasks."

Configuring Data-Sharing Settings

Within Google Analytics you have the option of sharing your data with Google. From the initial login page of your Google Analytics account, click the link "Edit Account Settings" (refer to Figure 4.2). The resulting configuration screen is shown in Figure 8.3.

By default, "Do Not Share My Google Analytics Data" is selected. However, as you might expect, by sharing your data with Google, there are some benefits for your account. Note that data is shared with Google only—not any third parties. Two sharing options are available:

- With Other Google Products Only
- Anonymously With Google And Others

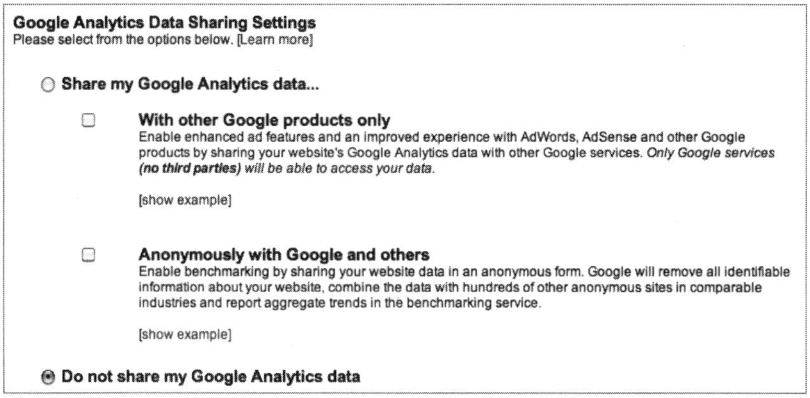

Figure 8.3 Data-sharing configuration

According to Google, the first option helps them improve the products and services they provide your organization. The rational is that products such as AdWords, AdSense, Ad Planner Publisher Center, and Website Optimizer can be improved and better integrated within Google Analytics if such data is shared. That is certainly a strong incentive if you use any of those products.

If you choose the anonymous data-sharing option, Google will remove all identifiable information about your website and then combine your data with other anonymous sites in comparable industries and report it in an aggregate form. This information is available in the Visitors > Benchmarking section of your Google Analytics reports. The Benchmarking report is discussed in Chapter 5, "Reports Explained."

Unless you operate in a monopoly situation or have only a small number of competitors, I recommend enabling both data-sharing options.

> **Note:** You are able to opt in or out from data sharing at any time. However, if you opt out, previously shared data is not removed. Google's position on privacy is discussed in Chapter 3, "Google Analytics Features, Benefits, and Limitations."

Goal Conversions and Funnels

As emphasized throughout this book, collecting data is only the first step in understanding the visitor performance of your website. Google Analytics has more than 100 built-in reports by default; that's impressive for fine-grain analysis, but it can be quite daunting to absorb all of this information, even for experienced users. In fact, I recommend you don't even attempt to do so.

Instead, you can distill visitor information by configuring Google Analytics to report on goal conversions. Think of goal conversions as *specific* measurable actions that can be applied to every visit. The path a visitor takes to reach a goal is known as the funnel; this is shown schematically in Figure 8.4. As you can see, the number of visitors entering the funnel process decreases at each step.

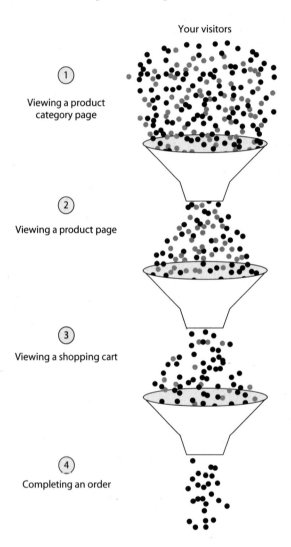

Figure 8.4 Schematic funnel and goal process

The Importance of Defining Goals

Defining your website goals is probably the single most important step of your configuration process, because it enables you to define success. Goal conversions, also referred to as simply *goals* or *conversions*, are any actions or engagements that build a relationship with your visitors. An obvious goal for an e-commerce site is the completion of a transaction. However, even without e-commerce, your website has goals, for example, the completion of a feedback form, a subscription request, leaving a comment on a blog post, downloading a PDF whitepaper, viewing a special-offers page, or clicking a `mailto:` link. Goal conversions are the de facto way to ascertain whether your website is engaging with your visitors. They are your "success" metrics.

A goal is typically the reason why you put up a website in the first place: Was it to sell directly, to generate leads, to keep your clients or shareholders up to date, to provide centralized product updates, or to attract new staff? As you begin this exercise, you will realize that you actually have many website goals.

Also consider that goals don't have to include the full conversion of a visitor into a customer—that is obviously very important, but it's only part of the picture. If your only goal is to gain customers, then how will you know just how close noncustomers came to converting? You can gain insight into this by using additional goals to measure the building of relationships with your visitors. For example, for most visitors arriving on your website, it is unlikely they will instantly convert, so the page needs to *persuade* them to go deeper—that is, get them one step closer to your goal. Table 8.1 lists some example goals.

▶ **Table 8.1** Sample website goals

Non-e-commerce Goals	Examples
Visitors downloading a document	Brochure, manual, whitepaper, price list (file types include PDF, XLS, DOC, PPT, etc.)
Visitors looking at specific pages or sections of pages	Jobs, price list, special offers, login page, admin page, location and contact details, terms and conditions, help desk or support area
Visitors completing a form	Login, registration, feedback form, subscription
Visitor engagement	Adding a blog comment, completing a survey, submitting a forum post, adding or editing a profile, uploading content, rating an article
Visitor thresholds	Staying on the site longer than XX seconds, viewing more than YY pages
E-commerce Goals	**Examples**
Transaction completed	Credit card thank-you page
Transaction failed	Credit card rejection page
Visitors entering shopping system	Adding to cart, getting to step x of y, using a promotional code or not

Further Reading on Designing Goal-Driven Websites

Bryan Eisenberg, his brother Jeffrey Eisenberg, and Lisa T. Davis have written extensively on the persuasion process technique and coined the phrase "persuasion architecture." Their books include *Call to Action* and *Waiting for Your Cat to Bark*.

Another worthwhile read when considering website goals and funnels is the excellent book *Don't Make Me Think* by Steve Krug (`www.sensible.com/about.html`). It's a commonsense approach to web usability written in an easy-to-read and humorous way.

Apart from the goals shown in Table 8.1, your website may possess negative goals—that is, goals for which you would like to decrease or minimize the conversion rate. For example, if onsite search is an important aspect of your website navigation structure, then minimizing the number of zero search results returned for a query is a valid ambition. Perhaps minimizing the number of searches per visitor is also an indication of an efficient onsite search tool; the theory could be that fewer searches conducted means visitors are finding what they are looking for more quickly. Negative goals are common for product-support websites—that is, when the best visitor experience is for the least amount of engagement, such as time on site or page depth.

Defining and measuring goals is the basis for building your key performance indicators (KPIs). Chapter 10 defines and discusses KPIs in more detail, but essentially they enable you to incorporate web data into your overall business model.

Your Google Analytics Profile Can Be Configured for up to 20 Goals

Your website should be focused enough that 20 goals cover your requirements. If they don't, then look again at the number of goals you wish to measure. An obvious efficiency is to use wildcards—for example, `*.pdf` rather than individual PDF file names.

If you truly need more than 20 goals to measure your website effectiveness, read "Monetizing a Non-E-commerce Website" in Chapter 11, which is applicable for all non-e-commerce goals.

What Funnel Shapes Can Tell You

Many website owners and marketers want to see a 100 percent goal conversion rate. In the real world, that just isn't feasible. In fact, it is not as desirable as you might think. Consider your funnel as acting like a sieve, qualifying visitors along the way. As with the offline world, it is important to qualify your web visitors so that your support or returns department is not swamped with calls from disappointed customers. Therefore, losing visitors via your funnel is not necessarily a bad thing.

Conversely, if you have verified all the qualifications before the visitor enters the funnel, then you would expect a high conversion rate. The outcome is highly dependent on how good your funnel pages are at doing their job—that is, persuading visitors to continue to the next step. Consider each funnel step as a "micro-conversion" towards the "macro-conversion" of achieving a goal completion. Figure 8.5 shows example schematic funnel shapes.

Note: A detailed funnel analysis for a website is performed in Chapter 11.

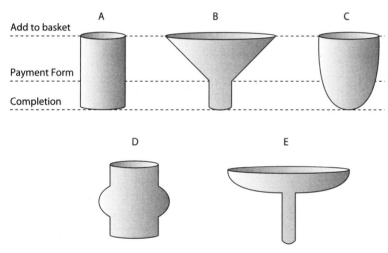

Figure 8.5 Schematic conversion funnel shapes

Figure 8.5 explained:

Shape A The impossible 100 percent conversion rate.

Shape B The most common funnel shape, showing a sharp decrease in visitors until the payment form step. Assuming there are no hidden surprises for the visitor at this point, the vast majority of visitors who reach this point should convert.

Shape C A well-optimized conversion-funnel process, with only a gradual decrease in visitors. This is the optimum shape you will wish to obtain for all your funnels.

Shape D An ill-defined funnel—visitors are entering the funnel midway through the process.

Shape E A poorly converting funnel with a serious barrier to progress.

The most common shapes I have come across are B, D, and E. Shape A occurs only for a small section of an overall funnel process (if at all). Shape C is very rare and is where your greatest opportunity lies.

The Goal and Funnel Setup Process

To set up your goals, log in to your Google Analytics account and click Edit in the Settings column, next to the profile to which you want to add a goal (or funnel). Scroll down to view the Goals section, shown in Figure 8.6. Here you can define up to 20 goals. You can also group your goals into four categories (5 goals per category). Grouping similar goals together in the same category provides easier report interpretation. Apart from this, there is no other difference.

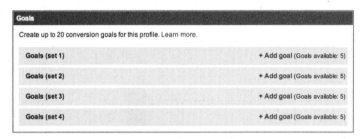

Figure 8.6 The Goals section of an account profile

In the Goals section, click Add Goal for a goal set. This takes you to Figure 8.7—I assume you will choose Set 1.

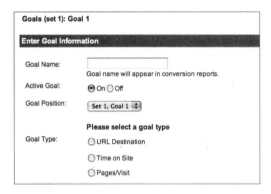

Figure 8.7 Initial goal-configuration screen

Goal Details

In this area you define what constitutes a goal, indicate how Google Analytics identifies it, and associate a value, if applicable, when the goal is triggered.

Goal Name and Type

First, define a Goal Name that you will recognize when viewing reports. Examples include "Email sign-up," "Article AB123 download," "Inquiry form sent," and "Purchase complete." Ensure that Active Goal is set to On. Then select a Goal Type—either URL Destination, Time On Site, or Pages/Visit.

Time On Site and Pages/Visit are *threshold* goal types. With these, you can specify a value that the web visit must be greater than, less than, or equal to in order to trigger a goal match, for example, Time On Site greater than 5 minutes, Pages/Visit greater than 10. These could indicate strong interest from visitors whom you wish to identify. However, think carefully before reaching a conclusion on threshold goals; you should correlate with other data, because a high Time On Site or Pages/Visit value could mean your visitors are lost or confused and cannot find what they are looking for.

For the purposes of this example, select URL Destination as the Goal Type, which then expands out as per Figure 8.8. This is a page URL that can be reached only by achieving a goal. Clearly, if your goal page can be reached by visitors who have not completed the goal, then your conversion rates will be inflated and not representative.

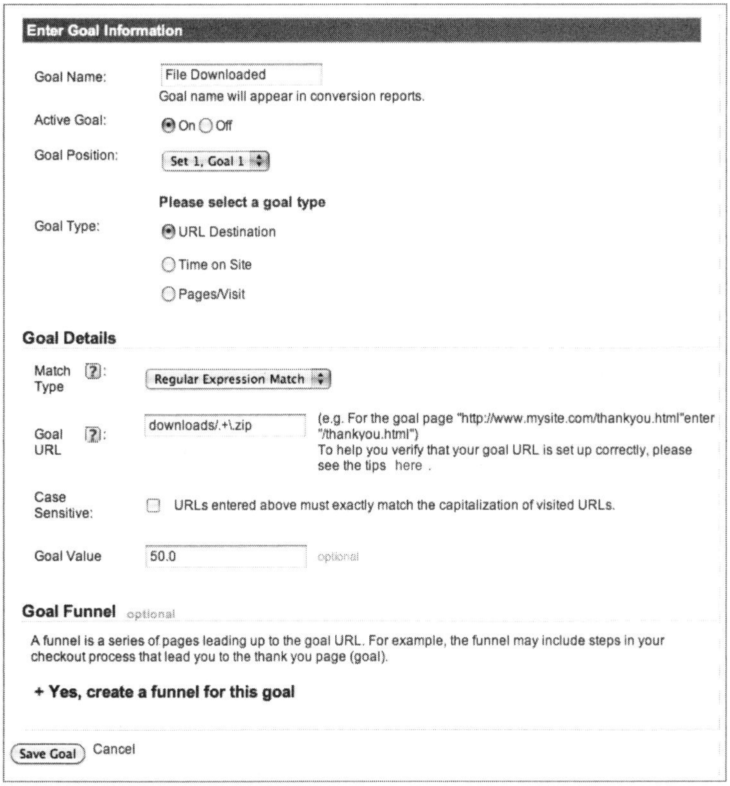

Enter Goal Information

Goal Name:	File Downloaded
	Goal name will appear in conversion reports.
Active Goal:	● On ○ Off
Goal Position:	Set 1, Goal 1
	Please select a goal type
Goal Type:	● URL Destination
	○ Time on Site
	○ Pages/Visit

Goal Details

Match [?] Type	Regular Expression Match
Goal [?] URL	downloads/.+\.zip (e.g. For the goal page "http://www.mysite.com/thankyou.html" enter "/thankyou.html") To help you verify that your goal URL is set up correctly, please see the tips here .
Case Sensitive:	☐ URLs entered above must exactly match the capitalization of visited URLs.
Goal Value	50.0 optional

Goal Funnel optional

A funnel is a series of pages leading up to the goal URL. For example, the funnel may include steps in your checkout process that lead you to the thank you page (goal).

+ Yes, create a funnel for this goal

(Save Goal) Cancel

Figure 8.8 Second goal-configuration screen

Defining Matches

Before entering the URL Destination value, you need to decide on how Google Analytics will perform the match.

Match Type This determines how your defined URLs are matched. There are three ways to achieve this: Exact Match, Head Match, and Regular Expression Match.

> **Exact Match** This means exactly what it says—the exact URL of the page you want to define. No dynamic session identifiers and no wildcards can be used here, so it is best to cut and paste the URL from the address bar of your browser to define your goal.
>
> **Head Match** If your URL Destination is always the same but is followed by a unique session identifier or other parameters, use the Head Match filter and omit the unique values. For example, if the URL for a particular page is
>
> ```
> http://www.mysite.com/checkout.cgi?page=1&id=9982251615
> ```
>
> but the `id` varies for every user, enter
>
> ```
> http://www.mysite.com/checkout.cgi?page=1
> ```
>
> **Regular Expression Match** This uses regular expressions to match your URL Destination—for example, wildcards and metacharacters. This is useful when the URL, query parameters, or both vary between users:
>
> ```
> http://sports.mysite.com/checkout.cgi?page=1&id=002
> http://news.mysite.com/checkout.cgi?page=1&language=fr&id=119
> ```
>
> To match against a single goal for this example, you would use the regular expression `.+page=1+.` to define the constant element. In this case, one or more characters, followed by the string *page=1*, followed by one or more characters. If you are unfamiliar with the use of regular expressions, see the overview provided in Appendix A.

Head Match and Exact Match are by far the most common ways to define simple goal and funnel steps, but e-commerce systems often require the use of regular expressions. Figure 8.8 uses Regular Expression Match to treat all filenames in the `/downloads` directory that end in `.zip` as a goal. In this example, I have assumed file downloads are being tracked as virtual pageviews, as described in Chapter 7.

Case Sensitive

If you want to differentiate URL Destinations that are identical except for the fact that one uses uppercase characters and the other uses lowercase characters—for example, `productx.html` and `productX.html`—then you should check the Case Sensitive check box. Most people do not change this, but it is there if needed.

Goal Value

For non-e-commerce goals, Google Analytics uses your assigned goal value to calculate ROI, $Index, and other revenue-related metrics. A good way to value a goal is to determine how often the visitors who reach the goal become customers. If, for example, your sales team can close 10 percent of people who request to be contacted, and your average transaction is $500, then you might assign $50 (10 percent of $500) to your "Inquiry form sent" goal. Conversely, if only 1 percent of mailing list signups result in a sale, then you might assign only $5 to your "Email sign-up" goal.

Note: Monetizing goals is discussed in detail in "Monetizing a Non-e-commerce Website" in Chapter 11.

Tip: You may wish to differentiate conversions from transactions in your reports, that is, a visitor can convert to a customer only once during a session but can make several transactions. If this distinction is important to you, define an e-commerce goal by setting your transaction receipt page as the goal URL and leave the Goal Value field blank. Then set up your receipt page as described in "E-commerce Tracking" in Chapter 7.

That's it for setting up your first goal. If you are using the goal type URL Destination, you have the option to add a funnel. Therefore, if you have a well-defined path that you expect visitors to take on their way to your goal URL, define these by clicking "Yes, Create Funnel" and proceed as described next. Otherwise, save your goal setup now.

Use Funnels Where Appropriate

Not all URL Destination goals have funnels. That is, not all conversions are achieved by visitors following a clearly defined linear path. An obvious linear path to conversion is an e-commerce shopping cart. You should certainly configure a defined funnel to analyze such a process.

However, for non-e-commerce conversions, consider carefully whether a funnel is necessary. For example, if there are many paths to achieve a PDF download, then analyzing this with a funnel would be pointless at best and misleading at worst. It would make more sense to define the goal without a funnel. If knowing the path that leads to such downloads is a key element of measuring your website's success, then consider the addition of a registration form to gain download access. This provides a funnel process for analysis.

Goal Funnel (Optional)

You may specify up to 10 page URLs in a defined funnel. These pages represent the path that you expect visitors to take on their way to converting to the goal. Defining these pages enables you to see which pages lead to goal abandonment and where they go next. For an e-commerce goal, these pages might be the Begin Checkout page, Shipping Address Information page, and Credit Card Information page—a four-step funnel, that is, three funnel steps plus the goal conversion. Each step of the funnel has its own conversion rate that you can focus on.

Figure 8.9 shows two funnel-configuration examples. Notice that by using wild-cards, I have extended the e-commerce funnel example with a View Category page and a View Product Detail page. This provides a six-step funnel for analysis—five funnel steps plus the goal conversion. A corresponding Funnel Visualization report is shown in Figure 8.10.

Note: Whichever match type you selected for URL Destination is continued throughout the funnel configuration. For example, if you selected Regular Expression Match, this is the same match type for each funnel step. Therefore, ensure that you check your funnel URLs for correctness, for example, escaping periods in filenames. See Appendix A for an overview of regular expressions.

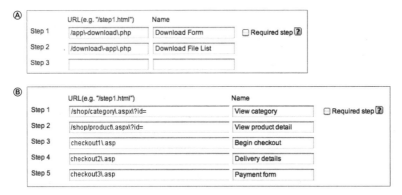

Figure 8.9 (a) Example three-step funnel configuration for a file download, (b) example six-step funnel configuration for an e-commerce checkout. Note that the final goal page is not shown.

Funnel Backfill Behavior

If you define a funnel for a goal and visitors are able to directly access that goal page, Google Analytics will backfill the funnel steps as if the visitor had gone through those steps. This is also the case for individual funnel steps. That is, if a visitor directly views step 3 of a funnel, Google Analytics will backfill that visit data into funnel steps 1 and 2. Hence, you should define a funnel only where a clear linear path exists.

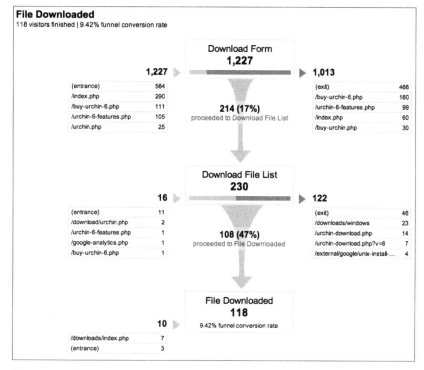

Figure 8.10 A three-step Funnel Visualization report corresponding to the configuration of Figure 8.9a

What Is a Required Step?

As you can see in Figure 8.9, there is a check box labeled "Required Step" next to the first funnel step. If this check box is selected, users reaching your goal page without traveling through this funnel page will not be counted as conversions in the Funnel Visualization report. Hence, the required step can be an important differentiator.

For example, consider visitors accessing a password-protected area of your website. You wish to define two goals:

- New signups for access to this area
- The log in of existing users

Both sets of visitors complete their action by arriving on the same page—the password-protected home page. This means the goal URL page must be defined the same way for each circumstance. However, the initial step is different. Therefore, you should use the Required Step check box to differentiate the different types of goals in this scenario.

> **Note:** Using this method to differentiate goals with the same URL will show only in reports that have funnel visualization in them. Other goal reports will show the same conversion rate for both examples, because only the funnel path differentiates them.

Tracking Funnels for Which Every Step Has the Same URL

You may encounter a situation where you need to track a visitor's progress through a funnel that has the same URL for each step. For example, your sign-up funnel might look like this:

Step 1 Sign Up

`www.mysite.com/sign_up.cgi`

Step 2 Accept Agreement

`www.mysite.com/sign_up.cgi`

Step 3 Finish

`www.mysite.com/sign_up.cgi`

To get around this, call the `_trackPageview()` function to track virtual pageviews within each step, as discussed in "Tracking Unreadable URLs with Virtual Pageviews," in Chapter 7. For example, within the GATC of the pages in question, you create virtual pageviews to be logged in Google Analytics as follows:

```
pageTracker._trackPageview("/funnel_G1/step1.html")
pageTracker._trackPageview("/funnel_G1/step2.html")
pageTracker._trackPageview("/funnel_G1/step3.html")
```

With these virtual pageviews now being logged instead of `sign_up.cgi`, you can configure each step of your funnel as follows:

Step 1 Sign Up

`http://www.mysite.com/funnel_G1/step1.html`

Step 2 Accept Agreement

`http://www.mysite.com/funnel_G1/step2.html`

Step 3 Finish

`http://www.mysite.com/funnel_G1/step3.html`

Why Segmentation Is Important

To understand the importance of segmentation, we first need to examine how averages are used in web analytics. When discussing averages, we are generally referring to the arithmetic mean that is computed by adding a group of values together and dividing by the total number of values in the group. It's used in mathematics to approximate the statistical norm or expected value.

The arithmetic mean works well when the distribution under consideration is close to normal, that is, Gaussian or bell-shaped. For normal distributions the average value is also the most common (modal) value. For example, assuming a normal distribution for visitor time onsite, if the average time is calculated at 95 seconds, then it is also true to say the average visitor spends 95 seconds on your website. However, this is not true when the distribution is not normal—see Figure 8.11. That is, for Figures 8.11b and c, it is not true to say that the average visitor spends 95 seconds on your site. The concept of "average visitor" is not applicable unless the distribution is close to normal.

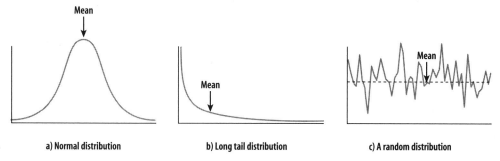

a) Normal distribution   b) Long tail distribution   c) A random distribution

Figure 8.11 Sample visitor distributions for time spent onsite

> **Note:** For the vast majority of web metrics, the distribution of values is not Gaussian. In many cases, when considering the whole data set, the distribution appears random. The whole data set can include new visitors, returning visitors, existing customers, people researching products, people purchasing products, job seekers, spammers, mistaken visitors (wrong address), employees, competitors, and so on.
>
> In addition, if you have ever tried to establish common visitor paths on your website, you will have noticed these are very hard to detect—usually only a small percentage of visitors share a common path. It seems almost every visitor has a unique way of viewing a website for all but the shortest of paths (funnels excepted).

Figure 8.11 shows that for nonnormal distributions, a typical visitor will not exhibit the average (mean) behavior, in other words, not stay on the site for the mean length of time.

Plans based on average assumptions are wrong on average.

—from "The Flaw of Averages" by Sam Savage, www.stanford.edu/ %7Esavage/faculty/savage/Flaw%20of%20averages.pdf.

For the random distribution in Figure 8.11c, quoting the mean value for the time spent onsite is misleading, because the distribution indicates many types of behavior are being exhibited. Perhaps the difference is indicating a mix of personas on your website—visitors, customers, blog readers, demographic differences, geographic differences. Whatever the reason, simply reporting an average is a blunt metric, and it is precisely the reason why you rarely see averages reported in Google Analytics. When averages are reported, they are segmented—for example, shown for a specific page URL.

To illustrate this, Figure 8.12a shows a significant number of one-page visits that are probably not representative of an interested website visitor. Quoting an average depth would hide the fuller picture. In Figure 8.12b, there are two maxima—indicating two types of visitor. If only an average is quoted without looking at the distribution, then you lose the clue that your site needs to cater to different visitor needs (personas).

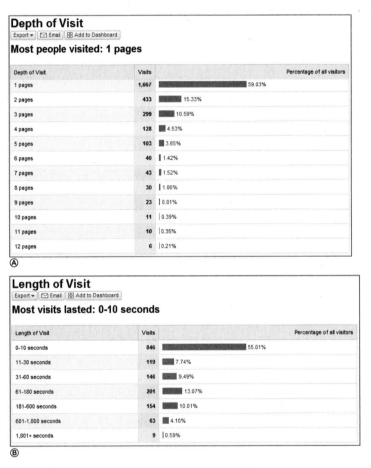

Figure 8.12 Typical nonnormal distributions of visitors to a website

In summary, the mean is sensitive to outliers—data points that are numerically distant from the rest of the data. A frequent cause of outliers is a mixture of distributions, which may be distinct subpopulations, that is, groups of visitors with different intentions. Therefore, when looking at averages, it is important to segment.

Within Google Analytics, there are three ways to segment your visitors:

- As you drill down through your reports (clicking data links)

- Using filters to provide a dedicated profile
- Using the Advanced Segments drop-down menu located at the top right of your report screen

Drilling down into your data is intuitive and self-explanatory—as discussed in Chapters 4 and 5. Therefore, the next sections describe how to segment based on using Profile Filters or Advanced Segments.

Choosing Advanced Segments versus Profile Filters

Profile Filters and Advanced Segments are complementary features to segment your visitors. Often I use both, first discovering segments within reports using the Advanced Segments menu. This is a quick and efficient method, because I segment the data immediately and can look back at historical data using the same segment. Then if required, I use Profile Filters to create dedicated report sets just for that segment.

I consider profile filters a longer-term segmentation technique—a permanent way of segmenting visitors. Though profile filters can be changed or removed at any time, the main difference is that once data is segmented out, for example, removing the filter does not restore historical un-filtered data—the removed segment is permanently lost. Advanced Segments on the other hand, allow you to apply and remove segments *without* removing data. Table 8.2 compares the usage of each and suggests when one method may be more appropriate than the other.

▶ **Table 8.2** Advanced Segments versus Profile Filters

Advanced Segments	Profile Filters
Modify a report view at the visit level.	Modify incoming data at the pageview level to create separate profiles (reports).
Applied to current and historical data.	Applied only to new data from the time the filter is created.
Instantaneous results—once they're created, you can view segmented data in your reports immediately.	Aimed at longer-term usage where once set, the segment is unlikely to change.
Allow the use of conditional values on metrics, for example, greater than, less than.	Only text string matches can be included—no numerical conditionals are available.
Set up by report users, making them safe—no data can be lost.	Set up by administrators, because data can be permanently deleted.
Test facility available.	Take 3–4 hours for data to populate reports.
Combine statements to meet multiple conditions.	Use cascading filters for combination effect.
Set on a per-user basis—segments can be shared with other report users, but cannot be used to hide data.	Set on a per-profile basis, therefore access to segmented data can be controlled separately from other data.
Regular expression statements are not limited, though the total combined for a segment with multiple statements must not exceed 30,000 characters.	Regular expression statement limited to 255 characters.

In summary, use profile filters to remove "noise" segments from your reports, such as your own staff visitors or your agency, which can be excluded from your target audience. Apply profile filters when the segment defined is a long-term one and unlikely to change—for example, your country offices wish to analyze only visits from within their region, or your support department wishes to focus only on help desk visitors. Use profile filters when you wish to control the level of access, such as providing paid search data to an external agency.

Conversely, use Advanced Segments when you are drilling down to understand visitor behavior, for example, comparing the performance of a particular marketing campaign against another, viewing mobile visitors versus desktop visitors, or determining whether customers browse differently from non-customers. Apply Advanced Segments when you need to use conditional operators, such as visitors who spend more than 30 seconds on site or visitors who spend more than $100 per transaction.

Profile Segments: Segmenting Visitors Using Filters

Everything discussed so far in this book has been concerned with the collection of good-quality data—ensuring that the report numbers are as comprehensive, accurate, and informative as possible. In this section, we consider the removal of data using filters.

Profile filters are applied to the information coming into your account, to manipulate the final data in order to provide specialized profiles (reports). By filtering, you gain a better understanding of visitor types in order to avoid interpreting an average of averages. In this case, think of it as segmenting out the "noise," or outliers. For example, you may want to remove visits to your website from your own employees because these visits can be significant, especially if your website is set as the default home page in their browsers.

In addition to having a data-cleansing role, profile filters can provide dedicated segmented reports. For example, if you run an overseas office, they may wish to have their own siloed set of reports relevant to their specific market, such as Asian visitors only or U.K. visitors only. That way, their conversion rates and ROI metrics will more accurately reflect their true value, rather than including visits from other regions.

To segment your visitors into separate profiles, you apply filters to the data. Filters are applied on new data only. That is, a profile filter cannot affect historical data, and it is not possible to reprocess your old data through the new filter.

 Note: Profile filters are not the same as table filters, as discussed in Chapter 4, "Using the Google Analytics Interface," Figure 4.2.

Best-Practice Tip: Keep a Profile without Filters

Always keep raw data intact. That is, keep your original profile and apply new filters to a duplicate profile in your account. That way, if you make a mistake in applying a new filter, you always have the original profile to fall back on.

To create a duplicate profile, log in to your account as administrator and click the Add Website Profile link. From the next page, select the option Add Profile For An Existing Domain. Select your existing domain and provide a new profile name.

Using this method, data will be imported simultaneously into both the original and the new report profiles. Note that any existing filters applied to the first profile will not be copied, so you will need to reapply these using the Filter Manager.

Creating a Profile Filter

To create a profile filter, log in to your Google Analytics account as an administrator, click Edit next to the profile name you wish to add a filter to, and then scroll down and click the Add Filter link. The Create New Filter dialog box is shown in Figure 8.13. Note that once you have created your filter, you will be able to apply it to other profiles within your account.

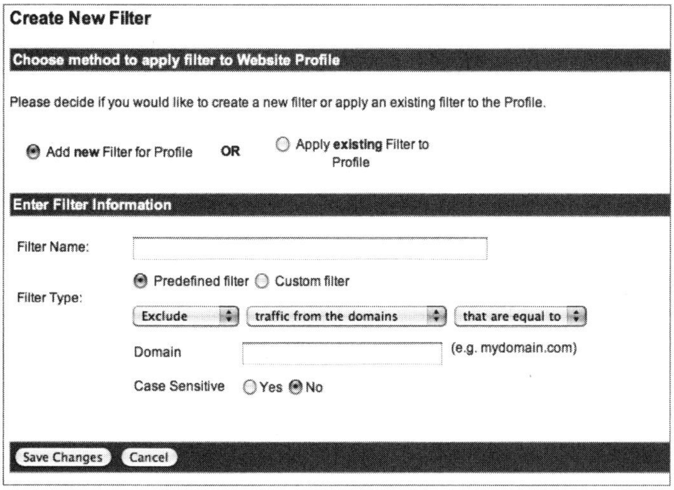

Figure 8.13 Adding a new filter

Google Analytics provides you with predefined filter types, as well as numerous options for a custom filter:

- Predefined filters are a quick and easy way to accomplish some of the most common filtering tasks, as shown in Table 8.3. Creating a predefined filter is covered online in "How do I create a predefined filter?"

  `www.google.com/support/googleanalytics/bin/answer.py?answer=55496`

- A custom filter allows for more advanced manipulation of data, and these are listed in Table 8.4. Creating a custom filter is covered online in "How do I create a custom filter?"

  `www.google.com/support/googleanalytics/bin/answer.py?answer=55492`

Most of the following filter examples use a custom filter.

▶ **Table 8.3** Predefined filters

Filter Type	Filter Name	Description
Include and exclude	Traffic from the domains	Includes or excludes traffic from a specific domain, such as an ISP or company network.
Include and exclude	Traffic from the IP address	Includes or excludes clicks from certain sources. You can enter a single IP address or a range of addresses.
Include and exclude	Traffic to the subdirectories	Includes or excludes visitors viewing only a particular subdirectory on your website, such as `www.mysite.com/helpdesk`.

▶ **Table 8.4** Custom filters

Custom Filter	Description
Exclude Pattern	This type of filter excludes log file lines (hits) that match the filter pattern. Matching lines are ignored in their entirety; for example, a filter that excludes Netscape will also exclude all other information in that log line, such as visitor, path, referral, and domain information.
Include Pattern	This type of filter includes log file lines (hits) that match the filter pattern. All nonmatching hits are ignored, and any data in nonmatching hits is unavailable.
Uppercase/Lowercase	Converts the contents of the field into all-uppercase or all-lowercase characters. These filters affect only letters, not special characters or numbers.
Search & Replace	This simple filter can be used to search for a pattern within a field and replace it with an alternate form.
Advanced	This type of filter enables you to build a field from one or two other fields. The filtering engine will apply the expressions defined in the two Extract fields and then construct a field using the Constructor expression. See Chapter 9, "Google Analytics Hacks," for examples of Advanced Custom Filters in use.

Filter Logic

If the filter being applied is an exclude filter and the pattern matches a data record, then the pageview entry is thrown away and Google Analytics continues processing with the next data record. If the pattern does not match, then the next filter is applied (if there is one) to that data row. This means that you can create either a single exclude filter with multiple patterns separated by pipe characters (|) or you can create multiple exclude filters with a single pattern for each. Here are some examples:

Single exclude filter Exclude all traffic from 217.158.66.33|21.7.158.67.1

In English this means exclude traffic from one IP address OR the other. This can also be achieved using two separate filters processed one after the other:

Filter 1 of 2 Exclude all traffic from 217.158.66.33

Filter 2 of 2 Exclude all traffic from 21.7.158.67.1

> **Note:** Filter patterns must not be longer than 255 characters. An overview of constructing regular expressions is given in Appendix A.

Include filters are applied with the reverse logic. When an include filter is applied, the data entry is thrown away if the pattern does *not* match the data. This is an important distinction if you apply multiple include filters, because then the data entry must match *every applied include filter* in order for the data entry to be saved.

For example, if you apply an include filter for your internal (staff) visitors using your network IP address, then it would not make sense to then add an additional include filter for, say, all Google search visitors. The combination will not result in reports of internal visitors plus Google visitors. The report will be only for internal visitors, assuming this filter is applied first, because everything else is discarded during processing at that point.

As for the case of exclude filters, to include multiple patterns for a specific field, create a single include filter that contains all of the individual expressions separated by pipe characters (|).

Using Multiple Include Filters

Best-practice advice is to assign a maximum of one include filter to each of your profiles unless you have a specific need and understand the resulting logic implementations.

Custom Filters: Available Fields

Building your own custom filter allows you go way beyond the default filters preconfigured in Google Analytics. Essentially, you can filter on any available data field present in your reports.

Tables 8.5 and 8.6 list all available fields and their purposes. Table 8.5 lists the regular fields—those automatically captured by Google Analytics—and Table 8.6 lists the user-defined variables whose values are determined by your implementation of Google Analytics, for example, landing page campaign parameters, e-commerce fields, and so on.

Examples of using these for a custom filter are discussed in the next section.

▶ **Table 8.5** Regular field list

Filter Name	Description
Request URI	Includes the relative URL (the piece of the URL after the hostname). For example, for `http://www.mysite.com/requestURL/index.html?sample=text`, the Request URI is `/requestURL/index.html?sample=text`.
Hostname	The full domain name of the page requested. For example, for `http://www.mysite.com/requestURL/index.html?sample=text`, the hostname is `www.mysite.com`.
Referral	The external referrer, if any. This field is populated only for the initial external referral at the beginning of a session.
Page Title	The contents of the <title> tags in the HTML of the delivered page.
Visitor Browser Program	The name of the browser program used by the visitor.
Visitor Browser Version	The version of the browser program used by the visitor.
Visitor Operating System Platform	The visitor's operating system platform.
Visitor Operating System Version	The visitor's operating system version.
Visitor Language Settings	The language setting in the visitor's browser preferences.
Visitor Screen Resolution	The resolution of the visitor's screen, as determined from the browser program.
Visitor Screen Colors	The color capabilities of the visitor's screen, as determined from the browser program
Visitor Java Enabled?	Whether Java is enabled in the visitor's browser program.
Visitor Flash version	The version of Flash installed in the visitor's browser program.
Visitor IP Address	The visitor's IP address.
Visitor Geographic Domain	The visitor's ISP, for example, aol.com or aol.co.uk for AOL users, derived from the geographic database.
Visitor ISP Organization	The ISP organization registered to the IP address of the user. This is the ISP the visitor is using to access the Internet.
Visitor Country	The visitor's geographic country location obtained by information registered with the IP address.

► **Table 8.5** Regular field list

Filter Name	Description
Visitor Region	The visitor's geographic region or state location, obtained by information registered with the IP address.
Visitor City	The visitor's geographic city location, obtained by information registered with the IP address.
Visitor Connection Speed	The visitor's connection speed, obtained by information registered with the IP address.
Visitor Type	Either New Visitor or Returning Visitor, based on Google Analytics identifiers.
Custom Field 1	An empty, custom field for storage of values during filter computation. Data is not stored permanently in this field but can be used by subsequent filters.
Custom Field 2	An empty, custom field for storage of values during filter computation. Data is not stored permanently in this field but can be used by subsequent filters.

► **Table 8.6** User-defined variables

Filter Name	Description
Campaign Source	The resource that provided the click, e.g., Google. This variable is automatically generated for AdWords hits when auto-tagging is turned on through the AdWords interface.
Campaign Medium	The medium used to generate the request, e.g., organic, cpc, or ppc. This variable is automatically generated for AdWords hits when auto-tagging is turned on through the AdWords interface.
Campaign Name	The name given to the marketing campaign or used to differentiate the campaign source, e.g., October Campaign. This variable is automatically generated for AdWords hits when auto-tagging is turned on through the AdWords interface.
Campaign Term	The term used to generate the ad from the referring source or campaign source, such as a keyword. This variable is automatically generated for AdWords hits when auto-tagging is turned on through the AdWords interface.
Campaign Content	Typically defines multivariate or split testing or is used to disseminate campaign target variables in an advertising campaign. This variable is automatically generated for AdWords hits when auto-tagging is turned on through the AdWords interface.
Campaign Code	Can be used to refer to a campaign lookup table (not yet implemented in Google Analytics).
User Defined	A custom variable name, for use by the end user.
E-Commerce Transaction ID	An unique ID variable correlated with a designated transaction.

Continues

Filter Name	Description
E-Commerce Transaction Country	Used to designate the country defined by the transaction process, obtained by information registered with the IP address.
E-Commerce Transaction Region	Used to designate the region defined by the transaction process, obtained by information registered with the IP address.
E-Commerce Transaction City	Represents the city where the commerce transaction occurred, obtained by information registered with the IP address.
E-Commerce Store or Order Location	Describes the store or affiliated site processing the transaction, e.g., U.S. store, U.K. store, Affiliate123.
E-Commerce Item Name	The item name purchased.
E-Commerce Item Code	The identifier or code number corresponding to the item purchased. Commonly referred to as the stock-keeping unit (SKU) code.

Five Common Profile Filters

The following list highlights, in no particular order, the five most common filters applied by most users of Google Analytics. The majority are custom filters:

Include only your website's traffic   At the very least you should apply this filter to all your profiles.

Exclude certain known visitors   For example, exclude your employees, your web agency, and so on.

Segment by geographical location   Make it easy for your country managers by creating profiles of visitors relevant only to them.

Segment by visitor campaign, medium, or referrer source   Visitors from different referrers may have different objectives.

Segment by content   Visitors viewing particular sections of your website may display different behavior, for example, purchase versus support sections.

These filters are discussed in more detail in the following sections. Before studying these, you should be familiar with regular expressions—see "Regular Expression Overview" in Appendix A.

Including Only Your Website's Traffic

This custom filter ensures that your data, and *only* your data, is collected into your Google Analytics profile. For example, it is possible for another person to hijack your GATC, placing the same code onto their own pages. This can happen deliberately or accidentally and is incredibly easy to do—a person simply copies your GATC by viewing your HTML source code. The consequence is that third-party traffic contaminates your results. Using the include filter shown in Figure 8.14 results in only traffic to `mysite.com` being reported. Note the backslash character (\) used to escape the delimiter character (.). This is an example of using regular expression syntax. Simply substitute `mysite.com` for your domain using the escape character for each "." in your domain.

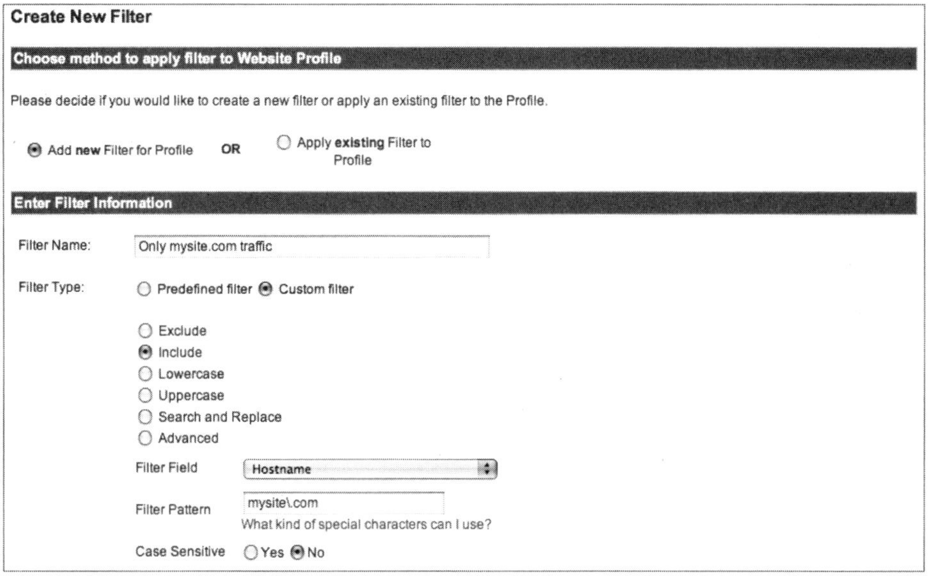

Create New Filter

Choose method to apply filter to Website Profile

Please decide if you would like to create a new filter or apply an existing filter to the Profile.

○ Add **new** Filter for Profile **OR**   ○ Apply **existing** Filter to Profile

Enter Filter Information

Filter Name: Only mysite.com traffic

Filter Type: ○ Predefined filter ● Custom filter

○ Exclude
● Include
○ Lowercase
○ Uppercase
○ Search and Replace
○ Advanced

Filter Field   [Hostname   ▲▼]

Filter Pattern   mysite\.com
                 What kind of special characters can I use?

Case Sensitive   ○ Yes ● No

Figure 8.14 Filter to include only your website's traffic

Of course, it may be desirable to collect data from multiple websites you control into one profile. In that case, add the multiple domains in the filter pattern separated with pipe characters—for example, `mysite\.com|mysite\.co\.uk`.

> **Tip:** In my view, this is the most important filter to apply to your profiles and is a required first step for a best-practice configuration. It ensures your data remains clean and prevents GATC hijacking. If you apply only one filter to your account, make sure it is this one.

Excluding Certain Known Visitors

Excluding visits from staff, your search marketing agency, or any known third parties, such as your web developers, is an important step when creating your profiles. These visitors generate a relatively high number of pageviews in areas that will greatly impact key metrics, such as your conversion rates.

For example, employees who have their browser home page set to the company website will show in your reports as retuning visitors every time they open their browser—and most likely as one-page visitors. Remember that the GATC deliberately breaks through any caching, so it's important to exclude employee visits from those of potential customers. Similarly, web developers heavily test checkout systems for troubleshooting purposes. These will also trigger GATC page requests, and most likely these will be for your goal-conversion pages. You should therefore exclude all such visits from your reports.

Excluding known visitors is straightforward if the visitor connects to the Internet via a fixed IP address. If this is the case, select the predefined filter Exclude Traffic From The IP Addresses from the Filter Manager, as shown in Figure 8.15a.

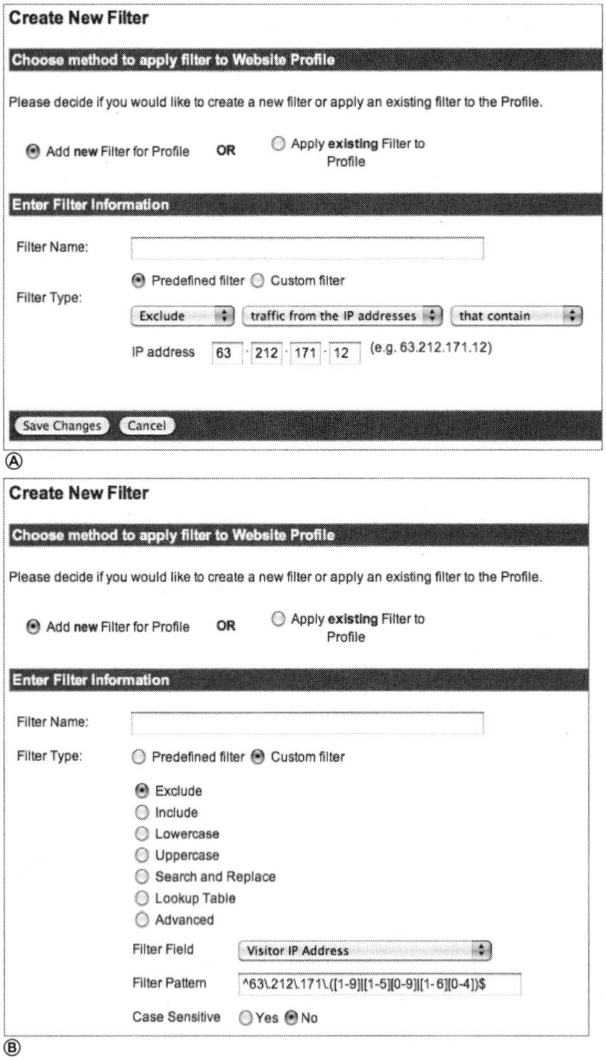

Figure 8.15 Excluding visitors from a known IP address (a) for a single IP address, b) for an IP range

The example shown in Figure 8.15a is suitable for a single IP address or when you have a handful of IP addresses to exclude (set up multiple exclude filters for this). However, for an IP range, use a custom filter with a regular expression. For example, excluding the IP range 63.212.171.1–64 is shown as a custom filter in Figure 8.15b. See Appendix A for an overview of regular expressions.

What If Visitors Do Not Have a Fixed IP Address?

This is often the case for home users, where the Internet service provider (ISP) assigns a different IP address each time the home user connects; this can also happen during a connected session. The solution is to use the function _setVar() in conjunction with a custom exclude filter. The principle is that you direct known visitors you want to exclude to a hidden page (not used by regular visitors) that contains a JavaScript label within the GATC. The label is stored as a persistent cookie on that visitor's computer and forms part of their pageview data. An exclude filter is then used to remove any pageview data that contains this label.

To assign a custom label to visitors, call the function _setVar() within the GATC on your hidden page as follows:

```
<script type="text/javascript">
    var gaJsHost = (("https:" == document.location.protocol) ? "https://ssl." :
    "http://www.");
    document.write("\<script src='" + gaJsHost + "google-analytics.com/ga.js'
    type='text/javascript'>\<\/script>" );
</script>

<script type="text/javascript">
try{
    var pageTracker = _gat._getTracker("UA-12345-1");
    pageTracker._trackPageview();
    pageTracker._setVar("dynamic");
}catch(err) {}</script>
```

In this way, only one visit to, for example, www.mysite.com/hiddenpage.htm is required to label the visitor until the cookie expires (24 months)—assuming the label cookie is not overwritten or deleted. Note that in this example _setVar() is called and set to the label dynamic. However, any value can be used in the brackets. With each pageview from your dynamic IP visitor now labeled, Figure 8.16 shows the filter required to exclude those visits from your profile. The value of _setVar() is stored in the Google Analytics field labeled User Defined.

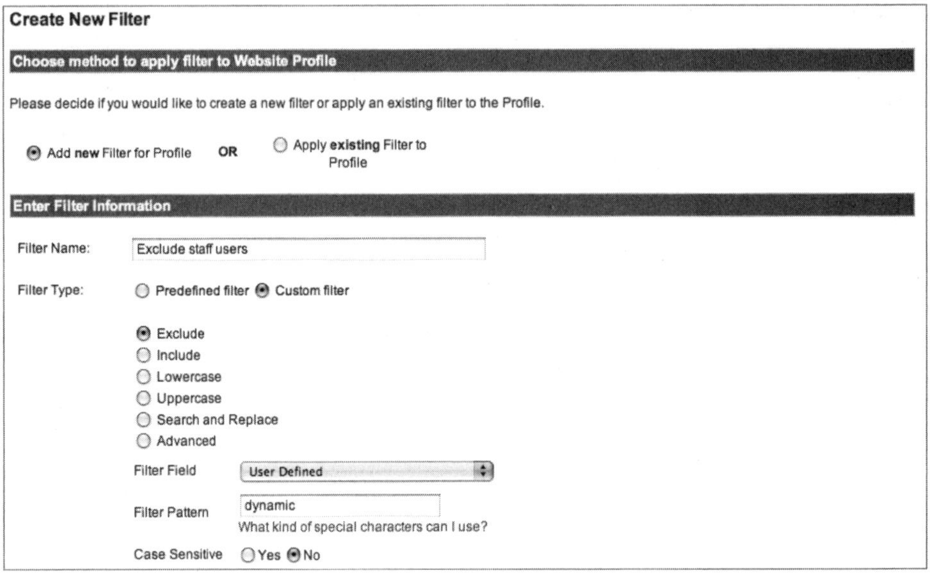

Create New Filter

Choose method to apply filter to Website Profile

Please decide if you would like to create a new filter or apply an existing filter to the Profile.

(•) Add **new** Filter for Profile   **OR**   ( ) Apply **existing** Filter to Profile

Enter Filter Information

Filter Name: | Exclude staff users

Filter Type: ( ) Predefined filter (•) Custom filter

- (•) Exclude
- ( ) Include
- ( ) Lowercase
- ( ) Uppercase
- ( ) Search and Replace
- ( ) Advanced

Filter Field | User Defined

Filter Pattern | dynamic
What kind of special characters can I use?

Case Sensitive   ( ) Yes (•) No

Figure 8.16 Excluding labeled visitors

Warning: The use of the _setVar has been superseded by the new Custom Variables feature of Google Analytics. However, at the time of writing it is not possible to filter by any Custom Variable. Therefore, _setVar is still of value. The Custom Variables feature is described in Chapter 9 in "Labeling Visitors, Sessions and Pages."

Segmenting by Geographical Location

Google Analytics performs an excellent job of showing you the countries from which your visitors are accessing your website. It even groups these into regions (continents: Americas, Europe, Asia, Oceania, Africa) and subregions (Northern Europe, Central Europe, Eastern Europe, Southern Europe), for example; refer to Figures 4.15 and 5.4. However, if your organization operates specifically in certain markets, you may want to create a profile that focuses on reporting visitors from just those countries. For example, North America (Canada and the United States) or BRIC Region (Brazil, Russia, India, China) can be included in a separate profile, as shown by the filter in Figure 8.17.

Filter Pattern Tip

When deciding what value to place in the Filter Pattern field, always consult your reports. For example, when cross segmenting a page by country, the available values are displayed. Note that these are all in English. For example, they are listed as Spain, Netherlands, Germany, and so on, not España, Nederland, Deutschland. Use only the values from your reports in the Filter Pattern field. Partial matches are also allowed.

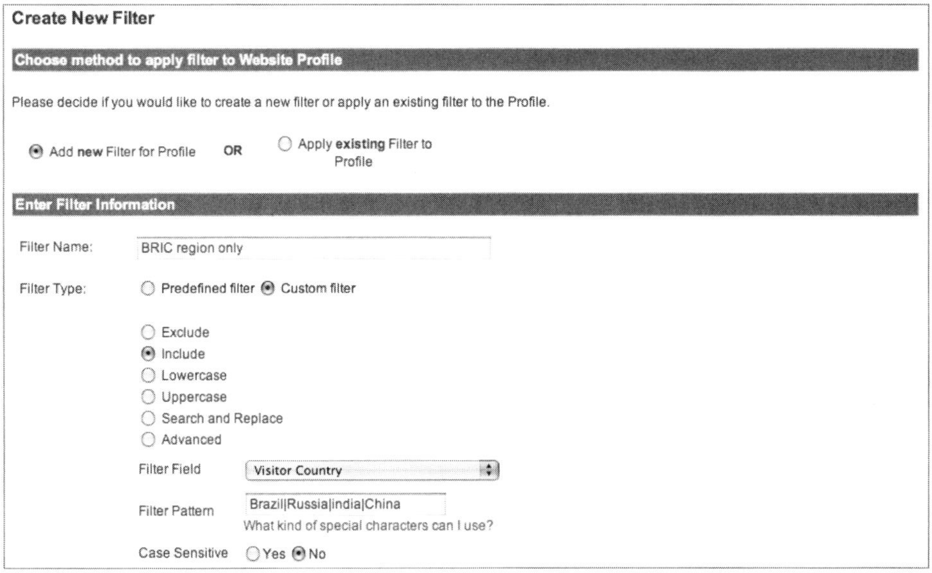

Figure 8.17 Segmenting visitors by country

By this method, country managers can better focus on the metrics without having to back out nonrelevant visits.

Segmenting by Campaign, Medium, or Referrer Source

As with the use of other filters discussed in this section, Google Analytics already does an excellent job of displaying different campaigns, mediums, or source referrers. However, in some scenarios it can be helpful to have a profile with dedicated reports for these, in order to help you optimize these better. For example, if have a search marketing agency helping you with paid search, you may wish to isolate just your paid search visitors for their view. Similarly, if you employ an email marketing agency, you can isolate just email referrals. Having a separate profile gives you control over the report access, allowing you to filter out noise and protect other potentially confidential data.

How you construct this filter depends on how you have tagged your landing page URLs (see "Campaign Tracking," in Chapter 7). The values you assigned for utm_source, utm_medium, and utm_campaign need to match the following filter fields:

- Campaign Name
- Campaign Source
- Campaign Medium

To filter Google-only visitors, both paid and nonpaid, into a separate profile, apply the filter shown in Figure 8.18.

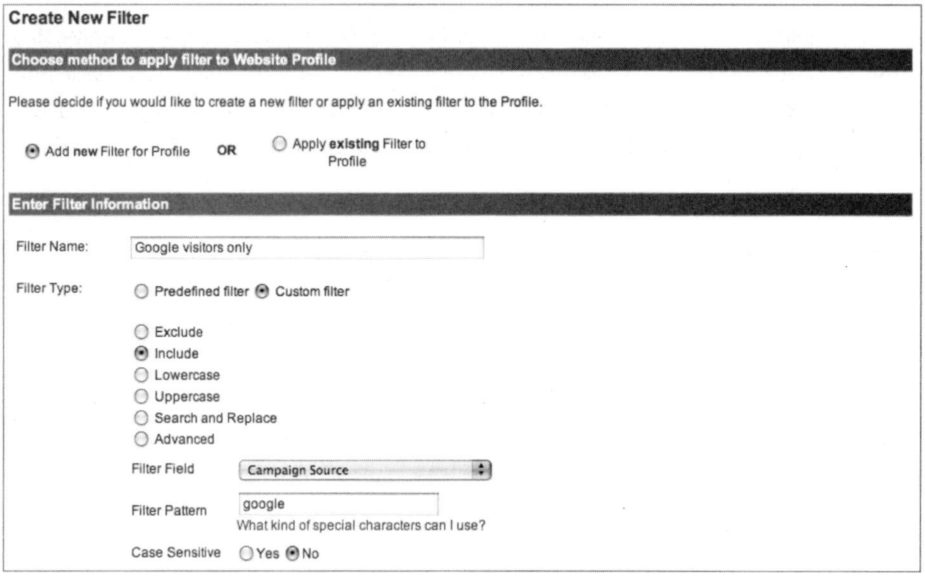

Create New Filter

Choose method to apply filter to Website Profile

Please decide if you would like to create a new filter or apply an existing filter to the Profile.

◉ Add **new** Filter for Profile   **OR**   ◯ Apply **existing** Filter to Profile

Enter Filter Information

Filter Name: Google visitors only

Filter Type: ◯ Predefined filter   ◉ Custom filter

     ◯ Exclude
     ◉ Include
     ◯ Lowercase
     ◯ Uppercase
     ◯ Search and Replace
     ◯ Advanced

       Filter Field   [Campaign Source   ▲▼]

       Filter Pattern   google
                  What kind of special characters can I use?

       Case Sensitive   ◯ Yes ◉ No

Figure 8.18   Filter to include only Google visitors

If you wish to track AdWords-only visitors, and this is the only paid search network you are running, apply the filter as shown in Figure 8.19. (I have assumed you have auto-tagging enabled in your AdWords account.)

If you are running other paid search networks (Microsoft adCenter, Yahoo Search Marketing, and so on) and these are labeled as utm_medium = cpc, you will need to apply both filters shown in Figures 8.18 and 8.19, in order.

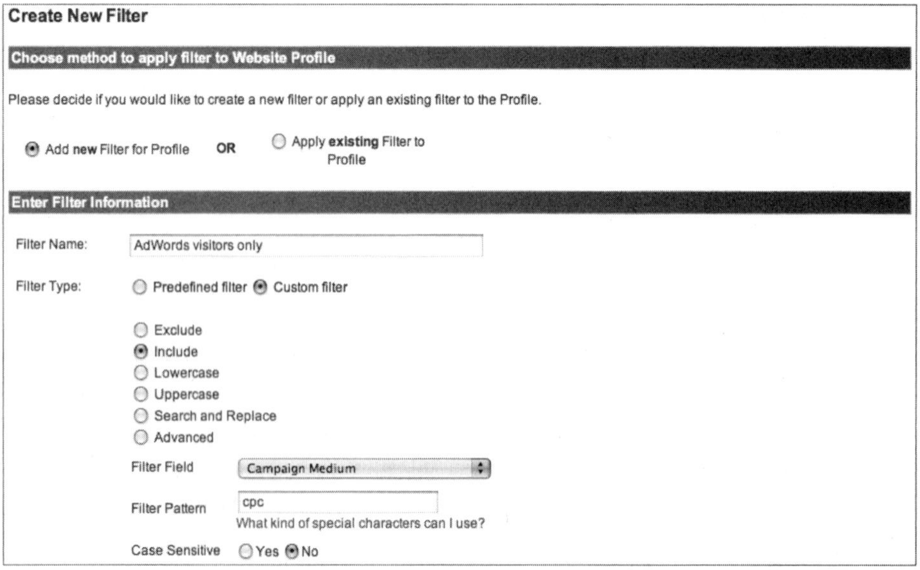

Create New Filter

Choose method to apply filter to Website Profile

Please decide if you would like to create a new filter or apply an existing filter to the Profile.

◉ Add **new** Filter for Profile   **OR**   ◯ Apply **existing** Filter to Profile

Enter Filter Information

Filter Name: AdWords visitors only

Filter Type: ◯ Predefined filter   ◉ Custom filter

     ◯ Exclude
     ◉ Include
     ◯ Lowercase
     ◯ Uppercase
     ◯ Search and Replace
     ◯ Advanced

       Filter Field   [Campaign Medium   ▲▼]

       Filter Pattern   cpc
                  What kind of special characters can I use?

       Case Sensitive   ◯ Yes ◉ No

Figure 8.19   Filter to include only AdWords visitors

Figure 8.20 shows how to segment only email visitors—that is, those visitors who have clicked a link to your website within an email message, assuming you tagged such links as utm_medium=email.

As you can see, segmenting by campaign, source, or medium is as simple as knowing what these values are in your corresponding landing page URLs and then applying them as field values to your include and exclude filters.

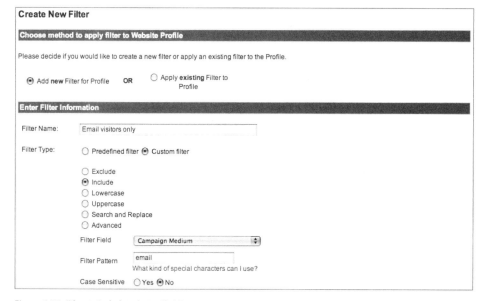

Figure 8.20 Filter to include only email visitors

Segmenting by Content

Often within one website, you will be trying to satisfy the needs of very different visitors—for example, product purchase versus product support or corporate information versus customer information. Effectively measuring such different needs requires the setting of very different goals for each section—hence the creation of separate profiles using filters. Figure 8.21 is an example filter that segments by content—in this case, a support blog.

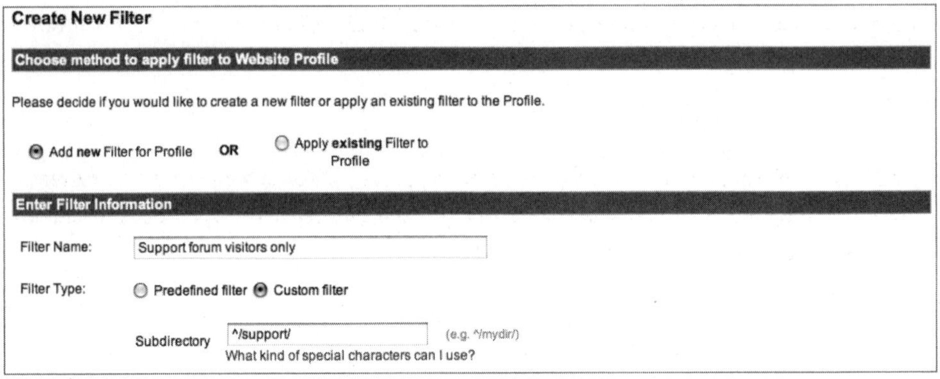

Figure 8.21 Filter to include only blog visitors

Of course, the success of this filter depends on you having a well-ordered website directory structure on which to filter content. If you do not, it is possible to achieve a virtual structure by using virtual pageviews, as described in "trackPageview(): the Google Analytics Workhorse," in Chapter 7.

Assigning a Filter Order

By default, a profile's filters are applied to the incoming data in the order in which the filters were added. However, you can easily modify the order from your Profile Settings page, using the Assign Filter Order link from within your profile settings (see Figure 8.22). Filter order is important for the filters described in Figures 8.18 and 8.19, if these filters are to be combined.

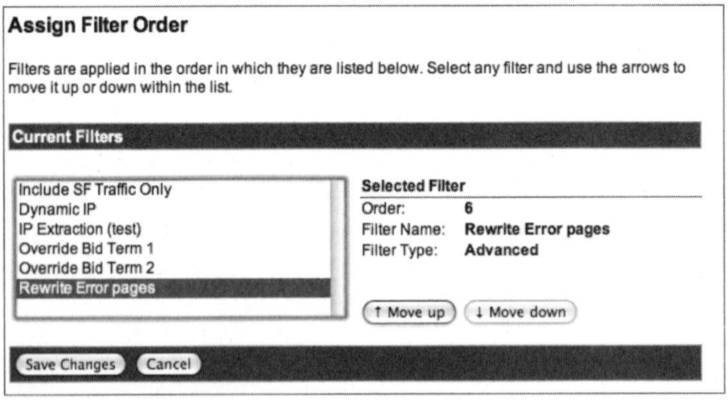

Figure 8.22 Assigning filter order

Report Segments: Segmenting Visitors Using Advanced Segments

The Advanced Segments menu allows you to segment your data *within* your reports. Unlike profile filters, you do not have to create separate profiles for an advanced segment because it leaves your original data untouched. Whereas profile filters modify data on the pageview level, Advanced Segments change a report's view of the data at the visit level.

> **Note:** To reiterate, Advanced Segments work on entire visits. For example, if you create an advanced segment equal to "Page Title matches X," the result shows you all visits in which pages with the title X were viewed, including all other pageviews that occurred during those visits.

Creating an Advanced Segment

The majority of Google Analytics reports contain an Advanced Segments drop-down menu at the top right of the screen (refer to Figure 4.4). By default "All Visits" is selected. If you click this option, the area beneath it expands, as shown in Figure 8.23. This is where you can select, create, and manage your advanced segments.

Figure 8.23 Advanced Segments management area

As you can see from Figure 8.23, two options are available: Default Segments are prebuilt and ready for immediate use; Custom Segments allow you create your own advanced segment for specific needs. The Custom Segments area will be empty if you have not previously created any.

Default Advanced Segments

As the name suggests, Google has included a number of prebuilt advanced segments for you to use:

All Visits No segmentation applied.

New Visitors Visitors who have not been to your site before, assuming they have not deleted their Google Analytics cookies since their last visit, or returning visitors using a different computer or browser.

Returning Visitors Visitors who have previously viewed your site using the same device and browser.

Paid Search Traffic Any visit whose referral medium value is set to cpc, ppc, cpa, cpm, cpv, or cpp.

Non-paid Search Traffic Any visit whose referral medium is set to organic.

Search Traffic Both paid and nonpaid searches, that is, any visit whose referral medium value is set to cpc, ppc, cpa, cpm, cpv, cpp, or organic.

Direct Traffic Visitors who typed your web URL directly or used a browser bookmark to arrive at your site. These could also be non-tagged visits. See Chapter 7 for a description of campaign tracking.

Referral Traffic Visitors who followed a link from other site (not a recognized search engine) to arrive at yours.

Visits with Conversions Your highest-value visitors.

Visits from iPhones Visits from iPhone users are straightforward to detect because their browser leaves its "signature" as operating system = iPhone.

Non-bounce Visits Visits that consisted of more than one page or one page plus an event. See Chapter 7 for a definition of Event Tracking.

This is not intended to be an exhaustive list, though it is very handy for common segmentation requirements. Check off the segments you want to select—currently limited to a maximum of four at any one time, and click Apply to finish. Your graph and tables reflect the segmented data, as shown in Figure 8.24.

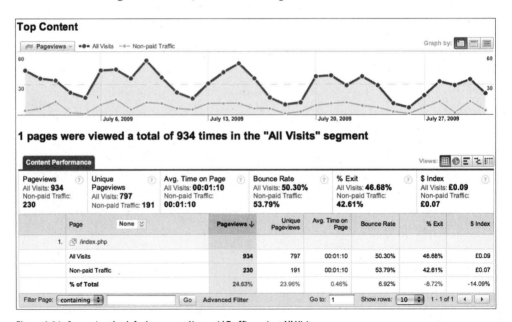

Figure 8.24 Comparing the default segment Non-paid Traffic against All Visits

If you wish to edit a default segment, click the link "Manage Your Advanced Segments," shown previously in Figure 8.23. Next to the default segment you wish to edit, select Copy. This provides the detail of how the segment was constructed. Edit this as required to include more conditions and values for your own purposes. Once you edit a copy of a default segment, it will be saved in the Custom Segments section of the Manage Your Advanced Segments page.

Creating a Custom Advanced Segment

From the screen shown in Figure 8.23, select "Create A New Advanced Segment." For this example, we will create a custom segment of visits with two or more unique purchases. Follow these steps, as shown in Figure 8.25:

1. Navigate to the Unique Purchases metric in the menu on the lower left by either selecting E-commerce from the Metrics area or searching for the word *unique* in the query field at the top of the list.

2. Select the Unique Purchases metric and drag it into the field bordered by the dotted lines. Note that the new field's Condition and Value property now become available.

3. Enter the comparison value for the segment. In this example, enter **2** in the Value field.

4. Test each segment to make sure conditions make sense for the segment you defined. Click Test Segment to view the effect once the advanced segment is applied.

5. Finally, name your segment with an informative name; then click Create Segment to finish.

Once saved, your new advanced segment is available to use in one of two ways: as a check box in the Custom Segments area, as shown in Figure 8.23, or by selecting Apply To Report from the menu of the Manage Your Advanced Segments page.

Dimensions versus Metrics

Two types of data are represented in Google Analytics reports: dimensions and metrics (refer to Figure 4.5). Dimensions are text strings that describe an item. Think of them as names, such as page URL, page title, hostname, browser type, connection speed, transaction ID, product name, and so on. Metrics are numbers, for example, time on page, time on site, bounce rate, or purchase total. The conditional operators less than and greater than can be applied only to metrics.

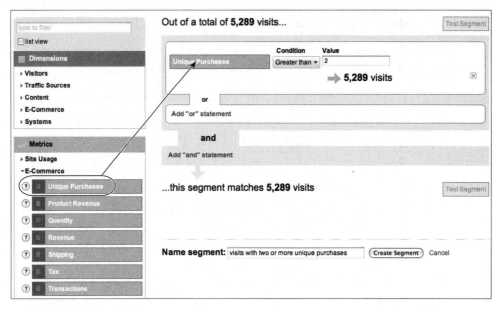

Figure 8.25 Building a custom segment

Example Custom Segments

Advanced segments can be incredibly powerful when it comes to drilling down into your data. It can seem like an endless supply of permutations and combinations is available. Which specific advanced segments meet your needs will be determined by your website type (lead generation, e-commerce, corporate information, content publisher, and so on) and the value such segments bring to your organization. The following four examples are ones that I commonly use.

Segmenting Mobile Phone Visits

As discussed in Chapter 2, "Available Methodologies and Their Accuracy," visits from older generations of Internet-enabled mobile phones cannot be tracked because they do not execute JavaScript or cookies—a major hurdle when trying to navigate the Web and a prerequisite for Google Analytics tracking. However, the newer generation of smartphones (iPhone, Blackberry, and the like) has driven the recent proliferation of web usage via mobile devices. Visitors using these can be tracked in the exact same way as desktop and laptop users.

Note: Google Analytics recently launched a server-side code snippet to track dedicated mobile websites, such as http://m.google.com and www.bbc.co.uk/mobile. Currently this supports PHP, Perl, JSP, and ASPX sites. The code is separate from tracking visits to your regular website from smartphone devices (JavaScript- and cookie-enabled phones). For further information see http://code.google.com/apis/analytics/docs/tracking/mobileAppsTracking.html.

Mobile Web Audience Statistics

Mobile web browsing as a proportion of total web browsing is currently very small at 0.72 percent, though growing (NetMarketingShare via Econsultancy.com blog, March 2009).

U.S. smartphone users spent an average of 4.6 hours per month on mobile Internet sites (M:Metrics via Marketing Charts, May 2008).

Global sales of smartphones are expected to reach 300 million by 2013 (Juniper Research, February 2009).

In the United States, 63.2 million people used their mobiles to find news and information in January 2009, more than double that of January 2008 (comScore, March 2009).

Of 182 million people in China with web-enabled mobile phones, 102 million (56 percent) use the devices to connect to the Web (Netpop Research via ClickZ, April 2009).

Despite the interest and growth of smartphone adoption, for the vast majority of websites, the number of pageviews from mobile phones is currently very small in comparison with normal computer access, typically less than 1 percent of total visits for European and U.S. websites.

However, this number will continue to grow in the coming years. The graph shows the explosive growth, albeit from a low baseline, in mobile Internet access for two similar (though unrelated) publisher websites. Both show a 1000 percent increase in visits from smartphone devices over six quarters. Overall visit traffic for the same period grew 25 and 30 percent, respectively.

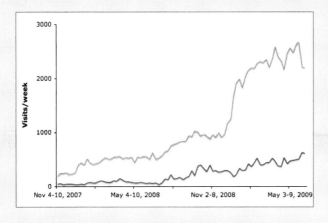

Designing a website for a mobile audience with a three-inch screen and potentially slower data connection is clearly very different from designing for other users. Therefore, studying this segment of visitors can have important implications for your web development. Figure 8.26 shows the advanced segment required to do this. It detects either the phone operating system or browser type and matches it against a known lookup list:

Operating system match `android|black|HTC|iphone|ipod|lg|nokia|palm|samsung|sony|symbian|vodafone|treo|xda|netfront`

Browser type match `android|black|HTC|iphone|ipod|lg|nokia|palm|samsung|sony|symbian|vodafone|treo|xda|netfront`

Out of a total of **?** visits...

Test Segment

Browser

Condition
Matches regular expression ▾
☐ case sensitive

Value
android|black|HTC|iphon ▾

⊠

or

Operating System

Condition
Matches regular expression ▾
☐ case sensitive

Value
android|black|HTC|iphon ▾

⊠

or

Add "or" statement

and

Add "and" statement

...this segment matches **?** visits

Test Segment

Name segment: Mobile phone visits   (Save Segment)   Cancel

Figure 8.26 A custom segment to highlight mobile phone visits

Just as for profile filters, you can use the regular expression pipe character (|) to separate multiple possible matches for the same metric or dimension. An overview of regular expressions is given in Appendix A.

The same lookup list is used for both operating system and browser type fields, because not all smartphones set these logically. For example, many do not broadcast their operating system name when viewing websites, while others identify their browsers as regular types, for example, Safari (Symbian, Android), which cannot be distinguished from ordinary desktop or laptop users. The use of both fields combined with an OR statement therefore ensures you capture most mobile visitors.

Note: The mobile match list for the preceding advanced segment example was compiled by analyzing the browser and operating system combinations of over 10 million visits during July–August 2009 from five independent websites. These were publisher websites, that is, those most likely to receive mobile visitors with a targeted audience of U.S. (one), U.K. (two), and Swedish (two) visitors.

The tracking of mobile visitors is discussed in Chapter 2 in the section "Issues Affecting Visitor Data Accuracy for Logfiles."

Segmenting Social Network Visits

In Google Analytics, all visits that originate from a social network website are tracked in the same way as any other referrals to your site. That is, they are grouped together with the plethora of visits from all the other referral links to your site. Because social networks can significantly impact your search engine rankings as well as rapidly create a buzz around your brand, studying this segment can be very revealing.

Figure 8.27 groups the social networks that are relevant to `www.advanced-web-metrics.com` as a single segment. That is:

```
wikipedia|stumbleupon|netvibes|groups.google|bloglines|groups.yahoo.com|link
edin|facebook|webmasterworld|del.icio.us|digg|feedburner|twitter|technorati|
blog|faves.com|wordpress|newsgator|PRweb|econsultancy|toprankblog|forums.
searchenginewatch
```

You will want to build your own regular expression list around the networks that are important to you.

Note: Key performance indicators (KPIs) for social network visits are covered in Chapter 10.

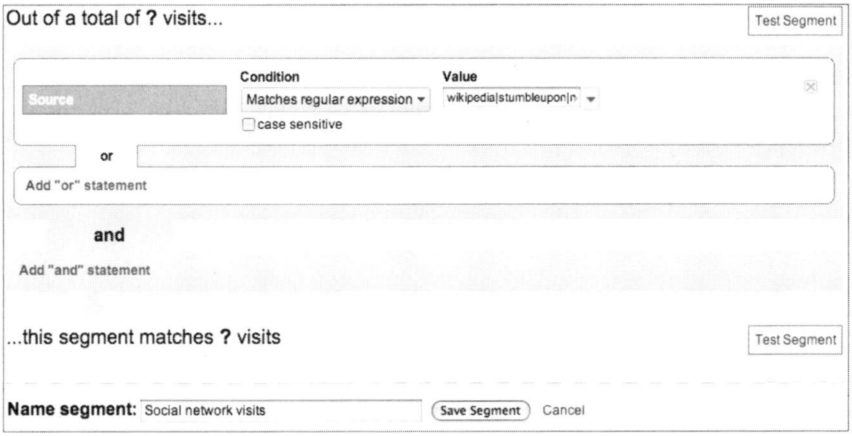

Out of a total of ? visits...   Test Segment

Source	Condition	Value	
	Matches regular expression ▼	wikipedia|stumbleupon|n ▼	☒
	☐ case sensitive		

    or

Add "or" statement

    and

Add "and" statement

...this segment matches ? visits   Test Segment

Name segment: Social network visits   (Save Segment)   Cancel

Figure 8.27 A custom segment highlighting social network visits

Grouping Visits from a Geographic Region

Google Analytics does an excellent job of showing geographically where your visitors come from. However, there are times when you need to group visitors as a single segment. For example, if you have North, South, and Central American offices, you may want to group visits from those regions. If you operate only on the East Coast, you may want to group visitors from relevant cities. You can apply this as well to Europe, the Middle East, Asia, and Africa.

Figure 8.28 generates a segment for Nordic customers. Notice in this case that I did not use "Matches Regular Expression" to build a single-condition field. Instead, I explicitly entered each country as a separate match. This can be useful for trouble-shooting purposes, that is, you can explicitly match each field and test to ensure you receive the expected result. Then you can combine the fields as a regular expression if required.

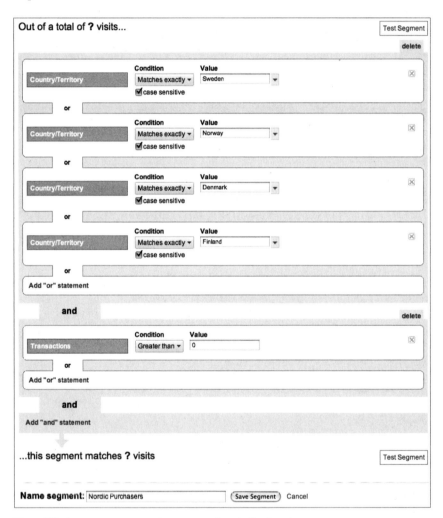

Figure 8.28 A custom segment grouping customers from the Nordic region

Segmenting Brand Visits

The number of people who arrive on your site as a result of knowing your brand name is an important segment. This includes visitors who type in your brand names or product names on search engines, as well people who arrive directly—either by typing in your web address directly or from a previously saved browser bookmark. Figure 8.29 is an example of reporting on a brand segment for this book.

Although I could have used a single regular expression to simplify the matching, I deliberately separated these into three groups: brand name matches (author name), product name matches (book name), and blog name matches. If you have a large number of brand names to match on, it can be useful to group your matches in this way in order to simplify understanding the advanced segment construction. A common use of this is when your brand or product name is known by a different name in other languages.

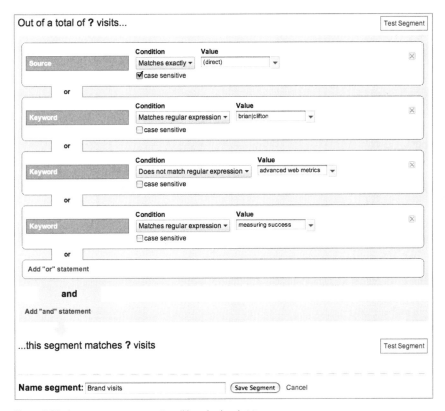

Figure 8.29 A custom segment grouping all brand-related visits

Note: KPIs for brand engagement are discussed in the section "Marketer KPI Examples" in Chapter 10.

Summary

In Chapter 8, you have learned the following:

Perform initial configuration You have learned how to set the initial configuration of your account, including localization, e-commerce, and Site Search settings.

Configure goals Configuring goals provides you with conversion and engagement rates. You have learned how to identify and set goals in order to benchmark yourself.

Configure funnels Funnels enable you to see what barriers exist on the path to achieving a goal. We discussed how to configure funnels and the significance of their shapes.

Configure filters Filtering keeps your data clean and, along with the Advanced Segments component, is the method of segmenting visitors:

- Set up filters to maintain the integrity of your data.
- Segment data to gain a deeper understanding of visitor behavior.
- Use filters for data cleansing as a method for long-term segmentation.
- Use Advanced Segments as an efficient way to focus on visitor types.

Google Analytics Hacks

Out of the box, Google Analytics is a powerful tool to add to your armory of search marketing, customer relationship, and other business-management firepower. With only a single page tag required to collect data, it is straightforward to set up, and with the addition of some filters, you can really gain an insight into your website performance.

If at this stage the reports answer all of your questions, that's great. However, you may find yourself asking further questions that are not answered by default in your reports. Fear not— you can still achieve a great deal more insight with a little bit of lateral thought; Google Analytics is incredibly flexible in that respect.

9

In Chapter 9, you will learn:

To customize the list of recognized search engines

To label and sessionize visitors for better segmentation

To track error pages and broken links

To gain a greater insight into your pay-per-click tracking

To improve site overlay, conversion, and e-commerce reports

Why Hack an Existing Product?

Google Analytics is a great product, but it does need to cater to the needs of a wide variety of report end-users—from traditional e-commerce sites, to publishers, blogs, forums, corporate, informational and lead-generation sites. Because of this diversity, certain compromises have to be made by the Google Analytics development team, as is the case for any web analytics product. Hence the need for a "hacks" chapter to pro-vide potential work-arounds for you.

Google Analytics hacks help you delve deep into analysis. To do that, you need to think laterally and be creative with applying filters. Because the GATC is written in JavaScript, Google Analytics is extremely flexible in this regard. There are numer-ous ways it can be altered or customized, and a good webmaster should be able to do this for you without too much trouble. Custom labeling of visitors on a per-visitor or per-session basis is very powerful, as is the ability to use advanced filters to manipulate reported data, such as adding referral source information to transaction IDs.

In this chapter I assume you have a strong understanding of JavaScript and HTML. The examples provided are only a sample of what you can achieve. Feel free to experiment and share your own experiences on the book blog site: www.advanced-web-metrics.com/blog.

Positioning and Updates of GATC hacks

When modifying the GATC, note that the placement of the code edits is important. Therefore, ensure that you follow the placement instructions carefully. In the vast majority of cases, edits to the GATC take place before the _trackPageview() call.

In addition, the exact syntax of the GATC is constantly in flux. Therefore, if you apply these hacks, or build your own, subscribe to the changelog feed at http://code.google.com/apis/analytics/docs/gaJS/changelog.html for relevant updates. When possible, updates to the hacks in this chapter will be made available at www.advanced-web-metrics.com/chapter9.

Customizing the List of Recognized Search Engines

Google Analytics currently identifies visitors from the following search engines in your reports. The target audience, if specific, is shown in parentheses:

- AOL
- About
- Alice
- AlltheWeb

- AltaVista
- Ask
- Baidu (China)
- Bing

- CNN
- Club-Internet
- Ekolay (Turkey)
- Gigablast

- Google
- Google.interia
- Kvasir (Norwegian)
- Live (now Bing)
- LookSmart
- Lycos
- MSN
- Mama
- Mamma
- Mynet (Turkey)
- Najdi (Slovenia)
- Netscape
- NetSprint
- Onet
- Ozu (Spain)
- PChome (China)
- Search
- Seznam
- Szukacz (Poland)
- Virgilio (Italy)
- Voila (France)
- Wp (Poland)
- Yahoo!
- Yam (Taiwan)
- Yandex (Russia)

Note: The search engine listed as "Search" is actually a catch-all name for all fully qualified domain names containing the word *search*. For example, in addition to www.search.com, it will match the subdomain search.anysite.com.

Although Google Analytics adds new recognized search engines to this list regularly, there are of course a great many more search engines in the world—language- and region-specific as well as niche search engines, such as price comparison and vertical portals. It is therefore possible to append or completely rewrite the list of recognized search engines as described in the following sections.

Appending New Search Engines

Suppose visitors from the Korean search engine, Naver, for example, are important to your website's marketing success. Such visitors will be tracked as referrals from naver.com because it is not part of the default search engine list. This means Naver will not be grouped with other search engines, and the visitor's search keywords will be lost.

To have Naver visitors recognized as search engine visitors with their keywords captured, follow these two steps:

1. Conduct a search on the naver.com website and view the resultant URL. For example, searching for "motorcycle" produces the following search result URL:

   ```
   http://search.naver.com/search.naver?where=nexearch&query=motocycle&x=0&y=
   0&sm=top_hty&fbm=1
   ```

2. To capture this URL and keyword as a search engine, add the following code to your page GATC:

   ```
   <script type="text/javascript">
       var gaJsHost = (("https:" == document.location.protocol) ? ↵
   "https://ssl.": "http://www.");
       document.write(unescape("%3Cscript src='" + gaJsHost + "google-↵
   analytics.com/ga.js' type='text/javascript'%3E%3C/script%3E"));
   ```

```
    </script>
    <script type="text/javascript">
    try{
        var pageTracker = _gat._getTracker("UA-12345-1");
        pageTracker._addOrganic("naver.com", "query");
        pageTracker._trackPageview();
    }catch(err) {}</script>
```

The line pageTracker._addOrganic("naver.com", "query") appends this search engine to the default list of search engines contained in the GATC. As you can see, the format is

```
pageTracker._addOrganic("search_engine_domain", "query_parameter_name");
```

The important step is to view the URL of a query on the search engine itself and extract the name of the variable containing your keywords. You can continue to add other search engines as needed by creating additional _addOrganic lines. For example, to add the price-comparison engine Kelkoo as a regular search engine, add the following:

```
<script type="text/javascript">
    var gaJsHost = (("https:" == document.location.protocol) ? "https://ssl."↵
 : "http://www.");
    document.write(unescape("%3Cscript src='" + gaJsHost + "google-↵
analytics.com/ga.js' type='text/javascript'%3E%3C/script%3E"));
</script>
<script type="text/javascript">
try{
    var pageTracker = _gat._getTracker("UA-12345-1");
    pageTracker._addOrganic("naver.com", "query");
    pageTracker._addOrganic("Kelkoo", "contextKeywords");
    pageTracker._trackPageview();
}catch(err) {}</script>
```

Note: By this method of appending, you cannot alter how the default list of recognized search engines is detected, because these are processed by Google Analytics first. To modify the default list, use the method described in the next section.

Rewriting the Search Engine List

Use this method if you need to modify the default list of recognized search engines as well as add new ones. You would need to do this if you wished to differentiate regional search engines. For example, being able to differentiate google.co.uk from google.com, google.de, and google.cn may be of importance to your marketing strategy.

You might think that adding the following to the GATC of your pages would provide this:

```
pageTracker._addOrganic("google.co.uk","q");
```

However, this won't work, because when adding regional variations to the search engine list, the order becomes important. Defining the custom _addOrganic variable as shown in your GATC appends google.co.uk (or any other variation) to the *end* of the default search engine list. By this time, the list has already assigned any google.* domain as "google"; therefore, appending is too late to change this.

The answer is to include a third parameter to each _addOrganic function: opt_ prepend. If set to true, this prepends the defined search engine to the *beginning* of the organic source list, as shown in this example:

```
try{   // Define new search domains first
    pageTracker._addOrganic("google.com","q",true);
    pageTracker._addOrganic("google.co.uk","q",true);
    pageTracker._addOrganic("google.es","q",true);
    pageTracker._addOrganic("google.pt","q",true);
    pageTracker._addOrganic("google.it","q",true);
     etc.
}catch(err) {}
```

With opt_prepend set to false, or omitted, the defined search engine is added to the end of the search engine list.

Rather than define a long list of additional search engines in your GATC, put these in a separate JavaScript file, named, for example, custom_se.js. Place this file in the root of your web-hosting account. Then call the file in all your web pages by adding the line in bold to your GATC:

```
<script type="text/javascript">
    var gaJsHost = (("https:" == document.location.protocol) ? "https://ssl." :
"http://www.");
    document.write(unescape("%3Cscript src='" + gaJsHost + "google-
analytics.com/ga.js' type='text/javascript'%3E%3C/script%3E"));
</script>

<script type="text/javascript">
try{
    var pageTracker = _gat._getTracker("UA-1190129-1");
}catch(err) {}</script>

<script src="/custom_se.js" type="text/javascript"></script>

<script type="text/javascript">
try{
    pageTracker._trackPageview();
}catch(err) {}</script>
```

Notice that the standard GATC has been split and the call to the custom_se.js file inserted between var pageTracker and _trackPageview. This placement is important, so do not change it.

A comprehensive list of more than 130 search engines is maintained at www.advanced-web-metrics.com/chapter9/ and includes assigning Google Local (maps.google.com) and Google News (news.google.com) as search engines. You can download and use this file as the starting point for your own custom search engine list. Also feel free to make additional suggestions.

Capturing Google Image Search

At present, Google Analytics shows all traffic from Google Image search as referrals—a standard click-through from a link like any other. That means any keyword information associated with the visitor's image search is not reported on. However, perhaps this information is important to your business model. If that describes your situation, consider the following.

Conduct a search at http://images.google.com for your website and select one of your images. The result is a framed window, as shown in Figure 9.1.

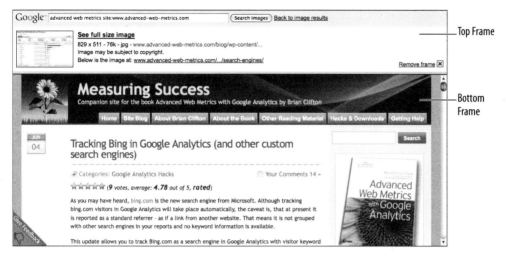

Figure 9.1 An image result from Google's Image search

The bottom frame contains the page on your website where Google found the image that is shown in the top frame. The resultant URL referrer for your site will look similar to this:

```
http://images.google.co.uk/imgres?imgurl=http://www.advanced-web-metrics.com/
blog/wp-content/uploads/2008/09/custom-search-engine-report.jpg&imgrefurl=
http://www.advanced-web-metrics.com/blog/tag/search-engines/&usg=__
MYksi-d3KEG5g8t-b-9F7gsE8o8=&h=511&w=829&sz=76&hl=en&start=1&um=1&tbnid=
d7DQ_U892-4ynM:&tbnh=89&tbnw=144&prev=/images%3Fq%3Dadvanced%2Bweb%2Bmetrics%
2Bsite:www.advanced-web-metrics.com%26hl%3Den%26rlz%3D1B3GGGL_enGB283GB284%26
sa%3DG%26um%3D1%26newwindow%3D1
```

Pretty it isn't! However, the referrer URL for a Google image search contains the search keyword in the parameter named prev, as highlighted, along with other surplus parameters that are not relevant to you. Because of this, viewing the Google Image search term in your reports requires a two-step process:

1. Add images.google to the search engine list of Google Analytics as previously described—either by modifying your GATC on all pages or adding to your custom_se.js, as follows:

```
<script type="text/javascript">
    var gaJsHost = (("https:" == document.location.protocol) ? "https://
ssl." : "http://www.");
    document.write(unescape("%3Cscript src='" + gaJsHost + "google-
analytics.com/ga.js' type='text/javascript'%3E%3C/script%3E"));
```

```
</script>
<script type="text/javascript">
try{
    var pageTracker = _gat._getTracker("UA-12345-1");
    pageTracker._addOrganic("images.google", "prev",true);
    pageTracker._trackPageview();
}catch(err) {}</script>
```

2. Use an advanced filter to extract the keyword from the prev parameter, as shown in Figure 9.2.

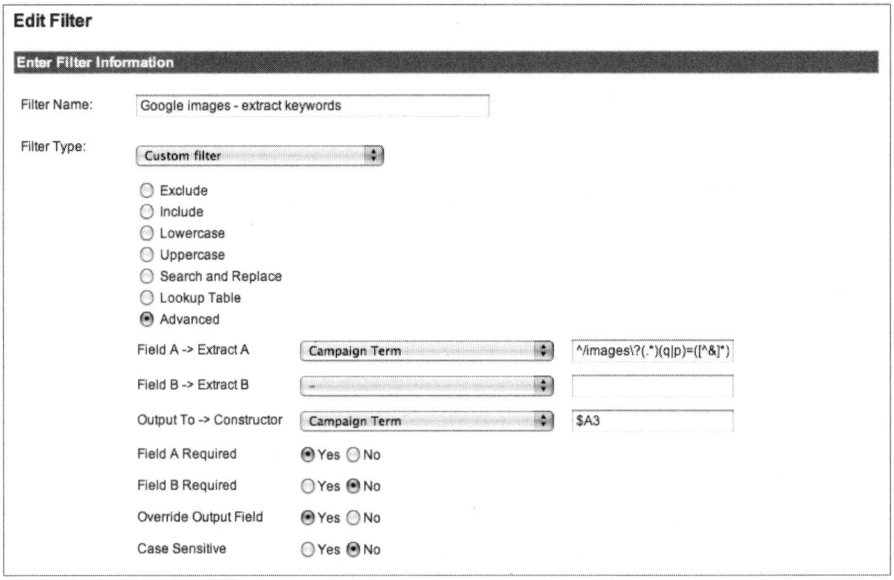

Edit Filter

Enter Filter Information

Filter Name:	Google images - extract keywords

Filter Type:	Custom filter

   ○ Exclude
   ○ Include
   ○ Lowercase
   ○ Uppercase
   ○ Search and Replace
   ○ Lookup Table
   ◉ Advanced

Field A -> Extract A	Campaign Term	^/images\?(.*)(q|p)=([^&]*)
Field B -> Extract B	-	
Output To -> Constructor	Campaign Term	$A3

Field A Required	◉ Yes ○ No
Field B Required	○ Yes ◉ No
Override Output Field	◉ Yes ○ No
Case Sensitive	○ Yes ◉ No

Figure 9.2 Advanced filter to extract the keyword from the prev parameter

In plain English, the advanced filter of Figure 9.2 reads:

a. From the referring site URL, extract from the campaign term (the prev parameter in the URL) the string that contains /images? followed by zero or more of any character, followed by a p or a q, followed by = and anything up to the next & character.

b. Overwrite the campaign term with the extracted contents from = to &.

Once this is implemented, you will see images.google (organic) show up in your search engine reports for visitors who use the Google Image search. Clicking its link will display the keywords used, as shown in Figure 9.3.

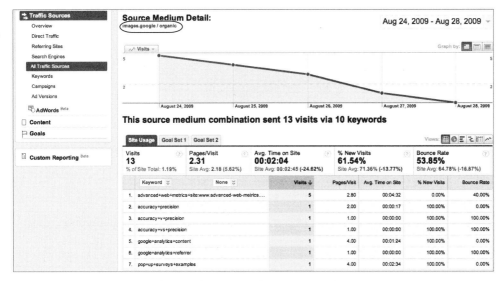

Figure 9.3 Keywords used by visitors from Google's Image search

Labeling Visitors, Sessions, and Pages

Labeling is first described in Chapter 8, "Best-Practices Configuration Guide," where it is used in conjunction with a filter to remove visitors with dynamic IP addresses (refer to the "Five Common Profile Filters" section). In that scenario we used the function _setVar() to label a visitor for the lifetime of their Google Analytics cookie—that is, permanent unless the visitor removes it. We chose this method because the label can be filtered later. However, in October 2009, the method for labeling visitors changed considerably. Although the original method (using _setVar) will still work, the new Custom Variables feature supersedes this and is the preferred technique.

Using the legacy function _setVar(), a label can be applied only at the visitor level. The power of Custom Variables is that in addition to the visitor level, you can also label sessions (with the label lasting for the duration of the current visit) and pages and even define multiple instances of all three. This means you can now use visitor labeling in many more circumstances.

To understand the potential of Custom Variables consider the following example: A publisher, a newspaper website, wishes to know which section of its site is most popular: Sports, Music, or Current Affairs. In addition, the publisher wants to know how visitors interact with various types of call to actions during their visit—do they click an ad, rate or comment on an article, and so on? Lastly, for all of the above, is the visitor a paying subscriber or an anonymous visitor?

This example demonstrates the three levels of interaction (hierarchies) for using custom variables: page, session, and visitor labels. These are known as the variable *scope* and are illustrated schematically in Figure 9.4.

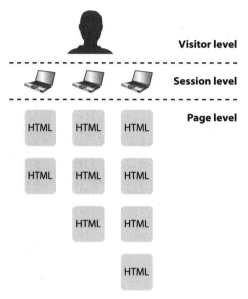

Visitor level

Session level

Page level

Figure 9.4 The use of scope when defining multiple custom variables

Understanding scope is important, because each custom variable is restricted to one particular scope level. From Figure 9.4, you can see that the custom variable set at the visitor level has only one value for that visitor. Set at the session level, it can have three values, because there are three sessions in this example. At the page level, each page can have its own associated custom variable—nine in total in this case. Table 9.1 illustrates how custom variables work, dependent on their scope.

 Note: I use the terms *custom variable* and *custom label* interchangeably. The correct terminology from Google Analytics is *custom variable*. However, I find the term *custom label* is easier to understand and convey to a stakeholder audience, especially when lots of other variables are being discussed.

▶ **Table 9.1** Custom variables by scope

Level	Duration	When Sharing a Slot with Other Custom Variables	Number Allowed
Page level	A single pageview, event, or transaction call.	The last page-level variable to be called on a page is the one applied to that page.	For any web property (collection of pages), many unique page-level variables can be set and slots can be reused, limited only by the number of hits in a given session. For any single page, you can set up to five simultaneous custom variables.

Level	Duration	When Sharing a Slot with Other Custom Variables	Number Allowed
Session level	The visit session of the visitor.	The last session-level variable called in a session is the one used for that session. For example: If login=false for slot #1 at the beginning of the session and login=true for slot #1 later on, the session is set to true for login. Overrides any previously set page-level variable called *in the same session*. For example: If slot #1 is first used for category=sports and then for login=true for a session, category=sports is ignored.	For any web property you can create as many distinct session-level custom variables as can be defined—up to the 50,000 unique aggregate table limit that exists in Google Analytics today. For any given user session, you can set up to five session-level variables.
Visitor level	The life of the visitor cookie. When set, applies to all visits onward (but not to previous visits or the current visit).	The last visitor-level variable set for a visitor is the one applied to the visitor. Overrides previously set custom variable types called *in the same session*.	For any web property, you can create up to five distinct visitor-level variables.

Note: The maximum combined length of the strings used for the name-value parameters must not exceed 64 bytes each. For Latin character sets this limit corresponds to 64 characters but will be reduced for double-byte character sets, that is, Chinese, Japanese, and Korean.

By defining your labels and scopes appropriately, all of these metrics can be viewed at a glance within your Visitors > Custom Variables report. An example is shown in Figure 9.5, which is taken from this book's website. In this case, a page-level custom variable is used to differentiate the two types of pages on the website—blog articles and regular content pages. Every page on the site has a page-level custom variable defined. As you can see, blog articles are much more popular in terms of visits than other content pages.

Of course, if the entire website content was nicely grouped in directories such as /pages and /blog, then it would be straightforward to view this information in your Content > Top Content report. However, that is rarely in the case for any website. In this example, pages are hosted in the root directory and various other subdirectories (and even sub-subdirectories), making it impossible to group content by its directory hierarchy. The use of page-level custom variables enables this.

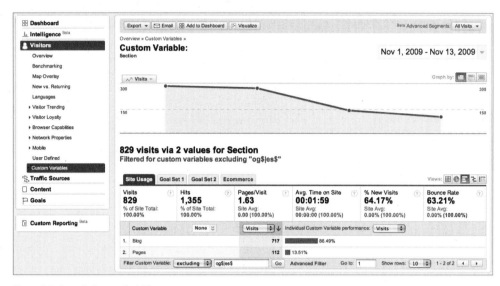

Figure 9.5 Example Custom Variables report

Implementing Custom Variables

You can add a custom label by using the function _setCustomVar() within the page where the label is applied, as shown in the following example,

    _setCustomVar(index, name, value, optional_scope)

where the parameters are defined as follows:

index The slot for the custom variable. This is a number whose value can range from 1 to 5, inclusive. A custom variable should be placed in one slot only and not be reused across different slots. The purpose is to allow multiple variables for the same scope.

name The name for the custom variable. This is a string that identifies the custom variable and appears in your top-level Custom Variables report, for example, "Section name", "Membership type", "Gender", and so on.

value The value for the custom variable. This is a string that is paired with a name. You can pair a number of values with a custom variable name. For example, for name=Section, values could be "Sports", "Music", or "Current Affairs".

optional_scope The scope defines the level of user engagement with your site. Available values are 1 (visitor level), 2 (session level), or 3 (page level). When left undefined, the custom variable scope defaults to page-level interaction.

Importantly, you must place _setCustomVar() before the pageTracker._ trackPageview() call of your GATC so that it gets delivered in the GIF request sent by _trackPageview(). The following defines a page-level custom variable with the name "Section" and a value of "Sports Pages" and is assigned to index=1:

```
<script type="text/javascript">
    var gaJsHost = (("https:" == document.location.protocol) ? "https://ssl." ↵
  : "http://www.");
    document.write(unescape("%3Cscript src='" + gaJsHost + "google-↵
analytics.com/ga.js' type='text/javascript'%3E%3C/script%3E"));
</script>
<script type="text/javascript">
try{
    var pageTracker = _gat._getTracker("UA-12345-1");
    pageTracker._setCustomVar(1, "Section", "Sports Pages", 3);


    pageTracker._trackPageView();
    }catch(err) {}</script>
```

This works when you know the value of the custom variable in advance. That is, it does not depend on a visitor's action such as onClick or onSubmit. If visitor action is required to set your custom variable, separate your GATC so that _setCustomVar() is called within your HTML *before* _trackPageview() (or _trackEvent()), for example:

```
<script type="text/javascript">
    var gaJsHost = (("https:" == document.location.protocol) ? "https://ssl." ↵
  : "http://www.");
    document.write(unescape("%3Cscript src='" + gaJsHost + "google-↵
analytics.com/ga.js' type='text/javascript'%3E%3C/script%3E"));
</script>

<body>
  .
  .
<a href="rate_track.php;" onclick="pageTracker._setCustomVar(3,'Engagement', ↵
'Contributor',2);"
  .
  .
<script type="text/javascript">
```

```
try{
    var pageTracker = _gat._getTracker("UA-12345-1");
    pageTracker._setCustomVar(1, "Section", "Music Pages", 3);
    pageTracker._setCustomVar(2, "Sub-Section", "Mowtown", 3);
    pageTracker._trackPageview();
}catch(err) {}</script>
</body>
```

In this example, a session-level custom variable is defined with the name "Engagement" and a value of "Contributor" and is assigned to index=3. In addition, two simultaneous page-level custom variables are assigned. For any single page, you can track up to five custom variables, each with a separate slot. This means that you could assign two additional custom variables on this same page.

 Note: Once you have set up custom variables, you can use the _deleteCustomVar(index) method to remove your custom variables.

The value placed in the name or value parameter can be any label you wish, though you should use only alphanumeric characters (as well as the space character) to avoid any potential encoding issues. The value you set will be displayed in the Visitors > Custom Variables report and can be cross-segmented as per other metrics.

Tracking Error Pages and Broken Links

With an out-of-the-box install of Google Analytics, you will not be tracking error pages or broken links on your website. This is because by default you probably have not added the GATC to your error pages. After all, how can you track a page that does not exist? To enable this, you need to add the GATC to the error-page templates that are delivered by your web server. A webmaster will typically do this. The GATC will then track your error-page URLs as if they were any other pageview request. That is the caveat: Without modification, error pages are reported as regular pages, not as errors, making them difficult to detect in your reports! You can highlight and separate error pages by modifying the GATC on your error page templates as follows.

Typically, a web server allows you to define a template for each error status code. For example, to track missing pages on your site, modify the standard GATC on your 404 template page as shown here:

```
<script type="text/javascript">
    var gaJsHost = (("https:" == document.location.protocol) ? "https://ssl." ↩
: "http://www.");
    document.write(unescape("%3Cscript src='" + gaJsHost + "google-↩
analytics.com/ga.js' type='text/javascript'%3E%3C/script%3E"));
```

```
</script>
<script type="text/javascript">
try{
    var pageTracker = _gat._getTracker("UA-12345-1");
    pageTracker._trackPageview("/error 404/" +document.location.pathname);
}catch(err) {}</script>
```

This is an example of the virtual pageview technique as discussed in Chapter 7, "Advanced Implementation." It allows you to create the virtual directory /error 404/ and the full path to the error page filename (URI). You modify other error templates in a similar way:

```
pageTracker._trackPageview("/error 500/" +document.location.pathname);
```

Web Server Status Codes

These are the status codes, defined in the HTTP 1.0 specification, returned by your web server in its headers (see www.w3.org/Protocols/Overview.html).

2xx Success

The requested action was successfully received and understood:

- 200 OK
- 201 Created
- 202 Accepted
- 203 Provisional Information
- 204 No Response
- 205 Deleted
- 206 Modified

3xx Redirection

Further action must be taken in order to complete the request:

- 301 Moved Permanently
- 302 Moved Temporarily
- 303 Method
- 304 Not Modified

Continues

Web Server Status Codes *(Continued)*

4xx Client Error

The request contains bad syntax or is inherently impossible to fulfill:

- 400 Bad Request
- 401 Unauthorized
- 402 Payment Required
- 403 Forbidden
- 404 Not Found
- 405 Method Not Allowed
- 406 None Acceptable
- 407 Proxy Authentication Required
- 408 Request Timeout

5xx Server Error

The server could not fulfill the request:

- 500 Internal Server Error
- 501 Not Implemented
- 502 Bad Gateway
- 503 Service Unavailable
- 504 Gateway Timeout

Using this technique enables you to differentiate error pages from other pageviews within your Google Analytics reports. Resultant entries for error pages will show in your Content > Top Content report as, for example, /error 404/noexisting-page.htm. This provides you with two very important pieces of information: the type of error (error code) and the URL of the page that produced this.

Figure 9.6 shows an example Top Content report for the error pages. Note that the report uses the table filter to highlight these, that is, bubble them up to the top of the report table. This is important, because error pages are usually buried at the bottom of your pageview listings—assuming they are a small fraction of the total!

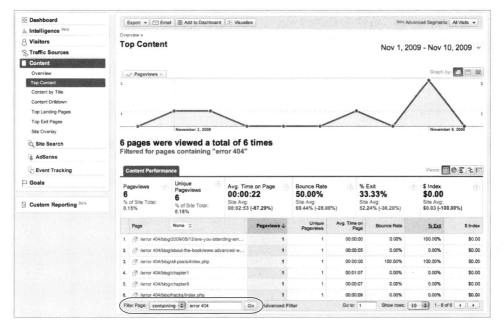

Figure 9.6 Viewing error pages

Of course, once you have identified error pages, you will want to know which links within your website point to these pages, that is, identify broken links. From the report shown in Figure 9.6, click any of the listed error pages to get the detail for that specific page (Figure 9.7), and then select Navigational Summary. The result is a list of pages that your visitors were on just prior to clicking through and receiving the error page, as shown in Figure 9.8.

What if you cannot use a different GATC in your error templates? Some host providers and even large corporations can be stuck in a one-size-fits-all control panel or content management system, where it is not possible (or too difficult) to have a different GATC on their error templates. If this describes your scenario, it may still be possible to track your error pages, so long as the error page title contains a hint that it is actually an error page being displayed. Most Apache configurations do this by default, as shown in Figure 9.9.

Figure 9.7 Specific page detail from the Top Content report

Figure 9.8 Pages leading to the error page

Because the error page template displays its error code in the HTML `<title>` tag, you can apply a filter to differentiate these from other pageviews in your reports, as shown in Figure 9.10.

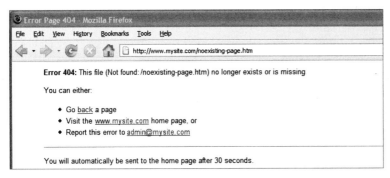

Figure 9.9 Typical 404 "not found" error page returned from the Apache web server

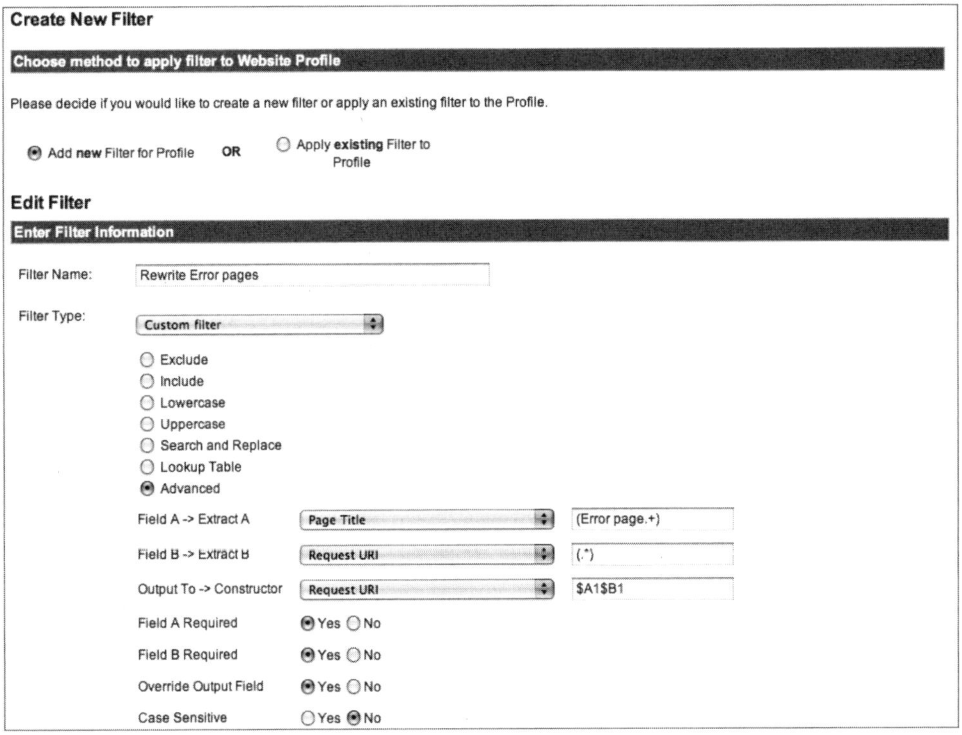

Create New Filter

Choose method to apply filter to Website Profile

Please decide if you would like to create a new filter or apply an existing filter to the Profile.

○ Add **new** Filter for Profile   **OR**   ○ Apply **existing** Filter to Profile

Edit Filter

Enter Filter Information

Filter Name: Rewrite Error pages

Filter Type: | Custom filter ▾ |

○ Exclude
○ Include
○ Lowercase
○ Uppercase
○ Search and Replace
○ Lookup Table
◉ Advanced

Field A -> Extract A | Page Title ▾ | (Error page.+)

Field B -> Extract B | Request URI ▾ | (.*)

Output To -> Constructor | Request URI ▾ | $A1$B1

Field A Required   ◉ Yes ○ No

Field B Required   ◉ Yes ○ No

Override Output Field   ◉ Yes ○ No

Case Sensitive   ○ Yes ◉ No

Figure 9.10 Filter to highlight error pages

In plain English, the filter is described as follows:

- Check whether the page title contains the phrase "Error page." If so, extract the page title and the page URI entries.

- Combine the page title and page URI entries and overwrite the original page URI field.

 Note: The section "Tracking Pay-Per-Click Search Terms and Bid Terms" from the first edition of the book is now deprecated. The new AdWords reporting section contains this information by default. See Chapter 5, "Reports Explained."

Tracking Referral URLs from Pay-Per-Click Networks

As well as displaying ads on their own search properties, pay-per-click networks often partner with other websites to display their advertisements, sharing revenue from resultant ad click-throughs with the partner. An example is the relationship between Google and Ask.com. Ask.com is an independent search engine with its own search technology for displaying organic search results (known as Teoma). However, for paid search, Ask.com partners with Google AdWords. If you advertise on AdWords, then your advertisement will also appear on the Ask.com website. In this way, pay-per-click partner networks are a great additional distribution channel for your advertisement, enabling you to reach a wider audience.

 Note: AdWords has a search network opt-out feature that enables you to advertise only on Google web properties if desired.

By default, reports in Google Analytics group all pay-per-click partner click-throughs for AdWords as google / cpc. For example, you will not see pay-per-click visitors who originate from Ask.com labeled as such—just google / cpc, as shown in Figure 9.11. The same is also true for other pay-per-click networks such as Bing and Yahoo!, which distribute their ads to AltaVista, Lycos, HotBot, A9, and others.

In addition, if your AdWords strategy spans more than one geography, for example, google.se and google.com, Google Analytics groups all such click-throughs as google/cpc.

Being able to view which partner site, or which specific Google domain, your AdWords visitors come from can help you optimize your advertising approach. If this level of detail is important to you, use two cascading filters (one applied after the other), to show more fully where your pay-per-click visitors are originating from, as shown in Figure 9.12.

In plain English, Figure 9.12 reads as follows:

a. For every pageview, where the medium is defined as cpc or ppc, extract the Referral domain, omitting the http:// text and anything after the next slash (/). Copy the contents of this match to Custom Field 1.

b. Append the referring domain to the Campaign Source variable and overwrite it.

Figure 9.11 Different paid networks

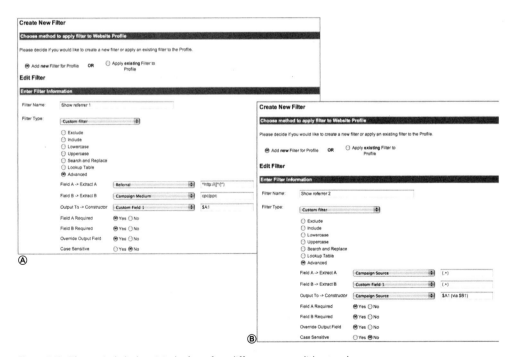

Figure 9.12 Filters to include the original referrer from different pay-per-click networks

Combining Pageview Fields with Session Fields

There is a slight caveat when working with the filters described in Figure 9.12: They combine a per-pageview field (Referral) with a per-session field (Campaign Source). A pageview field is populated with every pageview recorded by Google Analytics, whereas a session field is set and maintained throughout a visitor's time on the site.

For example, each time a pageview is viewed, the page title, URL, and referral are updated to match the current page, but the session fields (returning visitor versus new visitor indicator, or campaign name, for example) are the same regardless of the page currently being viewed. Referral is a pageview field, in that each pageview will have its own unique referral, whereas Campaign Source will have the same value across the entire session.

Because cookies can be altered during a session, for example, visitors can remove them or firewalls can restrict them, it is possible that applying an additional profile filter may alter a session field within a visitor's session. This can cause a data misalignment, potentially resulting in an unpredicted data value showing in the reports. This is rare, but it occasionally happens.

Notice that both filters A and B must be executed in order for the filter to work. The result is a report that lists both the original referral and the Google Analytics–defined campaign source, as shown in Figure 9.13.

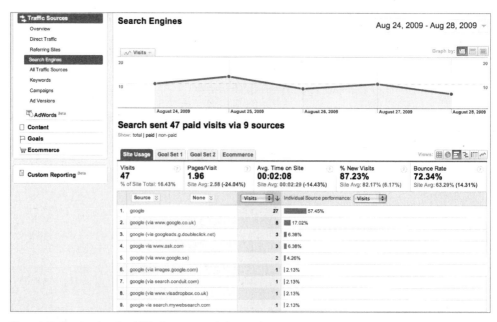

Figure 9.13 Showing the referral URLs from pay-per-click networks

As you can see, the structure of the report in Figure 9.13 is a referral source list of the form *ppc network source, (via referring website)*. The report shows visitors from the Google AdWords partner network, including ask.com, images.google.com, conduit.com, visadropbox.co.uk, and mywebsearch.com. Without these filters in place, the level of detail is limited to a single aggregate entry of google.

Search Engine Relationships

The relationships among search engines (paid and nonpaid), directories, and portals are quite complex—as the chart illustrates. To understand the relationship chart, try viewing only Google's relationships; Google provides organic search results for AOL and Netscape. AdWords results are displayed on AOL, Netscape, Ask.com, and many portal sites (via AdSense); Google receives directory results from DMOZ. The other search engines have similar multiple relationships.

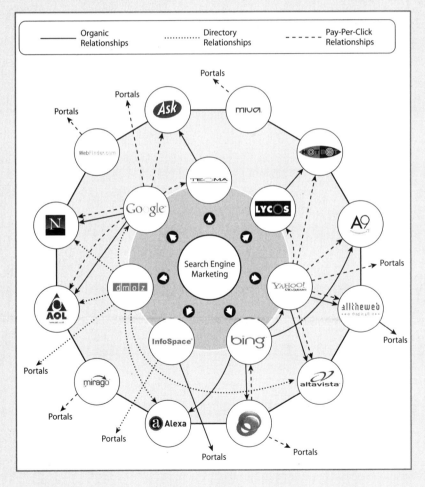

A color-coded, interactive version is available at www.advanced-web-metrics.com/ search-relationship-chart.

Site Overlay: Differentiating Links to the Same Page

Site overlay is an excellent way to visualize what links your visitors are clicking and which ones have the most value—that is, drive conversions. However, by default, if you have numerous links on a page all pointing to the same destination URL, the same metrics are shown for each link in the Site Overlay report. That is, you are unable to differentiate different links to the same URL. This can happen, for example, if you have an image link, a menu link, and a content link on a category page, all pointing to productA.html.

An example of this is shown in Figure 9.14, which shows a business directory portal with five links highlighted. All five point to the same URL—the Add form for creating a new business listing. Because these are all identical URLs, the site overlay report for these links will show identical metrics. However, by modifying each URL slightly with a different query parameter, we can differentiate these links. For example, here they are in numerical order:

```
http://www.mysite.com/product.htm?linkid=topMenu
http://www.mysite.com/product.htm?linkid=titleBox
http://www.mysite.com/product.htm?linkid=content
http://www.mysite.com/product.htm?linkid=listBottom
http://www.mysite.com/product.htm?linkid=bottomMenu
```

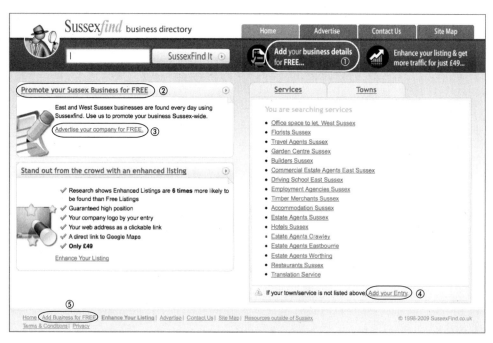

Figure 9.14 Business portal site with five identical link URLs

With this method, your Site Overlay report will be able to clarify whether a text link has more of an impact than an image link or menu link to the same page, as per Figure 9.15.

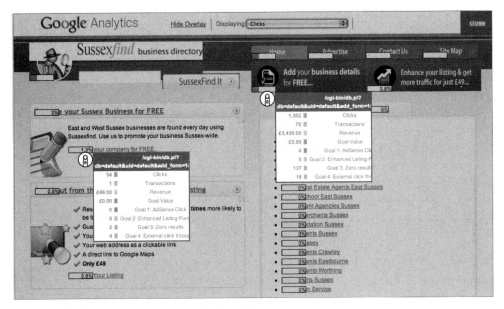

Figure 9.15 Site Overlay report with identical links differentiated

Bear in mind that when applying this method and viewing other reports, such as the Top Content report, you will need to sum the pageview data for these links to determine the page total—that is, aggregate the index.php pageviews as shown in Figure 9.16.

Figure 9.16 Result of adding query parameters to differentiate links to the same page

If the links you wish to differentiate already contain query parameters, simply append your differentiator as follows, for example:

```
http://www.mysite.com/product.php?id=101&linkid=topMenu
```

Matching Specific Transactions to Specific Referral Data

As discussed in Chapters 1 and 2 ("Why Understanding Your Web Traffic Is Important to Your Business" and "Available Methodologies and Their Accuracy"), web analytics is about identifying trends, so you shouldn't get hung up on precise numbers. Understand the strength and accuracy limitations of your data and get comfortable with it. For Google Analytics, Google's strong stance on privacy means that individuals are not tracked and all data is reported at the aggregate level.

However, for e-commerce transactions, e-commerce and marketing managers usually desire a little more detail. Without identifying individuals, the following hack enables you to view your transaction list and identify which referrer source, medium, and keywords were used by the purchaser to find your website in the first place.

Note: This technique was originally discussed in an article by Shawn Purtell from ROI Revolution (www.roirevolution.com/blog/2007/05/matching_specific_transactions_to_specific_keyword.html) and is reproduced here with permission.

The hack works by cascading three advanced filters as follows:

Filter 1 Figure 9.17 shows the first filter, which grabs the campaign source and medium of a visit and places this in a custom field.

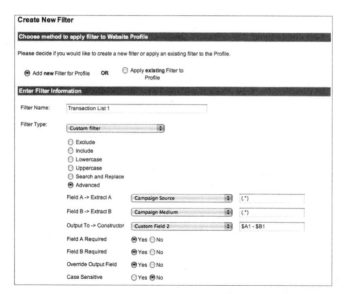

Figure 9.17 Capturing the campaign source and medium and storing these in a custom field

Filter 2 Figure 9.18 shows the second filter, which adds the keyword to the custom field. The custom field then contains the referrer source, medium, and keyword.

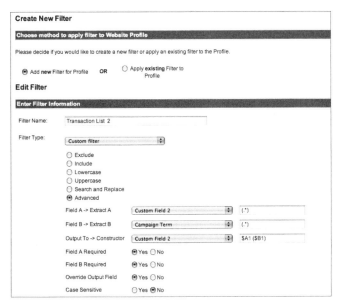

Figure 9.18 Appending the referral keyword to the custom field

Filter 3 Figure 9.19 shows the third and final filter, which takes the custom field created and appends it to the transaction order ID. This matches sources with specific transactions.

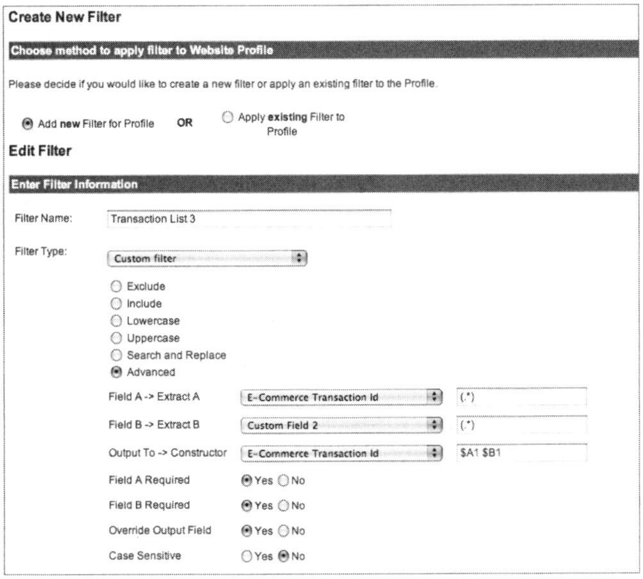

Figure 9.19 Appending the custom field information to the transaction ID

Of course, the order of the filters is important, and these should be maintained as described. When done correctly, the cumulative result is an Ecommerce > Transactions report that is transformed from just showing the list of transaction IDs to including details of the referring source, medium, and keyword, as shown in Figure 9.20. The format is:

```
Transaction-ID referral source - medium (keywords)
```

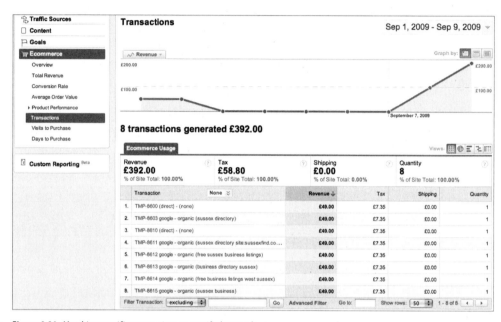

Figure 9.20 Matching specific transactions to specific keywords

Tracking Links to Direct Downloads

What if your campaigns send visitors directly to a file that does not accept the GATC JavaScript page tag? This can be the case with email marketing or other specialized types of campaigns whereby visitors are referred directly to a PDF, EXE, ZIP, DOC, XLS, or PPT download—or any other file type that is not a website landing page. Without the GATC in place, Google Analytics will not detect a visitor from such a campaign. However, you can address this challenge by creating an intermediate landing page to capture the campaign variables *before* forwarding the visitor to the actual file download.

Figure 9.21 shows an example intermediate landing page generated by a link from an email message that points to the following URL:

```
www.mysite.com/forwarder.php?file=catalogue.pdf&utm_source=sales&utm_campaign=
first-followup&utm_medium=email
```

Figure 9.21 Example use of an intermediate landing page for file downloads

As you can see, the URL contains a list of parameters that includes the filename to be downloaded (catalogue.pdf) and Google Analytics campaign parameters, as discussed in Chapter 7. Table 9.2 describes the individual elements.

▶ **Table 9.2** URL breakdown for Figure 9.21

Element	Description
forwarder.php	Name of the page that will redirect the visitor to the correct file
catalogue.pdf	Name of the file requested by the visitor
utm_source	Campaign source identifier
utm_medium	Campaign medium identifier
utm_campaign	Campaign name identifier

In this example, the forwarding page, forwarder.php, contains your GATC with the following code in the HTML <head> section tag:

```
<script type="text/javascript">
    var filename=("<? echo $_GET['file']; ?>") ? ↵
     "<? echo $_GET['file']; ?>" : "";
    var source=("<? echo $_GET['utm_source']; ?>") ? ↵
     "<? echo $_GET['utm_source']; ?>" : "";
    var medium=("<? echo $_GET['utm_medium']; ?>") ? ↵
     "<? echo $_GET['utm_medium']; ?>" : "";
    var campaign=("<? echo $ GET['utm_campaign']; ?>") ? ↵
     "<? echo $_GET['utm_campaign']; ?>" : "";
    window.onload = trackFile();

    function trackFile(){
        if (filename) {
            track = "/downloads/direct/" +filename+ "?utm_source="↵
             +source+ "&utm_medium="+medium+ "&utm_campaign=" +campaign;
            pageTracker._trackPageview(track);
```

```
        window.location = "http://" +document.domain +"/"+ filename
    }else{
        alert('No download file specified');
    }
  }

</script>
```

The purpose of the script is to immediately redirect the visitor to the speci-fied download file using window.location. However, before doing so, it sets a virtual pageview for Google Analytics to track and report on and also appends campaign vari-ables, captured from the landing page URL. No other content is required for this page, although as Figure 9.21 shows, also providing the option of a download link is good practice in case the redirect fails.

The beauty of this method is that you can view each file download as a pageview in your Google Analytics reports with the referral campaign, medium, and source cor-rectly attributed to the referring campaign. See Figure 9.22.

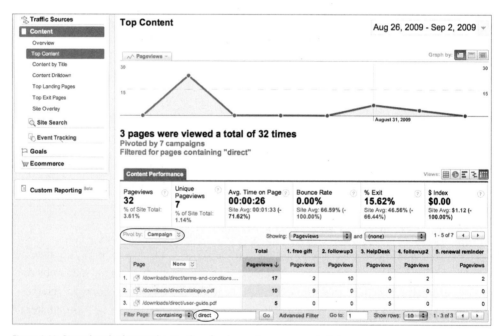

Figure 9.22 Direct download report showing the referral campaign name as a pivot view

In addition, forwarder.php will be listed with all the aggregate referral informa-tion; however, you might want to remove this page from your reports with an exclude filter to prevent double counting, because it is effectively a non-page.

> **Note:** Although PHP is used in the example, the technique is equally applicable for any server-side web-scripting language you might use, such as ASP, .NET, CGI-Perl, Python, and so on. It is also easy to modify for tracking downloads as events. Essentially, you modify the line
>
> ```
> pageTracker._trackPageview(track);
> ```
>
> to something similar to the following example:
>
> ```
> pageTracker._trackEvent('File downloads', source, filename);
> ```
>
> See Chapter 7 for details on event tracking.

Changing the Referrer Credited for a Goal Conversion

Defining goals for your website is discussed in Chapter 7. By default, Google Analytics gives credit for a conversion to the last referrer a visitor used. For example, consider the following search scenario for a user who visits your website by way of a different referrer each time:

- Google organic search—visitor leaves your website (referrer 1).
- Google paid search—visitor leaves your website (referrer 2).
- Email follow-up—visitor converts (referrer 3).

All visit referrals are tracked, with credit for the conversion given to referrer 3. This is the case except when the last referrer is direct—that is, the visitor uses their bookmark or types your URL directly into their browser address bar, for example:

- Google organic search—visitor leaves your website (referrer 1).
- Google paid search—visitor leaves your website (referrer 2).
- Email follow-up—visitor leaves your website (referrer 3).
- Direct (bookmark)—visitor converts (referrer 4).

Credit for the conversion is still given to referrer 3. That makes sense, because it is most likely referrer 3 that led to the bookmarking (or remembering) of your website address. In the next section, you'll see what you can do if viewing the previous referrer is more important to your conversions, and you want to see this in your reports instead of the last referrer.

Capturing the Previous Referrer for a Conversion

For tagged landing page URLs only (that is, not organic landing pages), you can change the referrer given credit for a conversion to the previous referrer by appending your landing page URLs with the utm_nooveride=1 parameter.

When Google Analytics detects the utm_nooverride=1 parameter, it retains the previous referrer campaign information. That is, only if there are no existing campaign variables will new ones be written. The key here is to be consistent, that is, all landing page URLs having utm_nooveride=1. Otherwise, you create a confused report that is impossible to decipher.

Consider, for example, an online marketing campaign using AdWords to drive visitors to your site, where the call to action is an email subscription. You then follow up by emailing your newsletter to new subscribers. In this scenario, you will probably want to maintain the original AdWords campaign details about how visitors came to subscribe in the first place and have these associated with any future activity. If you make no changes, future activity, including conversions and transactions, will be credited to the last campaign—in this case, your email follow-up.

To override this behavior and prevent your email marketing from overwriting the previous campaign details, append your landing page URLs within your email message with the utm_nooveride=1 parameter, for example:

```
http://www.mysite.com/product1.php?utm_source=sales&utm_campaign=
first-followup&utm_medium=email&utm_nooverride=1
```

The manual tagging of landing page URLs for email is discussed in the section "Campaign Tracking," in Chapter 7.

For your AdWords landing pages (for which auto-tagging is enabled), you also need to append the utm_nooveride=1 parameter to your landing pages as follows:

- Example AdWords landing page URL for a static web page with auto-tagging on:

  ```
  http://www.mysite.com/product1.php?utm_nooverride=1
  ```

- Example AdWords landing page URL for a dynamic web page with auto-tagging on:

  ```
  http://www.mysite.com/product.php?id=101&lang=en&utm_nooverride=1
  ```

 Note: If you are using a third-party ad-tracking system with your AdWords campaigns, read "Testing after Enabling Auto-tagging," in Chapter 6, "Getting Up and Running with Google Analytics."

By this method, if your email recipient has not previously been associated with any other online marketing activity, then they will be correctly reported as coming from your email marketing should they click through on a link to your website. Otherwise, the original referral details (initial AdWords campaign in this example) will be maintained. Further click-throughs from these AdWords campaigns will not overwrite the initial campaign information.

Capturing the First and Last Referrer of a Visitor

The previous section describes overriding which referrer is given credit for a conversion—from the last referrer (default) to the previous referrer. The hack in this section is an extension of that by capturing both the first *and* last referrer together. Also, an important difference is that this method works whether a conversion takes place or not and captures all referrers, including organic visitors—not just those that result from tagged landing pages. The caveat is that it requires a little more work. First you have to modify your GATC, and then you apply an advanced filter:

1. To capture and store the first referrer, modify your GATC on all pages, as follows:

```
<script type="text/javascript">
    var gaJsHost = (("https:" == document.location.protocol) ? "https://↵
ssl." : "http://www.");
    document.write(unescape("%3Cscript src='" + gaJsHost + "google-↵
analytics.com/ga.js' type='text/javascript'%3E%3C/script%3E"));

function _uGC(l,n,s) {
    // used to obtain a value form a string of key=value pairs
    if (!l || l=="" || !n || n=="" || !s || s=="") return "-";
    var i,i2,i3,c="-";
    i=l.indexOf(n);
    i3=n.indexOf("=")+1;
    if (i > -1) {
        i2=l.indexOf(s,i); if (i2 < 0) { i2=l.length; }
        c=l.substring((i+i3),i2);
    }
    return c;
}

function checkFirst(){
    // check if this is a first time visitor and if so, set flag
    newVisitor = 0;
    var myCookie = " " + document.cookie + ";";
    var searchName = "__utma=";
    var startOfCookie = myCookie.indexOf(searchName)
    if (startOfCookie == -1) {    // i.e. first time visitor
        newVisitor = 1;
    }
}
```

```
function grabReferrer(){
    // if first visit, grab utmz cookie values and put in utmv
    if (newVisitor) {
        var z = _uGC(document.cookie, "__utmz=", ";");
        urchin_source = _uGC(z,"utmcsr=", "|");
        urchin_medium = _uGC(z,"utmcmd=", "|");
        urchin_term = _uGC(z,"utmctr=", "|");
        urchin_content = _uGC(z,"utmcct=", "|");
        urchin_campaign = _uGC(z,"utmccn=", "|");
        var gclid = _uGC(z,"utmgclid=","|");
        if (gclid) {
            urchin_source = "google";
            urchin_medium = "cpc";
        }
        if (urchin_term != "-"){
            term = urchin_term.replace(/%27/g, "'");        //decode
            term = urchin_term.replace(/%22/g, "'");        //decode
            term = urchin_term.replace(/\+/g, " ");         //decode
            pageTracker._setVar(term);
        }
    }
}
try{
    var pageTracker = _gat._getTracker("UA-12345-1");
    checkFirst();
    pageTracker._trackPageview();
    grabReferrer();
}catch(err) {}</script>
```

Warning: This hack makes use of the Google Analytics _setVar() function that was first discussed in Chapter 8 in the section "Five Common Profile Filters." At the time of this writing, the general use of this function has been superseded by custom variables, described in "Labeling Visitors, Sessions, and Pages" earlier in this chapter. However, custom variables cannot be used in this hack because at present these are not available as filter fields. This should change in the not-too-distant future. If and when that happens, it should be straightforward to substitute custom variables for the use of _setVar().

The function checkFirst() checks whether this is a first-time visitor by looking for the presence of the _utma cookie. This is always set for a visitor, so its presence indicates a returning visitor. Hence it is called prior to _trackpageView, which sets cookies for the current visit. The function `grabReferrer()` is called if this is a first-time visitor and, if so, grabs all the current referral information and stores these as local variables. The last line of this function stores the keyword term, if it exists, as a visitor label by calling `_setVar()`.

Notice that in the function `grabReferrer()`, only the campaign term (the keyword) is stored as a visitor label. However, you can store any of the campaign variables listed, or combinations of them, by modifying the `_setVar()` line accordingly.

2. Use the advanced filter as per Figure 9.23.

When you implement this filter, you will see the first and last referral keywords displayed in your Keywords reports, as shown in Figure 9.24, that is, `last_keywords_used, first = first_keywords_used`.

Note: The advanced segment "Returning Visitors" has been selected in Figure 9.24. This makes sense because first-time visitors, that is, new visitors, will also be labeled in the same way by the JavaScript code, even though they have visited your site only once. Hence, new visitors are not relevant for this analysis.

Create New Filter

Choose method to apply filter to Website Profile

Please decide if you would like to create a new filter or apply an existing filter to the Profile.

◉ Add **new** Filter for Profile   **OR**   ○ Apply **existing** Filter to Profile

Enter Filter Information

Filter Name: `Append first search term used`

Filter Type: `Custom filter` ▼

     ○ Exclude
     ○ Include
     ○ Lowercase
     ○ Uppercase
     ○ Search and Replace
     ○ Lookup Table
     ◉ Advanced

Field A -> Extract A	`Campaign Term` ▼	`(.*)`
Field B -> Extract B	`User Defined` ▼	`(.*)`
Output To -> Constructor	`Campaign Term` ▼	`$A1, first = $B1`
Field A Required	◉ Yes ○ No	
Field B Required	◉ Yes ○ No	
Override Output Field	◉ Yes ○ No	
Case Sensitive	○ Yes ◉ No	

Figure 9.23 Advanced filter to combine the first and last referrer

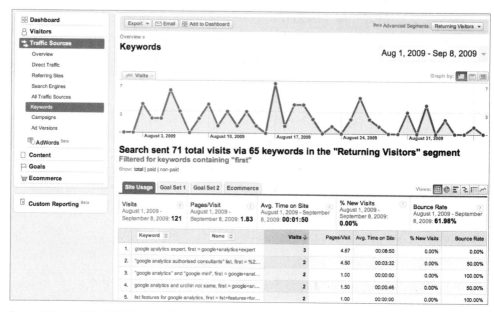

Figure 9.24 A modified Traffic Sources > Keywords report showing first and last search engine keywords used

Note: A slight quirk of Google Analytics at present is that the value of the User Defined variable, as saved by the `_setVar` function, remains encoded in the reports. This results in + and %27 characters showing in the data tables, representing space and single-quote marks, respectively. The JavaScript presented in the "Capturing the First and Last Referrer" hack decodes the most common encoded characters found. However, you may see others in your reports. If so, and you wish to remove them, append more decode lines as required.

Because the Keywords report now has many more characters per row, it is better to export the data in order to analyze relationships. Table 9.3 is an export of data from Figure 9.24 to highlight interesting combinations:

▶ **Table 9.3** Keyword export from Figure 9.24 highlighting first and last search engine keyword combinations for returning visitors

Last Search Term	First Search Term
"google analytics" and "google mini"	google analytics security concerns
michael clifton google analytics	michael clifton google
acquisition filters google analytics	technical google analytics course
buy urchin5	download urchin 5
google analytics course	google analytics training london

Table 9.3 highlights some interesting combinations. For example:

- The connection between security concerns and two Google products.
- Is there a Michael Clifton who specializes in Google Analytics?
- The connection that Google Analytics technical courses should focus on specialized filters.
- The connection between downloading Urchin and buying it.
- The interchangeable use of "training" and "course" by visitors.

The caveat here is that the number of visitors is very low for this sample set of data. For a more meaningful analysis, look for combinations that represent a significant proportion of your total search engine visitor volume—though by its nature, this analysis is very "long tail"–like.

To view a list of only the first keywords, use the Visitors > User Defined report.

Tip: If you want to maintain your keyword reports in their original state, you could place the `last_keywords_used, first = first_keywords_used` information in the User Defined report instead. Simply change the Output To constructor of Figure 9.23 to User Defined so that it overwrites the User Defined field rather than the Campaign Term field.

Roll-up Reporting

Roll-up reporting was initially discussed in Chapter 6. In summary, roll-up reporting answers a very specific requirement of enterprise clients, that is, autonomous offices or departments that wish to manage their own reporting needs (typically for region-specific domains—the United States, Europe, Asia, and so on) separately from HQ, which requires a bigger picture of all activity.

The principle to achieving this is to add multiple GATCs to your pages—more accurately described as adding a second tracker object. In this way, each autonomous office logs into its own stand-alone Google Analytics account, while HQ logs into a "catch-all" Google Analytics roll-up account. Each manages its own reporting needs without impacting the other. However, there are a number of caveats with this method, and these more-advanced issues are highlighted here. First, though, review the initial details of the section "Roll-up Reporting" in Chapter 6 before proceeding.

Tracking Roll-up Transactions

If yours is a transactional site, special consideration is required for e-commerce because you will need to call the e-commerce tracking code for each account—once for your stand-alone account and once for your roll-up account. So _addTrans, _addItem, and _trackTrans are required for both firstTracker and secondTracker objects. Schematically you need to add the following to your transaction receipt or confirmation page (see Chapter 7 for help with e-commerce tracking):

```
firstTracker._addTrans(enter transaction values as array);
firstTracker._addItem(enter item values as an array);
firstTracker._trackTrans();


secondTracker._addTrans(enter transaction values as array);
secondTracker._addItem(enter item values as an array);
secondTracker._trackTrans();
```

And that's it except for the following implications.

Implications of the Roll-up Technique

The following implications sound daunting at first, but in many cases they are not. Apart from unifying your e-commerce data (the second item that follows), you probably will not drill down deep enough in a roll-up report for these implications to be noticed. However, you should be aware of them.

Pageview aggregation Pageviews on your different websites that have the same page title or name (for example, index.htm, contact.htm) will be aggregated. That is, you will see only one entry in your roll-up report for index.htm and contact.htm, with the sum of their pageviews. Generally for roll-up reporting, this is not a problem because the account is used to get the bigger picture, or aggregate overview. However, if you still need the page name detail, apply the filter shown in Figure 7.13 of Chapter 7. This is the same filter for differentiating pageviews from subdomains.

Transactions in different currencies Similar to pageview aggregation, e-commerce data will be aggregated. That is, if you have transactions in different currencies, the revenue totals become meaningless at the aggregate roll-up level. Thus, dollars, pounds, Euros, and so on are all combined regardless of exchange rates. Therefore, for your roll-up account, unify your transaction data into a single base currency. This base currency should remain fixed so that long-term comparisons can be made—don't change this to reflect currency exchange rates.

Time zone alignment If your stand-alone accounts operate in different time zones, ignore time-of-day reports in the roll-up account. They won't make sense!

AdWords ROI in different currencies If you run AdWords accounts in different currencies for your stand-alone Google Analytics account, ignore the ROI and margin metrics from the Traffic Sources > AdWords reports. They won't make sense!

Cookie manipulation The roll-up reporting method results in cookies being shared between both your stand-alone and roll-up Google Analytics accounts. Therefore, any cookie manipulation on one—changing timeout values or expiry date, for example—results in changes impacting both sets of reports. This issue can arise, for example, if you have an agency collecting data for its own internal purposes (stand-alone account). They may wish to experiment, not realizing the wider impact. If this happens, a great deal of time and money can be wasted trying to troubleshoot data anomalies. Therefore, ensure that such changes are managed centrally. One option is to use the Custom tab of the GATC Wizard, as discussed in the section "Customizing the GATC" in Chapter 7.

Improvement Tip: Simplify with Pageview Roll-up

If you have dozens or even hundreds of product micro sites, you may wish to simplify your roll-up pageview reports even further. Rather than collecting detail of every page on each micro site into the roll-up account, "concertina" this into a per-site view. That is, roll up your pageviews.

In this way, instead of having pageA = 30 views, pageB = 20 views, pageC = 10 views, and so on, you would have pageview for www.mysite.co.uk = 60, www.mysite.com = 13, and so on. This simplifies the Top Content report, so that you see overall pageview volumes on a per-site basis. You can use the following GATC modification for simplifying pageview reports:

```
<script type="text/javascript">
    var gaJsHost = (("https:" == document.location.protocol) ? "https://ssl." ↵
: "http://www.");
    document.write(unescape("%3Cscript src='" + gaJsHost + "google-↵
analytics.com/ga.js' type='text/javascript'%3E%3C/script%3E"));
</script>

<script type="text/javascript">
try{
    var firstTracker = _gat._getTracker("UA-123456-1"); // for mysite.com
    firstTracker._trackPageview();
    var secondTracker = _gat._getTracker("UA-987654-1"); // for catch-all
    secondTracker._trackPageview(location.host);
</script>
```

Summary

In Chapter 9, you have learned the following:

Customizing the list of recognized search engines You have learned to add new and regional variations to the default search engine list so that you can differentiate visitors from, for example, google.com and google.co.uk, among others.

Labeling You know how to apply labels via the use of custom variables to visitors, sessions, and pages, allowing you to group these for better segmentation and analysis.

Tracking error pages and broken links You can now identify and highlight things that don't work on your site so they can be fixed quickly.

Tracking referral URLs from pay-per-click networks You understand which niche pay-per-click sites are driving traffic and conversions for you when they are part of a greater network.

Site overlay: differentiating links to the same page We discussed how the performance of a link differs by its format and placement on a page.

Matching transactions to specific keywords You learned how to determine which source, medium, and keywords are driving revenue at the specific transaction level.

Tracking links to direct downloads You saw how to ensure that a link in an email leading directly to a file download is tracked.

Changing which referrer is given credit for a conversion You can now manipulate the referrer attribution model to credit the first referrer or the last referrer or capture both.

Using roll-up reports You learned how to use roll-up reports for catchall overviews of multiple websites.

Using Visitor Data to Drive Website Improvement

Reporting, although important, is only half the story. The real power of web analytics lies in what you do with the data. Having a clear understanding of visitor behavior enables you to identify bottlenecks in conversion processes and marketing campaigns so you can improve them. That is, you can turn inert data into actionable information.

Part IV is about using data, from determining the most important metrics of performance (how to measure success) to optimizing pages, processes, and online and offline marketing campaigns. In addition, integrating Google Analytics data with third-party applications is a recent phenomenon that is on the increase.

In Part IV, you will learn the following:

IV

Focusing on Key Performance Indicators

By now you understand what web analytics tools can do, how to set up Google Analytics using best practices, and how to navigate its interface so that you feel comfortable with the data.

What we have discussed so far has been fairly straightforward—dare I say easy? The next step, providing key performance indicators (KPIs), *is the difficult part—not from a technical perspective but purely in terms of communication.*

KPIs enable your colleagues to focus on the parts of their online strategy that are most effective at increasing visitors, leads, conversions, and revenue for the business. The key for large organizations is delivering different KPI reports to each stakeholder and ensuring that these are hierarchical.

10

In Chapter 10, you will learn:

To set objectives and key results

To select and prepare KPIs

To present hierarchical KPIs

About example KPIs segmented by stakeholder job roles

About KPIs for a web 2.0 environment

Setting Objectives and Key Results

To summarize the story so far, the best-practice implementation principles are as follows:

- Tag everything—get the most complete picture of your website visitors possible.

- Clean and segment your data—apply filters.

- Define goals—distill the 100-plus reports of Google Analytics into performance benchmarks.

If you have followed these steps, that's excellent. However, the usual problem is that few other people in your organization know what you've done or appreciate your work. To many people, you have created a set of nice charts and reports. Even if they don't say it aloud, they may be thinking, "So what?"

The unfortunate truth is that you will have wasted your time unless you can get the buy-in to use the visitor data to drive business decisions and be the focal point for instigating change on your website. With your initial understanding of your visitor data, this is your next step—that is, to set key performance indicators for your website and align these with the objectives and key results (OKRs) of your organization. For this you need to bring in stakeholders from the other parts of the business.

What Is a Stakeholder?

A stakeholder is anyone who has an interest in your measurement project. Stakeholders can be internal or external to your organization, for example, a search marketing agency. They can be actively involved, or they may be end users of your reports attempting to make strategic business decisions from it. In this context, stakeholders are managers who have the organizational authority to allocate resources (people, budget) and can prioritize change. They are the people who make or break a change.

This is precisely why you need stakeholders on board. As discussed in Chapter 1, "Why Understanding Web Traffic Is Important to Your Business," web measurement is all about providing the foundation and yardstick for instigating change.

Most people are using web analytics as a benchmark: how did we do yesterday, and how are we doing today? Smart people are actually analyzing to optimize their website. The advanced people are using Web data to optimize all of their marketing.

—JIM STERNE, founding director and chairman of the Web Analytics Association

Objectives and key results are about understanding your business goals. This is an important prerequisite before you delve into the specific key performance indicators for your website. Essentially, you need to ensure that the two are in alignment, and the setting of OKRs prepares the way. Once you have your list of OKRs, the business language of your organization, you can use these to build your KPIs, the analyst language of your website.

The process of defining your OKRs consists of four steps:

1. Map your stakeholders.

2. Brainstorm with them.

3. Set your OKRs.

4. Distill and refine your OKRs.

Step 1: Map your stakeholders. Who are your stakeholders? These may be marketing, sales, PR, operations, web development and design agencies, e-commerce managers, content creators—even the CEO. Of course, it may be only the CEO, but if not, select one person from each department as the key contact for initial discussions. Your first choice may not end up being the right person, but you can change that later. The important thing is to get people on board from those departments. A key initial stakeholder is the person or department responsible for your Google Analytics implementation. If changes to your setup are required, this person should be involved from the start so they understand the vision and direction of your other stakeholders.

Your key contacts are the individuals who represent the interests of that department within your organization. They can canvass opinion from the rest of the organization on your behalf; in other words, they do not have to be the most senior people in their departments, though they should have a strategic and overview role, such as managerial. Try to make this a two-way street, with you setting the scene with your initial data and thoughts on the current situation and stakeholders providing their perspective on how it fits with their department. For example, they may provide information from CRM systems, call center figures, web server performance, and so on.

Step 2: Brainstorm with your stakeholders. Determine their requirements and expectations, and, importantly, manage these to ensure your project is a success. Accomplish this by arranging regular meetings with your stakeholders. For the first meeting, bring everyone together and aim to get a consensus of opinion. This should focus on what is currently happening—not whether it is good or bad, but rather what information is available. By the end of the session, you and your stakeholders should start to understand each other with respect to terminology, what data can be collected, and its accuracy and limitations.

For the second and subsequent meetings, meet with each stakeholder separately. In broad terms, you will be guiding the stakeholder as to what information can be gleaned from your reports and how it can be useful to the business. The trick is to get them to realize the opportunity that data insights can bring, so take some ideas into the meeting with you. Often your stakeholders will ask for more information, or possibly less, but usually they want to see data cross-referenced against other metrics—something to prepare for the next meeting. This brainstorming process usually takes from one to three meetings and is an important period in which to manage expectations, such as timeline and budget.

Step 3: Set your OKRs. With expectations managed and stakeholders on board and feeling engaged with the project, you should be ready to ask the question, "What is the objective of our website from your point of view?" With this, ask them to define what performance constitutes good and bad. If you can answer those three questions from each stakeholder, you have done a great job. Don't worry if you need a few more meetings to achieve this. Every organization is different. But try not to let this process drag on, or you risk losing momentum. The process taking place is not set in stone and can be reviewed and modified in six months or whenever necessary.

Encourage your stakeholders to give measurable answers to your objectives question or suggest some yourself; these form the *results* part of the OKRs. Beyond the obvious objectives of generating more transactional revenue, sales leads, and traffic volumes, the following are example OKRs I have come across:

- A main-street retail store carries literally tens of thousands of products. It is not feasible to have all of these on their e-commerce-enabled website because some are not cost-effective to ship, for example. By analyzing their site's transaction and feedback data (the objective), they wish to select the most popular product categories to focus their online efforts on (the result).

- A home furniture store that does *not* have a transactional website produces a printed catalogue each year (at great expense!). However, which products make it into the printed version is a mixture of experienced guesswork and luck, based largely on the whims of fashion trends. By analyzing the interests of their web visitors (objective), they wish to better predict and select with greater confidence which items should go into their next catalogue (result).

- A gaming company wants to understand which is the next hot market to establish operations in. By understanding the geographies and language demographics of its web visitors (objective), it wishes to select candidate markets for further research and tests (result).

- A waste-disposal company wishes to emphasize the environmental friendliness of their work on their corporate website. But what are visitors who visit a waste-disposal website interested in (objective)? Understanding this will enable them to better tailor content to get their environmental message across (result).

- A government information site, a nonprofit, is struggling to cope with the inquiry volume of its visitors and has requested an investment in new support staff. However, the funding department wants to know whether this is a cost-effective option or whether they should alter how their website operates, such as provide more self-help articles (objective). The web team needs to understand which visitor actions are of most value to support their funding request (result).

Step 4: Distill and refine your OKRs. With a long list of objectives and key results from your stakeholders (such lists are always long to start with), distill it down to the five most important OKRs for each. This should be your maximum because it is likely that each OKR will require more than one KPI to measure it. Therefore, focusing your efforts on the five most important OKRs will stand you in good stead because managers generally cannot cope with a long list of directives to act on. Where possible, group OKRs and keep them directional by avoiding the temptation of overspecifying.

Selecting and Preparing KPIs

Google Analytics is your free data-gathering and reporting tool, but it will not optimize your website for you. That requires smart people (you!) to analyze, interpret, and act on the reported findings. To act on your Google Analytics information—that is, instigate changes—you need to present your findings in a clear, understandable format to stakeholders. These are a diverse group of people who sit at different levels in your organization—all the way up to the board, one hopes. That's the caveat: Presenting web analytics data outside of your immediate team is a challenge because most businesspeople simply do not have the time to understand the details that such reports offer.

To communicate your story effectively to your stakeholders, create reports in a format and language that business managers understand—that is, KPI reports. These are abridged versions of your web analytics reports, usually summarized in Microsoft Excel or PowerPoint.

What Is a KPI?

Web analytics aside, organizations around the world use key performance indicators to assess their performance. Also sometimes referred to as key success indicators (KSI) or balanced score cards (BSC), KPIs are used in business intelligence to appraise the state of a business. Once an organization has set its OKRs, it needs a way to measure progress. Key performance indicators are those measurements.

Similarly, in web analytics, a key performance indicator is a web metric that is essential for your organization's online success. The emphasis here is on the word *essential*. If a 10 percent change—positive or negative—in a KPI doesn't make you sit up and call someone to find out what happened, then it is not well defined. Good KPIs create expectations and drive action, and because of this they are a small subset of information from your reports.

When considering your KPIs, bear in mind the following:

- In most cases a KPI is a ratio, percentage, or average, rather than a raw number. This allows data to be presented in context.
- A KPI needs to be temporal, that is, time bound. This highlights change and its speed.
- A KPI drives business-critical actions. Many things are measurable, but that does not make them key to your organization's success.

Use KPIs to put your data into context. For example, saying "we had 10,000 visitors this week" provides a piece of data, but it is not a KPI because it has no context. How do you know whether this number is good or bad? A KPI based on this data could be "our visitor numbers are up 10 percent month on month." This is a temporal indication that things are looking good over the time span of one month. In this example, the raw number should still be part of the KPI report, but it is not the KPI itself.

For the reasons just given, the vast majority of KPIs are ratios, percentages, or averages. However, sometimes a raw number can have a much greater impact. Consider the following examples:

- Our website lost 15 orders yesterday because our e-commerce server was down for 34 minutes.
- We lost $10,000 in potential revenue last week because our booking system does not work for visitors who use Firefox.
- We spent $36,000 last month on PPC keywords that did not convert.

Clearly, knowing whether any of these numbers are increasing or decreasing and what fraction of the total they represent is important, but the impact of these raw numbers is far greater at obtaining action and therefore should be the KPI in these examples.

The key point is that you should develop KPIs relevant to *your* particular business and *your* stakeholders. Any metric, percentage, ratio, or average that can help your organization quickly understand visitor data and is in context and temporal should be considered a KPI. Try to use monetary values where possible; everybody understands $$$.

Preparing KPIs

Most of the hard work of preparing KPIs consists of defining OKRs—the dialogue you had with your stakeholders in obtaining the business objectives of your company. The key results used to establish OKR success are in fact your KPIs; you just need to turn these into actual web metrics that are available to you.

Sometimes (actually, quite often) discussing KPIs with stakeholders instills fear in your colleagues. They think you are performing the web equivalent of a time and motion study that is going to spotlight their deficiencies and single them out as not doing a good job. That fear is understandable: Being measured is not a comfortable feeling. However, my approach has always been to dispel that image. Evangelize web analytics KPIs as the tools to help your stakeholders shine and be rewarded for their efforts. Wield a carrot, not a stick.

The art of building and presenting a KPI report lies in being able to distill the plethora of website visitor data into metrics that align with your OKRs. For small organizations, having a report of 10 KPIs aligning with 10 OKRs is usually sufficient. For organizations with many stakeholders, having only one KPI report will not cover the requirements of your entire business—there are simply too many stakeholders to reach a consensus about what the KPI short list should contain. Therefore, ensure that you tailor your KPI reports to specific needs by having individual stakeholder and hierarchical KPI reports.

Here is a six-point KPI preparation checklist:

1. Set your OKRs.

I repeat this here because of its importance. Identifying your stakeholders, discussing their needs, and being aware of the overall business plan for your organization enables you to put in place relevant metrics. This is an essential first step to ensure that your KPIs align with the business objectives of your organization. Otherwise, you are just a hit counter collator—looking backward and not forward.

2. Translate OKRs into KPIs.

This means setting specific web metrics against the business OKRs. Some metrics will be directly accessible from your Google Analytics reports; for example, if your e-commerce department says they want to "increase the amount of money each customer spends," then you will look for the average order value (AOV) from within the e-commerce section and monitor this over time. However, not all KPI metrics can be obtained in this way; sometimes segmentation is required or the multiplication or division of one number by another. Table 10.1 is a useful translation tool.

▶ **Table 10.1** Sample OKR-to-KPI translation

Stakeholder OKR	Suggested KPIs
To see more traffic from search engines	Percentage of visits from search engines Percentage of conversions from search engine visitors
To sell more products	Percentage of visits that add to shopping cart Percentage of visits that complete the shopping cart Percentage of visits in which shopping cart is abandoned

Continues

Stakeholder OKR	Suggested KPIs
To see visitors engaging with our website more	Percentage of visits that leave a blog comment or download a document Percentage of visits that complete a Contact Us form or click a mailto link Average time on site per visit Average page depth per visit
To cross-sell more products to our customers	Average order value Average number of items per transaction
Improve the customer experience	Percentage of visits that bounce (single-page visits) Percentage of internal site searches that produce zero results Percentage of visits that result in a support ticket being submitted

3. Ensure KPIs are actionable and accountable.

For each translated KPI, always go back and ask the stakeholder, "Who would you contact if this metric fell by 10 percent?" and "Who would you *formally* congratulate if it rose by 10 percent?" If a good answer for both is not forthcoming, then the suggested KPI is not a good one to include in your short list. I emphasize the word *formally* because this is a good way to focus the minds of your stakeholders on KPIs that lead to actions. A formal recognition could be a department-wide email bulletin or a performance bonus—that usually does the trick.

4. Create hierarchical KPI reports.

Ensure that each recipient of your KPI report receives only the data they need; the more relevant the information presented, the more attention and buy-in you will gain. It follows that a chief marketing officer will need a different, though similar, KPI report than a marketing strategist or account manager.

5. Define partial KPIs.

A frequently requested OKR is to increase the website conversion rate, usually sales or leads. This is often straightforward to measure, but it is also black and white—the visitor either converts or doesn't. By providing partial KPIs, also known as micro conversions, you can preempt your stakeholder's next question: "Why is the conversion rate so low?" I refer to these as partial KPIs because they relate to the partial completion of a full KPI. For example, if the conversion is to purchase, then adding an item to the shopping basket is a partial KPI—it's the first step of the conversion process. Similar partial KPIs include the following:

- Reaching a certain point in a checkout process
- Adding additional items (up-sell products) to the shopping cart
- For a multipage subscription form, the completion of step x of y

- Navigating to the download area or special offers section
- Completing an onsite search successfully, that is, nonzero results

Tip: Tracking partially completed forms is discussed in the section "Tracking Partially Completed Forms with Virtual Pageviews" in Chapter 7, "Advanced Implementation."

6. Consolidate.

After forming a list of required KPIs for each stakeholder, consolidate them by looking for overlaps. The point of KPIs is to focus on the important metrics to your business. To be significant, each KPI should represent at least 10 percent of the whole—so no more than 10 KPIs are allowed. If a single KPI is much less than 10 percent in importance, then drop it or consolidate it into a more important one. I cannot emphasize the importance of having no more than 10 KPIs. Having more than 10 will cost you the interest of your stakeholder by your third report!

Remember that initial KPI reports are not set in stone—they can and should evolve as your audience learns to understand the metrics of their website and develop their actions to effect change. Review your KPI short list quarterly, at the very least.

Tip: As part of your role as a web analyst, you might also want to include KPIs that are not part of your Google Analytics reports—for example, search engine rankings, notes of any offline campaigns or PR, website updates, new product launches, user feedback, news and events that impact your business, server uptime, and response speed. All of these can help explain what you see and therefore add value to your data.

Presenting Your KPIs

The best way to present KPI reports is by using Microsoft Excel or a similar spreadsheet program. Every strategist, manager, or executive is familiar with the spreadsheet format and recognizes its layout immediately. It is far better to present your KPI reports using Excel than to try to teach a new interface (Google Analytics) to old hands. In addition to using Google Analytics, you may be collecting data from different sources, such as visitor surveys or search engine–ranking reports. Combining all of them into one familiar interface will make it easy for everyone to understand the material you are presenting.

Figure 10.1 is an example KPI report for an online marketing executive containing 10 key metrics. Color coding (using Excel's conditional formatting) and arrows have been used to highlight positive and negative changes, with a threshold of 5 percent used to "double highlight" values.

	A	B	C	D	E	F	G	H
1	**KPI Report**							
2		May	June	% Change		July	% Change	
3	Conversion rate	n/a	3.7%			4.1%	10.8% ① ▲	
4	Booking income	n/a	£464,823			£377,995	-18.7% ▼▼	
5								
6								
7	SE Visitors as a % of total	90.4%	90.1%	-0.3%	▼	② 87.6%	-2.8%	▼
8	Non SE Visitors as a % of total	9.6%	9.9%	2.9%	▲	12.4%	25.6%	▲
9								
10								
11	Quality of SE Visitors (% entering booking system)	n/a	26.7%			③ 26.5%	-0.5%	▼
12	Quality of Non-SE Visitors (% entering booking system)	n/a	5.1%			6.8%	34.3%	▲
13								
14								
15	Quality of PPC Visitors (% entering booking system)	n/a	34.8%			④ 33.8%	-3.0%	▼
16	Quality of Organic Visitors (% entering booking system)	n/a	23.3%			27.2%	16.7%	▲
17								
18								
19	% unable to book (non-IE browser)	n/a	5.0%			⑤ 4.7%	-6.0%	▼▼
20	Money lost from non-IE visitors entering booking system	n/a	£23,078			£17,638	-23.6%	▼▼
21								
22	**Key & Defintions:**						*time*	
23	▲ = An increase							
24	▲▲ = An increase of 5%+							
25	▼ = A fall of 0% to 5%							
26	▼▼ = A fall of greater than 5%							

Figure 10.1 Example KPI report using Excel

All the data shown in Figure 10.1 is readily available from within Google Analytics, but using a spreadsheet to combine exactly what data elements your stakeholder wants to see enables you to deliver a concise report within a familiar interface.

Tip: Once you have built your KPI spreadsheet, you may wish to have its metrics refreshed automatically each time it is viewed. To achieve this, read Chapter 12, "Integrating Google Analytics with Third-Party Applications." You can download the example spreadsheet used in Figure 10.1 from the book blog site at www.advanced-web-metrics.com/chapter10.

The stakeholder (online marketer for a travel website) who receives the KPI report shown in Figure 10.1 is interested in the performance of his online marketing efforts—SEO and PPC—specifically, the propensity to book a vacation.

Interpreting the KPI report from Figure 10.1:

1. Online revenue is down 18.7 percent for July compared with June.

2. Approximately 90 percent of all visitors who arrive at the website do so from search engines.

3. Visitors from search engines are almost five times more likely to enter the booking system than non-search-engine visitors.

4. Visitors from pay-per-click sources are 24–49 percent more likely to enter the booking system than organic search engine visitors.

5. Because the website booking engine does not work with non–Internet Explorer web browsers, the website is losing £17,000–23,000 per month.

Action points for stakeholders of this KPI report:

- Check whether the drop in online revenue is a seasonal fluctuation experienced across the whole business or unique to the online channel. Note that the conversion rate is slightly up by 10.8 percent.

- Ninety percent of visitors arriving via a search engine appears at first glance to be too high a figure; share this statistic with the rest of the marketing department for discussion. Is this the result of a great search engine marketing strategy or are other channels not working very well?

- Increase the budget for pay-per-click campaigns—they work! However, PPC may be working better here because of failings with organic search optimization. For example, are the organic landing pages meeting the expectation of the visitor, or perhaps are they too generalized? Regardless, in the short term, raising the pay-per-click budget makes sense.

- Set up a meeting with the web development department to investigate an improved booking engine that will work for Firefox users.

As you can see, significant action points are required as a result of the KPI report presented. Without this data being shown in such a clear and concise way, discovering the action points from the wealth of Google Analytics reports available would be like finding a needle in a haystack and could even be missed.

As the volume of KPI data increases over time, plot your KPIs to spot long-term trends.

Tip: Consider delivering your KPI reports on a quarterly basis if you are a corporate or governmental organization and monthly if your website is a key part of your business model. If you are a transactional e-commerce site, certain stakeholders will want to receive reports weekly, even daily for very high-volume websites. Consider which report frequency is realistic for you. If your organization cannot take action on a daily basis, particularly your web development and design team, then daily KPI reports do not make sense. Bear in mind the issues discussed under "Understanding Web Analytics Data Accuracy," in Chapter 2, "Available Methodologies and Their Accuracy."

Presenting Hierarchical KPIs via Segmentation

There are hundreds of potential KPIs for your business. Which ones are relevant to your organization is an important discussion you will need to have with your company stakeholders. A key point stressed earlier is that you must deliver hierarchical KPI reports. That is, KPI reports for the chief marketing officer will differ from those for departmental managers, and they will differ from those for the account managers and strategists within each department.

For example, the CMO of a retail site would want to see the average conversion rate, average order value, and cost per acquisition. A marketing strategist would like to see this same information segmented by referral medium type (paid search versus organic search versus email marketing versus display banners, and so on). Without wishing to insult any chief marketing officer's intelligence, segmentation detail is generally too much information and is not required in order to give direction to the team, that is, to balance the investment of TV, radio, print, and digital marketing. However, it is required for the digital strategists to be effective in their role.

Detailed KPIs are obtained by segmentation, and a great deal of segmentation is available within the Google Analytics interface. As described in Chapter 4, "Using the Google Analytics Interface," rather than use a menu-style navigation system, Google Analytics encourages you to drill down through the data itself, automatically cross-segmenting by each click-through of the reports. Where applicable, you will often see a drop-down menu for further analysis. For example, Figure 10.2 highlights the 24 ways to cross-segment visitors for medium = organic. In addition, using Advanced Segments allow you to segment data at the visit level.

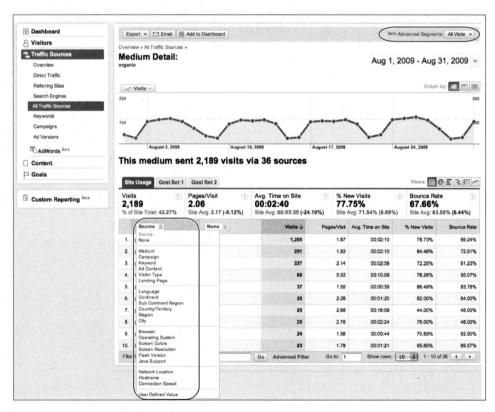

Figure 10.2 Segmenting with Advanced Segments and the 24 cross-segmentation options for organic search visitors

Most segmentation for KPI building involves the visitor type, referring source, or visitor geography. Segmenting on the fly via the user interface is a great tactic for quickly understanding the behavior of different visitor segments. Once you have identified the key ones that affect your website, you may wish to create specific profiles that report on only these. Having dedicated segmented reports enables you to investigate visitor behavior in greater detail, more efficiently, and more quickly. Segmentation is discussed in detail in the section "Why Segmentation Is Important" in Chapter 8, "Best-Practices Configuration Guide."

Figure 10.3 illustrates this model for an e-commerce website. Both the Account Strategist and Head of Department have six KPIs. That does not mean six metrics each, because that would be oversimplifying. For example, the Head of Department will wish to review sales performance by both volume and revenue, that is, the highest-selling products by quantity may not be the most profitable. For the Account Strategist, each KPI is further subdivided by referral source (segmented).

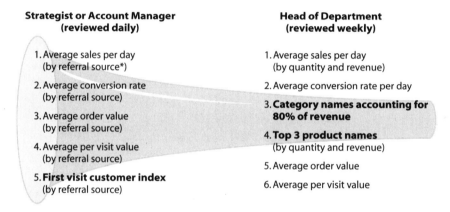

Strategist or Account Manager
(reviewed daily)

1. Average sales per day
   (by referral source*)

2. Average conversion rate
   (by referral source)

3. Average order value
   (by referral source)

4. Average per visit value
   (by referral source)

5. **First visit customer index**
   (by referral source)

Head of Department
(reviewed weekly)

1. Average sales per day
   (by quantity and revenue)

2. Average conversion rate per day

3. **Category names accounting for**
   80% of revenue

4. **Top 3 product names**
   (by quantity and revenue)

5. Average order value

6. Average per visit value

*Referral source values are organic search, PPC, email, banners, referral link, direct

Figure 10.3 Hierarchical example e-commerce KPI with differences highlighted

In addition, each recipient does not review these KPIs in isolation—the Account Strategists have their weekly meeting with the Head of Department. Hence there is a strong overlap in metrics. Highlighted in Figure 10.3 are the ones that do not overlap. For example, even if the three top-selling products change on a daily basis, the Account Strategist cannot take action. Therefore this is not on their KPI list. Instead, product selection and promotion is a decision the Head of Department will make, following a review of seven days' worth of data. Thus this KPI is on the Head of Department's list.

Explanations of the KPIs shown in Figure 10.3 are expounded upon later in this section.

Performing segmentation for hierarchical KPIs is a fine balance between obtaining clarity about visitor behavior and generating information overload. Clearly, Google Analytics offers a great number of segmentation options. However, whenever you segment data, you multiply the information reported—double it, triple it, and so on. This is clearly contrary to the purpose of KPI reporting. Therefore, you should apply a good deal of thought and investigation prior to segmenting. For example, ask yourself, how is this going to enhance my understanding of visitors, and what will I do with such information? If you are not satisfied with your own answers, don't overload yourself with more segmented data.

Benchmark Considerations

Keep in mind that KPIs are important to drive improvement for your *own* website. Although it is obviously interesting and insightful to compare how your website is performing against those of your peers and competitors, in my opinion it is a mistake to place too much emphasis on external industry benchmarks. These can be misleading and often end up with you finding the benchmark that fits your story—giving a false impression of success.

KPIs vary greatly by business sector—for example, retail, travel, technology, B2B, finance, and so on. Even within subsectors there is wide variance: think flights versus vacations or food retail versus clothing retail. Even comparing against your competitors with *identically defined goals* is fraught with gross approximations. The exact path that visitors will take to complete a goal and the quality of their user experience along the way will vary for every website. Slight changes in these can have a major impact on conversion rates. I deliberately emphasize the phrase *identically defined goals* here, because definitions from different organizations can become blurred. For example, retail managers will often wish to differentiate existing customer visits from noncustomer visits. Quoting an average conversion rate across an industry can therefore be misleading.

Also, consider that e-commerce conversion rates can be measured in a variety of ways:

- The number of conversions / total number of visits to the website
- The number of conversions / total number of visitors to the website
- The number of conversions / total number of visits that add to cart
- The number of conversions / total number of visitors who add to cart

In the preceding list you can also substitute the word *transactions* for *conversions*. That is, a visitor may complete a purchase and enjoy the experience so much that they return to make an additional purchase within the same visit session. Depending on the web analytics tool used and the preference of the organization, that can be defined as one conversion with two transactions or two conversions with two transactions.

 Note: For the preceding scenario, Google Analytics would show one conversion and two transactions, because the visitor has converted to a customer and this can happen only once during their session.

Other onsite factors that can greatly affect conversion rates, and therefore muddy the waters for benchmarking, include the following:

- Your website's search engine visibility (organic and paid search listings).

- You website's usability and accessibility (is your site easy to navigate?).

- Whether a purchase requires registration up front—it's exasperating to see how many sites require this. Put it at the end of the transaction process.

- Your page response and download times—page bloat is a conversion killer.

- Page content quality and imagery—it goes without saying that these should be a professional standard.

- The use of trust factors such as safe-shopping logos, a privacy policy, a warranty, use of encryption for payment pages, client testimonials, and so on.

- The existence of broken links or broken images—these destroy the user experience.

- Quick and accurate onsite product searching.

- Whether your website works in all major browsers.

As you can see, comparing apples with apples is complicated. By all means, benchmark yourself against your peers. It can be an interesting and energizing comparison. However, I emphasize the need for internal benchmarking as the main driver for your website's success.

KPI Examples by Job Role

Rather than produce a dictionary-style list of every potential KPI metric, I have focused on a small group that requires a little more thought in preparation—that is, it cannot be simply plucked from your Google Analytics reports—or requires further explanation. This is not intended to be an exhaustive list; rather, it is a sample to demonstrate how KPIs are defined and used—KPIs tell an easy-to-follow story. The story you need to tell will be very specific to your organization and your stakeholder relationships.

For job roles, I have grouped and differentiated the KPIs into four stakeholders: e-commerce manager, marketing manager, content creator, and webmaster. These should not be considered mutually exclusive, though. For example, marketers want to know the bottom line and e-commerce managers need to prioritize. As discussed previously, the level of segmentation applied will determine the hierarchy. As a Web Analyst, your role covers all of the above with regular "deep dives" to support your stakeholders.

Lastly, there is almost always more than one way to discover the KPI information within Google Analytics, and quite often the data points lie within several overlapping reports. In the following examples, I list the most obvious or most likely way to access the data.

Note: In Google Analytics, goal conversions and revenue (if you have monetized your goals) are reported separately from purchaser (e-commerce) conversions and revenue. Metrics that require the total revenue use the e-commerce plus goal revenue amounts.

E-commerce Manager KPI Examples

An e-commerce site probably has the most potential KPIs to choose from, because the main goal (purchase) is relatively easy to measure and the site objective (driving visitors into the shopping-cart system) is so clearly defined. Google Analytics has an entire section dedicated to the reporting of e-commerce activity. However, most of my KPIs come from other reporting areas.

Looking beyond visitor volume, some suggested KPIs for an e-commerce manager include the following:

- Average conversion rate
- Average order value
- Average per-visit value
- Average ROI
- Customer on first visit index

Average Conversion Rate

This is a high-level metric that every retailer watches with a keen eye in the offline world and is very easy to identify for online transactions. View the Ecommerce Conversion Rate report or the Ecommerce Overview report; the latter is shown in Figure 10.4.

Although useful, the conversion rate quoted in your reports is a blunt instrument. The calculation by Google Analytics is straightforward: the number of transactions divided by the total number of visits (expressed as a percentage); for example, 31 transactions from 798 web visits is a conversion rate of 3.88 percent.

However, this calculation includes *all* visitors to your website—even those who came for the wrong reasons and therefore have no intention of purchasing. To provide more insight, it would be useful to remove such visitors. You can achieve this by looking at your sitewide bounce rate. For example, if your site bounce rate for the same time period is 20 percent, the number of "prospect" visitors is actually 638 and your conversion rate recalculates as 4.86 percent.

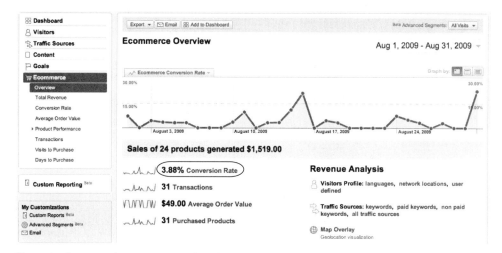

Figure 10.4 Ecommerce Overview report graphing the conversion rate KPI over time

For a partial KPI, you can further refine your conversion rate by including only those visits that begin the purchase process, such as add to cart. This tells you how good your checkout process is at converting, rather than your entire site. Replace the denominator by the number of visits that get to page 1 of your checkout system (from your Content > Top Content report). Similarly, to measure how good your site's content is at driving conversions, your calculation would be number of visits that add to cart divided by total number of visits that do not bounce.

Average Order Value

Like the average conversion rate, the average order value is an important high-level KPI that retailers watch closely. It is listed here because it is such an important metric for e-commerce managers. However, it is straightforward to calculate, and it can be obtained directly from your Google Analytics reports, as shown in Figure 10.4.

Average per-Visit Value

Understanding the average value per visit to your website is a strong KPI. Every visit has a value to your organization. Even if a visitor does not purchase, you can monetize your goals to evaluate your lead generation, registrations, and downloads. These all contribute to being able to differentiate your visitors and therefore target them better in future campaigns.

Knowing the value of your visitors and segmenting these by referral source and campaign (as well as other dimensions) is a powerful aide to both your e-commerce and marketing departments. By default, Google Analytics measures two types of per-visit value: Per Visit Goal Value (based on the value of your goals) and Per Visit Value (based on e-commerce transaction data). These can be obtained directly from your reports. Figure 10.5 shows both types. You add the two together for the *overall average per-visit value* KPI. Visitors who achieve neither a monetized goal nor a purchase will have a zero value for that visit.

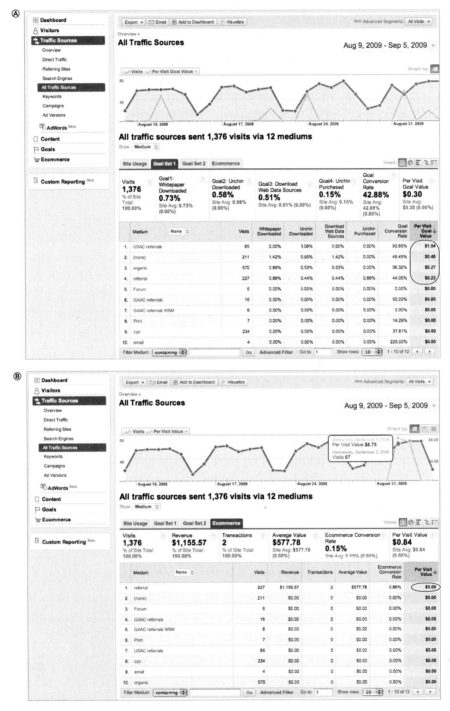

Figure 10.5 Obtaining (a) the Per Visit Goal Value, (b) the Per Visit Value

Figures 10.5a and 10.5b show the respective per-visit values segmented by medium in the tables and graphed against overall traffic. From Figure 10.5a, four referral mediums are driving goal conversions. In monetized order these are USAC referrals (a particular referral type specific to this website), direct, organic, and referral (general referrals). Comparing this with Figure 10.5b, you can see that only general referrals purchase in this time frame. Clearly word of mouth, that is, referrals, is very important to the success of this example website.

> **Note:** Although you can define up to four different goal sets, the overall goal conversion rate and per-visit goal values are not set-specific. That is, the calculation is based on all defined goals.

Average Return on Investment

Return on investment (ROI) is a KPI that all business managers understand. It tells you how much, as a percentage, you are getting back for every dollar you spend acquiring visitors. For clarity, the formula used for calculating return on investment in Google Analytics, expressed as a percentage, is as follows:

ROI = (revenue - cost) / cost

where cost is the amount spent acquiring Google AdWords visitors—currently Google AdWords is the only cost data that can be imported into Google Analytics. For example, if for every $1 you spend on AdWords, you get $2 back in sales from your website, your ROI would be 100 percent. If you received $3 back for the same outlay, your ROI would be 200 percent, and so forth. Obviously, you want to maximize your ROI—the greater this number, the better.

A negative ROI means you are losing money: Your costs of acquisition are greater than your returns. However, bear in mind that when launching a new AdWords campaign, ROI is likely to be negative until repeat visitors or brand awareness starts to grow and leads to more conversions (see Figure 10.6). Reaching the break-even point (0 percent ROI) could take hours, days, weeks, or even months, depending on many (visitor-centric, online, offline) factors. For mature campaigns, keep your ROI above 0 percent unless there is a clear reason not to do so. For example, you may be a new entry in the market and want to buy market share to gain customers at a later date.

Within Google Analytics you can drill down to view ROI reports for AdWords at three levels: Campaign, Ad Group, and Keyword. Figure 10.7 shows data at the Ad Group level. The report table clearly shows that although the Ad Group for "Book Terms" brings in more clicks from more impressions, the ROI is negative at -79.37 percent, whereas for the same time period the Ad Group for "My Name" is large and positive at 498.80 percent. That is to say, for every dollar invested in the AdWords "My Name" campaign, an average of nearly $6 is returned—a pretty good investment! From the data graph, Figure 10.7 also shows when the vast majority of ROI was earned—on two particular days, one in July and one in August.

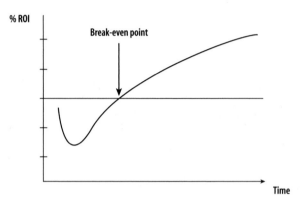

Figure 10.6 Possible change in ROI over time for a new AdWords campaign

Figure 10.7 AdWords ROI report shown for each Ad Group

You can further drill down and view your ROI on a per-keywords basis, as shown in Figure 10.8.

Of course, ROI is a top-level indication of performance from your total income. It does not take into account what profit margin you make on your sales. Nor does it take into account the volume of transactions or visitors received. For example, a high ROI campaign may be so specific that it generates only a small revenue. A lower ROI (less-specific) campaign may in fact produce greater revenue because of the higher visitor volume it generates.

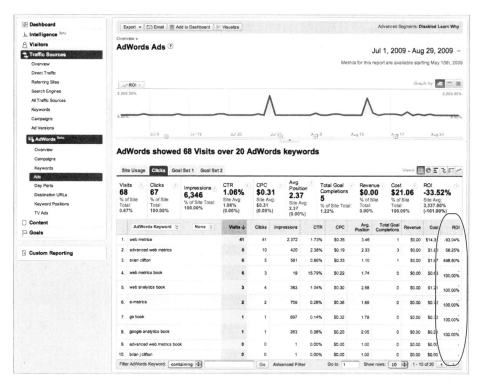

Figure 10.8 AdWords ROI report shown for each keyword

Modifying ROI to take into account profit margins is further discussed in the section "Optimizing Your Search Engine Marketing" in Chapter 11, "Real-World Tasks."

Customer on First Visit Index

Use this KPI when you are evaluating the impact of promotion codes, discounted pricing, and trust factors—those things that can help convert a new visitor into a new customer on their first visit. It answers the question, "What is the likelihood of a new visitor becoming a customer on their very first visit?"

You may notice from your reports a high proportion of transactions generated by new (first-time) visitors, as per Figure 10.9. But how does that relate to the *number* of first-time visitors? For example, by viewing Figure 10.9, although it is correct to say that 96.77 percent of transactions are from new visitors, it is not true to also interpret this as 96.77 percent of new visitors are generating your transactions—unless the number of new visitors to the site is also exactly 96.77 percent. It could be that only a small percentage of new visitors are generating your income.

Figure 10.9 Percent revenue and transactions from new visitors

The customer on first visit index KPI allows you to understand this relationship better. It is defined as follows:

$$\text{customer on first visit index} = \frac{\text{percentage transactions from new visitors}}{\text{percentage of new visitors}}$$

From the data in Figure 10.9 and knowing the percentage of new visitors, the value is calculated as follows:

customer on first visit index = 96.77 / 87.97

customer on first visit index = 1.10

Interpretation: A value of 1.0 indicates that a new visitor is equally likely to become a customer as a returning visitor. A value less than 1.0 indicates that a new visitor is less likely to become a customer than a returning visitor, and a value greater than 1.0 indicates that a new visitor is more likely to become a customer than a returning visitor.

Hence, for this example business, a business directory website, this KPI shows that a new visitor is 10 percent more likely to purchase than a returning visitor. This is not surprising in this case, because the average order value for purchasing an enhanced business listing is low at $49, meaning that low deliberation time is required. This indicates that the value proposition is very high.

Would new visitors be more likely to purchase on their first visit if the cost were reduced to $39? Following this KPI allows you to highlight any impact of promotion codes, discounted pricing, and trust factors on your site's propensity to convert.

Marketer KPI Examples

Bringing good-quality visitors—that is, qualified leads—to your website is the bread and butter of your marketing department. Putting offline marketing to one side, the "bringing" part is achieved with online marketing and may include any or all of the following sources: search engine optimization (free search rankings), pay-per-click advertising (paid search), social network interactions (groups, forums, blogs), press releases, banner advertising, affiliate networks, links from site referrals, and email marketing.

Determining which traffic is qualified means looking at the conversion rates, campaign costs, revenue generated (e-commerce or goal values), and ROI. KPIs for the marketer therefore overlap strongly with KPIs for the e-commerce manager. An important difference is that marketers look not only at purchaser transaction rates but also at goal conversions, because these build visitor relationships that, it is hoped, will later lead to purchases. Because e-commerce conversions have been discussed in the previous section, only KPIs related to goal conversions are considered here.

In most cases, online marketing is grouped under the general marketing department. It is therefore critical here to use hierarchical KPIs to differentiate those members of your audience familiar with the online channel from those who need to consider it against other channels. Looking beyond the overall visitor volume to a site, some suggested KPIs for marketers include the following:

- Percentage brand engagement
- Conversion quality index
- Average ROI by campaign type
- Percentage of new versus returning visitors (or customers)

Percentage Brand Engagement

In his blog at www.webanalyticsdemystified.com, Eric T. Peterson describes brand engagement as the brand index KPI. Visitors who know your brand and have arrived at your site because of it have, by definition, engaged with you. This KPI is defined as follows:

$$\text{percentage brand engagement} = \frac{\text{number of visits with search terms containing brand names} + \text{number of direct visits}}{\text{total number of visits from search engines} + \text{number of direct visits}}$$

Note that when referring to search terms here, I am referring to search engine referral keywords. Direct-access visits are also included because these are people who know your website address and therefore your brand. I have assumed all campaigns are being tracked and that you have excluded access of your own staff from your reports (see "Profile Segments: Segmenting Visitors Using Filters," in Chapter 8).

A percentage brand engagement report is not yet directly available within Google Analytics, but it is straightforward to calculate from two other reports. First, from the Traffic Sources > Keywords report, use the table filter to enter your regular expression of brand keywords (see Figure 10.10a). The number of direct visits is taken from the Traffic Sources > Direct Traffic report (see Figure 10.10b).

Constructing Regular Expressions

Because a maximum of 255 characters is allowed within the table filter box, you should construct your regular expression with some thought. For example, in Figure 10.10a, the brand term I am actually looking for is "Advanced Web Metrics with Google Analytics"—one brand name of the book website. I require the term "advanced web metrics" in this case only because this will pick up both terms (and other brand terms with this phrase) and is unlikely to match nonbrand terms. Once you have filtered this way, you could define an advanced segment to keep these terms permanently at hand for easy comparison. Advanced segments have much greater character limits for constructing regular expressions (see Table 8.2).

Using advanced segments and profile filters is discussed in Chapter 8.

Using the data from Figures 10.10a and 10.10b and knowing that the total number of search engine visitors to this example website is 2227 (taken from the Traffic Sources > Search Engines report),

percentage brand index = (323 + 1244) / (2227 + 1244)

percentage brand index = 45.15%

Figure 10.10 (a) Search keywords used by visitors, (b) Direct Traffic metrics

This illustrates how important branding is for the site in question. It may be that I would wish to increase this metric (a common request from marketers and brand managers), though often you may actually wish to reduce this. That is, you would want to increase the volume of traffic from visitors who are new to your brand.

By selecting a "Goal Set" tab within the reports of Figures 10.10a and 10.10b, you can also quickly calculate the brand index KPI on a per-goal basis.

Conversion Quality Index

Viewing a breakdown of visitors by referrer is an extremely effective set of KPIs for the marketer. For example, what's driving your traffic acquisition—email marketing, organic search, paid advertising, social networks, affiliates, or your offline marketing? Going beyond visitor volumes, the conversion quality index (CQI) is all about measuring how well targeted your campaigns are at driving conversion on your website.

For example, suppose 50 percent of your visitors are from AdWords (labeled in your reports as google / cpc), but only 20 percent of conversions are from this campaign source. That's an underperforming campaign because given two equally targeted campaigns, each producing 50 percent of your visitor traffic, both should produce 50 percent of your conversions. If one outperforms the other by generating more than its share of conversions, then by definition that campaign must be better targeted.

The conversion quality index, shown here, enables you to view these differences so you can better understand the effectiveness of your visitor-acquisition strategy:

$$\text{conversion quality index (for referrer X)} = \frac{\text{percent goal conversions from referrer X}}{\text{percent visits from referrer X}}$$

This report does not yet exist in Google Analytics. However, it is easy to calculate from the available reports using the data in Figure 10.11a and 10.11b. The values from these reports are then used to populate the rows of Table 10.2. Think of this as dividing one chart by the other in order to standardize the data. In this example, I have selected referral "medium" for the quality index. If individual campaign detail is important to you, drill down into a specific source to obtain these numbers.

Interpretation for the conversion quality index KPI: A value of 1.0 tells us that a visitor from the referral is as likely to convert as a visitor from any other. A value of less than 1.0 indicates that a visitor is less likely to convert than a visitor from any other referral, and a value of greater than 1.0 indicates that a visitor is more likely to convert than a visitor from any other referral. As a marketer, you should be aiming for a value of 1.0 for each referral set up.

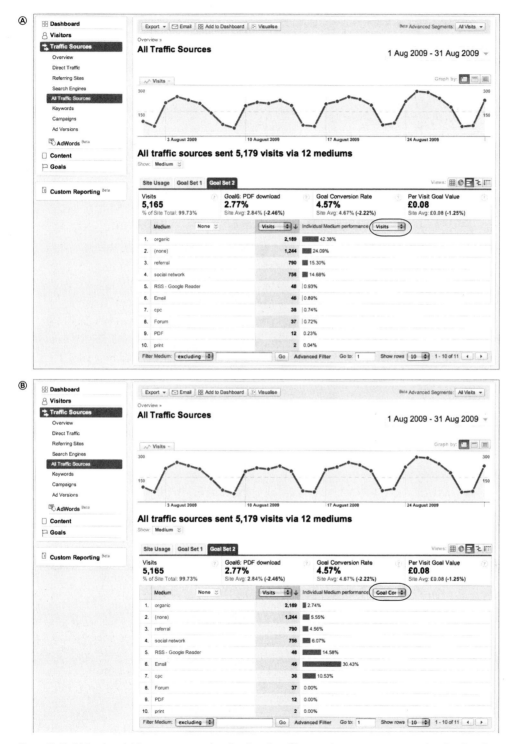

Figure 10.11 (a) Number of visits as a percentage by referral medium, (b) conversion rates as a percentage by referral medium

By using this method, Table 10.2 highlights two distinct types of referral performance:

High performing RSS - Google Reader, Email, CPC (AdWords)

Low performing All other referral mediums

▶ **Table 10.2** Conversion quality index (CQI)

Campaign	A % Visits (Figure 10.11a)	B % Conversions (Figure 10.11b)	C Conversion Quality Index (B/A)	D CQI Normalized
Organic	42.38	2.74	0.06	0.00
(none)	24.09	5.55	0.23	0.01
Referral	15.30	4.56	0.30	0.01
Social network	14.68	6.07	0.41	0.01
RSS - Google Reader	0.93	14.58	15.69	0.46
Email	0.89	30.43	34.17	1.00
CPC	0.74	10.53	14.31	0.42
Forum	0.72	0.00	0.00	0.00
PDF	0.23	0.00	0.00	0.00
Print	0.04	0.00	0.00	0.00

Column D of Table 10.2 normalizes the CQI to the highest value, in this case email referrals. Viewing this data for advanced-web-metrics.com, it is understandable that email referrals, that is, direct marketing, is the highest performer—by its nature, it provides highly qualified leads. Similarly, blog readers, in this case subscribers who click through to the site from their RSS reader, can be described as already highly engaged. Therefore, a high performance is expected from RSS readers. What is interesting from this analysis is the high performance of AdWords referrals, labeled as medium = cpc in Google Analytics, compared to other referrers—for example, organic search or social networks.

However, there is a large caveat with this particular example. As Figure 10.11 shows, the visit numbers for email, RSS readers, and CPC are very low. These should be disregarded until more data is collected. I left these in to highlight the need to keep raw numbers close at hand when calculating KPIs that are averages, ratios, or percentages. Taking the CQI at face value, it could be argued that social network participation should be dropped in favor of increasing the AdWords budget. While that may still be true, the sample size so far is too small to come to that conclusion just yet.

Assuming you have enough conversion data (at least hundreds of goal completions, for each data point) to mitigate random fluctuations, the conversion quality index is a valuable KPI to use to benchmark your referral source, medium, and campaign data against. It allows marketing managers to ask the question, "Does the distribution of our marketing budget match our conversions?" If, for example, little of your budget is being spent on email marketing, then you know from Figure 10.11 that this source provides a great goal conversion rate for you and so should be exploited further.

Average ROI by Campaign Type

This KPI is the same as the one discussed for e-commerce managers and shown in Figure 10.7. I list it here for completeness.

Percentage of New versus Returning Visitors (or Customers)

Knowing whether new or returning visitors are driving your website metrics is an important top-level guide to the success of your online marketing strategy (see Figure 10.12). If your marketing focus is on acquiring new visitors, then you would expect a greater proportion of these. If you focus on visitor retention, then you would expect the number of returning visitors to be higher.

Unless you are embarking on a new online marketing initiative, these metrics should remain fairly stable. Generally speaking, the more proactive your organization is at search engine marketing, the higher the percentage of new visitors—typically, 70 percent plus. Exceptions to this are customer-support websites and content-publishing websites that have a more even mix of new versus returning visitors.

Be careful when interpreting changes in percentage of visitor types. For example, a decrease in percentage of new visitors could in fact be due to an increase in percentage of returning visitors, rather than any change in your new-visitor acquisition strategy. To check, compare different date ranges and examine the raw numbers. By viewing the raw visit numbers of Figure 10.13, you can see that new visitors have decreased by 246 visits, so this is a genuine drop, albeit a small one.

Figure 10.12 Understanding new versus returning visitors

Figure 10.13 Comparing new versus returning visitors over time

In addition to traffic volume, you can also view the ratio of new versus returning customers—provided you are labeling visitors who purchase, as described in Chapter 9, "Google Analytics Hacks." By this method, select the Customer label in the Visitors > User-Defined report and cross-segment by Visitor Type.

Content Creator KPI Examples

If you create content—that is, you are an author, journalist, or copywriter for a content-driven website—then audience engagement is your goal. How long people spend reading your content and how much of it they consume are key indicators for measuring engagement.

Essentially, there are three categories of content-driven websites:

Product and organization information Examples include corporate website information, product review sites, blogs, help-desk support, online training sites, and so on.

Advertising-based content These include free-to-read content websites that derive revenue from selling advertisements (banner or text ads) alongside content. Examples include cnet.com, myspace.com, and most TV, newspaper, and magazine websites such as nytimes.com, ft.com, and cnn.com. Some blogs also embed contextual advertising within their articles—for example, using AdSense.

Subscription-based content As an alternative to deriving income from advertising, content-driven websites can offer subscription-based content; that is, you pay as a subscriber to access the material (or perhaps a more complete version of an article). Examples include jupiterresearch.com, e-consultancy.com, forrester.com, and many daily newspaper sites.

The latter two categories I classify as publishers, and they usually employ both methods of generating income. As a publisher, if you provide advertising-based content, then you have a dilemma: If you write the perfect article to fit on one page, visitors will read that single page, be satisfied, and move on to another site or activity. They will be single-page visitors. However, single-page visits are not good for business when you derive your revenue from advertising. To increase your revenue, you want visitors to read more pages so that they are exposed to more advertisements (greater inventory), increasing the likelihood that they will click one. That makes your website more attractive to advertisers.

Regardless of your content site's business model, greater engagement with your visitors is the key. Consequently, content managers are always looking at ways to include complementary subject matter with each article or page to encourage this. Clearly for content sites, visit volume—the number of visits per day, week, or month—is an important KPI, along with how this varies over time. However, the following sample KPIs focus on helping you measure engagement:

- Bounce rate
- Percent engagement
- Average time on site and pageviews per visit
- Advertisement performance
- Percent new versus returning visitors
- Percent high, medium, low visitor recency

Bounce Rate

A *bounce* in Google Analytics terminology is a one-page, zero-action visit—that is, a visitor arrives on your website, views one page, has no further action, and then bounces off to another site or closes their browser. It's an important, very-easy-to-understand KPI that every stakeholder wishes to reduce. Bounced visitors have no value to your business (assuming you have a well-crafted article that entices further click-throughs) and are important to minimize because an e-commerce manager wishes to maximize revenue. Web analysts love analyzing bounce rates—such a simple metric that can be so telling for web performance.

The bounce-rate calculation can vary for different web analytics vendors, so I clarify the formula here for Google Analytics:

$$\text{percentage bounce rate for a page} = \frac{\text{number of single page visits to that page with zero actions}}{\text{number of times that page was an entry page}}$$

I emphasize the use of the term *zero actions*. By *action*, I mean any non-pageview action that can be tracked by Google Analytics—such as an event (file download, Flash movie interaction, and so on) or e-commerce transaction. See Chapter 7 for further details on e-commerce and event tracking.

 Note: Labeling a visitor, as described in Chapter 9, is not defined as an action in this context (as of early 2009).

The average website bounce rate (a weighted average of all your page bounce rates) is quoted in numerous places throughout Google Analytics reports (for example, in the Content Overview report). To view the bounce rate for a particular page, view the Content > Top Content report, as shown in Figure 10.14. Because bounce rates can vary quite widely from page to page, I maintain focus by using an advanced filter in Figure 10.14 to exclude outliers (very high or very low bounce rates and pages with low pageview traffic).

From a content creator's point of view, a high percentage of bounced visitors means poor engagement. But what constitutes a high bounce rate? I use a traffic-light system as follows:

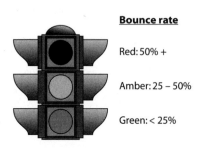

Bounce rate

Red: 50% +

Amber: 25 – 50%

Green: < 25%

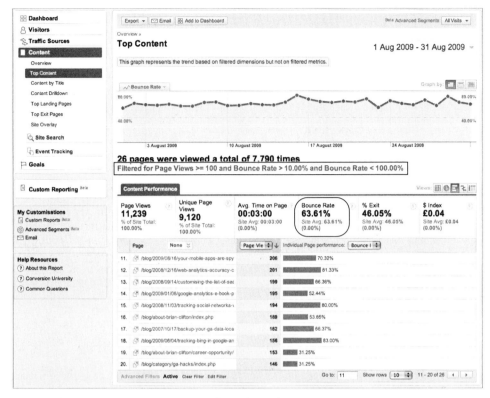

Figure 10.14 Top Content report using an advanced filter to focus on bounce rates

High bounce rate pages (red, greater than 50 percent) obviously need to be prioritized for review. Perhaps there is out-of-date content or errors on the page. If you cannot find a reason for a visitor's bounce, consider culling the content—remove pages that have a high bounce rate. After all, producing and maintaining content has a cost. If visitors are not interested in reading more than one page from you, then maybe the content is not relevant to your website.

Medium bounce rate pages (amber, 25–50 percent) hopefully constitute the bulk of your Top Content report. Thus, it can be some time before you optimize these for improvement—lower bounce rates.

Low bounce rate pages (green, less than 25 percent), although performing well, should not be ignored. Target these for new promotions, major news updates, or key announcements, because these have the greatest traction with your visitors.

Note: Anil Batra has written a report on typical industry bounce rates by surveying 80 companies across five industry sectors. Bearing in mind my caveats of external benchmarking discussed earlier in this chapter, his report makes interesting reading and is free to download from www.anilbatra.com/digitalmarketing/bounce-rates.asp.

Crafting Your Article to Entice Click-throughs

If you write the perfect one-page article, visitors will read the content, be perfectly satisfied and engaged, and then leave your website. Clearly that is not desirable—you want them to click around, see other great content from you, subscribe, and click an advertisement or two. By doing so they not only generate income for you but also differentiate themselves from visitors who truly are not interested in your content.

Facilitate this by tailoring your post to entice click-throughs, not by using special offers or give-aways (though that can, of course, be a method) but by how you craft your content. For example:

- For longer articles, use a natural break or continue point, such as "click to read page 2," to break up your content onto multiple pages.

- Reference previous articles on your site for the visitor to refer to (click to) for more detail. You can also do this for external links so long as you track these as virtual pageviews or events—see Chapter 7.

- Use thumbnail images that require a click-through to your site to view it properly, or "view this article in full" link.

- Avoid "ad blindness," that is, the overuse of animation on advertisements that cause visitors to ignore that section of the page in order to concentrate.

Percentage Engagement

Percent engagement has the opposite meaning of bounce rate. However, it is not simply the inverse of the bounce rate calculation. That is, just because a visitor does not bounce does not mean they are engaged—that would be far too simplistic.

Apart from visitors reading your content, how else could you determine their engagement? Examples include downloads, subscriptions, article ratings, blog comments, social share (Twitter, Del.ici.os, Digg, StumbleUpon, email, and so on), or visitors who provide unsolicited feedback in some other way. Whatever the method, visitors who connect with your website are a valuable metric of engagement. Expressed as a percentage, the calculation is as follows:

$$\text{percentage engaged visits} = \frac{\text{total number of engagements}}{\text{total number of visits}}$$

Google Analytics tracks all data at the aggregate level, so it is best to track this KPI on a per-visit basis rather than a per-visitor basis. Hence, it is not possible to determine whether a small number of visitors, for example, one visitor, is making all the engagements. Such a scenario is highly unlikely but something to bear in mind.

If all of your engagements are defined as goals, a simple way to obtain this KPI is to view the Goals > Goal Verification report, shown in Figure 10.15.

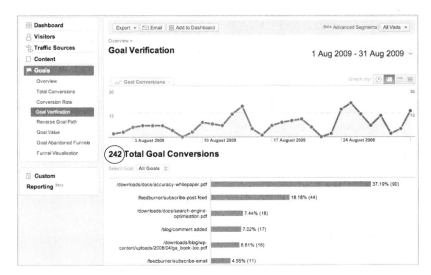

Figure 10.15 Goal conversion rates

The Goal Verification report shows the number of goal completions, or engagements. Note that you should not use the goal conversion rate in this calculation because this counts only unique conversions—a visitor can convert only once during their session even though they may have completed numerous goals.

Divided by the total number of visits (taken from Figure 10.12), the percent engaged visits for this example data is:

percentage engaged visits = 242 / 5179

percentage engaged visits = 4.67%

If some of your engagements are not defined as goals, use the table filter technique (refer to Figure 10.10a) to determine the number of engagements.

Percent Engaged Visitors

It is possible to be clever here and use the _setCustomVar() function as a label to track whether a visitor has engaged with your website (see "Labeling Visitors, Sessions, and Pages," in Chapter 9 for the use of visitor labeling). The KPI could then be changed to percentage engaged visitors by substituting for the number of visits:

$$\text{percentage engaged visitors} = \frac{\text{total number of engaged visitors}}{\text{total number of visitors}}$$

The total number of engaged visitors would show in the Visitors > Custom Variables report.

Average Time on Site and Pageviews per Visit

The average time on site is the length of time visitors spend interacting with your website, and it is a good base metric to help you understand whether your visitors are engaging with your site. All content creators want to increase this KPI—assuming, of course, the visitor experience is a good one.

The calculation is straightforward, though it is worth mentioning how it is determined. In order to calculate the time on site, Google Analytics uses the difference in time between the last and first pageview a visitor requests (or event if you are also tracking these). Note that times are measured when the page or event is *requested*, not when a visitor leaves a page. That complicates matters when the page in question is the last one visited—you know when the visitor made the request but not when they left. Perhaps the visitor opened another site in a new browser window or new browser tab or just minimized their browser while continuing with other work. These are very common scenarios resulting in the tracking session being closed by a cookie timeout—set at 30 minutes by default in Google Analytics though it can be adjusted; see "Customizing the GATC" in Chapter 7. Having a final pageview last 30 minutes would clearly skew the time-on-site metrics. To avoid the situation, Google Analytics ignores the last pageview for all time-on-site calculations. In fact, this is a common approach throughout the web analytics industry.

The depth of visit—that is, the average pages per visit—is closely related to the time on site. If one increases, you would expect the other to also increase. Hence, they are displayed together when viewing your Google Analytics reports. For example, if your depth of visit KPI causes you to ask further questions, you should also refer to the time on site. It could be that a low-average pages per visit KPI is a bad thing. However, if these visitors also display a high time on site or trigger other on-page events such as watching a Flash movie clip, then it could be good thing.

As with all KPIs, don't use the site-wide average, because that is too broad to be useful. A more informative view is to compare how these vary by visitor segment. For example, compare average time on site and pages per visit for new versus returning visitors or by referring traffic sources. To illustrate this, Figure 10.16 shows how these vary by referring source medium. An interesting observation is that visitors from a print ad campaign have the lowest pages per visit and lowest time on site, whereas visitors from social network sites have much higher rates. Initial thought—drop the print ad; marketing is changing!

By comparing segments for these KPIs, you can better tailor your website content, advertising, and overall usability for each visitor type. If you believe your content is already well structured and intuitive to use (everyone initially thinks that about their website), yet the average time on site or page depth is low, then consider how you are acquiring your visitors. Examine whether they are qualified visitors and whether the landing page they first arrive at is suitable for them.

Figure 10.16 Average time on site and pages per visit by referring source medium

---

A Higher Time on Site or Page Depth Is Not Always a Good Thing

It's difficult to tell if a higher value for these metrics is a good thing or not. On the one hand, spending more time on your site and viewing more pages could mean visitors are highly engaged and interested in your content; on the other, they could be confused and lost in your navigation. Therefore, take care before drawing conclusions from these metrics. Always attempt to cross-reference with other KPIs that can provide further insight—particularly bounce rate and engagement KPIs.

Advertisement Performance

If you are an AdSense user, that is, you are displaying Google AdWords alongside your content and benefiting from a share of the advertising revenue, there is a set of Google Analytics reports dedicated just for you. Assuming you have followed the integration steps described in Chapter 6, "Getting Up and Running with Google Analytics," the Content > AdSense report contains a host of KPI metrics, all of which can be of use straight out of the box—see Figure 10.17.

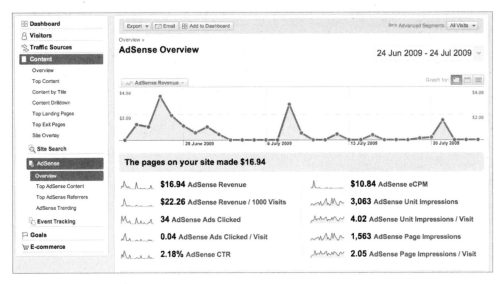

Figure 10.17 AdSense report

I always prefer monetized KPIs, so the AdSense Revenue / 1000 Visits and the AdSense eCPM metrics are particular favorites from this report. These two metrics tell you how much advertising revenue you are making from AdSense click-throughs per 1000 visits and per 1000 AdSense page impressions, respectively. Clearly you will want to increase these.

Because AdSense is contextual advertising, the key to improving these metrics is to provide good-quality content (isn't it always!), so that Google's ad network can find a relevant ad match. The stronger that correlation, the more relevant the ad will be and hence the more likely a visitor will click it.

If you are not an AdSense user, then a little more work is required to obtain these metrics for yourself. Assuming your advertisements lead a visitor to an external website, you will need to track these outbound links as discussed in Chapter 7—either as virtual pageviews or as events. With this tracking in place, performing calculations is straightforward using the Content > Top Content report (virtual pageviews) or from the Content > Event Tracking report (events). For example:

$$\text{Number of advertisements clicked per 1000 visits} = \frac{\text{total number of advertisements clicked}}{\text{total number of visits}} \times 1000$$

Extending the method, you can obtain your advertising revenue per 1000 visits by multiplying this value by the average value of your advertising sales. You can even differentiate ad formats, that is, you can take into account your rate card and have a different advertising revenue per 1000 visits for each format, by using the technique described in Chapter 7 in "Tracking Banners and Other Outgoing Links as Events."

The reason for multiplying the average by 1000 is that this metric is usually very small and does not convey the information well as a KPI. In addition, advertising rate cards for content and media sites are usually priced according to a cost-per-thousand-impressions model (CPM—cost per mille; *mille* is Latin for "thousand"). Having this KPI with the same multiplier is clearly beneficial to help establish your rate card.

If you feel these KPIs are low, then investigate the quality, quantity, relevance, and placement of advertisements.

> **Note:** For non-AdSense users, these calculations do not take into account that a single visit could produce all advertisement click-throughs—an unlikely scenario, but something to bear in mind if you spot a large anomaly.

Percent New versus Returning Visitors

This KPI is the same as the one discussed for e-commerce managers and shown in Figure 10.12. I list it here for completeness.

Percent High, Medium, Low Visitor Recency

Recency is defined as the amount of time that passes between sequential visits—that is, when were the current visitors last on your site? From experience, many people struggle to understand what recency is telling them or how to interpret the chart. Maybe it is because the terminology is not widely used in business. Nonetheless, it is an essential metric for measuring engagement. The report in Figure 10.18 illustrates this.

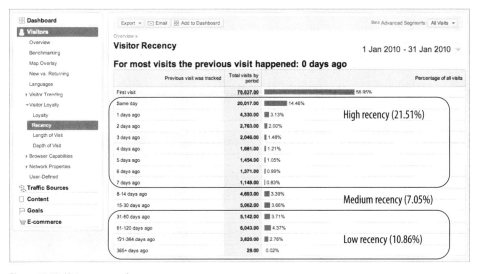

Figure 10.18 Visitor recency chart

Interpreting the chart in Figure 10.18 of the visits made in the period shown, the vast majority (56.95 percent) of them are same-day first-time visits; 14.46 percent are same-day repeat visits; 3.13 percent also visited one day before; 2.00 percent visited two days ago, and so on. For visitor recency KPI reports, group this chart into high, medium, and low categories. The boundaries for each group will depend on your business model, though I tend to use the following:

High = within one week

Medium = between 8 and 30 days

Low = more than 30 days

In all examples, the higher the recency the better, that is, the fewer days between previous visits, the more engagement you have. For e-commerce websites this could be the amount of time between visit and purchase. However, not all sites exhibit this behavior; high-value purchase items tend to have long visitor recency, because visitors take longer to consider their purchase.

Often when viewing this report, I wish to see metrics for returning visitors only. This makes sense when considering recency, that is, the time period since the *last* visit, because new visitors are not relevant in this instance. In which case, select the advanced segment of Returning Visitors.

 Note: According to a July 2007 ScanAlert report, online shoppers take an average of 34 hours and 19 minutes from their first visit to purchase.

Webmaster KPI Examples

Your webmaster department includes the people responsible for keeping your website up and running smoothly. Therefore, they need to know the expected visitor load on their servers. They also need to advise your design and content-creation departments on visitor profiles from a technical perspective, such as which browsers are most commonly used and what language settings visitors have on their computers. This is how the industry of web analytics got started—webmasters wanting to know "how many?"

Webmaster KPIs are usually nonhierarchical because of their technical importance and intended audience: technical people for whom high-level summary indicators raise more questions. For this audience, you may also consider bringing in other nonvisitor metrics to supplement the Google Analytics pageview data, such as web server uptime, server response speed, bandwidth used, and so on. These are not considered here.

Sample KPIs for webmasters include the following:

- Volume of visitors, visits, and pageviews

- Percentage of visitors without English language settings
- Percentage of visitors not using Microsoft
- Percentage of visitors with a broadband connection
- Percentage of visitors receiving an error page
- Internal search performance and quality

Volume of Visitors, Visits, and Pageviews

This is a classic base metric that enables webmasters to quickly get a handle on the volume of traffic the website receives. Such metrics are important in determining the load on your web servers and network infrastructure and the potential importance of your website compared to other parts of your business. For example, if you measure your customer base in the thousands, and one week you suddenly received 100,000 visits, your business needs to know about this!

The following metrics can be obtained directly from the Visitors > Overview report:

- Average number of visits per time frame
- Average number of unique visitors per time frame
- Average number of pageviews per time frame
- Average pageviews per visit

For such metrics, collect data over long periods to diminish the effects of large fluctuations. If you are a B2B website, the number of visits per day averaged over a week will be skewed by the weekend. In this case, it would be better to consider the average over the working week (Monday–Friday).

Percentage of Visits without English-Language Settings

The more insight you have about your website visitor demographics the better, and this KPI strongly overlaps with the goals of the marketing department. The visitor language setting is an excellent way of determining your international reach and whether your content matches this. Of course, if your main website language is not English, then simply replace the KPI name "English" with the appropriate language.

You can view the distribution of visitor languages directly from the Visitors > Languages report (see Figure 10.19). You will need to do some grouping here, because all language types are reported. For example, British English (en-gb) is reported separately from American English (en-us). Similarly, Spanish, Portuguese, and French have different varieties, as do many other languages. It is therefore important to group (or not) different language versions according to your requirements.

Note: Don't infer too much from the difference between en-gb and en-us, because a great many non-U.S. users have their browser settings set as en-us by default and never bother to change this. For example, I noticed that when I access my Google Analytics reports, I do so in U.S. English. In over two years I have not bothered to change this to U.K. English.

Figure 10.19 Distribution of visitor language settings

From Figure 10.19 you might assume that the vast majority of visitor language requirements (70 percent) are accounted for. However, you should always assess this further by viewing the Goal Set tabs. You would expect that all things being equal, the same proportion of conversions should occur for English visitors as for non-English visitors (if not higher). If that is not the case, there may be an opportunity for you to market in other languages.

To view your grouped data trended over time, use an advanced segment as per Figure 10.20 and applied as in Figure 10.21. As you can see from the long-term plot of Figure 10.21, the international reach of the example website has been increasing steadily, that is, as a proportion of total visits, more visitors now have non-English browser settings.

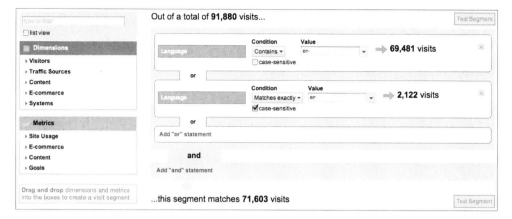

Figure 10.20 Advanced segment for grouping English-language visits

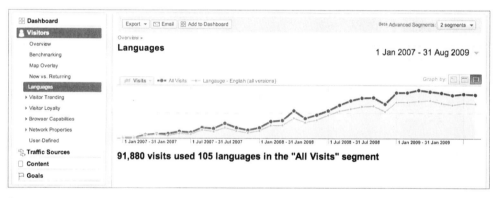

Figure 10.21 Long-term plot of English-language visits

341
■
KPI EXAMPLES BY JOB ROLE

> **Note:** An excellent resource for comparing Internet world statistics is www.internetworldstats.com. See, for example, http://www.internetworldstats.com/stats7.htm, where English accounts for 28.7 percent of world Internet usage (June 2009).

Percentage of Visits Not Using Microsoft

Microsoft has contributed hugely to the proliferation of the Internet because of its ubiquitous operating systems and free browser software (Internet Explorer). However, times are changing—the once-dominant use of the software giant's products is being eroded by alternative operating systems from Apple and Ubuntu (Linux for the desk/laptop) and the abundance of browsers such as Firefox, Opera, Safari, and Chrome.

Various web browsers and operating systems render web pages differently. This means pages can look different from that intended or not even work—the browser usually has the greatest impact here. Despite the use of Internet Explorer being globally estimated at 67 percent (see the sidebar "The Price of Incompatibility"), it still amazes me to visit websites of well-known brands that cannot process orders from non–Internet Explorer visitors. Simply put, they are losing out on significant revenue and damaging their brand reputation to boot. Perhaps it is because testing web pages on different browsers and operating system platforms is a laborious job for webmasters and therefore rarely prioritized.

Whatever the reasons, you can access this KPI at a glance from the Visitors > Browser Capabilities > Browsers report, shown in Figure 10.22. Knowing what your visitors use to access your website enables you to prioritize resources effectively. As you can see from Figure 10.22, the majority of visitors do not use Internet Explorer (74 percent).

Figure 10.22 Visitor browser types

In this case, having the website working well in both MS Internet Explorer and Firefox is important—accounting for 81 percent of all visits. In addition, you should assess this further by viewing the Goal Set tabs. That is, for this example, visitors from MS Internet Explorer and visitors from Firefox should result in approximately the same proportion of conversions: two to one. If not, then likely your website does not work equally well for both browsers.

The Price of Incompatibility

Browser market share data from Net Applications for August 2009 (http://marketshare.hitslink.com/browser-market-share.aspx?qprid=0) shows a global average of 33 percent of non–Internet Explorer users. Assuming these visitors behave in the same way as Internet Explorer visitors (there is no reason to suppose otherwise for the same website), that equates to a 50 percent loss of revenue if your website cannot work in these browsers (100/67). Even if your percentage of visitors not using Internet Explorer is lower than the global average, say 20 percent, that is still 25 percent (100/80) of your money left on the table. A crime in my view!

Putting this into perspective, consider the percentage gains your marketing department is trying to squeeze out from optimizing online marketing campaigns—typically an additional 1–2 percentage point improvement, an order of magnitude smaller.

With browser standards now well established, there really is no excuse for not making your website work well in at least two of your visitors' most popular browsers.

Percentage Visits with Broadband Connection

The speed at which your visitors access the Internet has obvious implications for webmasters when you are considering adding rich media content to website pages. However, not all parts of the world have broadband access, so even without rich media, slow page download times adversely affect the user experience.

Note: The Internet World Stats website, www.internetworldstats.com/dsl.htm, shows that of the countries with the highest Internet usage, the top five for broadband penetration are the Netherlands, South Korea, Sweden, Canada, and the United Kingdom, respectively. The United States ranks seventh (September 2007).

Regardless of connection speed, the latest study by Forrester Consulting for Akamai Technologies (September 2009) reveals that two seconds is the new threshold in terms of an average online shopper's expectation for a web page to load (www.akamai.com/html/about/press/releases/2009/press_091409.html). In addition, their report reveals that 79 percent of online shoppers who experience a dissatisfying visit are less likely to buy from that site again. Interestingly, their similar study of 2006 revealed a four-second rule—web users have increased their speed expectations. Whether you have a transactional website or not, I suggest the two-second rule be applied to your web pages.

You can view the distribution of visitor connection speeds directly from the Visitors > Network Properties > Connection Speeds report (see Figure 10.23). As you saw when viewing visitors by language settings, you need to do some grouping here. For example, DSL, cable, T1, and OC3 are all broadband connection speeds (see Table 10.3).

> Broadband = DSL, cable, T1, OC3

> Dialup = dialup, ISDN

▶ **Table 10.3** Connection type acronyms defined

Term	Description
DSL	Digital Subscriber Line (broadband)
Cable	Similar to DSL (broadband)
T1	Corporate leased line or private wire (fast broadband)
Dialup	Modem (slow band)
OC3	Optical Carrier 3 (very fast broadband)
ISDN	Integrated Services Digital Network (slow band, though twice as fast as dialup)

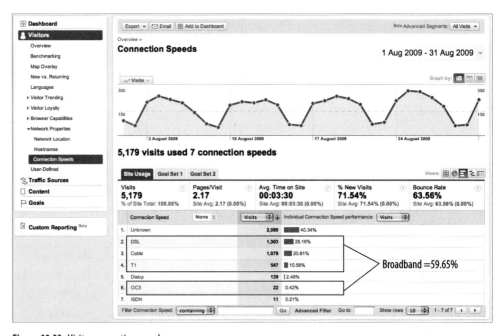

Figure 10.23 Visitor connection speeds

Percentage of Error Pages Served

This is an obvious metric any webmaster would wish to minimize. It is defined as follows and quoted as a percentage:

$$\text{percentage error pages served} = \frac{\text{total number of error pages served}}{\text{total number of pageviews served}}$$

Tracking error pages is discussed in "Tracking Error Pages and Broken Links" in Chapter 9. Essentially, you track them as virtual pageviews so they can be viewed in your Content > Top Content report—refer to Figure 9.5. A target for this KPI could be to maintain this level at less than 0.1 percent of your total pageviews.

Internal Search Performance

Onsite search is now so important for large websites that it has become an integral part of the navigation system. Even for smaller sites, a good internal search engine can improve the user experience and hence your bottom line, so measuring the internal search experience is a key metric.

Important site search KPIs are available in the Content > Site Search > Overview report, shown in Figure 10.24.

Figure 10.24 is a great starting point to evaluate your site search performance. For example, from this report you obtain the following:

- Percentage of visits that use site search (3.09 percent).
- Average number of search results viewed per search (1.30).
- Percentage of people exiting the site after viewing search results (28.04 percent).
- Percentage of people conducting multiple searches during their visit (21.15 percent). This excludes multiple searches for the same keyword.
- Average time on site for a visit following a search (00:03:38).
- Average number of pages visitors view after performing a search (1.79). If this is less than 1, then a significant number of visitors searching are not going beyond your results page.

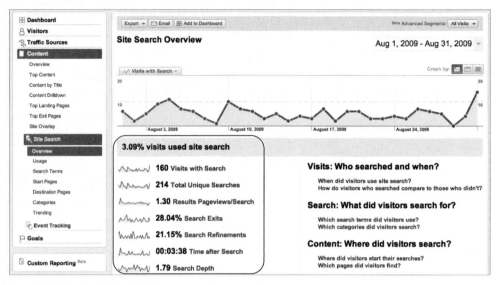

Figure 10.24 Site Search Overview report

Other important KPIs for site search include how visitors who use this facility compare with those who do not. For example, are site search visitors more likely to convert, spend more money, spend more time on site, or view more pages, that is, less likely to bounce? You can see these rates by viewing the Site Search > Usage report, as shown in Figure 10.25.

Figure 10.25 Site Search Usage report

From Figure 10.25, you can see that visitors who use the site search facility do indeed behave quite differently from those who do not. The Pages/Visit and Average Time on Site metrics are more than twice as high, while the Bounce Rate is significantly lower. Site search users clearly have a positive impact on the user experience for this example site—unless the quality of your search results is poor (see later in this section).

Why Site Search Visits May Not Have Zero Bounce Rates

A lower bounce rate is expected for site search visitors, because by definition visitors who perform an onsite search will view at least two pages—one to conduct the search and one to view the results. So why is the bounce rate not zero?

Two common explanations are that your search result pages are indexed by the search engine robots and therefore can be accessed directly from a Google search, for example. In addition, visitors can bookmark search results and therefore view them directly at a later date. For both of these scenarios, if the visitors do not view any further pages from you (or trigger any events), they are counted as bounced visits.

Note: Be aware that when selecting different metrics from the drop-down menu, the row order (and color key) may change depending on which is the highest value. For example, "Visits With Site Search" may be displayed as the first row when revenue is selected but as the second row when bounce rate is selected. This is the same behavior for all reports. That is, the highest value is always displayed first in the data table by default.

To compare site search usage against visits that do not search the site, take the site search metric and divide by the equivalent non–site search metric. This provides you with the ratio of how much more valuable (or not) site search is for your site. For example, Figure 10.26 shows that for the Per Visit Goal Value, visits that use site search are 2.57 times more valuable than those that do not (0.18 / 0.07). Other useful metrics for this calculation are Conversion Rate, Revenue, and Number of Transactions, if applicable.

Internal Search Quality

Determining your site search's result quality is harder to ascertain. Without asking your visitors what they think (discussed in Chapter 12), a useful KPI is the number of zero-result search pages delivered. The theory is that searches producing zero results reflect a poorly configured internal site search engine.

Tracking zero results for site search is discussed in Chapter 8. Essentially, a different URL is required for search terms that generate a zero result than for those that do not. I use the Category field for this, as shown in Figure 10.27. From this example data, 22 percent of visits that used the search facility received a zero result. You can investigate this further by clicking the Zero category label and viewing the search terms that generated this result. Measuring the success of site search is described in Chapter 11.

Figure 10.26 Valuing the impact of site search usage

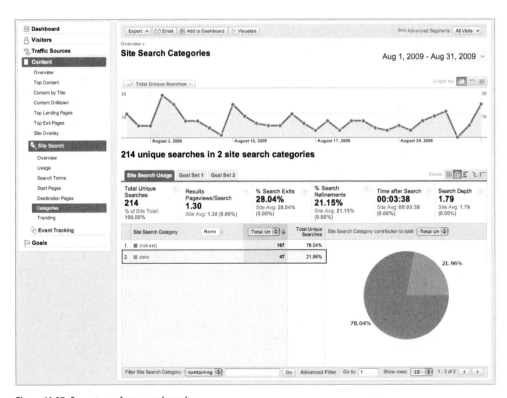

Figure 10.27 Percentage of zero search results

Note that it is possible that zero site search results could also be due to acquiring poor-quality traffic, though I have not considered this possibility here.

Using KPIs for Web 2.0

Web 2.0 is a phrase attributed to Tim O'Reilly (see www.oreillynet.com/lpt/a/6228 and www.oreillynet.com/pub/a/oreilly/tim/news/2005/09/30/what-is-web-20.html). In effect, Web 2.0 is a buzzword for the next generation of browser applications. According to Wikipedia, "Web 2.0 is a term often applied to a perceived ongoing transition of the World Wide Web from a collection of websites to a full-fledged computing platform serving web applications to end users. Ultimately Web 2.0 services are expected to replace desktop computing applications for many purposes."

The irony is that the technology that drives Web 2.0 is part of the original Web 1.0 technology and has been around for many years—that is, JavaScript and XML. Thus, Web 2.0 does not refer to any technical advancements of the Web or the Internet infrastructure it runs on but refers to changes in the way the medium is used. That's not to devalue the significance of Web 2.0, because this major shift in how users participate and surf the Web is driving the second generation of interactive web applications.

Example Web 2.0 Sites

Excellent examples of Web 2.0 websites with RIAs include the following:

Google Maps: http://maps.google.com (Ajax)

Google Mail: http://mail.google.com (Ajax)

Yahoo Mail: http://mail.yahoo.com (Ajax)

Google Docs: http://docs.google.com (Ajax)

YouTube: www.youtube.com (Flash and Ajax)

Photosynth: http://photosynth.net (Silverlight)

MobileMe: www.mobileme.com (Ajax)

Flickr: www.flickr.com (Ajax)

Fox Movies Trailer Library: http://silverlight.net/fox/ (Silverlight)

As you can see, Google is a great proponent for Web 2.0 technologies. In fact, Google Analytics itself is a prime example—combining Flash and Ajax.

Web 2.0 applications are usually built using Ajax (asynchronous JavaScript and XML) techniques. Similar to LAMP and DHTML, Ajax is not a technology in itself but a collection of technologies and methodologies combining JavaScript, XML, XHTML, and CSS. Another Web 2.0 technology is Flash. As with Ajax, it has been around for over 10 years but has only recently emerged as something more than just cool animation, with its ability to stream video and interact with XML. New up-and-coming technologies include Adobe Flex, Adobe AIR, and Microsoft Silverlight. Collectively, all these technologies are referred to as rich Internet applications (RIAs).

Why the Fuss about Web 2.0?

The techniques employed when developing a website using Web 2.0 technologies separate the components of data, format, style, and function. Instead of a web server loading a discrete page of information combining all those elements, each element is pulled separately. This has tremendous implications when it comes to defining KPIs, because the concept of a pageview all but disappears.

For example, load `http://maps.google.com` in your browser and navigate to your hometown (usually in the format of "town, country"). Then zoom in and out and pan around by dragging the map. You can also change to satellite view or a hybrid of both. It is difficult to describe this in words, but if you try it out you very quickly get the idea.

Google Maps is an excellent example of the power and interaction of a Web 2.0 website. When you load the first page, there is an initial delay while a JavaScript file is downloaded in the background. This is the controlling file that interacts with your mouse instructions. Note that the page and controlling JavaScript file are only loaded once. Then, as you interact with the map (zoom, pan around, and so on), further data is requested on the fly and inserted into the existing page. (The page URL does not change while you do this; the web page itself has become part of the delivery process.) By contrast, a traditional Web 1.0 website would require the reloading of the page to insert each additional map image.

This is an example of a visitor requesting one HTML page yet interacting in many different ways—perhaps creating dozens of actions or events (zooming and panning around) and gaining significant benefit from the experience. Clearly, using only pageview data for your KPIs is not going to work if your website contains RIAs.

 Note: Tracking Web 2.0 websites is not an issue for Google Analytics. These can even be monetized. See "Event Tracking" in Chapter 7.

Web 2.0 sites are still relatively rare, but they can have a huge impact. For example, not many people are unaware of Google Maps, Yahoo! Mail, or YouTube. The key

to their growing success is that the user experience is "cool." Visitors find and interact with content quickly and without waiting for page refreshes. I often refer to Web 2.0 as drag-and-drop technology.

Consider the screen shot from YouTube shown in Figure 10.28. The six areas highlighted are actions or events that the visitor can interact with; that is, they are not pageviews. Essentially, the visitor can multitask with all of these on the same page (only one pageview).

Figure 10.28 Visitor engagements on YouTube

As the number of Web 2.0 RIA sites grows, the requirement to define KPIs for them grows. Rather than think in terms of pageviews, analysts need to think in terms of actions and events that indicate engagement. In other words, what actions do you want your visitors to perform in order to classify an engagement?

Another implication of Web 2.0 has been the proliferation of user-generated content (UGC) sites—collectively referred to as social networks. Examples include Twitter, YouTube, Facebook, MySpace, Bebo, Orkut, and the plethora of Blogger and WordPress blogs. Measuring visitors from social networks is straightforward because they are tracked just like any other visitor to your site. The caveat is that without segmentation or rewrite filters, such visitors are buried deep within all your other referral traffic. Chapter 8 discusses how to bubble these up in your reports in the section "Example Custom Segments."

Social Marketing Is Different

Social marketing is very different from traditional marketing techniques. Essentially you attempt to influence active participants by putting your side of the story—be it to announce something new and newsworthy, to defuse criticism, or to provide comment on an existing story. You do this by interacting with others, instigating discussions, and responding to conversations. Whichever method you use, the key to success is to always have more content as a follow-up on your own website. That way, visitors will click through from the social network site onto yours. In doing so, what is happening away from your website on social networks becomes trackable within your onsite web analytics tool, Google Analytics.

Onsite web analytics tools such as Google Analytics cannot track what people are saying about your products or organization on social networks, away from your site. That is a separate form of measurement and is discussed in Chapter 1.

KPIs for Web 2.0 are actually no different from existing KPIs for a Web 1.0 world. True, you may be tracking them as events rather than pageviews; however, beyond visitor volume and transactions numbers, key metrics boil down to engagements, that is, determining how strong your virtual relationship is with your anonymous visitors. Engagement is exactly what savvy marketing managers and content creators are already focusing on with Web 1.0 technologies. If that describes you (I hope it does if you have read this far), any changes planned for your site involving RIAs or UGC will be easy for you to accommodate within your existing KPI strategy.

We discussed engagement in detail in the section "Content Creator KPI Examples." The principle is the same for RIAs and UGC. Without changing your analytical thinking, current KPIs suited to a Web 2.0 environment include the following:

- Percentage of visitors with content interaction—for example, zoom, pan around, view next message, customize

- Percentage of visitors triggering an event—for example, play, pause, next, upload, advertisement click-through, drag to cart

- Percentage engagement—for example, subscribe, register, comment, rate, add to favorites, share on Facebook

Summary

In Chapter 10, you have learned the following:

Setting objectives and key results Setting OKRs is an important prerequisite for aligning KPIs with your business, allowing you to manage expectations and gain the support of the business as a whole.

Defining KPIs based on business goals We discussed selecting and preparing KPIs by translating OKRs into actionable and accountable metrics, allowing success metrics from the Web to be incorporated into the rest of the business.

Making KPIs easy to understand You learned how to present KPIs in a clear format that business managers recognize and understand.

Defining KPIs by stakeholder job roles We examined KPI examples by job role to help you get started with important metrics.

Understanding the new KPIs You learned how Web 2.0 and rich Internet applications are changing metrics and KPI definitions.

Real-World Tasks

By now you may find your eyes glazing over at the scale of the project you have undertaken. However, Google Analytics is one of the easiest web analytics tools to configure, use, and understand. This chapter includes real-world examples of tasks most web analysts regularly need to perform. In this way, I hope to demystify the complexities of web analytics. As long as you dedicate the time and resources, you will find that this isn't rocket science. Even better, you will have a profound impact on the performance of your organization's website.

The tasks presented here are not intended to be an exhaustive or definitive list; rather, their purpose is help you obtain useful information you can act on. Acting on your data is the single most important aspect of web analytics, yet it is this aspect that most people stumble with.

11

In Chapter 11, you will learn:

To identify and optimize poorly performing pages

To measure the success of internal site search

To optimize your search-engine marketing

To monetize a non-e-commerce website

To track offline spending

To use Website Optimizer

Identifying and Optimizing Poorly Performing Pages

With all that visitor data coming in, one thing you will want to do is optimize your pages for the best possible user experience. Often the improvements are straightforward—for example, fixing broken links, changing landing-page URLs to match the visitor's intent, or aligning page content with your advertising message. But which pages should you optimize and how? If your website has more than a handful of pages, where do you start?

Traditionally for web analytics solutions, identifying pages that underperform from the plethora of other pageview data has been a difficult task. However, Google Analytics has several resources and reports to help you. This is not as an exhaustive list, but the following highlights the areas I most commonly turn to:

- $ Index values
- Top landing pages (bounce rates)
- Funnel visualization

Using $ Index Values

The importance of $ Index was discussed in Chapter 5, "Reports Explained," in the section "Understanding Page Value." In summary, it is a measure of the value of a page and is calculated as follows:

$$\$ \text{ Index} = \frac{\text{Goal Value} + \text{E-commerce Revenue}}{\text{Unique Pageviews}}$$

Essentially, if page A is viewed by visitors who go on to achieve a goal, the value of that goal counts toward the value of page A. The more times page A is viewed by visitors who achieve goals and the higher the goal value, the greater $ Index becomes. This technique is a great way to value pages that are not goals or conversions themselves. Ranking pages by their $ Index value enables you to prioritize them for optimization.

 Note: It is important to monetize goals in order for the true significance of $ Index to be realized. To define a goal value, see "Goal Conversions and Funnels," in Chapter 8, "Best-Practices Configuration Guide."

To view the $ Index values of your website pages, go to the Content > Top Content report and sort by the $ Index column (click the heading). This shows your most valuable pages. By default, pages you've defined as your goals are also included, so these will always be your highest $ Index pages. Therefore, you should remove these from the list using an inline report filter. The resultant report then reflects your most valuable pages, as shown in Figure 11.1.

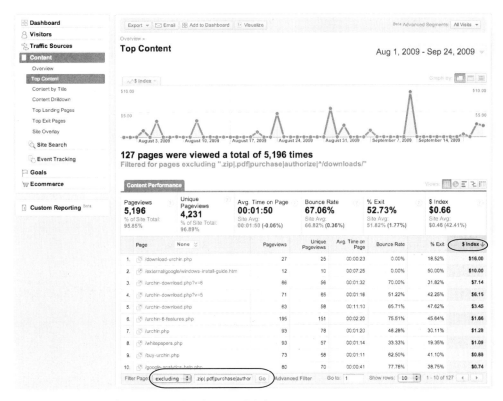

Figure 11.1 Viewing high $ Index pages with goal pages excluded

Unexpected high $ Index pages in this report—that is, those not obviously related to your goals—indicate an issue with your website structure or its content. Investigate further by clicking the page link in question within the report table. This takes you to the summary view for this page, as shown in Figure 11.2a. From here select the Navigation Summary report (see Figure 11.2b), which tells you the visitor's previous and next pages viewed—in other words, how the visitor got to that page and where they went next. From the summary view shown in Figure 11.2a, you can also select the Entrance Paths report (see Figure 11.2c). This extends the Navigation Summary report further by showing visitors who started their visit on the selected page, which pages they viewed next, and on which page they finished their visit.

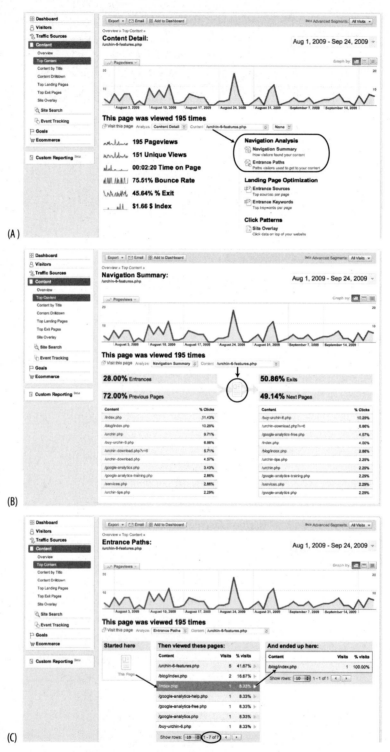

Figure 11.2 (a) A specific page summary report displayed by clicking a page link from the Top Content report, (b) Navigation Summary report, and (c) Entrance Paths report

Explanation of Figure 11.2c

Visitors who started their visit on the website in question at the page /urchin-6-features. php viewed a total of seven other pages next. Selecting one of these (/index.php), shows that one visitor went on to complete their visit on the blog home page (/blog/index.php).

Selecting Pages for Optimization

With your pages ranked in order of their $ Index values, it is tempting to simply select the least-valuable pages (lowest $ Index values) for optimization review. For example, you might assume that starting from such a low baseline might provide you with the quickest wins. However, perhaps low-performing pages are not required and these can be culled, saving you the trouble of optimizing them.

Similarly, it is also tempting to think that high $ Index value pages are looking after themselves. You may find that your payment-failure page also has a high $ Index, meaning that visitors often see this before finally completing their purchase. Likewise, this could be your contact page or terms-and-conditions page, meaning visitors need further information before completing their order.

If you notice these in your report, it indicates a problem with the conversion process. Perhaps your payment form has an unclear layout or visitors do not have enough confidence in your site to complete their purchase. Whatever the reason, you should review pages with both low and high $ Index values. Start the process by selecting your highest and lowest 10 pages by $ Index value. Then when these have been optimized (or culled), work your way inward, that is, the next 10 highest/lowest pages by $ Index.

Exercises for Page Optimization

Once you have a list of the 10 most valuable pages for your website as listed by their $ Index values, bring in your design or agency team to discuss improvements. Include a member of your sales team and your customer service department in the meeting, and ask them to bring a list of the five most common questions customers ask. Then spend a morning brainstorming.

As an initial exercise, ask the teams to map out what they consider the 10 most important pages for the website and rank them accordingly—remember to exclude the goal-completion pages. For each page, solicit a few bullet points explaining why it is important. When these are complete, compare them with your report of the 10 most valuable pages that visitors use—the highest $ Index pages. Hopefully a strong overlap is apparent, and you can move on to looking at your least-valuable pages. Unfortunately, often this is not the case. If this describes your situation, as a group use a browser to view the high $ Index pages that your team did not predict, and try to come up with three reasons why each page is so valuable from a visitor's perspective. Use the Navigation Summary report to assist in this (Figure 11.2b).

The important lesson from this exercise is understanding why visitors value pages that you as a team did not consider valuable. Your next meeting will discuss how to improve this, that is, to increase the value of those pages the team thought were valuable but visitors did not. Also discuss the alternative. That is, is it better to focus resources on the pages visitors preferred that your team missed?

The process just described is an excellent way to get your teams thinking about the value of a page in relation to the end goals for your website, rather than as a page in isolation, which is often the case. Each page must have a purpose and that is to help drive goal conversions. An obvious contribution is to present product information, but it may also be providing trust and credibility for your organization and products, as well as managing the visitor's expectations.

If your team suggests improvements that are not obviously beneficial—for example, "Let's try the sign-up process in Flash,"—consider testing the hypothesis first on a small sample of visitors (see "An Introduction to Google Website Optimizer," later in the chapter). If the tested change raises the $ Index value of the page for the sampled visitors, then it makes sense to apply the change for all visitors.

Having looked at your most valuable pages, it is straightforward to view your least valuable ones. From the Content > Top Content report, reverse the $ Index sort order by clicking again on the column heading. There's one important thing to avoid: Do not combine the assessment of high $ Index pages and low $ Index pages into one meeting. Although the objectives are the same (page improvement), I have found that mixing these page types into one meeting confuses the issue. Focus each meeting on 10 pages only—either high or low $ Index values.

Improving your least-valuable pages is an obvious ambition. First, check the difference in average $ Index values for your least-valuable pages compared to your most valuable. Maybe there is little difference, in which case all your pages are valuable!

 Tip: As a rule of thumb, I consider a significant difference between your highest- and lowest-value $ Index pages to be approximately the sum of your average daily goal value plus average daily transaction value. Remember to exclude your goal pages from your $ Index report for this calculation.

With your list of least-valuable pages, conduct another meeting with your design or agency team to discuss improvements. View each page in a browser as a group, and consider the page from the visitor's perspective. That is, how is the page related to the goals you wish them to complete? It may be that the information contained on those pages isn't relevant and can therefore be removed from your website or combined with another more valuable page. If you are an e-tailer with a large stock portfolio, perhaps the number of product pages can be reduced.

Pruning poor-performing pages in this way helps maintain focus on the remaining website pages—both for your visitors and for your organization's point of view. Maintaining irrelevant content has some overhead. Therefore, if you go through a pruning process, monetize the cost savings you have made. For example, assuming each page requires one hour of maintenance per quarter at a rate of $100 per hour, removing 25 pages saves your organization $10,000 in the first year alone!

Summary of Methodology

The use of $ Index is a powerful metric for understanding your website's content performance that I find is often underutilized, if used at all. As well as using $ Index for selecting pages that can have the greatest impact for special promotions, $ Index is your guide for optimizing poorly performing pages when there are so many pages to consider. The following is a summary of the points discussed in this section:

- If you are a non-transactional site, ensure your goals are monetized or this method won't work! Even if you have an e-commerce facility, you should also consider monetizing goals to measure the broader impact of site content. See Chapter 8 for details.

- Remove goal pages from your Top Content report by using an inline filter or advanced segment, because these will always be your top-valued pages.

- From the remaining list, select 10 pages at a time for review—alternating between the 10 highest and 10 lowest $ Index pages. Avoid the temptation of combining both into one review.

- Investigate any unexpected pages in your top 10 list by viewing Navigation Summary and Entrance Paths reports.

- Meet with your design team (plus sales and customer service persons) to brainstorm the list. From your group's point of view, which pages are missing from the report and which pages are surprises?

- View the content of each page and determine how to increase its value. Ask the team what its contribution is to your goals and how these can be strengthened. Add or modify the conversion contributing factors or consider removing the page.

- Where page improvements are not obvious, consider showing alternatives to a small sample of your visitors by using an A/B or multivariate testing tool—see "An Introduction to Google Website Optimizer" later in this chapter.

- Conduct this entire exercise quarterly. For example, you may select 20 pages in the first quarter (10 most valuable and 10 least valuable), followed by the next 10 of each in the second quarter, and so forth. Considering that most websites obey the 20/80 rule, that is, 20 percent of content responsible for 80 percent of revenue, you should find your optimization efforts being rewarded quickly. Expect a bonus or promotion by the end of the first year!

This methodology for identifying and optimizing pages using $ Index values can also be applied to other metrics, such as bounce rates, as discussed next.

Using Top Landing Pages (Bounce Rates)

As the name suggests, the Content > Top Landing Pages report shows the most popular entrance pages for your visitors (see Figure 11.3).

Figure 11.3 Top Landing Pages report

For this report, the bounce rate is the *key* metric; if visitors are arriving at the landing page and then leaving the site after viewing only that one page, it is poor engagement. If a landing page has a high bounce rate, then it means that the content of that page did not meet the visitors' expectations. Beyond looking for page errors, you need insight as to what the visitors' expectations were, which means looking at the referral details.

What constitutes a high bounce rate is discussed in the section entitled "Content Creator KPI Examples" in Chapter 10, "Focusing on Key Performance Indicators." My rule of thumb is to define *high* as a bounce rate of greater than 50 percent. From Figure 11.3, for each page with a high bounce rate, click its link in the report. This takes you to the same Content Detail report shown in Figure 11.2a.

For assessing bounce rates, the Navigation Analysis report of Figure 11.2a is not required, because the entry point and exit point are the same page for those visits that bounce. Similarly, click patterns (entrance paths) are not relevant for bounced visits. The key reports to view are within the Landing Page Optimization section—namely, entrance sources and entrance keywords—because these refer to your visitors' expectations before arriving on your website.

At this point, adopt a similar approach as described in the previous section for identifying and optimizing $ Index values. Substitute Bounce Rate for $ Index, and analyze this against referral source and referral keywords (as opposed to page name). This time bring in your marketing team and dive into the following reports.

Assessing Entrance Sources

As the term suggests, *entrance sources* are the referring websites and campaigns that lead visitors to your site—for example, search engines, paid advertising, social networks, affiliates, and email links. An example report for a website home page is shown in Figure 11.4.

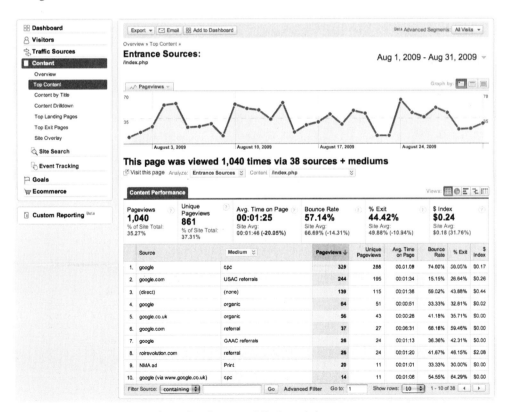

Figure 11.4 Entrance Sources report for a website home page (/index.php)

Discuss this report with your marketing team by considering the following perspectives:

- Offline marketing initiatives
- Paid search campaigns
- Search engine optimization (SEO)
- Social network participation

In the report shown in Figure 11.4, the source labeled (direct) could be the result of offline marketing efforts whereby people have seen your ad and remembered your web address. If you observe a high bounce rate from this source, then look at how you are targeting visitors by offline methods. A common mistake is to send visitors for a specific campaign to a generic home page, leading to poor traction with the visitor. Later in this chapter I discuss how to overcome this (see "Tracking Offline Marketing").

Note: The label (direct) will also be applied to visitors who bookmark your website (add to favorites) and any non-web referral link that has not been tagged correctly, such as email links and embedded links within digital collateral. To ensure that these are tracked, refer to "Campaign Tracking" in Chapter 7, "Advanced Implementation."

From Figure 11.4, identify any paid search campaigns. Rows 1 and 10 are examples from the Google AdWords pay-per-click network. Pay-per-click advertising is an excellent way to target search-engine visitors with a specific message (ad creative) and specific content (landing-page URL). Any high bounce rates observed from these sources should be investigated immediately, because they reflect poor targeting or a misaligned message. A common mistake is using time- or price-sensitive information in your ad creatives that is outdated when the visitor clicks through. Therefore, you should review your ads carefully.

In addition, are your ad landing-page URLs targeted for your campaigns? In the example of Figure 11.4, the high bounce rate from cpc (AdWords) visitors indicates that use of the generic home page as a landing-page URL is a poor choice, and it should be changed to a more specific one. Another area to look at is how you target your visitors with geotargeting; for example, do your pricing and delivery options match the expectations of visitors from different locations? These are discussed later in this chapter in "Optimizing Your Search Engine Marketing."

From an SEO perspective, think in terms of the visitor experience, because ultimately this is what search engines are trying to emulate with their ranking algorithms. For high-bounce-rate pages, view the source code and read the content within the HTML `<title>` and `<meta name="description"...>` tag sections. Are your page title tag and description metatag in alignment with the rest of your page content? This is important, because it is the only information about your organization a visitor sees on a search-engine-results page—the text of the clickable link is taken from your page title tag, while the snippet of text underneath is taken from your meta description tag. Hence, these are important qualifiers for visitors before clicking through to your site. Discuss with your marketing team making adjustments to these HTML tags.

Also consider link referrals from other websites. A visitor who follows a link from another website that turns out to be out of context is obviously a poor experience and waste of time for the visitor (it can also have a negative impact on your SEO rankings). If you find referral links with high bounce rates, use the Traffic Sources > Referring Sites report to investigate further. From there you can identify the referring site and view the exact page that visitors clicked through to arrive on your website (see Figure 11.5). Sometimes a simple, polite email to the webmaster of the referring site can pay you dividends. Specify that you want to ensure that links are in context and point to a relevant, specific landing page on your website. Provide any necessary details in your email.

Figure 11.5 Referring Link report

Assessing Entrance Keywords

The Entrance Keywords report focuses on those visitors who have used search engines to arrive on your website—both paid and nonpaid (organic) search engines. In effect, this report is direct market research—visitors are informing you exactly what content they expect to see on the page they arrive at on your site, as shown in Figure 11.6.

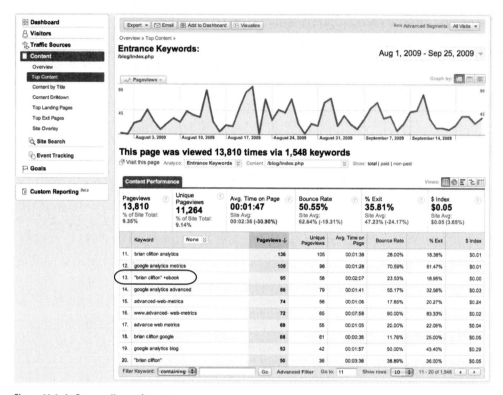

Figure 11.6 An Entrance Keywords report

As with the Entrance Sources report, high bounce rates here (greater than 50 percent) are an indicator that something may be amiss with your online marketing. Assuming your web server performance is not an issue, look at your visitor targeting, message alignment, and page relevancy, as described in the previous section.

Following this, consider the Entrance Keywords report as an opportunity to build page content around the listed keywords. For example, in Figure 11.6, row 13 for www.advanced-web-metrics.com shows a search term of "brian clifton +ebook," yet I had not considered the term "ebook" in my content—instead I had been referencing the format terminology as PDF. I now know "ebook" is an important term to my visitors and so have been including it ever since on relevant pages.

This is an example of where viewing low-bounce-rate pages can also provide important information (row 13 shows a low bounce rate). Generally speaking, you will focus your efforts on analyzing high-bounce-rate pages because these are the ones killing your visitors' user experience. However, as described in the previous section for using $ Index values, it's important to look at both ends of the spectrum when searching for insights. Then work your way inward, that is, consider the next 10 high- or low-bounce-rate pages.

Funnel Visualization Case Study

As discussed in Chapter 5, funnel analysis is an important process that helps you recognize barriers to conversion on your website, including the checkout process. I have often seen how understanding the visitor's journey within a website, followed by subsequent changes to improve the process, can lead to dramatic improvements in conversion rates and therefore the bottom line. The fourfold increase in bookings for the travel website example shown in Figure 1.1 was the result of the following funnel visualization and optimization case study performed at my company (omegadm.com).

Note: According to 2009 data from Coremetrics (`http://www.coremetrics.co.uk/solutions/benchmarking.php`), the average shopping cart abandonment rate for U.S. online retailers is 65.4 percent. Interestingly, for the UK it is smaller, at 50.1 percent. In other words, the transaction revenue obtained by site owners is a third, and half of the revenue that customers are willing to, and are in the process of, spending respectively.

Schematic funnel shapes and their meanings are discussed in Chapter 8 in "What Funnel Shapes Can Tell You." An ideal funnel process would schematically look like Figure 11.7, where there is a gradual decrease in visitors (width of funnel) because of self-qualification through the various steps (height of funnel). The process of self-qualification could be by, for example, price, feature list, delivery location, stock availability, and so on.

Figure 11.7 An ideal schematic wine goblet funnel shape

For this travel website case study, Figure 11.8 illustrates the checkout process (booking a vacation).

The customer follows these steps:

1. Search for a vacation rental.
2. View search results.
3. Check the availability of rental.
4. Book the trip.
5. Confirm the booking.
6. Make payment.
7. Receive confirmation of payment.

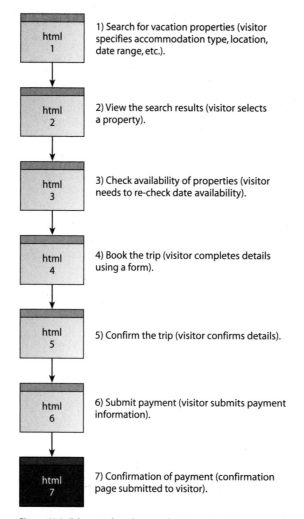

html 1	1) Search for vacation properties (visitor specifies accommodation type, location, date range, etc.).
html 2	2) View the search results (visitor selects a property).
html 3	3) Check availability of properties (visitor needs to re-check date availability).
html 4	4) Book the trip (visitor completes details using a form).
html 5	5) Confirm the trip (visitor confirms details).
html 6	6) Submit payment (visitor submits payment information).
html 7	7) Confirmation of payment (confirmation page submitted to visitor).

Figure 11.8 Schematic funnel process for the travel website case study

Figure 11.9 is the actual funnel process reported in Google Analytics for the travel website.

Note: I am quite biased when it comes to travel websites. On the whole, they tend to be poorly built from a user's viewpoint. They are pretty, with a lot of colorful images and inspiring photographs, but I never seem to have a good experience when it comes to actually booking my travel plans, let alone a great one. However, as a wise person (Sara Andersson) once said to me, "Your biggest obstacle is also your greatest opportunity."

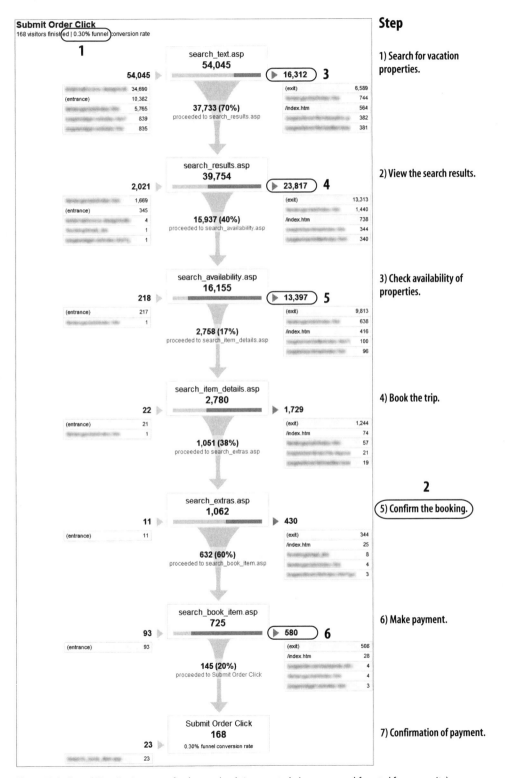

Figure 11.9 Funnel Visualization report for the travel website case study (page names obfuscated for anonymity)

Issues with the Funnel Presented

The steps from the funnel visualization in Figure 11.8 are discussed in the context of the following six issues, indicated by the large numerals in Figure 11.9:

Issue 1 The most obvious metric that stands out in Figure 11.9 is the end conversion rate—a woefully poor 0.30 percent. Put another way, 99.70 percent of all visitors abandon the booking process. Considering the cost of acquiring those visitors by both paid and nonpaid search, that means a very, very negative return on investment.

> **Note:** Although this funnel example is an extreme case, it never ceases to amaze me that online purchase rates can be so low and are accepted as such. For example, a July 2007 Forrester Research report showed U.S. retail websites convert an average of 2–3 percent of their site visitors into buyers. Surely we can do better than have 97-plus percent of visitors leave a website without conversion? I hope that having read this far, you will agree that it is laudable and entirely possible to improve this percentage significantly.

Issue 2 Looking at the entire booking process, the length of the funnel, at seven steps, appears overly long. From user-experience experiments, it is widely known that users do not like long checkout processes. That's obvious to anyone who uses the Web! The most effective method to reduce cart abandonment is to streamline the number of steps in the process, and this is applicable here. For example, step 5 (Confirm the Booking) is superfluous because all booking details are displayed at each preceding step.

Issue 3 The first step in the process begins with the search_text.asp page. This is the page where visitors search for their vacation rental (hotel, villa, apartment). From this page, 30 percent drop out of the funnel.

Issue 4 Following step 1, the search results page (step 2) loses 60 percent of remaining visitors; over half of these (13,313) exit the site completely.

Issue 5 Looking at the check-availability page (step 3), 83 percent of remaining visitors drop out of the funnel; again, the vast majority are site exits (60 percent). This is clearly a pain point and should be red-flagged as a problem page.

Issue 6 The next steps in the system have similar problems, but the killer is step 6, which is when payment details from the visitor are requested. Out of the 725 visitors who have had the stamina and persistence to get through what is obviously a difficult process, 80 percent of them (580) abandon at this final step; the vast majority leave the website completely.

Seeing the result of these issues represented schematically, rather than seeing the ideal funnel shape of Figure 11.7, we observe a funnel shape more like what is shown in Figure 11.10, with two clear pain points in the process, step 3 and step 6, that lead to large-scale abandonment.

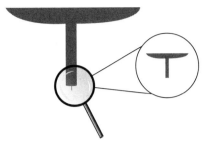

Figure 11.10 Stacked champagne glass schematic funnel shape

Action Points from the Funnel Visualization

Understanding the real-world funnel process of Figure 11.9 and its problems took less than one hour because the data is so clearly presented. Of course, correcting such issues obviously takes longer; you need to understand why this happened. This is something that web analytics tools cannot do; they cannot tell you why visitors are abandoning your booking process.

To address this, you could deploy a feedback system—a survey that pops up when a visitor abandons the booking process or leaves your website. Example survey tools include Clicktools, Kampyle, SurveyMonkey, and UserVoice. However, if your visitors are leaving because of a bad experience, they usually won't want to spend further time on your site explaining what went wrong. That said, any feedback from visitors *within* your shopping-cart system who are abandoning is gold dust and worth pursuing. See Chapter 12, "Integrating Google Analytics With Third-Party Applications," for an example integration with the Kampyle feedback system.

Putting aside having to deploy a feedback survey system, a little lateral thought and visiting your own website as if you were a potential customer can go a long way. For example, in this scenario I focused on steps 3 and 6, where the vast majority of visitors were abandoning the booking process. This led to the development of four key recommendations for improvement:

Improve the availability checker page. Step 3 (the availability checker) indicates either a total lack of accommodation availability, in which case the website owners should turn down the visitor acquisition "tap" and save marketing budget, or a malfunction in the process of selecting available dates.

Lack of availability was not an issue. By viewing the availability checker manually, no errors were found, but the process was quite clunky and difficult to interpret. For example, dates themselves were non-clickable. Instead, date-selection controls were located below the fold of the page—that is, not visible without scrolling down.

Correct the layout of the payment form. Step 6 (the payment form) required some additional thought. Although the form was considered to be overly long at seven steps, it did not make sense that such persistent visitors would bail out at the penultimate step (visitors were aware of their progress by the numbering of the steps—for example, with the heading "Step X of Y"). To test for problems, I tried the process of booking a vacation myself.

What I immediately discovered when clicking to submit my dummy payment details was an error page. In addition, the error page did not indicate what caused the problem. Using the Back button, I checked all the required fields and tried again—same error page, no message indicating what the error was. This process was repeated many times with no further insight. It really did appear to be a mystery as to why I could not complete my payment.

In fact, the problem was staring me in the face. The credit card type (Amex, Visa, MasterCard) was preselected as Amex by default. However, the HTML drop-down list for selecting the card type was not aligned with the other form fields—it was to the extreme right of the page when everything else was left justified.

Despite repeatedly testing the payment system and staring frustratedly at the page, I simply didn't see the right-justified card selector. I was filling in all my details correctly and hadn't noticed the default setting for the credit card as Amex while I was using Visa. In fact, I hadn't noticed the card type drop-down list at all.

Now the explanation of large-scale abandonment at step 6 is clear. Visitors were receiving the error page, which was probably the straw that broke the camel's back after such a difficult and tortuous booking process, and so they simply abandoned the site.

Streamlining the Checkout Process

Although selecting your card type on a payment form is almost always a manual process, it is possible to automate this and remove any potential errors. You can do this by using the initial digits of the card number, as shown in the following table:

Card Types	Prefix	Number of digits
American Express	34, 37	15
Diners Club	300 to 305, 36	14
Carte Blanche	38	14
Discover	6011	16
EnRoute	2014, 2149	15
JCB	3	16
JCB	2131, 1800	15
MasterCard	51 to 55	16
Visa	4	13, 16

Track error pages. Part of the difficulty in identifying the problem visitors were experiencing in step 6 was because the subsequent error page was not being tracked. Had it been, using the methods described in Chapter 9, "Google Analytics Hacks," the investigation could have taken place much more quickly.

Show clear instructions in your error pages. Even if an investigation into the low conversion rate had not been undertaken, visitors could have corrected the payment problem themselves—that is, if they were told what the problem was. Clearly this is not a solution to the problem, but it is certainly better than slamming the door in their face with nothing more informative than "Error—please try again."

Summary of Funnel Visualization

Presenting these findings to the client was groundbreaking. They had hired and fired several search-engine marketing agencies in the belief that they were receiving poorly qualified leads, resulting in such a low (0.3 percent) conversion rate. In fact, the problem was entirely on their site: a poor user experience. Once fixed, their conversion rate jumped by four-fold, with a concomitant revenue increase of millions of extra dollars per year. I should have billed by commission!

Funnel analysis shows both the power and the weakness of web analytics as a technique for understanding visitor behavior on your website. The power is in identifying the problem areas during a typical path visitors take; for that, your web analytics is capable of telling you what happened and when. That in turn enables you to focus your efforts on improving the particular problem page. The weakness of web analytics is that it does not tell you why visitors made the choices they did. To understand why visitors behave in a non-anticipated way, you need to investigate—either directly yourself (try a checkout or booking on your own website) or by conducting a survey or usability experiment. Integrating data from Google Analytics with feedback surveys is discussed in Chapter 12.

> **Tip:** If *usability experiments* is a new term for you, check out the excellent book by Steve Krug, *Don't Make Me Think*, as a background read before contacting a specialist agency.

Measuring the Success of Site Search

Site search is the internal search engine of your website that visitors often substitute for a menu-navigation system. For large websites with hundreds or thousands of content pages (sometimes hundreds of thousands), internal search is a critical component for website visitors, enabling them to find what they are looking for quickly. Internal search engines generally use the same architecture as an external search engine such as Google. In fact, the major search-engine companies sell their search technology to organizations. See, for example, the Google Search Appliance (www.google.com/enterprise/gsa/).

Important site-search KPIs were discussed in the section "Webmaster KPI Examples," in Chapter 10. In addition to the Ecommerce Overview report (refer to Figure 10.24), one of the things you will want to know is what keywords visitors are typing once they arrive on your website. The idea is that once you know these keywords, you include them (or exclude them if they are not relevant to you) in your paid and organic campaigns, as well as ensure that landing pages are optimized for them. This is discussed in the next section, "Optimizing Your Search Engine Marketing." An example Site Search Terms report is shown in Figure 11.11.

Figure 11.11 Site Search Terms report showing keywords used

Note: The value of the Site Search Terms report shown in Figure 11.11 should not be underestimated. Visitors on your website are actually telling you what they would like to see, in their own language, using their own terminology. Perhaps you assumed "widgets" was the commonly known name of your product, but you find out that people are searching for "gadgets," or people are looking for "widgets with feature X," which your manufacturing team hadn't thought of. It's analogous to your potential customers walking into your store or office and providing you with direct feedback—without you having to ask or worry about infringing on visitor privacy.

In addition to viewing what search terms are used on your website, you should track how these convert by viewing the Goal Conversion and Ecommerce tabs. Useful metrics for this are the Per Search Value (for e-commerce sites) and Per Search Goal Value (for sites with monetized goals).

Per Search Values are similar in principal to $ Index, described earlier in this chapter. $ Index measures the value of a page according to whether that page is used by visitors who go on to complete monetized goals or e-commerce transactions. Per Search Values measure the value of a site-search term. That is, did visitors who used a particular site-search term go on to complete a transaction or monetized goal? The higher the Per Search Value or Per Search Goal Value, the greater value that term is to the success of your website, as shown in Figure 11.12. Therefore, make use of the Per Search Values when prioritizing which search terms to overlap with your website marketing.

Figure 11.12 The value of site-search terms

Beyond looking at site-search terms used, how do visitors who use your site-search facility compare to those who do not? I illustrate this with a series of screenshots taken from the Content > Site Search > Usage reports.

From Figure 11.13, you can see that the percentage of visits resulting in a site search is low at only 2.67 percent. However, the bounce rate for those visitors is much lower at 10.51 percent, compared to those who did not perform a search (64.07 percent). Hence, a better user experience is inferred for those visitors.

Note: Having a bounce rate reported for site-search visitors may sound contradictory. How can a visitor who conducts a search bounce if they landed on a page, conducted a site search, and viewed the results—that is, viewed a minimum of two pages? For this example website, site-search result pages are also directly listed on referrer sites and in search-engine result pages such as Google. Therefore, the landing page is a site-search result in itself. If a visitor views only this page—the search results—and then leaves the site, they will be reported as a bounced visitor.

Figure 11.13 Bounce rate comparison of visitors who use site search and visitors who do not

Select other key metrics from the drop-down list highlighted in Figure 11.14. The ones I focus on in addition to bounce rates are as follows:

Goal Conversion Rate

$$\text{Goal Conversion Rate} = \left(\frac{\text{Number of Conversions}}{\text{Number of Visits}} \right) \times 100$$

Revenue

Revenue = Goal Value + E-commerce Value

Average Value

$$\text{Average Value} = \left(\frac{\text{Goal Value} + \text{E-commerce Value}}{\text{Number of Conversions} + \text{Number of Transactions}} \right)$$

E-commerce Conversion Rate

$$\text{E-commerce Conversion Rate} = \left(\frac{\text{Number of Transactions}}{\text{Number of Visits}} \right) \times 100$$

Per Visit Value

$$\text{Per Visit Value} = \frac{\text{Goal Value} + \text{E-commerce Value}}{\text{Number of Visits}}$$

Figure 11.14 The Per Visit Value difference from using site search

A particular favorite of mine is the Per Visit Goal Value (and Per Visit Value if you are an e-commerce site). As shown in Figure 11.14, a visitor who uses site search is nearly 2.5 times as valuable as a visitor who does not. Armed with that information, meet with your web development team (those responsible for your internal site search engine) and discuss with them what plans they have for developing and growing the site-search service. Before doing so, use the following formula to calculate the revenue impact that site search is having on your website:

$$\begin{array}{c}\text{Revenue Impact} \\ \text{of Site Search}\end{array} = \left(\begin{array}{c}\text{Per Visit Goal Value} \\ \text{with Site Search}\end{array} - \begin{array}{c}\text{Per Visit Goal Value} \\ \text{without Site Search}\end{array} \right) \times \begin{array}{c}\text{Number of Visits} \\ \text{with Site Search}\end{array}$$

From the eight-week period shown in Figure 11.14 and knowing the number of visitors who used site search for this example website (1,865 taken from the Site Search Overview report), the calculation is

Revenue Impact of Site Search = $(0.22 - 0.09) \times 1865 = \$121.23$ per month

This metric puts you in a great position to help your development team budget for further investment in site search. To put this value into context, it represents only 2.67 percent of the total traffic to the site. If site-search participation can be increased, say to a quarter of all visits, their value becomes $1,210 per month—very significant for a small-business nontransactional website.

If you are an e-commerce site, perform the same calculation substituting Per Visit Value for the Per Visit Goal Value. Often for e-commerce websites, the dollar impact of site search can be dramatic.

What if the metrics are reversed—that is, visitors who use site search have lower Per Visit and Per Visit Goal Values than those who don't. This would result in a negative revenue impact of site search—its use is costing you money!

It is possible that such a result could be valid. That is, in some scenarios, finding information can best be served by a directory-type structure of navigation rather than a search engine (before search dominated the Web, this was the business model of Yahoo!—selling directory listings). For example, generic keywords—those with multiple contexts such as "golf clubs" (can mean equipment or associations) and location-specific keywords are a few examples where navigating a directory structure may serve the visitor better than using your site search. However, this is rare.

A negative revenue impact of site search usually indicates an issue with the quality of the results returned. So far, we have assumed that your internal site search engine is working well—producing accurate and informative results regarding visitors' searches. Unfortunately, this is rarely the case. To get a handle on whether this is valid, look at the zero results produced by your site-search engine. The method for tracking zero results is discussed in Chapter 8 under the "Initial Configuration" section. Assuming you have used the same setup, select the label "Zero" from your Site Search Category report. This reveals the keywords used that generated a zero result—as per Figure 11.15.

Export this list into Excel, and highlight the keywords that are directly related to your website content. Meet with your web development team to ascertain why such relevant terms produce zero results. Maybe you have overlooked misspellings, regional differences (think "holiday" versus "vacation"), or visitors using terminology they are not familiar with that needs to be considered. However, it may be that there is a problem with how your site-search engine works or is configured. Is it picking up newly created or modified pages? Can it index PDF files? How is it ranking results?

Figure 11.15 Site-search zero-result keywords

Site-search engines are often installed and configured once and then forgotten about—that's a mistake. I often find the greatest opportunity for site improvement, that is, conversion and revenue improvement, is found by looking at its site-search performance. Websites evolve rapidly, including new content and new technologies. If site-search visitors have a lower revenue impact without good reason, then site search is costing you money. Present this figure to the head of your web team and schedule a meeting to discuss enhancements or a replacement. Showing a dollar amount is a much better motivator than saying, "Our site search is not working as effectively as our navigation system."

With your export list of zero-result site-search terms, highlight the keywords visitors used that are *not* relevant to your organization but are related to the business you are in. If the number of these is significant (more than a few percentage points of the total number of unique searches), then meet with your product or service team to discuss their meaning. Perhaps the product team never thought people would want to search for feature X combined with product Y. Your site-search data could provide valuable insight into this. For example, an action item may be able to build a specific landing page for product XY to gain further feedback from those visitors.

Optimizing Your Search Engine Marketing

If you own a commercial website, then you want to drive as much qualified traffic to it as possible. Online marketing options include search-engine optimization (nonpaid search, also known as organic search), paid search advertising (also referred to as pay-per-click or cost-per-click), email marketing, banner displays, and social network participation (comments and links left on sites such as Twitter, LinkedIn, Facebook, forums, blogs, and so on).

All of these visitor-acquisition methods have a cost—either direct with the media owner or indirect in management fees—though there is nothing stopping you as a do-it-yourself enthusiast. Optimizing your marketing campaigns using Google Analytics data can achieve cost savings and expose significant opportunities for your business. This section focuses on the essential steps for optimizing your search engine marketing (SEM), both paid and nonpaid, including the following:

- Keyword discovery (paid and nonpaid search)
- Campaign optimization (paid search)
- Landing page optimization and SEO (paid and nonpaid search)
- AdWords ad positioning optimization (paid search)
- AdWords day-parting optimization (paid search)
- AdWords ad-version optimization (paid search)

Keyword Discovery

When optimizing for SEM, one of the things you will constantly be on the lookout for is ideas for adding new, relevant keywords to your campaigns. These can be broad (for example, "shoes"), bringing in low-qualified visitors in the hope they will bookmark your page or remember your brand and website address for later use, or very specific (for example "blue suede shoes"), which are highly targeted to one of your products and could lead to an immediate conversion on a visitor's first visit.

Several *offsite* tools are on the market, both free and commercial, to help you conduct keyword research, for example:

- Google AdWords Keyword Tool (https://adwords.google.com/select/KeywordToolExternal)
- Wordtracker (http://freekeywords.wordtracker.com/)
- Microsoft's adCenter Labs (http://adlab.microsoft.com/Keyword-Research.aspx)

These all enable you to discover what people are searching for on the Web as a whole (hence the term *offsite tool*) that may be related to your products or services and in what numbers. The tools help you determine which search keywords are most frequently used by search-engine visitors and then help you identify related keywords, synonyms, and misspellings that could also be useful to your marketing campaigns.

Clearly, being language and region specific is important; for example, *tap* and *holiday* are terms used in the UK that in the United States are more commonly known as *faucet* and *vacation*, respectively.

> **Note:** The differences between offsite and onsite web analytics are discussed in Chapter 1, "Why Understanding Your Web Traffic Is Important to Your Business."

In addition to these offsite tools, your Google Analytics reports contain a wealth of onsite information that can help you hunt for additional suitable keywords. There are two areas to look at: search terms used by visitors to find your website from a search engine and internal site-search queries, that is, those used by visitors within your website.

Farming from Organic Visitors

The Traffic Sources > Keywords report is dedicated to referral keywords—keywords used by visitors who come from all search engines, both paid and nonpaid (see Figure 11.16). As an initial exercise, click the "non-paid" link from the Show menu, and then export all of your non-paid keywords. Compare these with those targeted by your paid campaigns. Nonpaid terms (organic terms), which are not in your paid campaigns, are excellent candidates to be added to your pay-per-click account. After all, you will wish to maximize your exposure to relevant search terms.

Note that when adding keywords used by organic search visitors to your pay-per-click campaigns, you should consider your current organic search rankings for those terms. For example, if you are number one for your brand or product name in the organic results, should you also add this to your paid campaigns? If you do, you are likely to cannibalize your own free organic traffic. On the other hand, you would remove a competitor from the search engine paid results; that is, you would occupy more "shelf space" on the results page.

If you are in organic position 1, 2, or 3, test whether an additional paid listing brings you benefit—add the organic term to a paid campaign and measure the total traffic (organic + paid search) for that keyword. If you notice a 1 + 1 = 3 effect in traffic volume or conversions, continue the paid campaign. Otherwise, abandon this strategy because you are paying for visitors you would normally receive free. As a rule, I advise not adding organic keywords to your pay-per-click campaigns when you already occupy the number-one organic position on that particular search engine.

Beyond exporting your list of organic keywords, the screen shown in Figure 11.16 is an excellent example of the wealth of information readily available within reports for improving your SEO efforts. In this case I have selected the pivot view to show visits and bounce rates on a per–search engine basis. The secondary dimension is also used to provide the landing page URL for each keyword. The result is a report that correlates keywords with landing pages on a per search engine basis, showing bounce rate and visit metrics. Information that will surely keep any marketer busy for several hours!

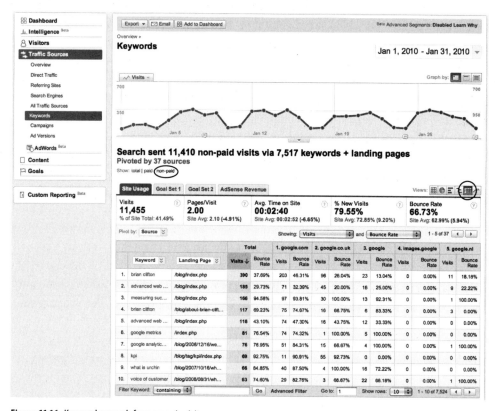

Figure 11.16 Keyword research from organic visitors

Farming from Site-Search Visitors

If your site has an internal search engine to help visitors find what they are looking for, then this is an excellent feedback mechanism for your marketing department—that is, visitors telling you exactly what they want to see on your website. Your Content > Site Search > Search Terms report is a rich seam of invaluable keyword information for you to mine. We looked at measuring the success of site search in the preceding section and also in Chapter 10, in the section "Webmaster KPI Examples."

From within your Google Analytics account, export your site-search keywords and compare them with those in your paid search accounts (pay-per-click). Site-search keywords not in your pay-per-click accounts are strong candidates to be added. You can prioritize these by considering not only their prevalence in site-usage reports but also whether they produce goal conversions and e-commerce transactions. The use of

Per Visit Value and Per Visit Goal Value for this was discussed earlier in the section "Measuring the Success of Site Search."

When selecting new keywords from your Site Search reports, also check your organic rankings for these. If you have a relevant landing page ranked in one of the top three organic search-engine positions for a particular search engine, I suggest that you do not add that term to your paid campaigns for that search engine. As mentioned in the previous section, this is likely to cannibalize your own free organic traffic.

In addition to comparing keywords from site search with your paid campaigns, also compare them with your nonpaid search terms. Perhaps there are variations in usage or spelling you can take account of in your page content. Perhaps visitors are using relevant keywords after they are on your site that you are not aware of. For example, visitors looking for books may also use keywords such as "how-to guides," "manuals," "whitepapers," and "tech sheets" on your internal site search. This is a perfect opportunity to build and optimize your website content for those additional, related terms.

Campaign Optimization (Paid Search)

After farming for new keywords from organic search engines and site-search users, and adding these to your paid campaigns (if applicable) and to the content of relevant pages, the next stage is to ensure that these keywords are optimized—that is, that they give you the best possible chance of conversion.

Within the Traffic Sources report is a dedicated section for AdWords. This enables you to drill down into Campaign, Ad Group, and Keyword levels for details of conversion rates, return on investment, margin, and more. As a business entity, you want to invest more in campaigns that produce more conversions and leads for you than in those that merely create visibility for your brand. However, you must take care here because by default Google Analytics gives credit for a conversion to the last referrer. In other words, spending more on campaigns that are reported as generating conversions and culling those that don't may result in you chopping off the head that feeds the tail. For methods of changing the default attribution model, see the section entitled "Changing the Referrer Credited for a Goal Conversion" in Chapter 9.

What about Other PPC Networks?

Currently, within Google Analytics you can track visitors from any search engine, indeed any referral. You can track not only which search engine visitors came from but also their paths and conversion rates, down to campaign and keyword levels. However, at present, cost data can be imported only from AdWords. That is, ROI data can be calculated only for AdWords visitors.

For those keywords that convert, you should optimize your investment by setting the maximum cost-per-click (CPC) you can afford within AdWords. The caveat is that your return on investment should be positive—that is, revenue generated being greater than your costs. The following is an example:

ROI = (Revenue − Cost) / Cost

If your ROI for a keyword is 500 percent, this means you are receiving a $5 return for every $1 spent on AdWords. Assuming your revenue is $600 from $100 spent, this is calculated as follows:

ROI = (600 − 100) / 100

= 500% expressed as a percentage

However, Google Analytics has no idea what margins you operate under, so you need to factor these in. That is, unless you are selling services, you need to take into account your operating profit margin to get the true ROI figure. For example, taking into account your manufacturing costs or reseller purchase price, if your profit margin (excluding marketing costs) is 40 percent, your true gross profit ROI is calculated as

$\text{ROI}_{\text{gross profit}}$ = (Revenue × Margin − Cost) / Cost
$\text{ROI}_{\text{gross profit}}$ = (600 × 0.4 − 100) / 100
$\text{ROI}_{\text{gross profit}}$ = 140% expressed as a percentage

This means you can afford to spend up to 140 percent more money (2.4 times as much) on this keyword in AdWords without producing a negative ROI.

Note: At the beginning of a campaign launch, your ROI may be negative as you build up brand awareness and visibility for your website. Visitors to a new website (new to them) usually require multiple visits before they convert. However, a negative ROI should be acceptable for only a short period of time—of the order of weeks, depending on your circumstances. See also Figure 10.6 in the section entitled, "E-Commerce Manager KPI Examples," in Chapter 10.

Clearly, you do not want to reach this maximum—zero percent ROI—otherwise, what's the point of being in business? Therefore, select a value that you are comfortable with—that is, one that drives more traffic to your website while still being profitable. With your preferred $\text{ROI}_{\text{gross profit}}$ set, calculate the maximum amount this allows you to spend on customer acquisition—the maximum cost per acquisition (cpa_{max})—by using the following procedure:

$$\text{cpa}_{\text{max}} = \frac{\text{Average Order Value} \times \text{Margin}}{\text{ROI}_{\text{gross profit}} + 1}$$

CHAPTER 11: REAL-WORLD TASKS

For this calculation, I have used the Keyword 1 data from the e-commerce report shown in Figure 11.17. Setting a target $\text{ROI}_{\text{gross profit}}$ of 25 percent (making $0.25 profit for every $1 spent) and a profit margin of 40 percent, the calculation is

$$\text{cpa}_{\text{max}} = 5.21 \times 0.4 / 0.25 + 1$$
$$\text{cpa}_{\text{max}} = \$1.67$$

This is the total cost you are willing to pay for a visitor with this keyword in order to achieve an average order of $5.21.

Figure 11.17 AdWords Keywords report

Knowing your conversion rate for each keyword, you can now calculate your maximum cost-per-click (cpc_{max}) allowed for that keyword. The conversion rate for purchases arising from keyword 1 is taken from Figure 11.17.

$$\text{cpc}_{\text{max}} = \text{cpa}_{\text{max}} \times (\text{Ecommerce Conversion Rate} / 100)$$
$$\text{cpc}_{\text{max}} = \$1.67 \times (12.31 / 100)$$
$$\text{cpc}_{\text{max}} = \$0.21$$

For this example keyword, you could bid up to $0.21 in AdWords to generate as much traffic as possible and be assured that you will make a gross profit of $1.25 for every $1 spent. You will never overbid for your AdWords keywords—even if you reach your cpc_{max} within your AdWords account, you will still maintain a 125 percent $\text{ROI}_{\text{gross profit}}$. Of course, the actual bid you pay in AdWords is determined by the market—that is, how many competitors are also bidding on the same keyword and how effective their ads are at gaining click-throughs. This is the basis of the AdWords Quality Score system. Hence, your $ROI_{gross\ profit}$ could turn out to be higher.

Without taking your profit margin into account, Google Analytics will report an ROI at your cpc_{max} as follows:

$$ROI = (5.21 - 0.21) / 0.21$$

That is, of 2380 percent! Clearly that is overstating the reality, so the modified calculation is an important adjustment for your AdWords campaign management.

Tip: If you are a nontransactional site, substitute Total Goal Value for Revenue, Per Visit Goal Value for Average Order Value, and Goal Conversion Rate for Ecommerce Conversion Rate in the calculations. Your goals will need to be monetized for this to work—see Chapter 8.

Simplifying the Task

The calculations of cpc_{max} appear cumbersome when written on paper, but with a spreadsheet they are actually quite simple, as shown in Figure 11.18. First, within the Traffic Sources > AdWords > AdWords Campaigns report, drill down to the keyword level by clicking through on the report table. Export your AdWords data from Google Analytics to a CSV file (or schedule a report email on a regular basis). Note that when you do this, all AdWords data is exported together—that is, the data contained in all the tabs of Figure 11.17 (Site Usage, Goal Conversion, Ecommerce) will be included in the CSV file. Open the file in Excel. From this spreadsheet, you require only three columns of data: the Keyword, the Average Value, and the Ecommerce Conversion Rate; the rest can be discarded unless you are a nontransactional site—see the sidebar tip. From the screen shown in Figure 11.18, inputting your profit margin (cell E2) and desired ROI (cell E3) will display the cpc_{max} (column F).

◇	A	B	C	D	E	F
1	# ————————					
2	www.mysite.com			Profit Margin %	40.00	
3	AdWords Keywords:			ROI (gross profit) %	125.00	
4		1-Jan-10	31-Jan-10			
5	# ————————					
6						
7	# ————————					
8	# Table					
9	# ————————					
10	Keyword	Visits	Average Value ($)	Ecommerce Conversion Rate	CPAmax ($)	CPCmax ($)
11	keyword 1	1380	49	0.065217391	8.71	0.57
12	keyword 2	520	55	0.01	9.78	0.10
13	keyword 3	10	34	0.05	6.04	0.30
14	# ————————————————					
15						

Figure 11.18 Excel spreadsheet to calculate per-keyword cpc_{max}

Note: Note: You can download this Excel template from www.advanced-web-metrics.com/chapter11.

As you can see, the cpc_{max} calculation is at the keyword level throughout. However, if you are bidding on large volumes of keywords (I once reviewed an AdWords account with over a million bid terms!), it is more likely that you will be bidding a single cpc amount for groups of keywords—that is, ad groups. In that case, the more focused your ad groups are, the more accurate the cpc_{max} calculation will be. Consider the ad group examples in Table 11.1.

▶ **Table 11.1** Single AdWords ad group for a mix of generic and specific keywords

Blue suede shoes Go out on the town in style. High quality at online prices. mysite.com/shoes	Keywords targeted: (general shoes)	Bid terms: shoes, fun shoes, blue suede shoes, turquoise suede shoes, fancy dress shoes, stylish suede shoes, stylish shoes

Clearly, the average ROI, average value, and average conversion rate for this group will have a large variance, because a broad spread of keywords is targeted. To provide better targeting and receive improved metrics, this group should be split into two focused ad groups—for example, a specific shoe type ad group (suede shoes) and a less-specific ad group (general shoes), as shown in Table 11.2.

▶ **Table 11.2** Two AdWords ad groups for generic keywords and more-specific keywords

Blue suede shoes Go out on the town in style. High quality at online prices. mysite.com/shoes	Keywords targeted: (suede shoes)	Bid terms: blue suede shoes, turquoise suede shoes, stylish suede shoes
Stylish suede shoes Go out on the town in style. High quality at online prices. mysite.com/shoes	Keywords targeted: (general shoes)	Bid terms: shoes, fun shoes, fancy dress shoes, stylish shoes

By dividing your AdWords keyword list into more-focused keyword themes, you will get a much better handle on which keywords and campaigns are working for you and therefore better metrics (conversion rate, average value) to optimize your cpc_{max} values. Of course, your landing pages for each ad group should also be optimized for those keywords, and that is discussed next.

Landing-Page Optimization and SEO

For search-engine marketing, a landing page is defined as the page your visitors land on (arrive at) when they click through from a search-engine results page. As such, landing pages need to be focused on the keywords your visitors have used—that is, keywords relevant to what they are looking for—and be as close to the conversion point as possible. That way, you give yourself the best possible chance of converting your visitors into customers.

For paid search, controlling which landing page a visitor arrives at is straightforward: You enter the URL in your pay-per-click campaigns. For example, in AdWords, each ad group can have its own unique landing page relevant to the displayed advertisement. For all paid search campaigns, you need to append tracking parameters to your URLs. This is done automatically for you in AdWords, but you must apply this manually for other paid networks (see "Campaign Tracking" in Chapter 7).

For nonpaid search (organic search), controlling landing pages is much harder to achieve because search engines consider all pages on your website when deciding which are most relevant to a visitor's search query. If you describe a product on multiple pages, then any or all of these may appear in the search-engine results. However, the highest-ranked page may not be your best-converting page. By optimizing the content of your best-converting page, you can influence its position within the search-engine results, thereby gaining a higher position than other related pages from your site. Landing page optimization is therefore a subset of search engine optimization (SEO).

Robots.txt

Not all pages on your site are relevant to search-engine visitors, for example, your privacy policy or your mission statement to be carbon neutral by the end of this year. Although both are laudable, unless they are a key aspect of your business, consider removing such pages from the search engine indexes—the file robots.txt is used to do this.

The use of robots.txt stops search engines from indexing pages on your website. If you have an existing page indexed and you add it to your robots.txt file as an exclusion, then over time it will be removed from the indexes.

For example, create a text file in the root of your web space named robots.txt with the following contents:

```
User-agent: *
Disallow: /images/
Disallow: /offer_codeY.aspx
```

This file tells all search engines that follow the robots exclusion standard (all the main ones do this) to not index any files in the directory named /images or the specific file named offer_codeY.aspx. For more information on the robots exclusion standard, see www.robotstxt.org.

Principles of SEO and Landing-Page Optimization

For both paid and nonpaid search visitors, you want to ensure that the landing page is as effective as possible—optimized for conversion—once a visitor arrives. That does not mean the visitor's next step is necessarily to convert from this initial landing page; the landing page could be the beginning of the relationship, with the conversion happening much later or on a subsequent visit. By optimizing the content of your landing pages for a better user experience, you not only increase conversions for all visitor types but also improve your organic search-engine rankings. Often the effects of this optimization process can be dramatic.

A key part of the optimizing process is understanding why visitors landed on a particular page of your website in the first place. The keywords they used on the referring search engine tell you this. Within Google Analytics you can view keywords for your top landing pages in a couple of ways:

- From the Traffic Sources > Keywords report, click a keyword, and then cross-segment by landing page.
- From the Content > Top Landing Pages report, click a landing page and select Entrance Keywords from the Landing Page Optimization section.

Generally I prefer the latter: focusing on a landing page and viewing which search keywords led visitors to it. This method is referrer agnostic, meaning you cannot tell whether your visitors arrived on a particular landing page by clicking an organic listing or a paid ad. This difference is not important; a visitor arriving on your website by a well-targeted link (paid or nonpaid) should be just as likely to convert regardless of the referrer used.

For the optimal user experience, focus your landing pages on a particular keyword theme, such as a specific product or service. The exception to this would be your home page, which shouldn't be used as a landing page except for your company or brand-name keywords.

> **Note:** Your home page is generally poor as a landing page for anything other than your company name. This is simply because by its very nature your home page is a generalist page that focuses on creating the right image, branding, and mission statements. Usually you will notice low conversion rates, low $ Index values, and high bounce rates for this page, which is expected. Therefore, you should focus your efforts on your content pages.

A *keyword theme* is a term used in search-engine marketing to describe a collection of keywords that accurately describe the content of a page. For example, if you sell classic model cars, keyword themes would center on particular makes and models, such as the following:

"classic alpha romeo model car"

"replica model alpha romeo"

"classic alpha romeo toy car"

Less-product-specific pages—for example, a category page—would use a less-specific keyword theme:

"model cars for purchase

"classic toy cars for sale

"scale model cars to buy

As a rule of thumb, themes generally consist of 5–10 phrases per page that overlap in keywords (the preceding examples list three such phrases for each page). Having more than 10 overlapping phrases dilutes the impact and effectiveness of the page, from the perspective of both the user experience and search-engine ranking. If you already have a page that targets more than 10 keyword phrases, consider creating a separate page to cater to the additional keywords.

At this stage I am assuming you have been through the process described earlier in this chapter under the heading "Identifying and Optimizing Poorly Performing Pages." If not, do this first because it ensures the user experience for each page is optimized; improving the user experience often reaps large rewards. Then, as an exercise, view your top 10 landing pages from your Content > Top Landing Pages report.

For each page listed in the report, click through its link to its Content Detail report and then again on its Entrance Keywords report. Print out the top 10 entrance keywords and repeat this process for each of your landing pages. Visit your website and print out the content for each of your top 10 landing pages. That gives you your top 10 landing pages with a list of the top 10 keywords associated with each.

 Note: If your Entrance Keywords report for each landing page contains hundreds of table rows, it may be because it is poorly focused or targeted. Check the landing page URLs specified in your paid campaigns. Are they pointing to the most appropriate page? If not, change them accordingly.

For each landing page URL, view the two corresponding printouts. Is the page content tightly focused on its listed Entrance Keywords report? This is quite a subjective process, though as a guide, if you read the first three paragraphs (or approximately the first 200 words) of your landing page and you don't come across every one of your top 10 entrance keywords, then the page can be said to be unfocused. The extent of this is relative to the percentage of missing entrance keywords from those first paragraphs; for example, three keywords missed and you can say your page is 70 percent focused.

If you determine that a landing page is unfocused, revise its content, ensuring that all 10 of your top target keywords are placed within the first 200 human-readable words (that is, not part of the HTML syntax). Pay particular attention to placing keywords in your paragraph headings—for example, assuming a target keyword of "blue widget," use a heading of `<h1>Our blue widget selection</h1>`.

Use Text to Display Text—Not Images

Machine-readable text is text that can be selected within your browser and copied and pasted into another document or other application such as Word or TextPad. If you cannot do that, then the text is likely to be a rastered image (GIF, JPG, PNG, and so on) or another embedded format such as Flash. Often, brand managers prefer the image format when referring to a product or company name so that nonstandard fonts and smoothing or special effects can be applied. However, it is doubtful this has any impact on conversions over plaintext, so long as these are referenced as images or logos elsewhere.

For SEO rankings, machine-readable text is king. The inappropriate use of images or other embedded content as headings will be detrimental to your SEO efforts. Search engines ignore images for ranking purposes, and embedded objects such as Flash can be only partially indexed. To mitigate this, it is good practice to include an alt tag (alternative text attribute) for each image to improve the usefulness of your document for people who have reading disabilities. However, it has very little positive impact on search-engine ranking. Therefore, where possible, use HTML and CSS to style your text, because these are the right tools for the job. Use images to display pictures and Flash for movie or animation effects.

Other prominent areas where you should place your target keywords that are not visible on the page include the title tag and description metatag. Using the same keyword examples, these could be written as follows:

```
<title>Purchase blue widgets from ACME Corp</title>
<meta name="description" content=" ACME Corp, the blue widgets division
of BigCorp, is a US sales and support channel
for the industry-leading blue widget package." />
```

Page title tags are visible by reading the text in the title bar at the top of your browser (blue in Windows, silver on a Mac), but visitors generally do not read this on your page, because it is located above the browser menu and navigation buttons—separately from your content. However, the title tag is the same text that is listed as the clickable link on search-engine result pages and is therefore very important for SEO ranking purposes. Ensure each page has a unique title and description tag relevant to its content, with its most important keywords included.

A best-practice tip is to also include your target keywords within call-to-action statements and make these hyperlinks to the beginning of a goal process—an Add to Cart page, for example. This is illustrated with the following text examples:

Bad SEO example To purchase and get a free gift click here.

Good SEO example Purchase blue widgets and get a free gift with your first order.

The second example contains three important elements that have proven to be many times more effective than the first (see "An Introduction to Google Website Optimizer," later in the chapter, for ways to test this hypothesis):

- The call-to-action statement contains the target keywords.
- The call-to-action keywords are highlighted as a hyperlink.
- The hyperlink takes the visitor to the start of the goal-conversion process.

The techniques described here for optimizing and focusing your landing pages will undoubtedly increase your conversion rates and decrease page-bounce rates regardless of visitor referral source. In addition, as a consequence of improving the user experience, such changes also have a significant and positive impact on your search-engine rankings. Therefore, once you have optimized the top 10 landing pages, move on to the next 10.

From a paid-search point of view, you need to ensure that campaigns point to one of these optimized landing pages—or create new ones. The worst possible thing you can do is use your home page as the landing page. If you take away only one lesson from this section, it should be to avoid this mistake!

A Note on SEO Ethics

When optimizing your landing pages to place keyword phrases in more prominent positions, always consider the user experience. Overly repeating keywords or attempting to hide them (using CSS or matching against the background color, for example), though not illegal, will inevitably result in your entire website being penalized in ranking and possibly removed from search-engine indexes altogether—and this can happen at any time without warning, even years later.

Although it is possible to get back into the search-engine indexes once you have removed the offending code, this can be a long, drawn-out process that damages your reputation. Essentially, spamming the search engines is not going to win you any friends, either from your visitors or the search engines themselves, so avoid it.

Summary of Landing-Page Optimization and SEO Techniques

Optimizing landing pages for better performance is a complicated business; indeed, it's a specialized branch of marketing. However, here is a 10-point summary for you to follow that will give you a solid start:

- Always put your visitors and customers first; design for them, not search-engine robots.
- Use dedicated landing pages for your campaigns, for both paid and nonpaid visitors.

- Ensure that landing pages are close to the call to action.

- Structure your landing-page content around keyword themes of 5–10 overlapping keywords and phrases.

- Place your keyword-rich content near the top of the page, that is, within the first 200 words. Think like a journalist writing for a newspaper, with structured titles, headings, and subheadings that contain keywords.

- Use keywords in your HTML `<title>` tags.

- Use keywords in your anchor links—that is, HTML `<a>` tags.

- Avoid placing text in images or Flash or other embedded content.

- Use a `robots.txt` file to control what pages are indexed by search engines.

- Never "keyword stuff" or attempt to spam the search engines; it's not worth it, and you can achieve better results by legitimate means.

If you have completed all 10 steps and are still thirsting for improvement (pages can always be improved), consider testing alternative page elements, as discussed in "An Introduction to Google Website Optimizer" later in this chapter.

> **Note:** It's important to recognize that I have attempted to cover only the principles of SEO. Many factors affect your search-engine rankings. The more important ones are page content (keyword density, keyword prominence), site architecture, internal link structure, and the number and quality of incoming links from other websites—including social network sites. For further in-depth reading on the subject, see *Search Engine Optimization (SEO) - Best Practice Guide* by Dave Chaffey, Chris Lake, and Ashley Friedlein (Econsultancy, 2009) and *Search Engine Marketing, Inc.: Driving Search Traffic to Your Company's Web Site* by Bill Hunt and Mike Moran (IBM Press, 2008).

AdWords Ad Position Optimization

As discussed in Chapter 5, Google Analytics contains a unique AdWords report called Keyword Positions (see Figure 11.19). This report provides metrics for your AdWords keyword performance on a per-position basis—in other words, the number of visits you received while in ad position 1, 2, 3, and so on. In fact, it's not just visitor numbers you can view on a per-position basis; 15 metrics are available. These include the following:

- **Visits**
- Pages/Visit
- Average Time on Site
- **% New Visits**
- Bounce Rate
- Goal 1 Conversion Rate [conversion rates for goals 2–4]

- Overall Goal Conversion Rate

- [Revenue, Transactions, Average Value, Ecommerce Conversion rate, **Per Visit Value**]

- **Per Visit Goal Value**

Figure 11.19 AdWords > Keyword Positions report for the keyword "web metrics"

Values in square brackets [ ] may not be present in the report, because they depend on your specific configuration—for example, whether e-commerce is enabled or you have goals defined.

The three metrics I suggest you focus on for ad position optimization are highlighted in bold: Visits, Percent New Visits, and either the Per Visit Goal Value or the Per Visit Value if you have an e-commerce website. That is not to say that the others are not useful, but in an analyst's world of information overflow, I like to keep things as simple as possible, and these are my favorites.

For example, I deliberately avoid Pages Per Visit and Average Time on Site, because these metrics can be misleading without further detailed investigation. On the one hand, a high value for these metrics could indicate a visitor is engaging with you. On the other hand, it could mean that visitors are lost in your navigation or confused by your content. Bounce rates and individual goal-conversion rates are best viewed in other reports, such as the Traffic Sources > AdWords > AdWords Campaigns report.

For the remaining metrics, I use the Per Visit Value (or Per Visit Goal Value if you do not have e-commerce reporting) as an excellent proxy for Revenue, Transactions,

Average Value, and Conversion Rate metrics. If the Per Visit Value is healthy, then so are the others.

With an understanding of how your ads perform by position, you can set position preference within your AdWords account, as shown in Figure 11.20 and discussed next.

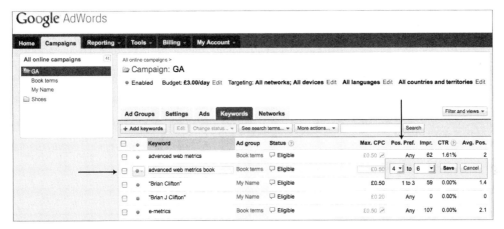

Figure 11.20 Setting the AdWords position preference for the keyword "advanced web metrics book"

Optimizing Positions by Visits

Acquiring the most traffic for the least cost is an obvious ambition of all marketers. A common misconception with pay-per-click advertising is that the higher the ad position, the more traffic you will receive. Certainly for focused keyword phrases with no ambiguity, that holds true most of the time. That is also the case for bids on brand terms, with the caveat that it is not necessary to bid on brand terms (and not advisable) if you already have a high organic placement—that is, a top-three organic ranking.

For more-generic terms, visitors tend not to follow this pattern of behavior; that is, most visitors do not click the highest-position ad. This is because generic terms can have different visitor intentions. For example, if a visitor searches for "blue suede shoes," are they interested in footwear or Elvis Presley? Similarly, searches for "golf" could be looking for a car, golf equipment, or golf associations.

Because of this ambiguity (use of less-focused keywords), advertisers tend to use broad match in their ad campaigns in order to capture as many visitors as possible who *may* be interested in their product. For example, you can find car dealerships and golf equipment suppliers advertising alongside search results for "golf driving." The same is true for "blue suede shoes"—footwear suppliers advertising alongside music download sites. The result is a blurring of the click-through distribution by position (see Figure 11.21).

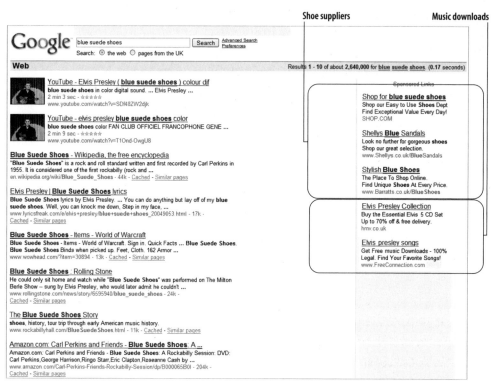

Figure 11.21 Advertising on ambiguous search terms can result in unexpected ad performance by ad position.

You can take advantage of this blurring by viewing your Google Analytics > Keyword Position reports and adjusting your bids within AdWords Position Preference to be placed in the most effective position for your target audience. For example, if you are a music retail site and the top three AdWords positions for the bid term "blue suede shoes" are for shoe suppliers, then you only need to bid to position four for your ad to be in the number-one position for your sector. There is no point in being number one overall, because you will be paying a premium to be placed higher than irrelevant competitors.

To determine whether most people searching for "blue suede shoes" are referring to Elvis or footwear, you can use the data available at Google Trends: http://trends. google.com. As indicated in Figure 11.22, currently and historically there is a considerably greater volume of search queries for footwear than music downloads. Therefore, a music retailer bidding to position four would avoid the expense of acquiring potentially irrelevant traffic from such an ambiguous search term.

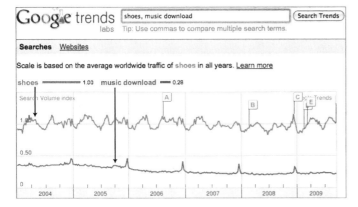

Figure 11.22 Google Trends data comparing query volumes on the Google search engine

Optimizing Positions by Percent New Visits

Percent New Visits is an interesting metric to view by ad position. When running a paid campaign, you hope that the visitors you are acquiring are almost all new visitors—people coming to your site for the first time. If instead significant proportions are repeat visitors (I consider this as greater than 25–30 percent), then you need to look at your visitor-acquisition strategy—why pay multiple times for the same visitor? If people are not ready to convert on their first visit, then you want them to either bookmark your website or at least remember your company or product name. That way, a follow-up search by visitors for your brand keywords should bring you to the top of the organic (free) results, saving you the cost of a repeat pay-per-click visitor.

Sometimes the top three ad positions on Google—those ad positions that occur at the top of a search-results page (as opposed to the right-hand side)—can attract significant numbers of repeat visitors. This is probably because they are at the top of the search-results page and in the direct line of sight for the searcher, just below the search box. Because of this, those positions can lead to significant click-throughs without the visitor bothering to view the rest of the results page—that is, without seeing your top organic position. If you find this is the case for your repeat visitors, consider not advertising in these positions by using the Position Preference settings of your AdWords campaigns. Perhaps the top-side position can prove more cost effective.

Optimizing Positions by Per Visit Value

The *Per Visit Value* is probably the most important metric to be viewed on a per-position basis and is calculated as follows:

$$\text{Per Visit Value} = \frac{\text{Goal Value} + \text{E-commerce Value}}{\text{Number of ad click-throughs while in Position X}}$$

If you are a nontransactional website, the Per Visit Goal Value is the equivalent for monetized goals. These metrics tell you how valuable an ad position is to your business on a per-visit basis, and it can vary wildly by position. For example, Figure 11.23 shows that the highest-value positions for the selected keyword ("web metrics") occur in positions 3–4. It therefore makes sense to focus the AdWords position preference for this keyword on those positions. However, the caveat here is that these positions will receive less traffic than positions 1–2, so before drawing conclusions, compare this metric with the Revenue By Position metric (select from the Position Breakdown drop-down menu) to see the total value of these positions to your business.

Figure 11.23 Per Visit Value by AdWords position

AdWords Day-Parting Optimization

By knowing at what time of day visitors are accessing your website, you can better tailor your advertising campaigns to match. For example, if you are a business-to-business website, then most of your visits will probably occur during normal working hours. Rather than display your ads in equal distribution throughout the day, it would make sense to run and maximize your pay-per-click campaigns at around the same time your potential audience is looking on the Web.

Other examples of day-parting optimization include targeting magazine readers who are likely to be online in the early evenings; targeting social networking sites whose potential audience is most likely to be online from 5:00 P.M. to 1:00 A.M.; and coinciding with radio advertisements, where remembering your website URL can be difficult and so the interested audience may subsequently conduct a search to find your site.

By viewing hourly reports, you can view the distribution of your visitors through-out the day. Hourly visitor reports are available in the Visitors > Visitor Trending section (see Figure 11.24). Of course, time zones should be taken into consideration. For example, if your audience is global, ensure your reports are first segmented by location (a proxy for time zone) for this exercise.

Figure 11.24 Viewing hourly reports for day-parting optimization

As with all data analysis, it is important to avoid looking at short time frames such as a single day. Visitors over short periods can vary significantly and randomly, making reports difficult (if not impossible) to interpret. Instead, select a longer period and ensure that the date range includes relevant days of the week for you. For a business-to-business website, for example, select Monday to Friday, or use Friday to Sunday if your target audience is more likely to be looking for your products or services in their leisure time. In addition, try to choose a discrete day range—one that does not overlap with national holidays if that would affect your visitor numbers. Whatever business you are in, also compare weekend visitors to weekday visitors, because this can reveal surprising insights.

From Figure 11.24, which is a business-to-business website with no day-parting optimization, you can see that there are fewer visitors in the early morning (midnight until 7:00 A.M.), significant numbers from then on (from 9:00 A.M. to 5:00 P.M.), with traffic dropping to a third of its daytime levels in the evenings. If you have e-commerce reporting enabled, compare your day-parting visitor information with when transactions take place: Go to the Ecommerce > Total Revenue report.

Use this information to optimize your paid campaigns by setting ads to display on or around these time frames, both when visitors are in a research frame of mind (just visiting) and when they are ready to purchase. Figure 11.25 shows you how to achieve this within the AdWords Ad Schedule page. Not only can you schedule when your ads are displayed, you can also vary your bids for ads on a given time or day. For example, if your default bid is $1.00, you can set a custom percent-of-bid entry for Tuesday from midnight until 8:00 A.M. at 20 percent—that is, your bid for Tuesday only prior to sunrise would be $0.20. By this method, you would be spending money on acquiring paid visitors at periods when they are most likely to be looking and purchasing and at a price that is most advantageous to you. You can customize any day or time frame in this way, using 15-minute intervals.

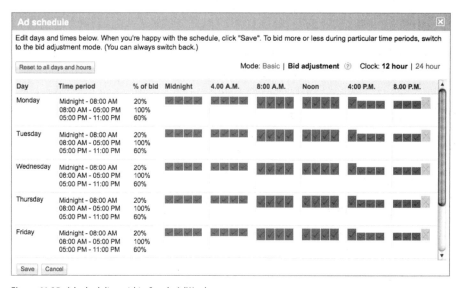

Figure 11.25 Ad scheduling within Google AdWords

Time Zone Considerations

To take advantage of day-parting reports, ensure that your paid campaigns are specific to a particular time zone. For example, don't mix your paid campaigns by displaying the same ad to both a U.S. and a U.K. audience. Time zone settings for AdWords are on a per-account basis. If you have audiences in different time zones, then create separate AdWords accounts for them.

You can configure time zone settings for Google Analytics on a per-profile basis. However, if you link your Google Analytics account to your AdWords account as described in Chapter 6, "Getting Up and Running with Google Analytics" then your AdWords time zone and country settings take precedence, and you cannot realign them within Google Analytics.

If time zone and other regional specifics (language, currency) are important for you, the best practice advice is to use a one-to-one relationship of Google Analytics and AdWords accounts. You can run an aggregate Google Analytics account by adding an additional GATC to your pages (see the section entitled "Roll-up Reporting" in Chapter 6).

AdWords Ad Version Optimization

When creating your pay-per-click campaigns in AdWords, how do you know whether one ad creative is more effective at generating click-throughs than another, similar ad? For example, is the headline "Blue suede shoes" better for you than "Turquoise suede shoes" or "Unique suede shoes"? Of course, you don't know the answer to this, and that's the point: No one does. It's up to your audience to decide. Even after you know the answer, it's like the English summer weather: It can still change quickly and without warning. To determine which ad performs best, use *ad-version testing*.

Ad version testing is a method used by pay-per-click networks that enables you to display different ad versions for the same target keywords. With Google AdWords, ads can be rotated in equal proportion to a random selection of visitors—for example, five ads each showing 20 percent of your total impressions. You can maintain this and view results in your Google Analytics reports. Alternatively, you can allow AdWords to optimize the display of your ads, favoring the better-performing ones by showing more impressions of the ad that receives more click-throughs.

Note: This is a simplified description of how ad-version testing works within AdWords. Optimized ad serving actually favors ads with higher historic click-through rates and quality scores. For more information on AdWords quality scores, see http://adwords.google.com/support/bin/answer.py?answer=21388.

Figure 11.26 shows four different ads for the same target keywords.

Stylish suede shoes
Go out on the town in style.
High quality at online prices.
mysite.com/shoes
Ad version 1

Suede shoes
Go out on the town in style.
High quality at online prices.
mysite.com/shoes
Ad version 2

Turquoise suede shoes
Go out on the town in style.
High quality at online prices.
mysite.com/shoes
Ad version 3

Blue suede shoes
Go out on the town in style.
High quality at online prices.
mysite.com/shoes
Ad version 4

Figure 11.26   Four different AdWords ad versions targeting the same keywords

Google Analytics tracks different AdWords ad versions with no additional configuration required. Ad version results appear automatically in your reports as long as you have the Google Analytics auto-tagging box checked within your AdWords account (see Chapter 6).

To track ad versions for other paid referral sources, such as Yahoo! Search Marketing and Microsoft adCenter, you need to add tracking codes to your landing page URLs as discussed in Chapter 7 in the section "Campaign Tracking." Specifically, the `utm_content` parameter is required to differentiate ad versions.

As you can see in Figure 11.27, "Stylish suede shoes" is receiving the vast majority of click-throughs from AdWords (no AdWords impression optimization applied). From the drop-down menu shown, you can also view other visit metrics for each ad version. In addition to the Site Usage report, you should view the ad version data in the Goal Conversion and Ecommerce reports.

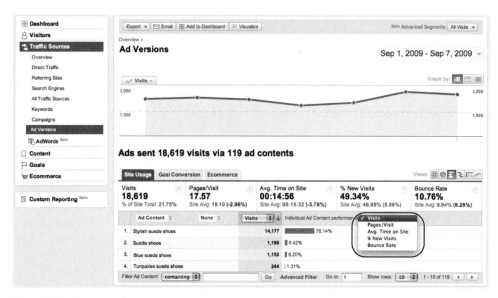

Figure 11.27 Ad version testing results

Tip: Each of the AdWords ad variations shown in Figure 11.26 has a unique headline. These headlines appear in your Google Analytics Ad Versions report. It is not yet possible to report on ad variations that use the same headline, differing only in body text. Note that turning off auto-tagging in AdWords and attempting to use manual tracking parameters as an alternative will not work.

Check the Goal Conversion and Ecommerce reports to confirm that "Stylish suede shoes" is performing better from a conversion and revenue point of view (click the tabs within the Ad Versions report). For example, it may be that the attractive headline of "Stylish suede shoes" is better for visitor acquisition (click-throughs), but when it comes to visitors interacting with your website, perhaps "Blue suede shoes" converts better and generates more revenue. If that is the case, then take advantage of this discrepancy and create separate ad groups for each, so you can run separate bidding strategies.

Assuming the Goal Conversion and Ecommerce reports show a similar trend as in Figure 11.27, you can then either enable Google's ad-serving optimization (ad rotation feature), which will favor "Stylish suede shoes," or disable (pause) the remaining ad versions and focus all your pay-per-click efforts on "Stylish suede shoes."

As an aside, you can also use ad-version testing for non-pay-per-click campaigns by using the utm_content tracking parameter. For example, if you use a mix of banners for a display campaign, you could test the effectiveness of different formats such as header versus skyscraper or static versus animated. You achieve this by appending utm_content values to the landing-page URLs on the banners, for example, utm_content=flash or utm_content=static. If you use the utm_campaign tracking parameter in this way, then also take advantage of using the other campaign-tracking parameters available to you (see "Campaign Tracking" in Chapter 7).

Monetizing a Non-E-commerce Website

For non-e-commerce websites, understanding and communicating website value throughout your organization are key to obtaining buy-in from senior management. After all, you want to make changes to improve your bottom line, but without an associated dollar value, that can be difficult to achieve. By gaining executive support, you will be able to procure investment for content, infrastructure, and online marketing. The problem is that many executives' eyes glaze over when they see yet another set of charts on visitor metrics. "Our site doesn't sell anything, so who cares?" is a common response, and you'll need to address this head on or face a very frustrating job role. Identifying the monetary value of your visitor sessions is a proven way to get executive attention, and it can help keep the company website from becoming just someone's pet project.

Google Analytics provides two mechanisms for demonstrating website monetary value:

- Assigning goal values
- Enabling e-commerce reporting for your non-e-commerce site

The key to both approaches lies in knowing the value of website goal conversions to your business. For example, if a PDF brochure is downloaded 1,000 times and you estimate that one of these downloads results in a customer with an average order value of $250, then each download is worth $0.25 ($250/1,000). If 1 in 100 downloads converts into a customer, then each PDF download is worth $2.50 to you and so on. Therefore, to attain a monetary value for each goal, you need to ask two fundamental questions: How many goal conversions are required to create a customer, and what is the average lifetime value (LTV) of a customer?

The Google Analytics Goals Overview report shows how many conversions you get to each of your site goals. From this, you'll need to estimate the percentage of goal conversions that result in paying customers. To get the process started, if a visitor's goal conversion provides personal information, such as name and email address, that you can later use as a sales follow-up, I guesstimate 10 percent of these will result in a sale. If no personal information is provided, for example, a visitor clicking a PDF download link, I use 1 percent for my guesstimate of sales. These are just initial guesstimates to start off the conversation with your organization's sales team. This process is not an exact science, and you'll be able to fine-tune later as you collect more information. However, aim to get these numbers formalized within a quarter—if you don't and they continue to change, you will not be able to compare long-term trends.

Determining the average value of a customer is more straightforward. Assuming a customer attributed as a lead from your website has the same value as any other customer, simply ask your sales team for the average LTV of your customers. If your business is new or your average customer lifetime is particularly long and convoluted, use the average revenue generated in 12 months per customer as your LTV.

Once you can estimate the value of each of your site goals, it is straightforward to monetize your website.

Tip: If you are struggling to estimate goal values, start off the process by first evaluating your least-significant goal. Give this a value of 1 (as with assigning all goals in Google Analytics, the actual amount is unitless—the symbols $, £, €, and the like are labels). For more valuable goals, use a multiple of the least-valuable one. For example, if your least-valuable goal is a PDF download and your next more valuable goal is a subscription request that is five times more valuable to you, then assign goal values of 1 and 5, respectively.

Approach 1: Assign Values to Your Goals

Every site has at least one goal; quite often it has several. Non-e-commerce sites have PDFs and other document files to download, product demonstrations, brochure requests, quote requests, subscription signups, registrations, account logins, blog comments, content ratings, printouts—even the humble mailto: link (email address link) can be considered a goal and tracked with Google Analytics (see "Event Tracking" in Chapter 7).

With your goals defined, assigning a goal value is straightforward and is described in "Goal Conversions and Funnels" in Chapter 8. Adding values to goals enables you to gain additional metrics in your Google Analytics reports, such as the average per-visit goal value ($/Visit) as shown in the Traffic Sources section, the average per-search goal value ($/Search) as shown in the Content > Site Search reports, and the average page value ($ Index) as shown in the Content report section. In addition, you can view individual and total goal values in the Goals > Goal Value report.

Assigning goal values is a fundamental configuration step and a prerequisite for understanding the value of your nontransactional website. However, you obtain far more detailed reporting by using the technique outlined in the second approach.

Approach 2: Enable E-commerce Reporting

By setting up your non-e-commerce site as an e-commerce website in Google Analytics, you'll be able to do the following:

- Have an unlimited set of goals
- See the amount of time and number of visits it takes for visitors to convert
- View a breakdown of how much each "product" (goal) contributes to your website revenue
- Group goals into categories
- List specific "transactions" (individual goals)

Here is an example to illustrate the last bullet point and the capability the expanded reports will give you. Imagine you are a publisher of content with hundreds of PDF files available for download (probably behind a registration system). Perhaps you also have abstracts available free. Using a wildcard such as *.pdf in your goal configuration setup will tell you how many goal conversions you receive for PDF files. However, it does not tell you how many PDF files were downloaded, because visitors can convert only once during a session for a particular goal, even though they may have downloaded several PDF files.

To ascertain the total number of downloads (goal completions), you need to view the Goals > Goal Verification report; if you wish to see the different types of PDF downloads (for example, specification, help, brochure, price guide), apply table filters or advanced segments. Clearly, this is not scalable. By enabling e-commerce tracking, more-detailed rich reports are available to you—for this example, each individual PDF file will be tracked as a product, grouped into categories, and monetized, as shown in Figure 11.28.

These are just a few examples of what you will see. Using this approach, you gain additional aggregate information as well as more specific goal and goal-conversion information. How this is achieved is discussed next.

Tracking a Non-E-commerce Site as Though It Were an E-commerce Site

The following examples were developed at www.omegadm.com for the corporate website of a global industrial manufacturer. Beyond content updates, investment in their website had tailed off a number of years ago because no one in the organization considered it an opportunity—more of a dot.com necessity. Omegadm.com was brought in to reinvigorate senior executive interest and allow the digital manager to seek additional budget for further development.

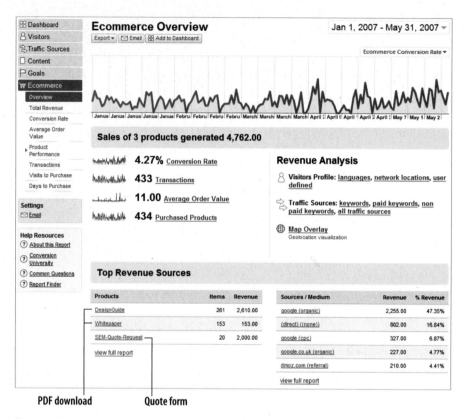

PDF download   **Quote form**

Figure 11.28 An e-commerce report for non-e-commerce goals

Essentially, the approach is to tag each goal page with e-commerce tracking information (see "Tracking E-commerce Transactions," in Chapter 7). Some of the e-commerce fields will be left blank. For example, assume that one of your goals is for a visitor to click a `mailto:` link. Visitors who click this do not leave their delivery address by this action, so you will not be entering anything for this particular e-commerce field. As an aside, as discussed in Chapter 3, "Google Analytics Features, Benefits, and Limitations," it is against the Google Analytics Terms of Service to track personally identifiable information.

There are two steps for implementing this technique: first, defining the e-commerce field values for your goals, and second, calling the function `_trackTrans()` so that Google Analytics tracks these when the goal is completed. The following are example goals that we'll track with e-commerce fields:

- Pseudo e-commerce for a `mailto:` goal

- Pseudo e-commerce for a file download goal

- Pseudo e-commerce for a form-submission goal

- Pseudo e-commerce for multiple file-goal downloads

Generating Unique Order IDs

In all of the pseudo e-commerce examples given, it is important that you assign a unique order ID to each transaction. An e-commerce system would do this for you automatically. However, here you will need to apply some additional code on your pages. Add the following just above the </head> HTML tag of each page that you are tracking with e-commerce fields:

```javascript
<script type="text/javascript">
function getOrderID(){
    // generate a random order id
    var randomnumber=Math.floor(Math.random()*1000);
    var currentTime = new Date();
    var month = currentTime.getMonth()+1
    var timeStamp =  currentTime.getFullYear() + month + currentTime.↵
      getDate() + "-" +currentTime.getHours() + currentTime.getMinutes()↵
      + currentTime.getSeconds() +"-" + randomnumber;
    return(timeStamp);
}
</script>
```

With this in place, when the goal page is loaded, a unique order ID is generated of the form YYYYMMDD-hhmmss-XXX, where XXX is a random number between 0 and 999. This provides tracking of up to 1,000 orders per second and enables you to keep order IDs in a logical structure that can be searched for later within the reports. If you receive much fewer than 1,000 orders per day, you can simplify the order ID by removing the hhmmss element.

With the script in place, generate an order ID by calling the JavaScript function getOrderID(), as shown in the examples.

Defining Your Pseudo E-commerce Values

For each example, add the e-commerce fields to the page with the goal to be tracked. You must place this after your GATC:

Pseudo e-commerce fields for an email click-through goal Add the following e-commerce fields to the page with the mailto: link to be tracked:

```javascript
<script type="text/javascript">
    orderNum = getOrderID();
    pageTracker._addTrans(
      orderNum,              // order ID - required
      "",                    // affiliation or store name
      "1",                   // total - required
      "",                    // tax
      "",                    // shipping
```

```
            "",                    // city
            "",                    // state or province
            ""                     // country
        );
        pageTracker._addItem(
            orderNum,              // order ID - required
            "brian@mysite.com",    // SKU (stock keeping unit)
            "Email link",          // product name
            "General enquiries",   // category or variation
            "1",                   // unit price - required
            "1"                    // quantity - required
        );
    </script>
```

The preceding code consists of text lists and can therefore be collapsed into single lines. From now on I use the abbreviated form of assigning e-commerce values as follows:

```
    <script type="text/javascript">
        orderNum = getOrderID();
        pageTracker._addTrans(orderNum, "", "1", "", "", "", "", "");
        pageTracker._addItem(orderNum, "brian@mysite.com", ↵
        "Email link", "General enquiries", "1", "1");
    </script>
```

As you can see, most of the e-commerce fields are blank—you cannot know the shipping address of someone who simply clicks your email link. A value of $1 and a quantity of 1 have been assigned and categorized under "General enquiries."

Pseudo e-commerce fields for a file-download goal In this case, I have used a PDF file as the example. Add the following e-commerce fields to the page with the download link to be tracked:

```
    <script type="text/javascript">
        orderNum = getOrderID();
        pageTracker._addTrans(orderNum, "", "10", "", "", "", "", "");
        pageTracker._addItem(orderNum, "", "PDF Brochure", ↵
        "Download", "10", "1");
    </script>
```

Here, a PDF download has been categorized as "Download" and given a value of $10; the quantity remains 1. If you have multiple PDF files on the same page, then you could categorize them and value each differently, perhaps by language or by content. This is discussed as a special case in the next section.

Pseudo e-commerce fields for a form-submission goal Add the following e-commerce fields to the page with the form submission to be tracked:

```
<script type="text/javascript">
    orderNum = getOrderID();
    pageTracker._addTrans(orderNum, "", "50", "", "", "", "", "");
    pageTracker._addItem(orderNum, "", "Form submission", ↵
    "Subscriptions", "50", "1");
</script>
```

This example assumes a value of $50 per form submission with a quantity of 1 and categorized under "Subscriptions."

Calling the Function _trackTrans()

With your e-commerce fields in place on the pages that contain goals, the second part of the implementation is to decide how to get these values into Google Analytics. This is done using the JavaScript call to the pageTracker._trackTrans() function. For the preceding three examples, use the following calls:

```
<a href = "mailto:email@address.com" onClick = "pageTracker._trackTrans();">

<a href = "file.pdf" onClick = ↵
 "pageTracker._trackPageview('/downloads/file.pdf');↵
  pageTracker._trackTrans();">

<form action = "formhandler.cgi" onSubmit = "pageTracker._trackTrans();">
```

Note the use of trackPageview for the second example. This is not directly related to what we wish to achieve, but it should be used as a best-practice technique—that is, capturing the PDF download as a virtual pageview. For more details on virtual pageviews, see "trackPageview( ): the Google Analytics Workhorse," in Chapter 7.

Special Case: Pseudo E-commerce Fields for Multiple File Downloads

The preceding file-download example is a simplified case that is useful to illustrate the method. However, if file downloads are important to your website performance, then it is highly likely you will have multiple links to downloads on the same page. This is a special case, because the e-commerce event handler needs to be called for *each* file download link. That way, each click on a download link receives a different transaction ID. This is an important requirement, because you cannot have multiple items for a single transaction by this method—this is not a shopping cart. To overcome this limitation, use the following format for each download link:

```
<a href = "file1.pdf" onClick =
"pageTracker._trackPageview('/downloads/file1.pdf');↵
orderNum=getOrderID();pageTracker._addTrans(orderNum, ↵
'', '10', '', '', '', '', ''); pageTracker._addItem(orderNum, '', 'PDF ↵
Brochure', 'Download', '10', '1');pageTracker._trackTrans();">
```

```
file1.pdf</a>
<br>
<a href = "file2.pdf" onClick =
"pageTracker._trackPageview('/downloads/file2.pdf'); ↩
orderNum=getOrderID();pageTracker._addTrans(orderNum, ↩
'', '5', '', '', '', '', ''); pageTracker._addItem(orderNum, '', 'PDF ↩
Specification Sheet', 'Download', '5', '1');pageTracker._trackTrans();">
file2.pdf</a>
```

Here, two PDF downloads have been categorized and given values of $10 and
$5, respectively. If a visitor clicks both of these files (or repeatedly clicks the same file),
then each is tracked as a separate transaction, because the function getOrderID() is
called on each occasion. Assuming there is a minimal delay in loading the HTML page
in question, the transaction IDs for these two files will be very similar—for example,
varying only in the ss-XXX part of the string YYYYMMDD-hhmmss-XXX.

Approach 2 Provides Significant Benefits

By enabling e-commerce reporting on your non-e-commerce website, you can see at a glance the
referring sources that lead to goal conversion, time to purchase, visits to purchase, average order
value, which keywords convert best, and more.

If you were to use the first approach only, you would need to navigate to each goal page and
determine the information separately—and that can be quite tricky with 500 PDF whitepapers, 10
application downloads, 3 mailing list subscriptions, 2 quote request forms, and a contact-us form!

Tracking Offline Marketing

Having a unified metrics system that can report on key performance indicators from
the Web, print, display, radio, and TV—all in one place—and one that can track the
correlation between all visitors who start in one channel and cross over into others
before converting has been a long-sought analytics nirvana for many a marketer.

Some vendors have attempted to achieve such a system, with varying degrees
of success. The barriers of technical difficulty (bringing information from disparate
systems together) and issues with data alignment (for example, how do you compare
a web visitor who has specifically searched for information to a passive TV viewer?)
mean that, to date, few organizations have made such a high-cost and resource-
intensive investment.

However, vendors are making many inroads to overcome these difficulties.
The open-source nature of Google's application programming interface (API) model

for making data accessible goes some way toward making this happen. Google APIs include AdWords, Google Maps, Google Earth, and more recently Google Analytics. With an API, Google Analytics users are able to stream their data directly out and into their own applications—and potentially in the future to import data back into Google Analytics. This could be as simple as real-time updates to KPI tables in Excel or the merging of web data with CRM data. The use of the Google Analytics API is discussed in Chapter 12.

Without getting into the technicalities of using the API in this chapter, let me just say that Google Analytics can still provide you with a great deal of insight in terms of measuring your offline marketing campaigns. Consider the chart shown in Figure 11.29. This chart measures the uplift in web visitor numbers while running a print advertising campaign.

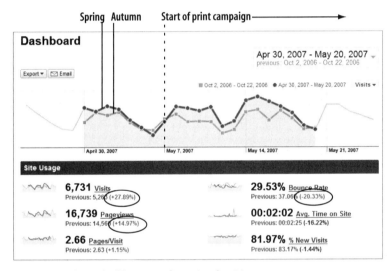

Figure 11.29 Observed uplift in visitors from print advertising

Both lines in Figure 11.29 represent a three-week time frame; one in autumn and one the following spring. A magazine ad ran for the last two weeks in spring (May 7 to May 20). As you can see, the uplift over the entire three-week period in visit and pageview numbers is significant, at plus 28 percent and plus 15 percent, respectively. Page bounce rates are also reduced, at minus 20 percent. Fluctuations due to seasonality or general visitor growth are taken into account by displaying data one week prior to the print ad campaign—that is, before the campaign the visit numbers closely align between the two time periods (including pageview data, though this is not shown). The hypothesis is therefore that the print campaign drove the uplift.

To confirm this hypothesis, examine uplifts from referral keywords (specifically branded terms) and direct traffic. Uplift from direct referrals represents people remembering your printed URL, while uplifts in search visitors using your brand terms are from people unable to remember this. Expect to see one or both of these trends in order to confirm the positive effect of the print campaign.

Tip: Take care when comparing date ranges because it is important to align with the days of the week; that is, compare Monday with Monday, and so on. Seasonality also needs to be considered; otherwise, you may be giving undue credit to an offline campaign. If possible, try to normalize your numbers by taking into account the background growth in visitor traffic received between the time periods considered.

The strong uplift observed in Figure 11.29 does not equal 100 percent causality. A better solution to gain more certainty is to combine offline campaigns with unique landing-page URLs that these visitors use. There are a number of ways to achieve this, using any or all of the following methods:

Vanity URLs Recommended when you have strong *product* brand awareness, with all web content hosted on a *single* central domain. Examples include ThinkPad, iPod, Castrol, Gillette, Colgate, Aquafresh, Big Mac, Fanta, Snickers, and so on.

Coded URLs Recommended when you have a strong *company* brand or when your products already have *separate* websites. Examples include IBM, Microsoft, Google, Kellogg's, Kodak, BMW, and any product that relies on model numbers for identification, such as cell phones, cars, printers, or cameras.

Combining with search Recommended when your brand values are less significant than your product or service values or your target audience is more price oriented than brand oriented. Examples include the vast majority of small- to medium-size businesses, the travel industry, the insurance sector, utilities, groceries, and office supplies. That is, industries where there is little brand loyalty.

Note: The example names given for tracking offline visitors are for brand recognition only. They do not reflect the actual website architecture or strategies of the sites in question.

Using Vanity URLs to Track Offline Visitors

If your website content is held at www.mysite.com and you have a strong product brand that has greater awareness than your company brand, consider using a vanity URL of www.myproduct.com for your offline campaigns such as television, radio, and print. Use your website (www.mysite.com) only to promote via online marketing.

Clearly, you don't want to build two separate websites to promote to offline and online audiences. Their needs are the same; the only difference is how they find your website. Apart from the resource overhead, you should not build duplicate pages, because the search engines will penalize you for this.

To avoid duplicate content, apply permanent redirects to your vanity URLs, such as www.myproduct.com. Redirects on your web server capture the different URLs used by your offline visitors, append tracking parameters, and then automatically forward them through to your main content website, such as www.mysite.com. The process takes a small fraction of a second to perform and shows no visible difference to your offline visitors. They type in a vanity URL (www.myproduct.com) and arrive on your official website (www.mysite.com) with tracking parameters appended. In effect, you are pretending to have product-specific websites for your offline visitors, using this to differentiate, and then redirecting them to your actual content.

With a redirect in place, you can view offline visitors by identifying the campaign variables used. In Figure 11.30, the offline ad is identified in the reports by the medium Print.

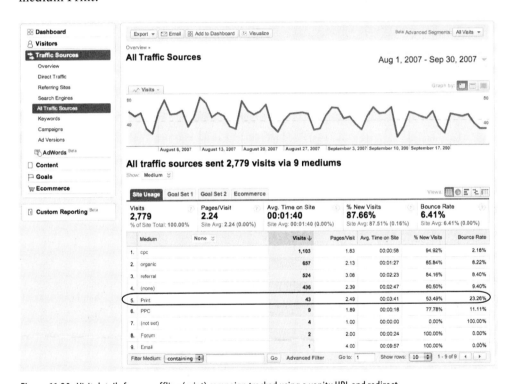

Figure 11.30 Visit details from an offline (print) campaign tracked using a vanity URL and redirect

Using vanity URLs for managing offline campaigns is very effective, assuming you have multiple domains to use and the product you are selling is not trademarked or protected by someone else, preventing you from using it as part of a domain. Don't use this method if you already have your products hosted on separate websites—see the following section on using coded URLs.

Using Redirects for Vanity URLs

Redirects are an important aspect of using vanity URLs, because they avoid any duplicate content issues (bad for SEO) and allow campaign variables to be appended to the final URL destination.

Two types of redirects are possible: permanent (status code = 301) and temporary (status code = 302). From a search engine optimization point of view, it is important to apply permanent redirects so that the final destination URL is the one that is indexed by the search engines; otherwise, the search engines ignore the content.

The following is an Apache example of redirecting the vanity URL www.myproduct.com, used only for print campaigns, to the official web address containing the actual content, www.mysite.com. The rewrite code is placed in the virtual host configuration section for www.myproduct.com in the httpd.conf file. Other web servers use a similar method:

```
<VirtualHost>
    ServerName www.myproduct.com
    RewriteEngine on
    RewriteCond %{HTTP_USER_AGENT} .*
    RewriteRule .* http://www.mysite.com/?utm_source=magazineX&utm_↵
    medium=print&utm_campaign=March%20print%20ad [R=301,QSA]
</VirtualHost>
```

The rewrite code requires the mod_rewrite module to be installed. Most Apache servers have this by default (see http://httpd.apache.org/docs/mod/mod_rewrite.html). Ensure that the RewriteRule is contained on one line within your configuration file (up to and including QSA]); and if spaces are required, use character encoding (%20).

In this example, Google Analytics campaign variables are used so that you can uniquely identify the offline campaign, as described in the section "Online Campaign Tracking," in Chapter 7. These are then permanently passed onto the official website using the Apache mod_rewrite option. The query string append (QSA) ensures that any other query parameters are also redirected. After a redirect takes place, you should see your campaign variables in the address bar of your browser. If not, the redirect has not worked correctly, and this will need to be resolved.

For the example redirect given, the offline visitor can be identified in your Google Analytics reports anywhere the source, medium, and campaign variables are displayed. In this case, the source is "magazine," the medium is "print," and the campaign is "March print ad." This is effective when the only offline campaign running is a print ad, that is, you can redirect to only one place at a time. If this vanity URL is required for other offline campaigns running at the same time, then change the utm_source, utm_medium, and utm_campaign tracking variables to the generic text "offline." You then track your offline marketing in aggregate.

Using Coded URLs to Track Offline Visitors

If your company brand has greater awareness than your products, then consider using coded URLs within your offline campaigns. These are of the following form:

```
www.mysite.com/offer_codeX
www.mysite.com/offer_codeY
```

Coded URLs are unique to your offline campaigns; they are not displayed anywhere on your website and are not visible to the search engines. That means your content should be visible to the search engines, but this will be via a different online-only URL such as www.mysite.com/productX.

By using coded URLs in your offline marketing, you will know that visitors to the subdirectory /offer_codeX must have come from your offline ad; there is nowhere else to find it. Of course, there is always the possibility that the visitor will remember only your domain (mysite.com) and not the specific landing page (offer_codeX) required to distinguish them from direct visitors; this is common for strong brands. It is therefore important that your offline campaign provide a compelling reason for the visitor to remember your specific URL. This can be the promotion of special-offer bundles, voucher codes, reduced pricing, free gifts, competitions, unique or personalized products, and so on that are available only by using the specific URL you display in your offline campaigns.

A useful tip when employing this technique is to use a landing-page URL that can be remembered easily, tying it in with your message and the medium. This sounds like common sense, but you would be surprised what a little thought can achieve for you. For example, for a TV campaign you could consider the following:

```
www.mysite.com/tvoffer
www.mysite.com/10percent
www.mysite.com/getonefree
www.mysite.com/twofourone (or /2for1, /241)
www.mysite.com/xmas
www.mysite.com/sale
```

Identifying with your TV branding slogan or campaign message can be a very effective way of keeping your full URL in the viewer's mind, because this associates your website with their viewing activity.

As with the use of vanity URLs, redirecting visitors is required. This enables you to avoid producing duplicate content and appends tracking parameters to the landing page. The only difference here is that the redirection is applied to a subdirectory, not the entire domain. This is desirable if your products are already hosted as separate websites.

Even without redirection, as long as the URLs remain unique to your offline campaigns and are neither shown as links within your website nor indexed by the search engines, you will still be able to measure the number of offline visitors to these specific pages. The purpose of the redirection is to help you compare different campaigns within your Google Analytics reports. This is key for marketers attempting to understand the performance of numerous marketing channels.

Redirecting Coded URLs

This example uses the Apache `mod_rewrite` module, which most Apache servers have installed by default. See `http://httpd.apache.org/docs/mod/mod_rewrite.html`.

```
<VirtualHost>
    ServerName www.myproduct.com
    RewriteEngine on
    RewriteCond %{HTTP_USER_AGENT} .*
    RewriteRule /xmas.* /productX/?utm_source=channel123↵
    &utm_medium=tv&utm_campaign=March%20tv%20ad [R=301,QSA]
</VirtualHost>
```

Ensure that the `RewriteRule` is contained on one line within your configuration file (up to and including QSA]), and if spaces are required within the URL, use character encoding (%20). Adjust your campaign-tracking parameters accordingly—as described in Chapter 7.

Combining with Search to Track Offline Visitors

When your brand values are less significant than your product or service values or your target audience is more price oriented than brand oriented, remembering a URL can be difficult for your potential visitors—your brand is simply not strong enough to gain traction. An alternative technique is to use search as part of your offline message, such as running a radio ad that uses something like "Find our ad on Google by searching for the word *productpromo* and receive 10 percent off your first order."

By creating an AdWords ad just for this campaign, targeting a unique word or phrase that is relevant only to people who have heard your ad, you not only provide a strong incentive for visitors but also directly assign these visitors to a specific offline marketing effort.

This extra step of asking your potential audience to first go elsewhere (to a search engine) has a small drawback: You pay for the click-through on your AdWords ad. However, using a unique search phrase means you should be the only bidder and hence would pay as little a one cent per click-through. For such a small price, the upside is considerable: You have full control of the ad message and landing-page URL. That means each campaign (print, TV, display, radio) can have a separate landing page and hence is completely traceable, *without* the need of going to your IT department and asking for redirections to be set up.

Example keywords to use in your AdWords campaign include the following:

- 10percent
- productX101
- whyCompanyName
- 1-800-123-BIKE—your toll free number (U.S.)
- 207-123-4567—your telephone number
- Signal House, London Road—the first line of your address

Tip: Check your AdWords listing regularly, because competitors may pick up your campaigns and start to bid on the same keywords!

Summary and Case Study

To help guide you through the decision-making process of which method to choose, I describe here the approach I used for this book. That is, I wanted to track whether readers use the URLs provided in the book text to visit www.advanced-web-metrics.com. Fortunately, I possess the skills to fully manage the IT requirements of my Apache server. Therefore, all three offline tracking methods were available to me: vanity URLs, coded URLs, and combining with search.

First, I ruled out combining with search because my offline marketing extends only to print—the book itself. In addition, my target keywords, for example, "Google Analytics," would attract a very broad and poorly qualified audience. I therefore needed to consider which type of redirection URLs are most suitable.

For my situation as an author of content wishing to track reader engagement, my brand is the book title and its web address, www.advanced-web-metrics.com. My "products" are chapters of this book, and I wish to track reader engagement on a per-chapter basis. Therefore, relatively speaking, I have strong company brand awareness and low product brand awareness ("Chapter 11" is meaningless unless you are aware of the book). Hence I use coded URLs in this book to track you. For example, www.advanced-web-metrics.com/ chapter11 redirects to the website with campaign parameters appended, allowing me to view the activity of offline readers in my Google Analytics reports. As you will see if you try this link, I use the parameter utm_id=81 to differentiate such visitors (campaign parameters are added in the background).

Using these methods, tracking offline marketing activity is relatively straightforward and most importantly scalable—1 thousand, 1 million, or 100 million offline visits can be tracked this way. However, despite this, tracking offline marketing efforts has long been a frustrating experience for marketers. Essentially you need a savvy IT person who understands the requirements of marketing and can advise on which of the three methods is the best fit for you on a per-campaign basis—a rare breed indeed.

If that is not available to you, or you are an organization where brand values are less significant than your product or service values, you should combine offline marketing with search marketing. This gives you complete control over tracking without any IT to worry about. Even large brands, for example, Pontiac, have used this technique to great effect.

An Introduction to Google Website Optimizer

Google Website Optimizer is a free web-page testing tool that enables you to seamlessly run experiments on your website visitors—comparing either different versions of the same page (A/B testing) or elements within a page, that is, multivariate testing (MVT). The technology displays a test version to your visitors at random, which is maintained throughout their visit. That is, they see only one particular test and are unaware of other versions. Hence, the process does not interfere with your visitors' browsing experience. By defining a goal—analogous to Google Analytics—the test that drives the most goal conversions is the one your visitors prefer. With this knowledge, the idea is that you adopt the winning test page as your permanent content.

Marketers will be familiar with A/B testing—a binary test to compare the effectiveness (usually a conversion rate) of a statistical element, such as one product image versus another. For example, page A is shown to 50 percent of new visitors selected at random, while page B is shown to the remaining 50 percent of visitors. If page A is better at generating conversions than page B, then page A is declared the winner and subsequently shown to all visitors. Another page, or page section, can then be tested, such as product title A versus product title B. Despite its name, you can also perform multiple side-by-side tests, that is, A/B/C/D... tests.

Multivariate testing is used to evaluate multiple page elements such as images, headlines, descriptions, colors, fonts, content, and so on *within* a page in order to understand which combinations provide better conversions. According to Wikipedia (http://en.wikipedia.org/wiki/Multivariate), multivariate statistical analysis describes "a collection of procedures which involve observation and analysis of more than one statistical variable at a time." The key phrase "more than one statistical variable at a time" is what distinguishes MVT from A/B testing.

If you have used AdWords or another pay-per-click search marketing network, you may have already experimented with A/B testing. AdWords Ad Version Optimization, discussed earlier in this chapter, uses the same statistical methods to display different ad creatives to Google search visitors, where you have more than one ad version available for the same keywords. AdWords Ad Version Optimization is a testing technology for visitor acquisition, while Google Website Optimizer extends the methodology for testing page effectiveness once a visitor has arrived on your website.

Similar to the launch of Google Analytics, the release of Website Optimizer was a pivotal moment in the short history of the landing page optimization industry. Previously, such tools were complicated to deploy and came with a hefty price tag to implement and use. Google changed that with a simplified setup and free availability to all. Unlike Google Analytics though, the launch of Website Optimizer in 2007 was the result of internal product development, not an acquisition.

Note: Google Website Optimizer allows you to run tests on your pages regardless of visitor referral source, not just AdWords visitors. In addition, you do not need to be an AdWords advertiser to use it.

AMAT: Where Does Testing Fit?

Consider the following scenario: You have set up your website, initiated marketing to bring relevant traffic, and viewed your visitor reports, and you notice an important page is underperforming. You've identified the problem, and various teams have come up with suggestions to improve the situation. These include changes to the page layout and its design, different product images, snappier headlines, revised descriptive text, and stronger calls to action (bigger buttons!). Now you have to advise which suggestion to pick as the replacement, or should you select all of them?

This common problem can sometimes halt the entire optimization process; people just don't know what to do next—there are too many choices and all (or none) could be right. Often the highest paid person in the room (HIPPO) or most vocal person determines the way forward. But the reality is that they know much less about the behavioral patterns of visitors on your website than you do, as you look at the data on a regular basis. Are you prepared to put your credibility on the line by taking an educated guess or going with the strongest opinion? That's a dilemma expert consultants as well as novice analysts face.

The answer is you don't need to and shouldn't. Let your visitors decide, because these are the "expert" opinions you need to listen to. This is precisely where testing comes in. Multivariate and A/B testing are crucial elements that dovetail into the web-marketing life cycle, known as AMAT:

1. Acquire visitors.
2. Measure interactions.
3. Analyze results.
4. Test improvements.

As Figure 11.31 shows, AMAT allows for a continuous cycle of improvement, providing a measurable process by which you can optimize conversion rates on your website, right down to a page-by-page basis if required.

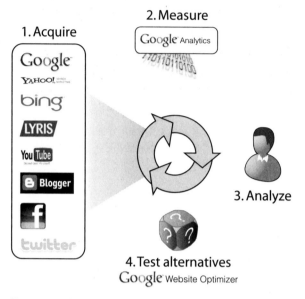

Figure 11.31 The web-marketing life cycle (AMAT)

Choosing a Test Type

At this stage I assume you have been through the process of optimizing poorly performing pages and search-engine marketing campaigns—as described earlier in this chapter.
Do these first to ensure you get the basics right before performing a test—there is no
point in testing just for the sake of it. Employ testing when you have a fundamental
best-practice web design and search marketing strategy in place. Otherwise, you waste
a great deal of time and effort looking for statistical significance in areas that are basic
and can be identified quickly by a good web consultant.

With these in place, next have a clear definition of what page you wish to test.
Some practitioners propose "test everything." However, for all but the smallest of websites, that is unrealistic. Instead, focus your efforts on pages with high and low $ Index
values, high and low bounce rates, and funnel steps to your goal completions.

Low $ Index and high-bounce-rate pages indicate poor performance and are
obvious candidates for testing. High $ Index and low-bounce-rate pages are strong-
performing pages that are excellent candidates for testing promotions, new ideas, and
so on. Funnel steps are the well-defined linear micro-conversions that take the visitor
to the end goal—the purpose of your website. Experimenting with any of these can
have a huge impact on your website performance—as discussed in "Identifying and
Optimizing Poorly Performing Pages" at the beginning of this chapter.

With a test page defined, log in to your Website Optimization account and
click Create a New Experiment. The first thing to decide is what type of test (referred
to as *experiment* from now on, with *test* used to describe a particular experiment

combination) is most suitable for your needs. As shown in Figure 11.32, you have two choices:

A/B Experiment A/B tests, often referred to as split testing within the industry, allow to you to test two (or more) entirely different versions of a page. Choose this if you are considering a page redesign or new layout, or if you simply wish to change one item on a page.

Multivariate Experiment Multivariate tests allow you try multiple combinations of content on the *same* page. Choose this to test combinations simultaneously where the design and layout remain constant.

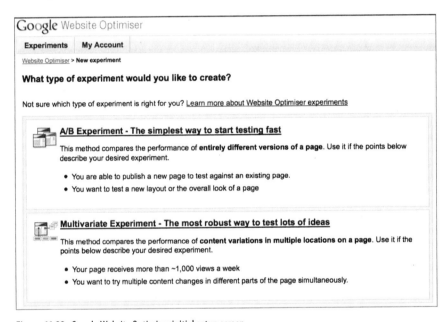

Figure 11.32 Google Website Optimizer initial setup screen

In both cases you define a conversion goal that signifies success.

When A/B Experiments Are Appropriate

The great advantage of A/B testing is that it is simple to set up, obtain results, and make a change. It is often used to test design layout—for example, should the menu-navigation system be at the top or left side of the page, or is a black-and-white theme preferred to a multicolored alternative? The iterative nature of A/B testing and the few alternatives presented to the visitors (as low as two—the original and an alternative) enable you to gain results quickly. This is particularly useful when answers to macro-questions are required—is version A better than version B or not?

The advantage of A/B experiments diminishes as the number of alternatives grows (A, B, C... Z), because each page must be created and hosted on your servers.

When Multivariate Experiments Are Appropriate

With multiple page elements—for example, multiple product images, titles, and descriptions on the same page—A/B testing is too laborious to implement and too time consuming to obtain results. Another caveat is that A/B testing cannot tell you whether one page element affects the conversion rate of another; for example, what if the product title affects how visitors perceive the product image?

Use multivariate testing to test multiple elements on a page simultaneously. It determines what, if any, correlations exist between elements and evaluates the best combination of all page elements to create a winning recipe—that is, generate more conversions.

Use A/B Testing for Dynamic Content

For multivariate (MVT) experiments, Website Optimizer hosts your alternative combinations on Google servers. In this way, when a visitor views a page under test, Website Optimizer replaces the original (control) version of the section you wish to test with one of your alternatives. Because this process takes place on the fly, test versions must be defined *within* Website Optimizer.

The advantage of this approach is that it removes a large part of the technical overhead required to perform a multivariate test—a savvy marketer can set up and control an MVT experiment without changes to the website architecture. However, a consequence is realized when the page alternatives depend on dynamic variables, such as the visitor's input prior to the test page being viewed.

For example, consider testing a product-page template of a shopping-cart system. Which image, headline, description, and so on are displayed depends on the link the visitor clicked in the preceding product-category page. Website Optimizer has no way to determine which product was selected, because this is dynamically generated at the point of click-through. Therefore, you cannot use MVT in this scenario. Instead, perform an A/B test with your alternative combinations.

Note: Depending on what elements you are specifically testing, there are advanced methods allowing you to run MVT tests on dynamically generated content, for example, using server-side logic in conjunction with JavaScript and CSS. In addition, if you use Website Optimizer to inject CSS and JavaScript rather than "content," you can rearrange elements on a page to present different variations to the visitor. However, these are advanced techniques.

Getting Started: Implementing a Multivariate Experiment

In the following sections I consider the setup of a multivariate experiment and two resulting case studies—a retail website (Calyx Flowers) and a content publisher (YouTube).

As you may have suspected, there is a close relationship between Website Optimizer and Google Analytics—the conversion data used in Website Optimizer reports comes from the same database system Google Analytics uses. In addition, a modified version of the GATC is used for tracking purposes.

Note: This section outlines the principles of a Website Optimizer implementation. A fuller description is available from www.google.com/websiteoptimizer with more technical information available at the official Website Optimizer blog: http://websiteoptimizer.blogspot.com/2009/03/introducing-techie-guide-to-google.html.

Similar to Google Analytics, Website Optimizer is integrated with AdWords and is accessed from within your AdWords account or directly from www.google.com/websiteoptimizer, as shown in Figure 11.32.

After selecting Multivariate Experiment, you have four steps to complete:

1. Set up a test page and conversion goal.
2. Install JavaScript tags on both pages.
3. Create alternative variations to test.
4. Review and launch.

Step 1: Set Up a Test Page and Conversion Goal

Your choice of a test page is determined during the consideration of test type, described previously. As already mentioned, don't test for the sake of it. Plan your experiments with care, or you risk being swamped with even more data (isn't Google Analytics enough for you?). Pages with a high bounce rate, high exit rate, or high $ Index value are suitable candidates for testing. If you are a transactional site, your checkout funnel is a prime starting point.

For your goal conversion page, you can use the same goal URLs as those defined in your Google Analytics configuration or define others. An important difference of Website Optimizer goals is that your goal must define success for your *test*—that's not always going to be the same as for Google Analytics, which uses goals to define success of your *website*.

Website Optimizer goals may be virtual pageviews and wildcards; /download/*.pdf and /cgi-bin/*.pl can be defined as goals as long as such files are being tracked by the Website Optimizer tracking script—for example, using an onClick event handler for PDF downloads. You can even define multiple goals on the same page or on subsequent pages. Each conversion is summed and added to the total, though it is currently not possible to weight different goals; all goals are considered equally.

Tip: A conversion goal does not have to immediately follow the test page—it can be much farther down the visitor journey. However, bear in mind the longer that path is, the fewer conversions the test will receive, and hence the longer the experiment will need to run in order to provide statistically significant results.

Step 2: Install JavaScript Tags on Both Pages

With your test and goal page URLs selected, you need to insert page tags to control the experiment and track the results. Figure 11.33 schematically shows the three different tags required for this. These tags are snippets of JavaScript code that are provided in the Website Optimizer interface during setup. The tracking and conversion scripts are simple modifications of the GATC.

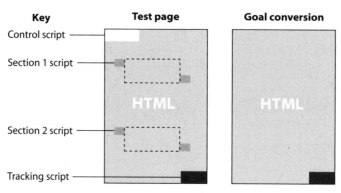

Figure 11.33 Schematic tagging of pages for a multivariate experiment

The three different page tags required are as follows:

Control script The control script governs the progress of the experiment. It contacts Google servers to retrieve appropriate content variations (the actual variations are maintained on Google servers). The control script also ensures that a repeat visitor views the same variation and that multiple views of the same page by the same user do not affect the experiment statistics.

The control script must be placed before any section scripts and before all displayable content. The recommended placement is in the HTML <head> section of the test page.

Section scripts Section scripts are used to define sections of page content that will vary in the experiment. Most things can be included within a section—for example, text, script, graphics, and so on—or all of these can be in one contiguous block. Currently the combined limit for all alternatives of a section is 150 KB, though this can vary depending on the size and number of other sections.

If you are testing more than one section, then each section requires a unique name. Section names are case sensitive and can be up to 25 characters long. Try to use meaningful names—for example, "headline 1" or "product photo X"—to make it easier to interpret your reports.

Tracker scripts (two) These scripts trigger Google Analytics data collection and ensure that page refreshes are counted properly. Add the tracker script to both the test page and the conversion page and immediately following your GATC—that is, place it after all displayable content in each page, just above the </body> tag. The order is not important, and you can also place the Website Optimizer tracking scripts just prior to your GATC.

A generic example illustrating the positioning of the scripts is shown here:

```
<html>
  <head>
    ...
    <script><!-- Control script ---><\script>
  </head>
  <body>
    ...
    <script><!-- Page section 1 script ---><\script>
    <script><!-- Page section 2 script ---><\script>

    <script><!-- Your regular GATC ---><\script>
    <script><!-- Optimizer tracking script ---><\script>
  </body>
</html>
```

Custom Variables

If you have the following custom variables in your GATC, then you will also need to customize the control script for your experiment:

```
pageTracker._setDomainName
pageTracker._setAllowHash
pageTracker._setCookiePath
```

To do this, create a new script setting the customized variables to the same values set in your GATC. This new script should be in its own set of `<script>` tags and placed immediately above the Website Optimizer control script, in the header area of your page. Note that the control script needs `urchin.js`-style customization, regardless of whether you are using `ga.js` or `urchin.js` for your tracking scripts.

```
<html>
<head>
<script>
    _udn = "none";            // from pageTracker._setDomainName
    _utcp = "/path/of/cookie"; // from pageTracker._setCookiePath
    _uhash = "off";           // from pageTracker._setAllowHash
</script>

<script><!-- Control script ---><\script>
    ...
</head>
```

Once you have installed all the tags, validate them within Website Optimizer. If errors are detected, fix these before continuing. Website Optimizer will not let you proceed to the next step without validation. There are two methods of doing this:

- Provide the URLs for your test and conversion pages. Website Optimizer will access them and validate.

- If your test pages are not externally visible—for example, if they are part of a purchase process, behind a login area, or inaccessible for some other reason—you can upload the HTML source files.

Step 3: Create Alternative Variations to Test

At this step, you add variations of section content within the user interface by simply pasting plaintext or HTML content into the box provided, as shown in Figure 11.34. This is required for each variation. Once you've completed this, you can preview each combination that your visitors might see.

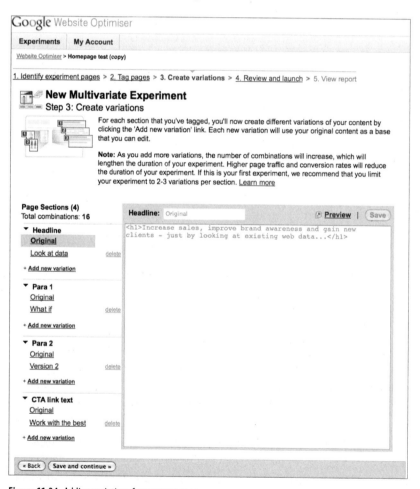

Figure 11.34 Adding variations for your test page

Note that the content variations used for testing are hosted on Google servers; the original content remains hosted by you or your hosting provider. Each time a visitor views your test page, Google servers insert your variations randomly. Once a visitor has received a particular combination, the combination remains fixed for that visitor. For example, if the visitor returns to the same test page later during their visit or at a later visit, the same combination will be displayed to that visitor—provided, that is, they use the same device and browser when viewing your site and have not deleted or lost their cookies. Otherwise, they will receive another random variation.

It is tempting to create lots of alternatives for a section under test because it is so easy to do. However, you should avoid making superfluous changes such as bold highlighted text versus nonbold or "Click here" versus "Read more" because the number of combinations is important. When your test page is displayed during an experiment, Website Optimizer is testing the performance of not only individual variations but also the combined effect of all page sections on the page. For example, in an experiment with two page sections—headline and image with two and three variations, respectively—the following six combinations will be tested (2×3 combinations):

- Original headline + original image
- Original headline + new image
- Original headline + new image2
- New headline + original image
- New headline + new image
- New headline + new image2

Extending this to four page sections with four variations for each, you will have 256 combinations ($4 \times 4 \times 4 \times 4$). As you can see, the number of combinations grows rapidly. This has obvious implications regarding the length of time the experiment needs to run in order to produce meaningful results (see the following section).

Step 4: Review and Launch

This is where you enter the percentage of traffic to include in the experiment (1–100 percent); the more traffic included, the faster the experiment will run. Before launching, it is worthwhile to make a final check of your experiment settings. Once you start the experiment, you will not be able to change the parameters; instead, you must create a new experiment.

Once you click Start, you will return to the experiment workflow page, which has an additional section describing the progress of this experiment and the number of impressions and conversions tracked so far. Your test page will start showing different combinations immediately, but there is a delay of about an hour before reports begin displaying data. Figure 11.35 is a schematic representation of how Website Optimizer works.

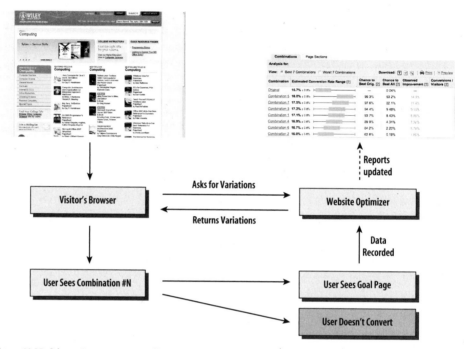

Figure 11.35 Schematic representation of how Website Optimizer works

How Long Will an Experiment Take?

The progress of the experiment and the estimated duration depend entirely on the amount of traffic seen on your test and conversion pages. As a guide, when selecting test pages choose pages that receive thousands of pageviews and are part of a conversion process that results in hundreds of goal conversions. The period it takes to achieve this in your Google Analytics reports is a good guide to how long it will take for your experiment to run for *each* variation.

For example, if you are testing three page sections, each with two variations, that is eight combinations to test in total ($2 \times 2 \times 2$). Each combination needs to receive approximately 100 conversions to show statistically significant test results. Assuming an average conversion rate from the test page to each goal page of 10 percent, then approximately 8,000 views of your test page are required. If that is achievable on your website within a week, then it will take approximately the same time to achieve meaningful results within Website Optimizer. If you have 256 combinations and a conversion rate of 5 percent, you require approximately 500,000 pageviews to your test page for the experiment to complete.

This highlights two important points when conducting multivariate experiments:

- Select high-traffic pages as candidates to test in order to obtain results in a reasonable time frame. As a guide, consider a multivariate test only for pages that receive in excess of 5,000 pageviews per week.
- Define a test goal as "close" as possible to the page being tested—as opposed to using your ultimate goal conversions defined in Google Analytics; for example, use "adding to the cart" or "proceeding to the next step" instead of "purchase confirmation."

Estimating Experiment Time

A handy calculator to help you estimate the potential duration of your experiment is available at www.google.com/analytics/siteopt/siteopt/help/calculator.html.

As a guide, a reasonable time frame for achieving useful experimental results is two to four weeks; otherwise you risk losing momentum. If you estimate an experiment taking considerably longer, use A/B testing instead. Once you have narrowed the combinations in this manner, you can return to a multivariate test with a smaller number of variations.

In addition, Website Optimizer has two pruning options to improve the speed of running experiments: auto-disable and manual disable. Auto-disable allows you to automatically prune variations that underperform. Manual disable allows you to manually achieve the same thing on a per-combination basis. These features are useful in decreasing the time it takes to run an experiment to statistical significance and when you wish to prevent underperforming pages from being served to visitors and distract them from the pages that have proven to be more effective.

Once you start seeing impressions and conversions recorded in Website Optimizer, view the preliminary results by clicking View Report. However, be careful drawing any conclusions at these early stages. At the beginning of an experiment, sample sizes will be small and results therefore highly inaccurate, that is, with large fluctuations.

For example, imagine spinning a coin 10 times. There is a possibility that all ten spins will result in heads showing. That does not mean that heads should be favored over tails and the experiment ended—such a result can be accounted to pure chance and the "butterfly effect." If you repeat the coin experiment 1,000 times, then overall you will observe a more even distribution, maybe 550 heads and 450 tails. Repeating the experiment a million times will give you a near-perfect prediction for the probability of receiving a head: 0.5.

The point is that patience is a virtue when it comes to testing. Allow enough data to be collected for each combination before analyzing, pruning, or selecting a winner—at least until the green or red conversion bars appear in your experiment reports.

The following case studies illustrate the abilities of Website Optimizer.

Calyx Flowers: A Retail Multivariate Case Study

This case study was produced by EpikOne (www.epikone.com) as part of their work for Calyx Flowers (www.calyxandcorolla.com) and is reproduced here with the kind permission of both parties.

As the name suggests, Calyx Flowers is a flower-distribution company, founded in 1988 and based in Vermont. Initially, Calyx Flowers had begun to invest significantly in its online marketing—particularly search-engine optimization and pay-per-click advertising. However, the company felt that the increase in visitor numbers did not match the modest increase in conversions received, that is, flowers purchased. Furthermore, Google Analytics revealed significant exit rates for visitors who had viewed a product page but did not add to the cart.

In designing the Website Optimizer experiment, EpikOne chose to test whether the product page could be more effective at producing conversions. In this example, a conversion was considered successful if a visitor added a product to the shopping cart. As shown in Figure 11.36, three sections of the product page were identified for testing:

1. Change of messaging

Would the addition of trust factors, such as customer testimonials, help?

2. Stronger call to action

Would larger, brighter buttons for "Buy Now" help?

3. Change of brand image

Would a different (more emotive) product image help?

For the experiment, each section had two combinations: the original and an alternative ($2 \times 2 \times 2 = 8$ combinations). Table 11.3 shows the combinations with all alternatives displayed.

▶ **Table 11.3** Multivariate test alternatives for Calyx Flowers

Section Name	Original	Alternative
Subhead	None	*Customer Favorites:* "Calyx Flowers has mastered the art of fresh flower design! I just adore this company." Juliet P. Verzolini, Linda, VA
Featured CTA	None	Order Now
Hero shot		

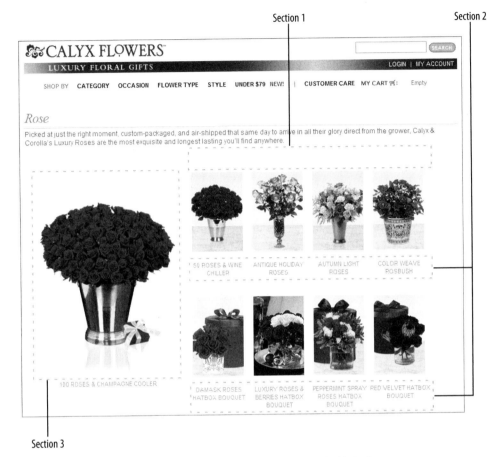

Figure 11.36 The Calyx Flowers original product page, with three test sections highlighted

The experiment was launched to test which sections and which combinations would lead to better conversions. For this test, a conversion was defined as adding a product to the shopping cart. Enough conversions were gathered to complete the experiment within a week.

Results and Impact

When viewing results, there are two reports to consider: the Page Sections report and the Combinations report. These are shown in Figures 11.37a and b, respectively.

The Page Sections report identifies which sections of the experiment have the greatest impact. This is indicated graphically with green and gray bar charts and numerically in the adjacent table. The Chance to Beat Orig. column is a measure of the overlap of the two (gray and green bars) conversion distributions. The smaller the overlap, the greater the separation of the distributions and therefore the higher the probability of beating the original variation. In other words, was the change in the observed conversion rate real, or did it just occur by chance (within error bars)? A clear separation of green and gray indicates it is real, with a 95 percent confidence level.

In Figure 11.37a, we can see that the addition of a testimonial has the greatest impact on conversion rate, closely followed by the change in product image. The enhanced call-to-action buttons show a negative impact (red bar)—that is, they decreased the conversion rate. However, the decrease is minimal (−0.48 percent) and the distribution overlap is large, as indicated by the Chance to Beat Orig. (42.9 percent). This means there is a 57.1 percent chance that the original section could have also had the same effect. Thus, the call-to-action section is considered to have no significant impact on conversions.

Viewing the Combinations report of Figure 11.37b, we can see that there are two superior combinations (5 and 7). Both of these contained the testimonial, with the winner also including the more emotive product image and the original call-to-action links; see Figure 11.38.

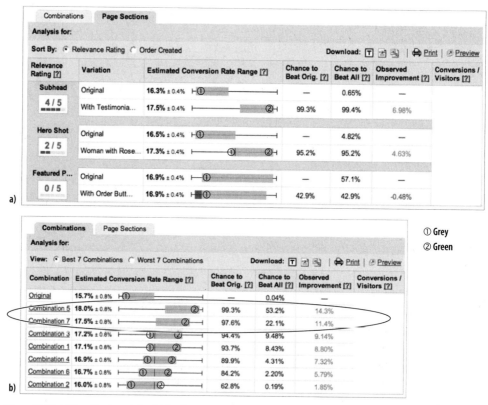

Figure 11.37 (a) Page Section results, (b) Combination results

Figure 11.38 Winning combination for the Calyx Flowers product page

The best improvement of a 14.3 percent increase in conversions equates to a significant dollar improvement for the Calyx Flowers bottom line—of the order of millions of dollars per year. This has provided the evidence required that their online marketing efforts are working and provided impetus to further invest in their online channel.

YouTube: A Content-Publishing Multivariate Case Study

This case study was produced by Google in association with VKI Studios (www.vkistudios.com) and is reproduced here with the kind permission of both parties.

YouTube is synonymous with video sharing and has grown into one of the most highly trafficked sites on the Web. To put this into perspective, by 2009 YouTube users were uploading 13 hours of video per minute. Think for a second about that statistic—it would take you more than two years just to watch one hour's worth of uploaded content. And that incredible bandwidth is happening 24 hours per day!

Because of its daily visitor volume, small changes on a website such as YouTube can make a very big difference, and it's an excellent case for a multivariate test. The goal was to increase the number of people who sign up for an account.

Three sections were tested on 100 percent of the YouTube US-English homepage. Figure 11.39 shows the original test page with test sections highlighted. The hypothesis was that if the prominence of the sign-up link were increased (via changes to sections 1 and 2) along with clearer highlighting of the benefits of having an account (via section 3), more people would sign up.

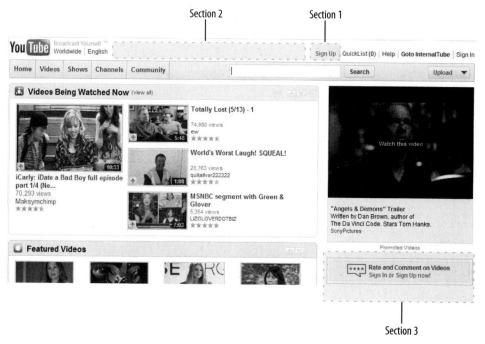

Figure 11.39 The YouTube home page with three test sections highlighted

For the experiment each section had multiple possible alternatives, giving a total of 1,024 combinations ($2 \times 16 \times 32 = 1024$). As shown in Figure 11.40, section 1 is a simple change of text style using all capitals for accentuation. Section 2 is new content that in the original is empty space. Its purpose is to highlight that having a YouTube account provides additional benefits and draw attention to the call to action. There are 16 alternatives (15 plus the original blank space). Section 3 provides additional supporting information of the benefits of having an account with 32 alternatives.

Results and Impact

The report of Figure 11.41 shows the presence of several winners. Although 12 are visible, the results page is paginated, so the winners stretch beyond what is shown in the screen shot. All of the top four provide a conversion uplift of greater than 15 percent and are predicted to beat the original 99.9 percent of the time, that is, almost certain. This high level of certainty is due to the very large sample size of pageviews and is therefore quite rare for most sites.

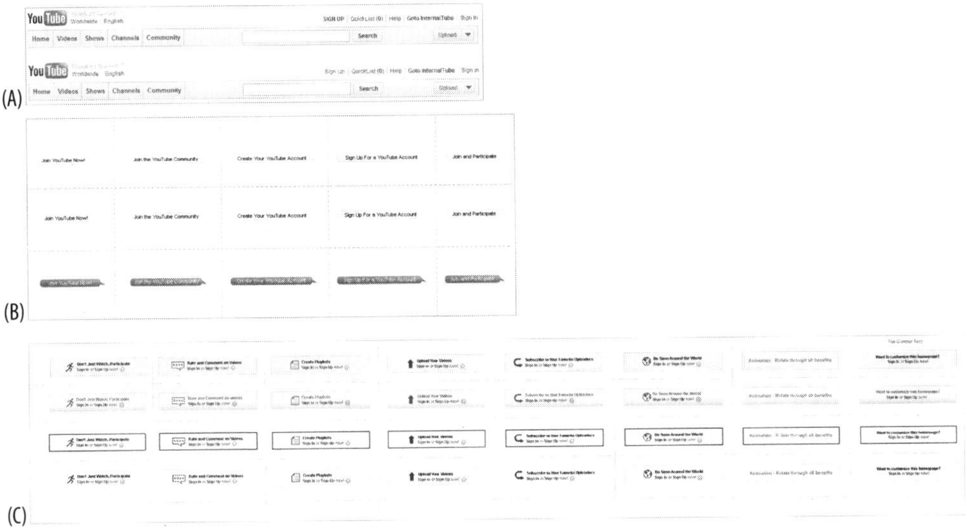

(A)

(B)

(C)

Figure 11.40 Experiment alternatives: (a) call-to-action texts, (b) encouragement banners, (c) engagement banners

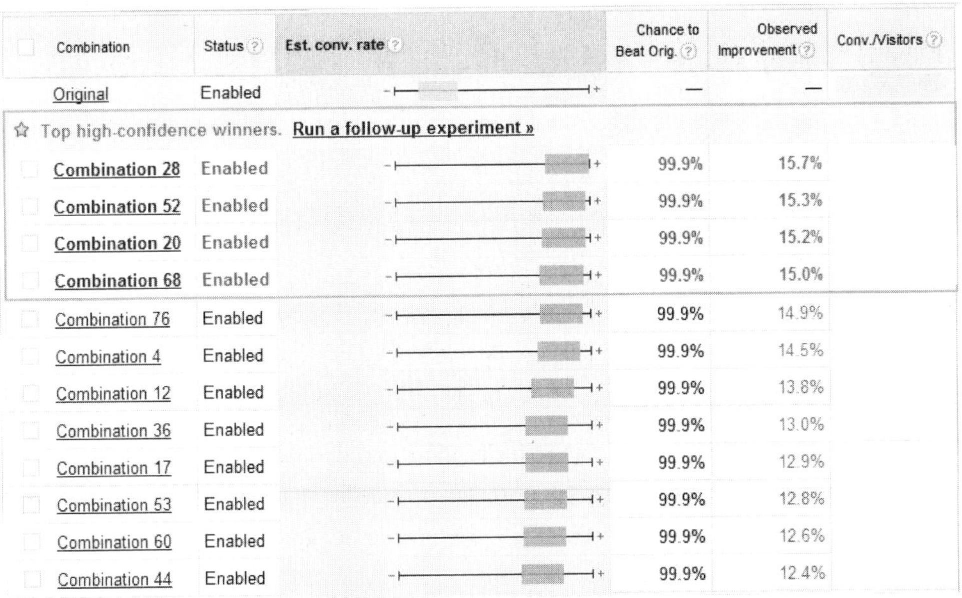

Combination	Status ?	Est. conv. rate ?	Chance to Beat Orig. ?	Observed Improvement ?	Conv./Visitors ?
Original	Enabled	– ⊢▭━━━━⊣ +	—	—	
☆ Top high-confidence winners. **Run a follow-up experiment »**					
Combination 28	Enabled	– ⊢━━━━▭⊣ +	99.9%	15.7%	
Combination 52	Enabled	– ⊢━━━━▭⊣ +	99.9%	15.3%	
Combination 20	Enabled	– ⊢━━━━▭⊣ +	99.9%	15.2%	
Combination 68	Enabled	– ⊢━━━▭⊣ +	99.9%	15.0%	
Combination 76	Enabled	– ⊢━━━━▭⊣ +	99.9%	14.9%	
Combination 4	Enabled	– ⊢━━━▭⊣ +	99.9%	14.5%	
Combination 12	Enabled	– ⊢━━━▭⊣ +	99.9%	13.8%	
Combination 36	Enabled	– ⊢━━▭⊣ +	99.9%	13.0%	
Combination 17	Enabled	– ⊢━━▭⊣ +	99.9%	12.9%	
Combination 53	Enabled	– ⊢━━▭⊣ +	99.9%	12.8%	
Combination 60	Enabled	– ⊢━━▭⊣ +	99.9%	12.6%	
Combination 44	Enabled	– ⊢━━▭⊣ +	99.9%	12.4%	

Figure 11.41 Combination results: Website Optimizer highlights the top four winners, though this is arbitrary.

Although Combination 28, shown in Figure 11.42, is the winner with an increase in performance of 15.7 percent, all 12 combinations show overlaps in predicted conversion rates. That is, the green bars representing the spread of conversion rates at 95 percent confidence overlap. This means it is entirely possible for, say, Combination 76 to outperform Combination 28. The report shows both are better than the original, but the difference between the two could be the result of random chance. If you wanted to conclusively select a winner, further testing would be needed on the top performers.

The increased sign-up rate for YouTube of 15.7 percent represents thousands of more signups every day for YouTube. Putting this achievement into perspective, the entire experiment, including planning, execution, and result analysis, lasted less than two weeks. In addition, this large experiment with 1,024 combinations (the largest Website Optimizer test to date) shows the robustness of the technique and the promise for very-large-scale multivariate experiments.

Figure 11.42 Winning combination for YouTube home page

Summary

In Chapter 11, you have learned the following:

To identify and optimize pages You have learned how to identify and optimize poorly performing pages using a mix of methods, including a detailed funnel analysis.

To benchmark internal site search We discussed how to measure the success of site search and put a dollar amount on its importance to your organization.

To optimize search-engine marketing You have seen how to optimize your search-engine marketing efforts for both paid and nonpaid search.

To monetize a non-e-commerce website You can ensure that your nontransactional site is not a pet project by monetizing it, either by assigning values to defined goals or by faking transaction calls to Google Analytics.

To track offline campaigns You have learned how to track offline marketing by using modified landing-page URLs and redirection or combining with search-engine marketing.

Multivariate and A/B testing We explored how to use Website Optimizer as a way to test a hypothesis or alternative design.

Integrating Google Analytics with Third-Party Applications

This book has so far focused on collecting, analyzing, and using web visitor data from within the Google Analytics user interface. You can import data from AdWords and AdSense and export individual reports in XML, CSV, TSV, or PDF format. This method of exporting is ideal for one-off needs or regular schedules via email. However, sometimes you require a regular "pull" of data, wish to integrate it into another system, or simply be creative and visualize your data in a completely different way.

In this chapter I explain the techniques used to auto-extract data and present case studies on how different organizations are pushing the envelope by adding extra functionality to Google Analytics.

12

In Chapter 12, you will learn:

To extract Google Analytics cookie information using JavaScript or PHP

To use the Google Analytics export API

To use the Google Analytics API via case studies from third-party applications

To use Google Analytics to track phone calls

To integrate Website Optimizer with Google Analytics

Extracting Google Analytics Information

The launch of the free Google Analytics export API in May 2009 was a pivotal moment in the history of Google Analytics. It paved the way for greater innovation by opening up the product so that third-party developers could build their own applications around the data. In addition, the API has provided Google with greater transparency in its data-collection methodology—you are able to query your own data as and when you wish.

If you have the necessary programming skills to develop API applications, go straight to the next section to learn which applications are already in the "wild" or to start building your own. However, sometimes a simple query of the Google Analytics cookies can be sufficient for your needs. For example, a visitor subscribes or makes a purchase on your website and you wish to pass the original referrer information, such as the search engine name and keywords used, into your CRM system. In such cases, consider using one of the following two approaches.

Importing Data into Your CRM Using JavaScript

Campaign variables (medium, referral source, keywords, and so on) captured by Google Analytics are stored in the campaign cookie named __utmz. Using standard JavaScript methods, you can extract this information at the point when a visitor submits a form request or confirms their purchase and transmit this into your CRM, help desk, or logfile system. The method is demonstrated using a submit form:

1. Copy the following two JavaScript functions into the <head> section of the HTML page containing your form:

```
<script type="text/javascript">
function _uGC(l,n,s) {
   // used to obtain a value form a string of key=value pairs
   if (!l || l=="" || !n || n=="" || !s || s=="") return "-";
   var i,i2,i3,c="-";
   i=l.indexOf(n);
   i3=n.indexOf("=")+1;
   if (i > -1) {
      i2=l.indexOf(s,i); if (i2 < 0) { i2=l.length; }
      c=l.substring((i+i3),i2);
   }
   return c;
}


function setHidden(f) {
   // set values for hidden form fields
   var z = _uGC(document.cookie, "utmz=",";");
   f.web_source.value = _uGC(z,"utmcsr=","|");
```

```
        f.web_medium.value = _uGC(z,"utmcmd=","|");
        f.web_term.value = _uGC(z,"utmctr=","|");
        f.web_content.value = _uGC(z,"utmcct=","|");
        f.web_campaign.value = _uGC(z,"utmccn=","|");

        var gclid = _uGC(z,"utmgclid=","|");
        if (gclid) {
            f.web_source.value = "google";
            f.web_medium.value = "cpc";
            //It is not possible to capture AdWords campaign details by this
            //method as GA processing is required for this. Therefore the
            //following lines are set to remove confusion should a visitor
            //use multiple referrals with the last one being AdWords.

            f.web_term.value = "";          // remove previous info if any
            f.web_content.value = "";       // remove previous info if any
            f.web_campaign.value = "";      // remove previous info if any
        }
    }
</script>
```

2. Within your HTML <form> tag of the same page, add the onSubmit event handler and hidden form fields as follows:

```
<form method="post" action="formhandler.cgi"
onSubmit="setHidden(this);">
    <input type=hidden name=web_source value="">
    <input type=hidden name=web_medium value="">
    <input type=hidden name=web_term value="">
    <input type=hidden name=web_content value="">
    <input type=hidden name=web_campaign value="">
...etc.
</form>
```

3. If you already have an onSubmit event handler, append the setHidden(this) call:

```
<form method="post" action="formhandler.cgi" onSubmit="validate();setHid
den(this);">
```

By this method, when a visitor submits the form to your CRM or other third-party system, a call is first made to the JavaScript function setHidden(this). This routine extracts the campaign variables from the Google Analytics __utmz cookie using the function _uGC. These are stored as hidden form fields and transmitted to your CRM system with the visitor's other form data.

Although in this example only campaign variables are extracted from the cookies and passed into your application, you can use the same method to query any of the Google Analytics __utmx cookies and include these in your import. For example, the contents of __utma contain timestamp information on a visitor's first and previous visit as well as how many times they have visited your site in total. An example of extracting this information is described next.

 Note: Even without a CRM system, you may want to use this method. For example, most formhandler scripts allow you to log the details of a form submission. Simply append the hidden form fields to your logfile.

Importing Data into Your CRM Using PHP

Similar to using client-side JavaScript to query and extract Google Analytics cookie information as described in the previous section, you can use server-side techniques. The following is an example using PHP, developed by Joao Correia and first discussed at http://joaocorreia.pt/blog/2009/09/google-analytics-php-cookie-parser/#english.

The method defines a PHP class to parse the __utma and __umtz cookie data. This class is used to provide the integration between Google Analytics and your CRM (or other third-party) application. The code is reproduced here with permission and is also available at www.advanced-web-metrics.com/chapter12.

To see this example working, follow these steps:

1. Place the following PHP code on the page where you wish to view the Google Analytics cookie information (for example, test.php):

```php
<?
require("class.gaparse.php");
$aux = new GA_Parse($_COOKIE);

echo "Campaign source: ".$aux->campaign_source."<br />";
echo "Campaign name: ".$aux->campaign_name."<br />";
echo "Campaign medium: ".$aux->campaign_medium."<br />";
echo "Campaign content: ".$aux->campaign_content."<br />";
echo "Campaign term: ".$aux->campaign_term."<br />";

echo "Date of first visit: ".$aux->first_visit."<br />";
echo "Date of previous visit: ".$aux->previous_visit."<br />";
echo "Date of current visit: ".$aux->current_visit_started."<br />";
echo "Times visited: ".$aux->times_visited."<br />";
?>
```

2. Place the following code in a file named `class.gaparse.php` **in the same directory as** `test.php`:

```php
<?
class GA_Parse
{
    var $campaign_source;        // Campaign Source
    var $campaign_name;          // Campaign Name
    var $campaign_medium;        // Campaign Medium
    var $campaign_content;       // Campaign Content
    var $campaign_term;          // Campaign Term
    var $first_visit;            // Date of first visit
    var $previous_visit;         // Date of previous visit
    var $current_visit_started;  // Current visit started at
    var $times_visited;          // Times visited

    function __construct($_COOKIE) {
        $this->utmz = $_COOKIE["__utmz"];
        $this->utma = $_COOKIE["__utma"];
        $this->ParseCookies();
    }

    function ParseCookies(){
    // Parse __utmz cookie
    list($domain_hash,$timestamp, $session_number, $campaign_number, ↵
    $campaign_data) = split('[\.]', $this->utmz);

    // Parse the campaign data
    $campaign_data = parse_str(strtr($campaign_data, "|", "&amp;amp;"));
    $this->campaign_source = $utmcsr;
    $this->campaign_name = $utmccn;
    $this->campaign_medium = $utmcmd;
    $this->campaign_term = $utmctr;
    $this->campaign_content = $utmcct;

    if($utmgclid) {
        $this->campaign_source = "google";
        $this->campaign_name = "";
        $this->campaign_medium = "cpc";
```

```
      $this->campaign_content = "";
      $this->campaign_term = $utmctr;
   }

   // Parse the __utma Cookie
   list($domain_hash,
      $random_id,
      $time_initial_visit,
      $time_beginning_previous_visit,
      $time_beginning_current_visit,
      $session_counter) = split('[\.]', $this->utma);

   $this->first_visit = date("d M Y - H:i",$time_initial_visit);
   $this->previous_visit = date("d M Y - H:i",↵
$time_beginning_previous_visit);
   $this->current_visit_started = date("d M Y - H:i",↵
$time_beginning_current_visit);
   $this->times_visited = $session_counter;
   }
}
?>
```

3.   Load test.php in your browser.

You will see something similar to Figure 12.1—simple and elegant! With the Google Analytics cookie values captured, you can then pass these into your CRM system as hidden form fields or environment variables.

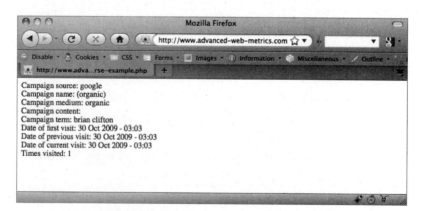

Figure 12.1 Example output from PHP parser for Google Analytics cookies

Working with the Google Analytics Export API

The previous section described quick and simple techniques for extracting Google Analytics cookies and importing this information into a third-party application. This section describes how to extract *all* your Google Analytics report data, by utilizing the recently launched Google Analytics export application programming interface (API).

This section is intended to give the reader an overview of the capabilities of the Google Analytics export API and illustrate this with examples of what smart people around the world are doing with it. Coding examples are kept to a minimum. For detailed instructions, view the online documentation at `http://code.google.com/apis/analytics`.

The Google Analytics export API launched in Google's famed beta format in May 2009. Built on the Google Data Protocol (`http://code.google.com/apis/gdata/docs/2.0/reference.html`) used by many other Google services, it allows developers, with the correct authorization, access to processed Google Analytics data. The purpose is to facilitate and propagate the use of Google Analytics data in ways the current user interface cannot provide. The export API achieves this by allowing data to be exported without the requirement of a user interacting with the Google Analytics user interface. This provides the infrastructure for developers to build their own applications for manipulating data, whether for integrating web visitor data with other third-party systems; providing auto-refresh functionality in Excel, PowerPoint, and custom dashboards; or creating new innovative ways of visualizing data. The possibilities are literally endless.

> **Note:** At present the API is a one-way street. That is, you can only export data from a Google Analytics account. It is hoped that one day an import API will be made available so that third-party data can be included in the Google Analytics user interface. Possibilities include importing cost data from non-Google campaigns—allowing you to view the return on investment on all marketing activities (email, SEO, Yahoo! Search Marketing, and the like), offsite web analytics data such as social media brand mentions, and sentiment information alongside your Google Analytics onsite data.

A schematic of the Google Analytics data-querying architecture is shown in Figure 12.2. Note that this is an extension of the schematic discussed in Figure 3.2 of Chapter 3, "Google Analytics Features, Benefits, and Limitations." For more information on BigTable, see `http://en.wikipedia.org/wiki/BigTable`.

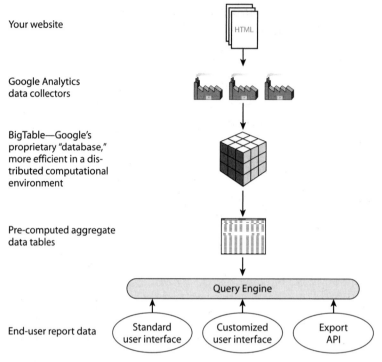

Your website

Google Analytics
data collectors

BigTable—Google's
proprietary "database,"
more efficient in a dis-
tributed computational
environment

Pre-computed aggregate
data tables

End-user report data

Figure 12.2 Schematic example of the Google Analytics API

To summarize the last row shown in Figure 12.2, there are currently three ways to obtain your web visitor data:

- Asking predefined questions and displaying the results in a fixed user-interface format

- Asking custom questions and displaying the results in a fixed user-interface format

- Asking custom questions that are not tied to a user interface

As you can see, whether you use the standard Google Analytics reports, custom reporting, or the export API, all data requests go to the Google Analytics Query Engine. This lookup engine knows where to find requested information from the processed (precomputed) data tables. The "secret source" Google has created makes the query engine extremely fast and super scalable—a huge engineering achievement for a service that must handle billions of queries every day. As an aside, this is one of the key differentiators between Google Analytics and its sibling product Urchin Software. Urchin is discussed in Chapter 3.

At this stage it is important to realize that querying the data, by whatever method, results in a query to the processed data, that is, data that has initial computations carried out—such as time on page; whether the page is an entrance, exit, or bounce page; whether it is a goal, part of a funnel, an event, or a transaction. The only exception to this is when building advanced segments, which results in a query to the raw (BigTable) data via the Query Engine.

How to Use the Export API—the Basics

The Google Analytics export API is a REST API, meaning that its software architecture corresponds to the Representational State Transfer style. In this case, it means that you send your data request as a URL with query parameters defining the content of your "question." The Google Analytics export API then returns an XML data feed corresponding to the "answer" of your question. See `wikipedia.org/wiki/Representational_State_Transfer` for more information on the REST architecture.

The use of the REST architecture provides a straightforward, efficient process that requires knowledge of only three steps, which are discussed next:

- Authorization
- Account query
- Report data query

Tip: Assuming you have a webmaster or web developer background, view Google's JavaScript tutorial at `http://code.google.com/apis/analytics/docs/gdata/1.0/gdataJavascript.html` (this is how I got started!). Other programming languages are also available.

Authorization

Similar to having to log in to Google Analytics, before users can view data from an application that uses the data export API, they must be granted access. The export API requires a user to grant an application access to their data. This is achieved with a request for an authorization "token" from the Google Accounts API. The method prevents user credentials being sent around the Internet for each request and is therefore more secure.

Note: It is important to know that authentication takes place via the Google Accounts API only, not the data export API.

Three types of authorization services are supported:

ClientLogin username/password authentication Used for applications that run on a user's computer only, that is, not distributed to other users.

AuthSub proxy authorization Used for distributed applications. A user's username and password are never revealed to the application. Instead, the application obtains special AuthSub tokens, which it uses to act on a particular user's behalf. The end user can revoke access by the third party from their Google Account configuration page (www.google.com/accounts).

OAuth authorization Similar to AuthSub though typically used for developing an application in an environment that uses a variety of services from multiple providers.

For the purpose of simplification, I consider only the ClientLogin method in this section.

To request an authorization token through ClientLogin, send a POST request to the following URL: https://www.google.com/accounts/ClientLogin. The POST body should contain a set of query parameters that appear as parameters passed by an HTML form, using the application/x-www-form-urlencoded content type. These parameters are

- *accountType*: Set to GOOGLE
- *Email*: The user's full email address of their Google Account
- *passwd*: The user's Google Account password
- *service*: Set to analytics
- *source*: A string identifying your application in the form companyName-applicationName-versionID

To see how straightforward communication is with the Google Analytics export API (you do not need a degree in software programming), use the following HTML form submission to authenticate:

```
<form action="https://www.google.com/accounts/ClientLogin" Method="POST">
    <input type="hidden" name="accountType" value="GOOGLE">
    <input type="hidden" name="service" value="analytics">
    <input type="hidden" name="source" value="BClifton-testApp-1.0">
    <input type="text" name="Email" value="">
    <input type="password" name="Passwd" value="">
    <input type="submit" value="Log me in">
</form>
```

If authorization succeeds, the server returns an HTTP 200 (OK Status) code, plus three long alphanumeric codes in the body of the response: SID, LSID, and Auth. If the authorization request fails, then the server returns an HTTP 401 (Unauthorized Status) code.

While this simple HTML form method illustrates the simplicity of the approach, it is not very practical, because you then need to cut and paste the returned token into your application! The following methods take this to the next level by handling the authentication within the script itself.

 Warning: At present API authentication must be via your Gmail account. That is, do not use a Google Apps For Your Domain account if you have one.

Account Query

Once your application has verified that the user has access, the next step is to find out which specific accounts the user has access to. To access the Google Analytics account feed, send an HTTP GET request to `https://www.google.com/analytics/feeds/accounts/default`. For this to work, you must add the authorization token to this request. Note that you cannot enter this URL via your browser address bar because the token must be inserted in the HTTP headers of the request. The following is an example of how to access the account feed through the `Bourne` shell using `cURL` (available from `www.advanced-web-metrics.com/chapter12`). Authorization takes place first, with the token inserted in the HTTP header of the subsequent account query.

Run the script using your preferred Linux environment—the Apple Terminal application will also suffice—and view the resulting output.

```
#!/bin/bash
USER_EMAIL="" #Insert your Google Account email here
USER_PASS="" #Insert your password here


googleAuthToken="$(curl https://www.google.com/accounts/ClientLogin -s \
    -d Email=$USER_EMAIL \
    -d Passwd=$USER_PASS \
    -d accountType=GOOGLE \
    -d source=curl-accountFeed-v1 \
    -d service=analytics \
    | awk /Auth=.*/)"


feedUri="https://www.google.com/analytics/feeds/accounts/default?↵
prettyprint=true"
curl $feedUri -s --header "Authorization: GoogleLogin $googleAuthToken"
```

Remember that users can have access to many different accounts—and within them, many different profiles. For this reason, your application cannot access any report information without first requesting the list of accounts available to the user. The resulting accounts feed returns this list. The list also contains the account profiles that the user can view.

Note: In the account and report query examples, JavaScript is not used because inserting the authorization token into the request HTTP header is harder to achieve. This is because JavaScript is unable to make cross-domain requests. However, a work-around for this is provided in the JavaScript client libraries available at `http://code.google.com/apis/gdata/client-js.html`.

Report Query

From the list of available profiles obtained from the account query, your application can request report data. The key to this request is the table ID for the profile obtained in the account feed. A difference to note between using the Google Analytics user interface and communicating via the export API is that within the user interface, profile names are employed and each profile has an ID number. In the export API, `ga:` is prepended to the profile ID in order to obtain the table ID. When working with the export API, you must specify the table ID for each profile you require access to. You can also view a particular profile ID in the Google Analytics user interface in the Profile Settings screen.

The data feed provides access to all data in a selected profile. To access the Google Analytics Report Feed send an HTTP GET request to `https://www.google.com/analytics/feeds/data`. As for the account query, you cannot achieve this using your browser address bar, because the authorization token must be inserted into the HTTP headers. Authorization takes place first, with the token inserted into the HTTP header of the subsequent account query.

The following is an example of how to access the report feed through the `Bourne` shell using `cURL` (available from `www.advanced-web-metrics.com/chapter12`):

```bash
#!/bin/bash
USER_EMAIL="" #Insert your Google Account email address here
USER_PASS="" #Insert your password here
PROFILE_ID="" #Insert your profile ID here

googleAuthToken="$(curl https://www.google.com/accounts/ClientLogin -s \
    -d Email=$USER_EMAIL \
    -d Passwd=$USER_PASS \
    -d accountType=GOOGLE \
    -d source=curl-accountFeed-v1 \
    -d service=analytics \
    | awk /Auth=.*/)"

feedUri="https://www.google.com/analytics/feeds/data\
?start-date=2008-10-01\
&end-date=2008-10-31\
&dimensions=ga:source,ga:medium\
&metrics=ga:visits,ga:bounces\
&sort=-ga:visits\
&filters=ga:medium%3D%3Dreferral\
&max-results=5\
```

```
&ids=ga:$PROFILE_ID\
&prettyprint=true"

curl $feedUri -s --header "Authorization: GoogleLogin $googleAuthToken"
```

As you can see in this example, you use query parameters to indicate what analytics data you want, as well as how you want it filtered and sorted.

Report Query Builder

Similar to the URL Builder used for helping you generate your campaign-tracking URLs (see "Campaign Tracking" in Chapter 7, "Advanced Implementation"), a Google Analytics report query builder also exists. This allows you to experiment with specifying different metrics, dimensions, filters, and so on and view the resulting query URL. See `tinyurl.com/apiquerybuilder`.

A list of all available dimensions and metrics exposed by the export API can be found at `http://tinyurl.com/apimetricsdimensions`.

Clearly there is a great deal more to the Google Analytics export API, and I have covered only the foundations here. An entire book can easily be dedicated to its use! However, my intention is to whet your appetite so that you can further explore its possibilities. Also bear in mind that the API is still a beta product (referred to as "Labs" by Google), and so exact syntax is still fluid. Refer to the Google Code site as necessary: `http://code.google.com/apis/analytics`.

In summary, the export API provides the opportunity for anyone to be innovative and creative with web visitor data. Often web measurement is considered a dry subject, which it certainly can be. Features such as Motion Charts, described in Chapter 5, "Reports Explained," go some way in improving the situation, but even Google cannot think of everything. The Google Analytics export API is your chance to change that. Don't be afraid of experimenting—applying a little lateral thinking and imagination can even surprise Google!

API Quota Policy

There is currently a quota policy in place to protect the robustness of the API system. Because the Google Analytics export API is still in beta, these limits are likely to change. Note that quotas apply to a single web property, not profiles, as follows:

- A maximum of 10,000 requests per 24 hours

- A maximum of 10 requests in any given one-second period

- Pagination limits of 10,000 entries per feed, with a default response of 1,000 entries

Continues

Examples of API Applications

The following are example applications of cool things people are doing with the Google Analytics export API. Most of these are freely available or operate on a *freemium* basis (free with upgrade options). All are creative and innovative. The first four in the list are presented in the next section as case studies written in conjunction with the original developers.

Visual Basic macros Microsoft Office applications (Word, Excel, PowerPoint, and Access) all support Visual Basic for Applications (VBA). Building import features into these applications using VBA allows you to automatically refresh KPI tables as well as expand on the visualization options offered within Google Analytics. As an alternative to plug-ins, it is virtually version independent, can operate faster, and allows the end user to experiment with modifications. A suite of such macros has been developed by Mikael Thuneberg. Further information is available at `http://gatoexcel.blogspot.com`.

Voice of customer Kampyle is an online Feedback Analytics platform that allows website owners to create their own advanced, branded, and customized feedback forms and put them on their websites. By integrating Kampyle feedback with the Google Analytics API, visitor feedback information is combined with Google Analytics geographic, visitor-loyalty, exit-page, and landing-page information. The result provides a more holistic picture of website performance—combing the "what" with the "why." Further information is available at `http://blog.kampyle.com/post_332`.

Excel plug-in The Tatvic Google Analytics Excel plug-in imports data into Excel. The tool comes with a three-step wizard to simplify the process and is targeted at Google

Analytics power users who need to invest a significant amount of time analyzing large data sets. With this plug-in, users can perform a one-time setup in Excel to pull data for a given period into a dashboard. The plug-in makes it easy to update the dashboard's data with a different date range. Works on Windows XP and above with Microsoft Office 2003 onward. Further information is available at www.gaexcelplugin.tatvic.com.

A similar product competing in the same market is Excellent Analytics. The plug-in works on Windows XP and Vista with Microsoft Office 2007 onward. Further information is available at http://excellentanalytics.com.

Custom applications and browser toolbars Youcalc connects to the Google Analytics data API to provide custom analytics applications that run in iGoogle, the iPhone, intranets, and blogs—pretty much anywhere. The applications allow you to access and analyze live Google Analytics data without opening Google Analytics. You can build custom applications on live data without coding, and mesh data from AdWords or salesforce.com into one analytics application. Further information is available at www.youcalc.com/solutions/webanalytics.

The seperia analytics toolbar was built to encourage Google Analytics users to view their website data more often. The free toolbar maintains key metrics visible on your browser and provides direct access to your Google Analytics reports for further information if needed. The toolbar is also certified by TRUSTe, the industry-recognized safe-software white list. Further information is available at http://www.seperia.com/toolbar/.

Blog publishing Google Analyticator adds Google Analytics tracking to a WordPress-powered blog. It comes with a customizable widget that can be used to display specific information gathered by Google Analytics. It supports all of the tracking mechanisms that Google Analytics supports, such as external link tracking, download tracking, tracking without counting administrative users, and any other advanced tracking the user wishes to add. Further information is available at http://plugins.spiralwebconsulting.com/analyticator.html.

CMS integration GX WebManager created a component that utilizes the Google Analytics API and displays metrics of pages and documents within its content management system. Metrics such as pageviews, time on page, search keywords, AdWords information, and so on are available to editors and marketers to enable them to understand what drives traffic to their websites and have contextual feedback about page content and keyword use. Further information is available at www.wcmexchange.com/googleanalytics.

Axiom CMS is a web-based content management system built on the Java Axiom Stack open-source development framework. By integrating with Google Analytics, content managers can see metrics as they are manipulating their content. Further information is available at www.axiomcms.com/google-analytics-integration.

Data visualization Trendly is an innovative monitoring and visualization tool that enables you to easily see what's changed in your Google Analytics data. In short, Trendly uses mathematical models to take noisy data and figure out when significant changes have happened. It prepares a news feed with attractive charts that put the changes into perspective relative to everything else that's going on. Further information is available at `http://trendly.com`.

Email marketing MailChimp's Analytics360 tool allows you to track the ROI of email marketing campaigns. Integration with Google Analytics gives a detailed report that shows how much revenue each campaign generates as customers click from email to website and make purchases. Email campaign reports include completed goals, value per transaction, and total ROI. Further information is available at `www.mailchimp.com/features/power_features/analytics360`.

ExactTarget is an alternative email marketing product that similarly provides integrated email-to-web behavior tracking. It allows you to understand the impact of your email marketing programs with aggregate subscriber tracking data and reports, including e-commerce tracking, geotargeting, trend analysis, and benchmarking in an easy-to-use interface. Further information is available at `http://email.exacttarget.com/Solutions/ByTechnology/Analytics/GoogleAnalytics.html`.

Microsoft Office and Gadgets ShufflePoint integrates Google Analytics with Microsoft Excel, PowerPoint, and Google Gadgets using its own powerful query language (GAQL) and a drag-and-drop query builder. Within Excel, you can associate web queries with spreadsheet ranges with refreshable GAQL queries—no add-ins or macros required. Similarly, for PowerPoint you can associate slide placeholders with GAQL queries. By using iGoogle, you can build your own Google Analytics dashboard. The ShufflePoint approach is encapsulated as "design once, refresh automatically." Further information is available at `www.shufflepoint.com/GoogleAnalytics.aspx`.

Mobile applications Mobile GA is an Android application that allows you to securely monitor your Google Analytics statistics directly from your mobile phone. Mobile Google Analytics does not use third-party servers to access or process your information and is designed to quickly produce your reports, using limited bandwidth, memory, and processor time. Further information is available at `www.analyticsmarket.com/mobileapps/mobile-ga/android`.

Analyze This! is an iPhone application that presents an executive overview of Google Analytics data to Directors on the go. It does not show you everything that is available in Google Analytics. Instead, it focuses on the measurements that matter—the ones that impact your bottom line. Further information is available at `http://analyzethisapp.com/download-it`.

Search marketing WordStream is a keyword-management solution, providing search marketers with integrated keyword tools for discovering, researching, analyzing, organizing, prioritizing, and acting on keyword data within their PPC and SEO campaigns. The latest version of WordStream integrates with both Google AdWords and Google Analytics. It automatically augments your existing keyword research every day with new, highly relevant keyword opportunities. WordStream also integrates your Google Analytics goal-tracking data so you can build on your initial keyword list and better understand which keyword niches are actually working (or not) on your site. Further information is available at www.wordstream.com/blog/ws/2009/11/10/future-keyword-research.

Concentrate is a long-tail search analytics tool designed for SEO and paid search professionals who want to make sense of search keyword data. Using the Google Analytics API, Concentrate exports Google Analytics keyword data and applies a unique pattern-identification algorithm to condense the long tail of search into keyword phrases with similar structures. A variety of analysis and visualization features gives users the tools to focus on the highest-performing keyword clusters. Further information is available at www.concentrateme.com/features.

Benchmarking and comparison TrakkBoard is an Adobe Air application that enables the simultaneous view of multiple reports from different websites—without logging in to Google Analytics. Targeted at agency environments, the application allows you to compare data of different accounts, websites, and profiles without permanently changing sites at Google Analytics. You can summarize your most important key performance indicators on one dashboard and follow current developments from your desktop. Further information is available at www.trakkboard.com.

SeeTheStats allows you to publish your Google Analytics data publicly—without the need for users to authenticate. Why do this? SeeTheStats is aimed at publishers wishing to be transparent to their advertisers. That is, you can view traffic levels before you purchase an ad. That is, you can also search for other participating websites and view their traffic for comparison. Further information is available at www.seethestats.com.

Note: Although not an API integration, Google FeedBurner is now integrated with Google Analytics—see www.google.com/support/feedburner/bin/answer.py?answer=165769.

If FeedBurner is enabled, clicks originating from your FeedBurner feed will show up in the All Traffic Sources and Campaigns views in your reports. Essentially, this is automatic campaign tracking in the same way AdWords operates with Google Analytics (see Chapter 7). The default tagging sets the utm_source as feedburner, the utm_medium as the channel in which your feed is distributed, such as feed or email, and the utm_content as the actual endpoint application in which the user viewed your feed content, such as Google Reader or Yahoo! Mail. However, you can customize these settings.

Example API Case Studies

The following case studies were provided by the creators of the solutions in question—all of whom are cited—and edited by me.

Visual Basic Macros

While Google Analytics offers a wide range of possibilities for reporting, there are many situations where additional analysis needs be conducted elsewhere. These situations include analyzing multiple metrics and dimensions at once, merging Google Analytics metrics with data from other sources, and simultaneously analyzing a large number of profiles. For the majority of people, the most convenient platform for this kind of additional analysis is Microsoft Excel.

There are several ways of importing data from Google Analytics into Excel. Most obvious is the Google Analytics built-in Excel export. However, this process has to be done manually for each report set and profile. Following the introduction of the export API, several solutions have been developed that involve installing Excel plug-ins. Mikael Thuneberg (`http://mikaelspage.blogspot.com`) has developed an alternative approach.

The alternative method of Thuneberg is to attach Visual Basic for Applications (VBA) code containing custom functions directly to an Excel workbook. This method allows the functions to be used in the workbook just as any other of Excel's built-in functions, such as SUM or COUNT. Reports can also easily be shared with other Excel users, who can refresh their data or modify queries without the need to install anything.

 Note: You can download the code for the functions and the files referred to in this section from `http://gatoexcel.blogspot.com`.

This solution works in Microsoft Office for Windows versions 2003 and later. You'll need to enable macros in the application settings. While using the functions is naturally easiest and most convenient in Excel, they also work in other Microsoft Office applications. Therefore, with some VBA skills, it is possible to create PowerPoint presentations that are always up to date or to import Google Analytics data into an Access database.

Instructions for Working with the VBA Functions

Only basic Excel skills are required in order to use the Thuneberg functions—no knowledge of VBA is needed. You will need to learn the various parameters for use with the functions and how to input array formulas in Excel—that is, formulas that fill more than one cell simultaneously. The easiest way to do this is to download a template

Excel file from `http://gatoexcel.blogspot.com` and start building on that. Each template file has the necessary VBA code already attached, so you can use it straight away. You can also view examples of the functions in use from within the file.

The first function required is `getGAauthenticationToken`, which is used to authenticate with Google Analytics by the `ClientLogin` method. To use this function, type the following into an Excel workbook cell

```
=getGAauthenticationToken (email,password)
```

where the two parameters are your email address and password to log in to your Google Analytics account. This function returns the authentication token. For importing data, use the `getGAdata` function to generate a report query by typing the following into a cell

```
=getGAdata(token,profile number,metrics,start date,end
date,filters,dimensions,sort)
```

where the following describes the fields used (left to right):

Token Type the address of the cell where you have typed the authentication function.

Profile number Type the ID number of the profile from which you want data. You can obtain this from your Google Analytics admin area.

Metrics Type the metrics you want to fetch, for example, **visits** or **visits&pageviews.**

Start date and end date Type the start and end dates of the period from which you want data. Typing dates can be cumbersome because of the various date formats. The easiest way is to write the dates in separate cells and put references to those cells here.

Filters (optional) If you want to include, for example, U.S. visits only, type **country== United States.** If this field is left blank, data for all visits is fetched.

Dimensions (optional) If you want to split the data by traffic source and medium, for example, type **source&medium.** If this field is left blank, the function fetches the site totals.

Sort (optional) By default, the results are shown in alphabetical order. If you'd rather sort by the metric, type **TRUE** here.

The `getGAdata` function makes a report query through the Google Analytics API and returns the data to Excel. If you have included just one metric and have not included any dimensions, then you can simply write this function to a single cell and the function will return the value to that one cell. If you have used multiple metrics or included dimensions, the results will not fit into a single cell. Therefore, you need to input the function as an array formula. To do this, follow these steps:

1. Select a range of cells.

2. Click the formula bar and write the function there.

3. Press Ctrl+Shift+Enter (simultaneously).

The function will now fill the range of cells with the query results.

VBA Usage Examples

The use cases for these VBA functions range from ad hoc analysis to elaborate dashboards that integrate data from Google Analytics and other sources. Here are some examples of common situations where the functions can help:

Custom dashboards As discussed in Chapter 10, "Focusing on Key Performance Indicators," it is not realistic to expect senior managers or executives to log in to Google Analytics directly. Therefore building a custom dashboard in Excel that automatically refreshes itself can be of enormous benefit. The dashboard can easily be shared throughout an organization because it does not require additional installs to be able to use it—just Excel with macros enabled.

Merging data from multiple Google Analytics profiles Google Analytics currently cannot easily compare or sum metrics from different profiles—unless you open multiple browser windows or use the roll-up reporting method described in Chapter 6. The VBA functions allow you to automate this by typing the ID numbers of the profiles into one column and getGAdata functions pointing to those profile numbers into another column.

Merging Google Analytics metrics with other data As an example, perhaps you know the cost of email marketing and would like to calculate the *cost per visit* from *email* for your site. Currently Google Analytics imports cost data only from AdWords and AdSense. However, by merging Google Analytics email visit data with data from your email marketing tool, this calculation becomes straightforward. You can calculate the return on investment for your email marketing right down to a per-campaign basis.

Innovative visualizing methods By importing data into Excel you can take advantage of its wide range of visualization features. One example is shown next.

An Innovative Visualization Method

While Google Analytics users with very basic Excel skills can get great value from using the VBA functions to automate data importing, people with more advanced skills can use them to make advanced reporting applications. For example, Mikael Thuneberg has created an application that illustrates how different Google Analytics metrics change over time, so you can quickly get a comprehensive view of how a site's traffic, usage, or sales are developing. As an example, see Figure 12.3, which shows how the country breakdown of traffic to a website has varied.

The purpose of this example is to show that with some basic Excel and VBA skills, it is possible to quickly create valuable reporting applications using the Thuneberg functions. Excel includes a wide range of data illustration and analysis features that can be accessed programmatically.

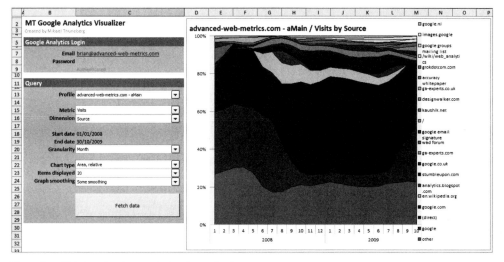

Figure 12.3 Visits by referral source displayed using Excel

Voice of Customer Integration

Kampyle (www.kampyle.com) is an online Feedback Analytics platform that allows website owners to create their own advanced, branded, and customized feedback forms and put them on their sites for the benefit of their users. Website visitors can quickly and simply submit their feedback with a general grade, feedback category, subcategory, text description, and the contact details. Visitors access the feedback form through the use of a non-invasive feedback button, which can be placed in various locations on the web page.

Once visitors submit feedback, it is processed to provide a high-level management view of the data and its context. Through advanced, automated analysis, the Kampyle dashboard helps website owners get the overview and perspective needed to improve their site. The system provides the qualitative "why" visitors do what they do, to complement the "what" and "when" provided by web analytics tools such as Google Analytics. Clearly, integrating Kampyle feedback data with Google Analytics provides a more complete picture of website performance.

The Integration Approach

In determining the type of integration needed, Kampyle considered the information Google Analytics experts would be looking for, such as what information they would want to know that they didn't already have in Google Analytics.

The first integration with Google Analytics was achieved using a Firefox extension called Greasemonkey. This Firefox add-on, using special scripts, could manipulate a HTML web page immediately after it was loaded by the visitor's browser. Often referred to as "page scraping," the technique allowed visitor feedback information to be displayed alongside relevant information from Google Analytics. Although providing some insight, it did not provide the complete picture.

By using the Google Analytics API, a fuller, more intelligent integration of data coming from two different sources can be achieved. It provides the freedom to use smart business logic to supply greater insights and display combined data in the most effective way possible. Using the export API, data can be manipulated from both sources to create intelligent reports and alerts that would let website owners know when something requires their attention.

The Kampyle system queries the client's Google Analytics information once per day. Reports on geographic distribution information, visitor loyalty, top exit pages, and top landing pages all have Kampyle feedback data incorporated. An example of this is shown in Figure 12.4.

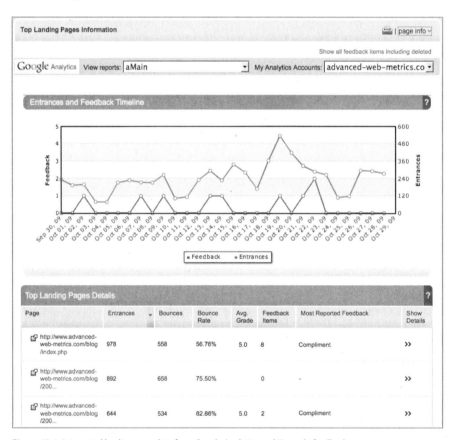

Figure 12.4 Integrated landing page data from Google Analytics and Kampyle feedback

Top exit and landing pages hold special importance for website owners because they are where users first arrive and where they leave from. Information on these pages can be invaluable for a website owner's efforts to bring users to the website and keep them there for as long as possible (or necessary). Google Analytics is responsible for identifying the pages to which most visitors first arrive at the site (landing pages) and the pages from which most users leave a site (exit page). For each of these pages, Kampyle can tell a website owner the average feedback grade as well as the most-reported issue. A simple drill-down procedure then allows the website owner to review all the feedback received on a specific landing or exit page.

Excel Plug-in

Tatvic (www.tatvic.com) offers a Microsoft Excel add-on to extract data from Google Analytics. The plug-in allows Google Analytics power users to choose and customize what data they want for analysis purposes and import this into Excel with different levels of granularity.

As an Internet marketing company and Google Analytics Authorized Consultant, Tatvic began its plug-in project from an internal need to analyze large data sets and run statistical applications on client data. The rationale was that exporting multiple data sets via the Google Analytics user interface is a procedure that requires the merging of multiple Excel datasheets. As with any such manual process, this can be laborious and error prone. By utilizing the Google Analytics API, Tatvic could avoid these limitations. Following internal development, Tatvic now offers their plug-in as a free-to-use, commercial-strength Excel application.

Plug-in Installation and Setup

Installation of the plug-in is straightforward; with your Excel application closed, download the plug-in file from http://gaexcelplugin.tatvic.com (Windows only) and double-click the install file. Then open Excel. The toolbar shown in Figure 12.5 should be present. Following login authentication, the Excel user is presented with the initial setup screen (Step 1 of 3) shown in Figure 12.6.

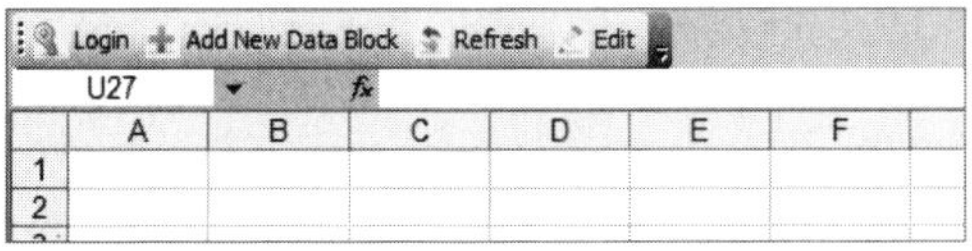

Figure 12.5 The Tatvic Google Analytics toolbar in Excel

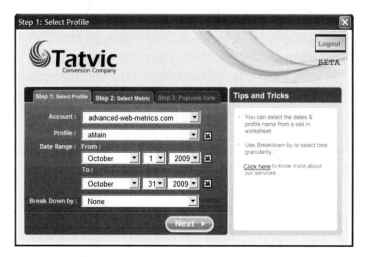

Figure 12.6 The Tatvic initial setup screen

Step 2 of 3 is to define the metrics and dimensions you wish to analyze. By selecting these fields from the drop-down menus shown in Figure 12.7, you append additional API query parameters to the report request URL in the background.

Figure 12.7 Step 2 of the Tatvic setup

As described earlier in this chapter, the Google Analytics export API operates via URL query parameters. That is, a user provides a specific data query as a URL request and Google Analytics responds with an XML feed containing the stipulated visit data. This plug-in handles the building of the API query for you. For example, the complete API query request for the user-defined parameters specified in Figure 12.7 is as follows:

```
https://www.google.com/analytics/feeds/data?ids=
ga%3A1234567&dimensions=ga%3Amedium%2Cga%3Asource&metrics=
ga%3Avisits&start-date=2009-10-01&end-date=2009-10-
31&sort=ga%3Avisits&start-index=1&max-results=500
```

Within this query request, each API report parameter is specified as a name/value pair separated by & in the usual way. However, you needn't be concerned with this level of detail in order to operate the plug-in. In fact, that is the point of the plug-in—to remove any complexity and allow you to analyze the data.

From Figure 12.7, the Dimension parameter defines the primary data keys for your Excel report, for example, referral source, medium, campaign, city, content, and so on. The Metrics parameter contains the aggregated statistics of website visitor activity in your Google Analytics profile, such as visits, pageviews, goal starts, goal completions, and so on. When queried alone, metrics provide aggregate values for the requested date range, such as overall pageviews or total bounces. However, when requested with dimensions, values are segmented by those dimensions. For example, number of pageviews (metric) requested with country (dimension) returns the total pageviews per country.

An early realization during the Tatvic plug-in development was that users wanted more than just plain data extraction into Excel—they required a tool to build an Excel dashboard with a "design once and update automatically" approach. To achieve this Tatvic used the cell-referencing ability of Microsoft Excel. The refresh data function allows users to prepare a dashboard once and then later simply refresh to update the data for the next time period—saving the analyst significant time. In addition, advanced features have been built into the plug-in that include the ability to create cascading advanced segments—similar to how the Google Analytics interface works, as shown in Figure 12.8.

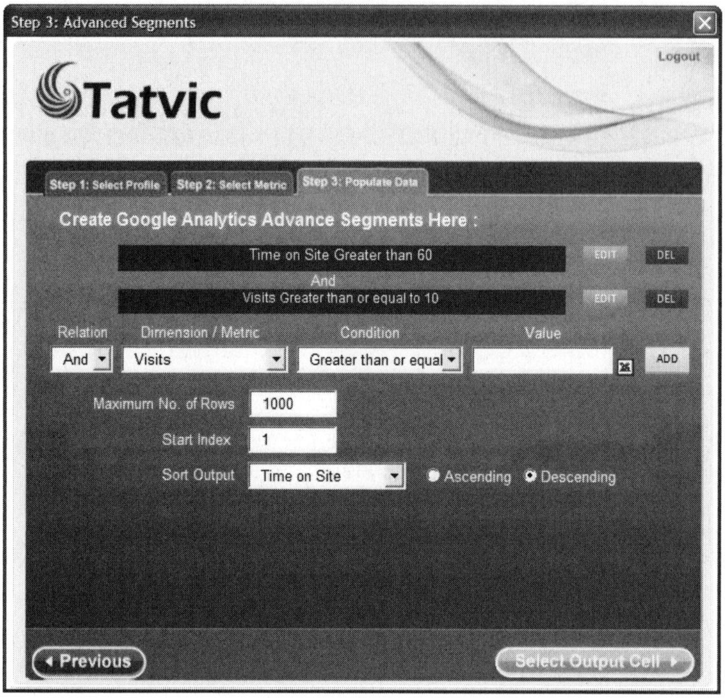

Figure 12.8 Step 3 of the Tatvic setup

Browser Toolbar

An area identified for improvement by easynet (seperia) Ltd., a Google Analytics Authorized Consultant from Israel, is that clients rarely log in to their Google Analytics account. It's a common concern when reporting back to an organization—getting report users to fend for themselves. Perhaps this is because of the overwhelming variety of reporting possibilities that Google Analytics has to offer and having to get over the initial fear factor that this can instill.

Certainly, defining goals, making use of the Google Analytics Dashboard, scheduling email exports, and viewing Intelligence reports can overcome a lack of self-engagement. However, the approach of seperia is to produce an analytics toolbar in order to keep metrics constantly visible in the website owner's browser. Think of it as a metrics teaser, with the objective of stirring enough curiosity for the user to drill deeper—that is, go on to view the full Google Analytics reports.

You can download the seperia analytics toolbar at `http://www.seperia.com/toolbar` (see Figure 12.9). Note that this toolbar is still in early beta and undergoing rapid development based on user feedback. Firefox, Safari, and Internet Explorer are supported on Windows, Mac, and Linux platforms.

Figure 12.9 The seperia analytics toolbar

The main factor considered when designing the toolbar was which metrics it should display. To qualify, each suggested metric had to meet the following criteria:

- It must be a primary metric a site owner or marketer needs to view regularly.
- The metric should be easy to understand at a glance so that action can be taken.
- The metric must change often. If it is relatively constant, do not include it.

By iterating through this process, the toolbar evolved and currently provides three Google Analytics mini-reports for users:

Performance trends A monthly trend of visits is shown within a mini-graphic on the toolbar itself. When you click the drop-down menu, this section reveals the trends of e-commerce total revenue and goal completions.

Top organic keywords This reports the top 10 organic keywords that drove the most traffic during the past week or month.

Top traffic sources The report on the top 10 traffic sources shows the percentage of traffic that was brought by each source/medium combination.

The toolbar helps website owners stay in touch with the performance of their website and its main sources of traffic. Next to each mini-report on the toolbar is a direct link to corresponding report inside Google Analytics for diving deeper into the data. Figure 12.10 shows all the toolbar menus expanded.

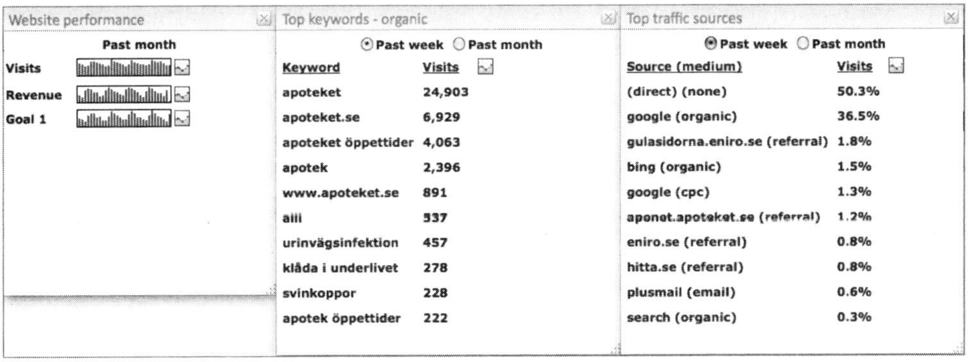

Website performance		Top keywords - organic		Top traffic sources	
Past month		●Past week ○Past month		●Past week ○Past month	
Visits		**Keyword**	**Visits**	**Source (medium)**	**Visits**
Revenue		apoteket	24,903	(direct) (none)	50.3%
Goal 1		apoteket.se	6,929	google (organic)	36.5%
		apoteket öppettider	4,063	gulasidorna.eniro.se (referral)	1.8%
		apotek	2,396	bing (organic)	1.5%
		www.apoteket.se	891	google (cpc)	1.3%
		aiii	337	aponet.apoteket.se (referral)	1.2%
		urinvägsinfektion	457	eniro.se (referral)	0.8%
		klåda i underlivet	278	hitta.se (referral)	0.8%
		svinkoppor	228	plusmail (email)	0.6%
		apotek öppettider	222	search (organic)	0.3%

Figure 12.10 Summarized Google Analytics data provided by the seperia analytics toolbar

Call Tracking with Google Analytics

Telephone calls are still an important call to action for a non-transactional commercial website. This is particularly so when an ID is required before a sale can be completed, for example, within the finance industry. However, this contact point is rarely tracked, and even when it is, the data is often siloed and not part of the web analytics reports where it can be compared against other forms of lead generation. Recently a number of vendors have started to address this issue by integrating call tracking with web analytics tools—most notably, Google Analytics.

Note: The following system and process information was provided by Fresh Egg Ltd for their product CallTrack ID, reproduced here with permission, with thanks to Nikki Rae, Andrew Heasman, David Grace, and Vaughan Luke (`www.freshegg.com/call-track-id.htm`).

The approach presented here, for CallTrack ID, is a typical one supplied by call-tracking providers that integrate with Google Analytics. Though specific system details vary among vendors, the following summarizes the methodology:

- A predefined callback number is displayed dynamically when a visitor views a page. That is, the number varies based on the visitor's referrer source—for example direct, organic, or AdWords.

- Your telecommunications provider logs calls made to these referral specific numbers.

- At regular intervals, an application is run to parse the logfile contents.

- For each logged call, the application generates a virtual pageview request (or event) to your Google Analytics account, with source, medium, and campaign-tracking variables appended.

- Call data is stored in a separate Google Analytics profile from other visit data because it represents calls made, not visits.

The last bullet point is important to fully understand. That is, this technique tracks calls logged by your telecommunications provider. It does not track website visit information and therefore cannot be associated with a caller's activity on your website—either before or after they made the call. Because of these limitations, all call-tracking data should be placed apart from your main Google Analytics visitor reports, that is, in a separate profile. Otherwise, you will be skewing your pageview count with data from new, single-session, one-page visitors.

To keep your call-tracking data separate, create an additional profile for a new domain, as described in Chapter 8, "Best-Practices Configuration Guide." In this example, www.yoursite.com/your-call-tracker/ is used as the URL of the call-tracking page being tracked. Make a note of the unique Google Analytics account number generated for this profile. This is the one you add to your CallTrackID profile, for example, UA-12345-2.

> **Note:** In addition to CallTrackID, which is U.K. specific, other Google Analytics phone-tracking solutions exist from vendors such as ClickPath (U.S.: http://clickpath.com), Mongoose Metrics LLC (U.S.: www.mongoosemetrics.com/solutions-web-analytics.php), AdCallTracker (U.K.: www.adcalltracker.com), Calltracks (U.K.: www.calltracks.com), AdInsight (U.K.: www.adinsight.eu), ifbyphone.com (U.S.: http://public.ifbyphone.com/services/google-analytics-call-tracking). As yet, no global provider exists for this approach, that is, one that can provide telephone numbers for multiple countries and integrate these with Google Analytics.

The CallTrackID Methodology

During the creation of your CallTrackID account, each route a visitor can take to arrive at your website is assigned a unique telephone number, as shown in Table 12.1.

▶ **Table 12.1** Telephone number format dependent on visitor referral source

Source	U.K. Format	U.S. Equivalent Format
Google organic	0845 ******1	1-800-******1
Google paid	0845 ******2	1-800-******2
My Top Keyword (paid search)	0845 ******3	1-800-******3
Direct	0845 ******4	1-800-******4
Any other channel	0845 ******5	1-800-******5

Then the following process occurs to collect call data:

1. A visitor clicks a link to your website from a search engine or any other referrer type. The contact telephone number displayed on your site when they arrive will depend on the route they took.

2. The visitor dials the specific telephone number presented to them. The call is routed to your main dedicated sales phone number to be answered as normal.

3. Your telecommunications provider logs the call. At regular intervals, the call data is emailed as a CSV file to CallTrackID servers, is parsed through a system

that converts it to XML, and then requests a call to a dedicated page on your website that contains your GATC.

4.   The data is recorded in Google Analytics in its own separate profile for you to use to create comparison reports between the referring routes. This allows you to determine which routes to the site generate the most telephone calls.

How CallTrackID Works

First, you will need to place CallTrackID's JavaScript snippet (available from www .freshegg.com/js/phonenumbers.js) on the pages where you display a telephone number. The number displayed varies by the snippet depending on the visitor's referral path. For example, to track an organic visitor from google.co.uk, the JavaScript simply reads the referring string (or Google Analytics __utmz cookie value) and assigns a predefined number. When a visitor calls one of these predefined numbers, it is recorded in your telephone supplier's call management system.

The CallTrackID approach is to have your logfile emailed in CSV format to their servers, where a Windows C# custom application monitors the mailbox. Once a new logfile is detected, it is moved into a folder for immediate processing. The result is converted into an XML file and sent as a stored procedure to a Microsoft SQL server. The application processes this with your corresponding CallTrackID account profile that contains your Google Analytics account ID, defined telephone numbers, and Google Analytics source and campaign values for each number.

For each logged call, an Internet Explorer engine automatically loads a landing page URL with campaign parameters appended. Your GATC is embedded in this page and registers a virtual pageview within your Google Analytics account. Campaign parameters are used in the usual way, as described in Chapter 7. These are utm_source, utm_medium, and utm_campaign. Values for these are taken from your CallTrackID account profile, where you predefine values for each telephone number. These can be any text string you would like displayed in your reports, though utm_campaign is usually omitted for all but the most proactive of lead-generation sites that vary telephone numbers based on specific campaigns. The value of utm_medium is set to phone.

Figure 12.11 shows an example call-tracking report. As you can see, only the visit data, representing calls made, is relevant in this report—time on site, bounce rate, and other visitor metrics are not applicable. Importantly, the report does allow you to measure return on investment for lead generation where the call to action is a phone call. You can then reallocate budgets according to results and adjust target keywords to pursue the most profitable terms.

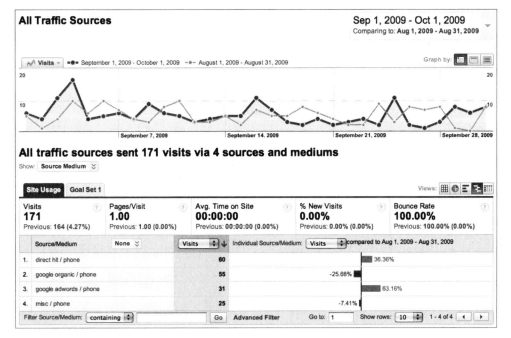

Figure 12.11 Call-tracking report within Google Analytics using the CallTrackID method

Integrating Website Optimizer with Google Analytics

An introduction to Google Website Optimizer is provided in Chapter 11, "Real-World Tasks," along with two case studies that show how, by testing alternatives, a page can be quickly optimized for better conversions—without guesswork, that is, using your visitors and customers as experiments. Ensure you are familiar with the terminology and methods described in Chapter 11 before reading this section.

While Website Optimizer is a great page-testing tool on its own, it may not have escaped your attention that results are very black and white. That is, a conversion either happens or it doesn't   the alternative headlines, layouts, images, and so on that produce the greatest uplift in conversion are considered the winner. There is no halfway house. But what if your conversion metric is not so clear cut? For example, maybe your test objective is to reduce a page's bounce rate, increase a visitor's time on page, or increase its $ Index value. For this, you need to integrate Website Optimizer with Google Analytics and bring in the additional metrics that Google Analytics has to offer.

Following is a summary of benefits when integrating Google Analytics with Website Optimizer:

- With Google Analytics, additional metrics become available for your test analysis, such as bounce rate, time on page, time on site, and revenue.

- You can segment data in any way available to Google Analytics, for example, a breakdown of test visits and conversions based on source or medium or a breakdown based on visitor type (new or returning visitor). Website Optimizer currently has no segmenting abilities.

- You can measure additional conversion goals. Maybe the test you are running impacts more than the single conversion defined in your Website Optimizer account. Google Analytics has the ability to measure up to 20 different goals.

- You are able to view the number of test visits or conversions for any time frame, for example, what happened last month versus this month. On its own, Website Optimizer considers visits from when the experiment is created, with no time-frame comparison.

The listed benefits are particularly helpful when you wish to test both micro-conversions and macro-conversions. Micro-conversions are the individual funnel steps that lead to a macro-conversion. For example, a micro-conversion could be how many people add a product to their shopping cart, how many of these go on to the next funnel step—your delivery details page, for example—and so forth. The macro-conversion for this process is how many people complete the checkout process, that is, become customers. Non-transactional sites work in the same way if they have funnel steps prior to reaching a goal conversion, for example, subscription sign-up or contact form completion.

If you use Website Optimizer in isolation, then you have to choose which one of these actions is defined as the test conversion and used as the benchmark for experiment success. By definition, if both micro- and macro-conversions are important, you would need to create two or more experiments. Unless you have very high traffic levels, a macro-conversion with many alternatives to test may take several months to produce statistically significant results. The advantage of combining with Google Analytics is that you can measure both the micro-conversion (add to cart) and the macro-conversion (make a purchase) simultaneously. This allows you to quickly identify alternatives that are underperforming and stop serving them—even before you have enough data on the macro-conversion for that alternative.

The Integration Method

When using Website Optimizer, you need to address two issues in order to integrate with Google Analytics:

- Generate a unique tracking URL for each test variation so alternatives can be analyzed in Google Analytics—using a separate profile.

- Tidy up Google Analytics reports so existing profile data tracks all test variations as a single page.

As you can see, the second point appears to contradict the first. However, the purpose is to first separate out the different Website Optimizer test combinations for analysis. This detail is not required in your main Google Analytics profile. Therefore, in order to maintain report simplicity, alternative test URLs are recombined in your main profile so that you receive an aggregate report for the single test page.

The approach adopted is to insert your Website Optimizer variation number into the Google Analytics tracking call. Note that you should employ this technique only when running multivariate tests. It is not required if you are running an A/B split test (or A/B/C/D ...), because each alternative already has its own unique URL.

> **Note:** This technique was originally discussed in the "The Techie Guide to Google Website Optimizer," coauthored by Ophir Prusak: www.google.com/websiteoptimizer/techieguide.pdf. Thanks go to Ophir Prusak and the team at POP for help with writing this section (www.pop.us). Credit for coding examples goes to Eric Vasilik at www.gwotricks.com/2009/02/poor-mans-gwoanalytics-integration.html.

Generating Unique URLs for Each Multivariate Test

Website Optimizer utilizes two cookies in order to manage test experiments; __utmx and __utmxx. By querying the value of __utmx, you can obtain the value identifying the test combination. For example, consider a page under multivariate test with three test sections. Section 1 has three alternatives including the original, section 2 has four alternatives, and section 3 has two alternatives. That's a total of 24 combinations being tested ($3 \times 4 \times 2$). By using the JavaScript function utmx("combination_string"), a string is returned corresponding to the combination displayed to the user, such as "0-3-1." In this example, that represents the original variation for the first section, the third test alternative in section 2, and the first test alternative in section 3. Note that the original variation of a test is always represented as combination 0.

With this knowledge, modify the Google Analytics _pageTracker() call within the GATC of the test page as follows:

```
<script type="text/javascript">
(function(){try {
 var l = document.location, s = l.search;
 if (utmx('combination_string') != undefined) {
  s = s +(s.length ? '&' : '?') +'combo=' +utmx('combination_string');
  s += '&testname= button-test-3';
  // the testname variable is to allow you to easily filter out
  // a specific experiment. Change this to your experiment name
  // defined in Website Optimizer
 }
```

```
var pageTracker = _gat._getTracker("UA-12345-1");
pageTracker._trackPageview(l.pathname + s);
}catch(err){}})();
</script>
```

Viewing Test Alternatives in Google Analytics

The side effect of having each test combination tracked using a unique URL is that multiple pages (each test combination) are reported in Google Analytics, for example:

/test-page.html?combo=0-0-1&testname=button-test-3

/test-page.html?combo=0-1-2&testname=button-test-3

/test-page.html?combo=1-0-2&testname=button-test-3

This, of course, is visit data for a single page: test-page.html. In order to avoid confusion in your main Google Analytics profile, track your Website Optimizer test data in a separate Google Analytics profile and modify your main profile so all combinations are combined and reported as a single page. To achieve this, create a new, carbon-copy profile in your Google Analytics account—see Chapter 8 for details on how to create additional profiles. When this is in place, no other change is necessary—by default each of your test page alternatives will be tracked separately for you to analyze in your new profile, as shown in Figure 12.12.

Figure 12.12 Website Optimizer test alternatives tracked in a separate Google Analytics profile

Tip: In your new profile, if you have goals, filters, or segments that use `test-page.html`, ensure they don't break. For example, if your goal includes `test-page.html`, do not use Exact Match as the goal match type. Instead use Head Match because this will trigger a goal for `test-page.html?combo=1&testname=button-test-3` as well as other combinations.

In order to combine all combinations and report them as a single page in your main profile, use the Google Analytics Exclude URL Query Parameters functionality. If you have used the example code presented so far, your original and test page alternatives differ only by the *combo* and *testname* parameters. Hence, add these to the list of parameters to ignore in your main profile—see Figure 12.13.

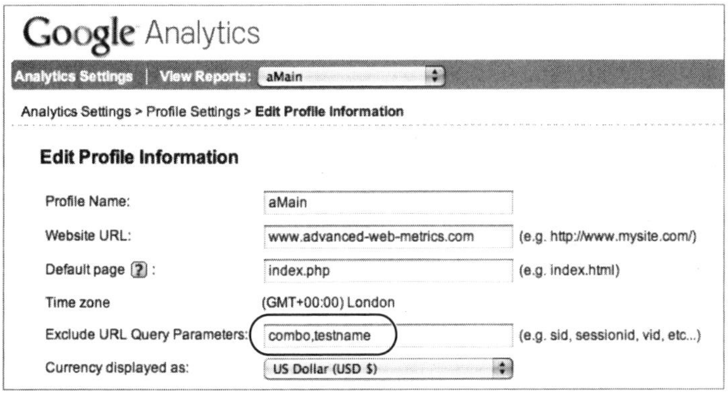

Figure 12.13 Ignoring Website Optimizer test parameters in Google Analytics

Summary

In Chapter 12, you have learned the following:

How to extract Google Analytics cookie information You have learned to use JavaScript or PHP to query and extract information from Google Analytics cookies.

An introduction to the Google Analytics API You have an overview of how to use the API and its capabilities.

Which example API solutions are available We discussed the kind of third-party applications currently available to augment and enhance Google Analytics data in clever ways.

How to track phone call usage You know how to track visitors where the website call to action is to make a phone call.

How to integrate Website Optimizer with Google Analytics You have learned how to combine the testing capabilities of Google Website Optimizer for conversion optimization with other metrics that Google Analytics provides.

Regular Expression Overview

Regular expressions, also referred to as regex, *are a way for computer languages to match strings of text, such as specific characters, words, or patterns of characters. A simple everyday example of regular expressions is using wildcards for matching filenames on your computer. For example,* *.pdf *matches all filenames that end in* .pdf. *However, regex can be much more powerful (and complex) than this.*

Within Google Analytics, regular expressions are primarily used when creating profile filters (Chapter 8, "Best-Practices Configuration Guide"), advanced segments (Chapter 8), and table filters (Chapter 4, "Using the Google Analytics Interface").

Note: This appendix is intended as a general introduction to the fundamentals of building regular expressions within Google Analytics. In most cases this will fit your needs. However, if you need more details there are numerous resources on the Web—for example, try a search for `http://www.google.co.uk/search?q=regular+expression+%2Btutorial`.

Understanding the Fundamentals

A solid understanding of regex syntax is required, and the syntax remains similar across the different flavors of regex engines (POSIX, PCRE). In addition, a number of tools are available to help you troubleshoot building your regular expressions—see Appendix B.

Google Analytics uses a partial implementation of the Perl Compatible Regular Expressions (PCRE) library. I use the word *partial* because a full implementation is more powerful and flexible than a Software as a Service vendor would want it to be! If its use is unrestricted, it can be used maliciously to hack or break a website. Hence, not every feature of PCRE is included, though you would be hard pressed to find what isn't.

Warning: Google Analytics uses only a partial implementation of PCRE, and hence advanced features may not be available. Unfortunately, the exact feature set of the regex engine is undocumented, so further guidance is difficult! However, we do know that "look ahead" and "negative look ahead" features are not available. That is, `google\.(?=com)` or `google\.(?!com)` will not work. The work-around for this particular regex when using table filters or advanced segments is to select Excluding or "Does not match regular expression" from the configuration drop-down menu and use `google.com` for the match.

An important point to grasp when using regular expressions is that there are two types of characters: *literals* and *metacharacters*. Most characters are treated as literals. That is, if you wanted to match a URL for *advanced*, you would type the characters as *a*, followed by *d*, followed by *v*, and so forth. The exceptions to this are metacharacters. These are characters of special meaning to the regex engine and therefore interpreted differently. The most common metacharacters are listed in Table A.1. Ensure you understand these before proceeding.

474

Metacharacter	Description
.	Matches any single character.
[ ]	Matches a single character that is contained within the square brackets. Referred to as a *class*.
[^]	Matches a single character that is *not* contained within the square brackets. Referred to as a *class*.
^	Matches the beginning of the string. This is referred to as an *anchor*.
$	Matches the end of the string. This is referred to as an *anchor*.
*	Matches zero or more of the previous item.
?	Matches zero or one of the previous item.
+	Matches one or more of the previous item.
|	The OR operator. Matches either the expression before or the expression after the operator.
\	The escape character. Allows you to use one of the metacharacters for your match.
( )	Groups characters into substrings.

Regex Examples

Using only literals, you can construct simple regular expressions. However, combining literals with metacharacters provides for more complex pattern matching. The best way to understand how regular expressions work is by example, and I use relevant Google Analytics matches to illustrate this.

> **Note:** The regex engine of Google Analytics is *not* case sensitive.

First, partial matches are allowed. For example, say you wanted to view only referrals from the website www.google.com. Using a regular expression, you could use the partial keyword goog in the table filter of your Traffic Sources > All Traffic Sources report. This will match all entries that have the letters goog in them, as shown in Figure A.1.

Although simple to implement, literals can be very powerful—as long as you can identify a unique pattern match that includes the string of interest. Taking the previous example, the use of goog still results in 117 rows of data. To be more specific, use the OR metacharacter, for example:

```
google\.(com|co\.uk|ca)
```

	Site Usage	Goal Set 1	Goal Set 2	AdSense Revenue				Views:

Visits	Pages/Visit	Avg. Time on Site	% New Visits	Bounce Rate
11,861	**1.88**	**00:02:12**	**78.53%**	**69.48%**
% of Site Total: 50.29%	Site Avg: 1.99 (-5.66%)	Site Avg: 00:02:52 (-23.24%)	Site Avg: 73.33% (7.08%)	Site Avg: 66.67% (4.21%)

	Source/Medium	None ⌄	Visits ↓	Pages/Visit	Avg. Time on Site	% New Visits	Bounce Rate
1.	google / organic		5,033	1.83	00:02:09	82.14%	70.97%
2.	google.com / organic		3,204	1.76	00:02:03	81.02%	72.07%
3.	google.co.uk / organic		857	1.92	00:02:05	74.10%	66.16%
4.	images.google / organic		296	3.14	00:04:58	81.42%	57.43%
5.	Google email signature / Email		282	1.70	00:01:43	55.32%	58.87%
6.	google.com / RSS - Google Reader		239	1.64	00:01:59	56.90%	74.48%
7.	google.com / referral		229	2.11	00:02:13	66.81%	63.32%
8.	google.co.in / organic		228	1.58	00:01:15	90.79%	75.88%
9.	trucosgoogleanalytics.com / referral		105	1.69	00:01:21	71.43%	71.43%
10.	google / cpc		103	2.17	00:02:17	71.84%	58.25%

Filter Source/Medium: [containing ⬍] (goog) [Go] Advanced Filter   Go to: [1]   Show rows: [10 ⬍] 1 - 10 of 117 [◄] [►]

Figure A.1 Table filter using a partial match

This matches the literal google, followed by a period (this must be escaped because it is also a metacharacter), followed by com OR co.uk (period also escaped) OR ca. The result is shown in Figure A.2.

	Site Usage	Goal Set 1	Goal Set 2	AdSense Revenue				Views:

Visits	Pages/Visit	Avg. Time on Site	% New Visits	Bounce Rate
11,861	**1.88**	**00:02:12**	**78.53%**	**69.48%**
% of Site Total: 50.29%	Site Avg: 1.99 (-5.66%)	Site Avg: 00:02:52 (-23.24%)	Site Avg: 73.33% (7.08%)	Site Avg: 66.67% (4.21%)

	Source/Medium	None ⌄	Visits ↓	Pages/Visit	Avg. Time on Site	% New Visits	Bounce Rate
1.	google.com / organic		5,033	1.83	00:02:09	82.14%	70.97%
2.	google.co.uk / organic		3,204	1.76	00:02:03	81.02%	72.07%
3.	google.ca / organic		857	1.92	00:02:05	74.10%	66.16%
4.	google.com.au / organic		296	3.14	00:04:58	81.42%	57.43%
5.	google.com / referral		282	1.70	00:01:43	55.32%	58.87%
6.	google.com / RSS - Google Reader		239	1.64	00:01:59	56.90%	74.48%
7.	google.com.br / organic		229	2.11	00:02:13	66.81%	63.32%
8.	google.co.uk / referral		228	1.58	00:01:15	90.79%	75.88%
9.	mail.google.com / referral		105	1.69	00:01:21	71.43%	71.43%
10.	spreadsheets.google.com / referral		103	2.17	00:02:17	71.84%	58.25%

Filter Source/Medium: [containing ⬍] (google\.(com|co\.uk|ca)) [Go] Advanced Filter   Go to: [1]   Show rows: [10 ⬍] 1 - 10 of 117 [◄] [►]

Figure A.2 Table filter using the OR metacharacter

Note: Google Analytics automatically escapes periods in the report table filter and advanced segments for you. Therefore, you can omit the escape charter (\) for these. However, when you are learning regex, I advise you to always escape these yourself as best practice. Profile filters and goal or funnel configurations do not have the automatic escape feature.

You will notice from Figure A.2 that subdomains of Google are present in the reports. Suppose you wish to remove these from your matches. Modify the regex query as follows:

```
^google\.(com|co\.uk|ca)
```

This results in only referrers that start with the pattern google being matched. Another example to practice with includes

```
^go.+le\.((com$)|(co\.uk)$|(ca)$)
```

This extends the previous example to explicitly match only Google domains that end in .com, .co.uk, and .ca. This removes referrers such as google.com.au, google.com.br, and so forth, as shown in Figure A.3. Note that I have also been a little lazy and used go.+le to illustrate how to use the + metacharacter. That is, it is used to match one or more of the previous character—in this case, any character.

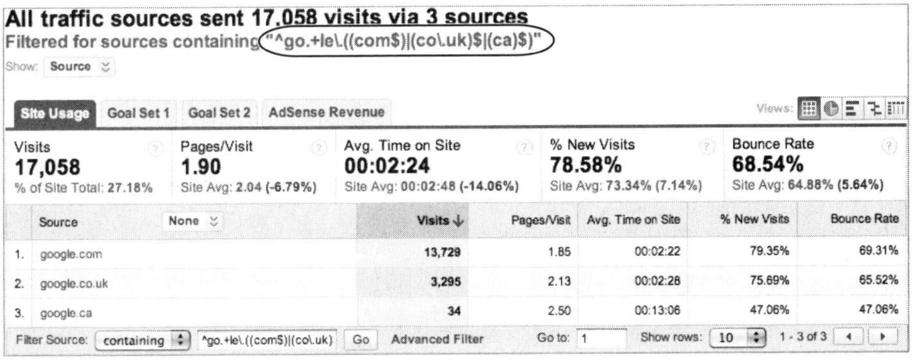

All traffic sources sent 17,058 visits via 3 sources
Filtered for sources containing "^go.+le\.((com$)|(co\.uk)$|(ca)$)"

Show: Source ⌄

| Site Usage | Goal Set 1 | Goal Set 2 | AdSense Revenue | | | Views: ▦ ◑ ☰ ⚞ ▥ |

Visits	Pages/Visit	Avg. Time on Site	% New Visits	Bounce Rate
17,058	**1.90**	**00:02:24**	**78.58%**	**68.54%**
% of Site Total: 27.18%	Site Avg: 2.04 (-6.79%)	Site Avg: 00:02:48 (-14.06%)	Site Avg: 73.34% (7.14%)	Site Avg: 64.88% (5.64%)

	Source	None ⌄	Visits ↓	Pages/Visit	Avg. Time on Site	% New Visits	Bounce Rate
1.	google.com		13,729	1.85	00:02:22	79.35%	69.31%
2.	google.co.uk		3,295	2.13	00:02:28	75.69%	65.52%
3.	google.ca		34	2.50	00:13:06	47.06%	47.06%

Filter Source: containing ⬍ ^go.+le\.((com$)|(co\.uk) Go Advanced Filter Go to: 1 Show rows: 10 ⬍ 1 - 3 of 3 ◄ ►

Figure A.3 Table filter using multiple metacharacters

The following are examples to consider when matching URLs listed in your Content > Top Content reports:

```
\?(id|pid)=[^&]*
```

This matches the filename followed by the first query parameter and its value if its name is equal to id or pid. If you have a report with URIs of the following form, this regex will match the two URIs highlighted:

```
/blog/post?pid=101
/blog/post?id=101&lang=en&cat=hacks
/blog/post?lang=en&cat=hacks&id=102
/blog/about-this-blog
```

Typically, this regex format is used when defining a goal or funnel step. Note the use of the negative class to stop the regex match. That is, this regex will match all characters after id= or pid= that do not contain &. An asterisk is used (*) to also match zero occurrences of & so that even if there is no second query parameter present, as per the first URI, the regex will still match.

An example that is useful when filtering within the Keyword reports (search engines and internal site search) is to consider misspellings. Perhaps you need to find all matches for "colour" and "color." The following regex will achieve this:

```
colo[u]*r
```

Here are some other misspelling examples:

```
Voda(ph|f)one
Ste(ph|v)en
Br[ai][ai]n
```

(My name is sometimes spelled Brain!)

Finally, although not directly relevant to Google Analytics, a common regex used in web development for processing forms is:

```
^(.+)@([^\(\);:,<>_]+\.[a-zA-Z.]{2,6})
```

Use this to test your understanding. Broken into its constituent parts, this regex checks an email address to ascertain if it is a valid format—that is, brian@mysite.com and not brian@@my_site:com, for example. From left to right, the English interpretation is as follows:

- Match one or more of any character before the @
- Match any character after the @ but do not include any of following characters:
  ( ) ; ; , < > _
- Followed by a period
- Followed by between two and six characters that must include an alphabetic character (A–Z as either upper- or lowercase) or a period

I have **highlighted** the middle section of this regex to help guide your eye, that is, the part between the @ and first period.

If you have followed these examples, you are well on your way to understanding regular expressions. If not, reread this section and use one of the regex tools listed in Appendix B. Further regex examples are shown throughout this book, though none are more complicated than those shown here.

Tips for Building Regular Expressions

- Make the regular expression as simple as possible. Complex expressions take longer to process or match than simple expressions.

- Avoid the use of . * if possible because this expression matches everything zero or more times and may slow processing of the expression. For instance, if you need to match all of the following

  ```
  index.html, index.htm, index.php, index.aspx, index.py, index.cgi
  ```
  use
  ```
  index\.(h|p|a|c)+.+
  ```
  not
  ```
  index.*
  ```

- Try to group patterns together when possible. For instance, if you wish to match a file suffix of .pdf, .doc, and .ppt use
  ```
  \.(pdf|doc|ppt)
  ```
  not
  ```
  \.pdf|\.doc|\.ppt
  ```

- Be sure to escape the regular expression wildcards or metacharacters if you wish to match those literal characters. Common ones are periods in filenames and parentheses in text.

- Use anchors whenever possible (^ and $, which match either the beginning or end of an expression), because these speed up processing.

Useful Tools

The tools and helper applications I have come across as a practitioner come in two flavors: those that help you with your implementation of Google Analytics—install and setup—and those that help you use or interpret reports—navigation aides, segmentation help, and so forth. Often these two scenarios overlap, and marketers frequently find themselves using the same toolset as webmasters and web developers. Regardless of your job role, all the tools I list here are straightforward to use.

Tools to Audit Your GATC Deployment

The key to being able to improve your website is having good, solid, accurate data that you can rely on. A fundamental step of implementing any web analytics tool is getting the data in—there simply is no point investing in analysis if the data is flawed. After all, garbage in equals garbage out. Maintaining data integrity is key. Adding page tags, the GATC, is therefore not a one-time, "set it and forget it" process. It requires careful deployment planning and regular maintenance checks to ensure data holes do not appear.

The following is a list of site scan and site audit tools that can verify the completeness of your GATC:

SiteScan by EpikOne Free and paid Software as a Service (SaaS) vendor. Performs a text search and regular expression match for the GATC:

www.sitescanga.com

Web Analytics Solution Profiler (WASP) A Firefox plug-in that detects the setting of the GATC cookies plus 100 other vendor tools. Works on a page-by-page (free) and site-scanning (paid) basis:

www.webanalyticssolutionprofiler.com

Joost de Valk's Statistics Detector Free Greasemonkey script for Firefox. Performs a text search and regular expression match for the GATC plus 34 other vendor tools. Works on a page-by-page basis only:

http://yoast.com/tools/seo/greasemonkey/statistics-detector/

ObservePoint Paid Software as a Service (SaaS) vendor. Detects the setting of the GATC cookies plus Omniture's. Works as a site-scanning and monitoring/alert tool:

www.observepoint.com

Accenture Digital Diagnostics (formerly Maxamine) Paid Software as a Service (SaaS) vendor. High-end site diagnostic tool:

www.accenture.com

A typical report from these tools would list the URLs scanned and show the following, for example:

- Pages scanned = 548 (100%)
- Pages with correctly functioning GATC = 522 (95.3%)
- Number of incorrect GATC = 14 (2.6%)
- Number of pages not found (error 404) = 12 (2.1%)

How Often Should I Audit My GATC Implementation?

The main factor to consider here is how often your content changes. If 10 percent of your website content changes each month, then by halfway through the year the majority of your website will have changed. The greater the change, the higher the possibility of errors. Even non-humans such as CMS, CRM systems, and web servers can, and do, make errors. And because page tags are a hidden piece of code, errors are not visible by simply visiting the page in your browser. The result is that page tag errors easily go unnoticed and build up rapidly on your website.

In the early stages of a GATC deployment (or redeployment) I recommend you scan your pages weekly. Assuming there are no holes in your data collection, or they have been fixed, move to a monthly scan after eight weeks. Again, assuming data holes and anomalies have been ironed out, you should be able to move to quarterly scanning frequency by Q3. Maintain quarterly scans until your next major site redesign or a replacement CMS comes online, and then increase the frequency again.

Firefox Add-ons

Add-ons are installable enhancements to the Firefox browser. Developed by third-parties, add-ons are capable of customizing Firefox by providing additional functionality and, best of all, the vast majority of add-ons are free to use. Because of this flexibility, I recommend Firefox when viewing Google Analytics reports. More information on Firefox add-ons is available at

> https://addons.mozilla.org/en-US/firefox/.

The following are add-ons that can help with your implementation and usage of Google Analytics. I use all of them:

Better Google Analytics This is the mother of all Google Analytics helper add-ons. It enhances Google Analytics with a compilation of Greasemonkey user scripts produced by various authors. At the last count, it incorporated 19 add-ons, including:

- Automatic access to your Google Analytics account.
- Automatic navigation expansion.
- Full-screen view: Removes the side menu.
- Content search direct from the side menu.
- Table sort: Sort only what you see, not the entire report data set.
- Integrated social media metrics: Includes Sphinn, Technorati, Digg, StumbleUpon metrics, and several others.

- Integrated Google Insights search: Perform Google Insights searches on keywords in your reports.
- Advanced date selection: Compare year-on-year data with one click.
- Google Docs export: Adds Google Spreadsheets as an export option.

Plus it offers a few helper scripts to ease your way around the `conversionuniversity.com` content.

Better Google Analytics is maintained at

`www.vkistudios.com/tools/firefox/betterga/`

Goal Copy Allows you to copy one set of configured goals over to another profile, and even a profile in another Google Analytics account. Useful when creating multiple carbon copies of profiles, for example, a profile for U.S. visitors separate from U.K. visitors.

`www.lunametrics.com/blog/2008/01/21/copying-goals-in-google-analytics-a-firefox-extension/`

Web Developer Toolkit This Firefox add-on adds a menu bar to your browser with a whole range of useful features for anyone who has an interest in creating web pages. It has an excellent browser error console and DOM inspector, as well as quick lookup tools for cookies, source code, and so forth:

`https://addons.mozilla.org/en-US/firefox/addon/60`

Firebug This free Firefox add-on adds debug capabilities for JavaScript, CSS, and HTML live in your browser. Currently with over 20 million downloads, it is one of the most popular Firefox add-ons:

`https://addons.mozilla.org/en-US/firefox/addon/1843`

Live HTTP Headers This add-on allows you to view HTTP headers of a page while you are browsing. All the communication requests sent and received by your browser can be viewed. These can be quite numerous and difficult to follow. Therefore, to follow only Google Analytics requests, set the configuration of this add-on to Filter URLs With Regexp set to `/__utm.gif.*`.

`https://addons.mozilla.org/en-US/firefox/addon/3829`

Note: Google Chrome is a new browser (released in September 2008) that I find myself using often. Though support for Mac computers is currently limited, Chrome uses extensions in the same way Firefox uses Add-ons. That is, allowing third-party developers to extend its capabilities. For example, the Analytics Helper extension displays a notification if a Google Analytics account code (UA number) is detected in a web page. See: `https://chrome.google.com/extensions/search?q=analytics+helper`.

Desktop Helper Applications

WebBug WebBug is a Windows application that allows you to enter a URL and see exactly what is sent to the web server and what response is sent back. This is the information that your browser takes care of when rendering a page. I use this mainly to check a web server's status code response. It is very useful for tracking redirection issues—a common problem that can result in the loss of campaign variables from your landing page URLs. WebBug is free to use, Windows only, and is available for download from

        www.cyberspyder.com/webbug.html

The Regex Coach Regular expressions (regex) are snippets of pseudo code that match patterns within text. In Google Analytics, regular expressions are used for filtering—both within a report (table filter) and for creating separate profile reports (profile filters), for defining advanced segments, and for configuring goal conversions and funnel steps. In other words, regular expressions are important, and I refer to them throughout this book.

Going beyond the basics, things can rapidly appear complex because regular expression often appear like algebra. Therefore, before implementing your regular expression, validate it through the excellent Regex Coach application (Windows only). Regex Coach is free to use and can be downloaded from http://weitz.de/regex-coach/.

Recommended
Further Reading

This is not intended as an exhaustive list of reading material but more a reflection of the books and resources I have read and the blogs I have participated in over the years. If you have a relevant reading resource that I am unaware of, please email me at brian@advanced-web-metrics.com *and I will endeavor to include it here and on the book website itself (*www.advanced-web-metrics.com/blog/ recommended-reading*).*

Books on Web Analytics and Related Areas

Listed in reverse published date order:

- Avinash Kaushik, *Web Analytics 2.0: The Art of Online Accountability and Science of Customer Centricity* (Sybex, 2009)
- Steve Jackson, *Cult of Analytics: Driving online marketing strategies using web analytics* (Butterworth-Heinemann, 2009)
- Stephen Moss and Mark Brimm, *AdWords University: The Complete Guide to AdWords* (Interface Communications Group, 2009)
- Tim Ash, *Landing Page Optimization: The Definitive Guide to Testing and Tuning for Conversions* (Sybex, 2008)
- Bill Hunt and Mike Moran, *Search Engine Marketing, Inc.: Driving Search Traffic to Your Company's Web Site* (IBM Press, 2008)
- Bryan Eisenberg, John Quarto-vonTivadar (Author), Lisa T. Davis, *Always Be Testing: The Complete Guide to Google Website Optimizer* (Sybex, 2008)
- Avinash Kaushik, *Web Analytics: An Hour a Day* (Sybex, 2007)
- Jason Burby and Shane Atchison, *Actionable Web Analytics: Using Data to Make Smart Business Decisions* (Sybex, 2007)
- David Bowen, *Spinning the Web: How to Transmit the Right Messages Online* (Bowen Craggs & Co. Limited, 2006)
- Bryan Eisenberg, Jeffrey Eisenberg, and Lisa T. Davis, *Waiting for Your Cat to Bark?: Persuading Customers When They Ignore Marketing* (Thomas Nelson, 2006)
- Hurol Inan, *Search Analytics: A Guide to Analyzing and Optimizing Website Search Engines* (BookSurge Publishing, 2006)
- Jakob Nielsen and Hoa Loranger, *Prioritizing Web Usability* (New Riders Press, 2006)
- Steve Krug, *Don't Make Me Think: A Common Sense Approach to Web Usability* (New Riders Press, 2005)
- Chris Sherman, *Google Power: Unleash the Full Potential of Google* (McGraw-Hill Osborne Media, 2005)
- Eric T. Peterson, *Web Analytics Demystified: A Marketer's Guide to Understanding How Your Web Site Affects Your Business* (Celilo Group Media, 2004)
- Hurol Inan, *Measuring the Success of Your Website: A Customer-centric Approach to Website Management* (Longman Publishing Group, 2002)
- Jim Sterne, *Web Metrics: Proven Methods for Measuring Web Site Success* (Wiley, 2002)

Web Resources

- CMO.com: www.cmo.com
- Econsultancy: www.econsultancy.com
- Interactive Advertising Bureau (IAB): www.iab.net
- Search Engine Marketing Professional Organization (SEMPO): www.sempo.org
- Web Analytics Association: www.webanalyticsassociation.org

Blog Roll for Web Analytics

Listed in alphabetical order. Most of these also have Twitter accounts.

Advanced Web Metrics by Brian Clifton	http://www.advanced-web-metrics.com/blog
AIMS Canada	http://www.blog.aimscanada.com/aims_canada/ analytics
Always Be Testing by Andy Edmonds	http://alwaysbetesting.com/abtest
Analytics by Adam Berlinger	http://analyticsbyadam.blogspot.com/
Analytics Insider—from the authors of *Web Analytics for Dummies*	http://www.analyticsinsider.com
Analytics Notes by Jacques Warren	http://www.waomarketing.com/blog
Analytics Talk by Justin Cutroni (EpikOne)	http://www.epikone.com/blog
Andy Beal's Marketing Pilgrim	http://www.marketingpilgrim.com
Blackbeaks Blog....All Things Analytics	http://www.blackbeak.com
BobPage.net—Information overload	http://bobpage.net
Business Analytics by Bhupendra Khanal	http://www.bhups.net
Cliff Allen on Marketing	http://blog.allen.com
Commerce360 by Craig Danuloff	http://blogs.commerce360.com
Conversion Rater	http://www.conversionrater.com
Data Mining Research by Sandro Saitta	http://www.dataminingblog.com
Data Sciences Analytics by John Aitchison	http://dsanalytics.com/dsblog
Digital Alex by Alex Cohen	http://www.alexlcohen.com
Econsultancy	http://www.econsultancy.com/blog
FutureNow's Marketing Optimization Blog	http://www.grokdotcom.com
Gilligan on Data by Tim Wilson	http://gilliganondata.com
Engage-Digital Blog by Hugh Gage	http://www.engage-digital.com/blog
Google Analytics Blog (Google's official blog)	http://analytics.blogspot.com
Greater Returns by Aaron Gray	http://blog.greaterreturns.me
How to Change the World: A practical blog for impractical people—by Guy Kawasaki	http://blog.guykawasaki.com
Immeria :: an immersion into web analytics by Stephane Hamel	http://blog.immeria.net
Instant Cognition	http://blog.instantcognition.com
June Dershewitz on Web Analytics	http://june.typepad.com

KISSmetrics	http://blog.kissmetrics.com
Lies, Damned Lies...	http://www.liesdamnedlies.com
LunaMetrics	http://www.lunametrics.com/blog
Market Motive	http://www.marketmotive.com/blog
Marketing Productivity Blog by Jim Novo	http://blog.jimnovo.com
My Analytics, Media and Marketing Blog by Dennis R. Mortensen	http://visualrevenue.com/blog
Mymotech by Michael Helbling	http://www.mymotech.com
Negligible Quantities by Julien Coquet (in French)	http://juliencoquet.com
Occam's Razor by Avinash Kaushik	http://www.kaushik.net/avinash
Pattern Finder	http://creese.typepad.com/pattern_finder
Random Analytics	http://randombits.typepad.com/webanalytics
Rich Page Rambling by Rich Page	http://www.rich-page.com
SemAngel by Gary Angel	http://semphonic.blogs.com/semangel
Share the Genie's Power :: ClickInsight Blog	http://blog.clickinsight.ca
The Analytics Ecology by Joseph Carrabis	http://theanalyticsecology.com/
The Big Integration by Jacques Warren	http://www.thebigintegration.com/blog
Trending Upward—Web analytics for higher education	http://www.trendingupward.net
Turn Up the Silence—iPerceptions Blog	http://blog.iperceptions.com
Unofficial Google Analytics Blog	http://www.roirevolution.com/blog
Web Analysis and Online Advertising by Anil Batra	http://webanalysis.blogspot.com
Web Analysts Info by Lars Johansson	http://www.webanalysts.info/webanalytics
Web Analytics Analyzed by Paul Strupp	http://blogs.sun.com/pstrupp
Web Analytics and Optimization Blog by Mike Sukmanowsky	http://analytics.mikesukmanowsky.com
Web Analytics Applied by Paul Legutko (Semphonic)	http://legutko.typepad.com
Web Analytics Association Blog	http://waablog.webanalyticsassociation.org
Web Analytics by Hurol Inan	http://www.hurolinan.com
Web Analytics by Matt Hopkins	http://www.webanalyticmatt.com
Web Analytics Demystified	http://www.webanalyticsdemystified.com/weblog
Web Analytics in China by Florian Pihs	http://longmarch.chinalytics.com/
Web Analytics Forum	http://groups.yahoo.com/group/webanalytics
Web Analytics: Information for the average user by Matt Lillig	http://mattlillig.blogspot.com
Web Analytics Inside by Timo Aden (in German)	http://www.timoaden.de
Web Analytics Management by Phil Kemelor (Semphonic)	http://wam.typepad.com/wam
Web Analytics Princess by Marianina Chaplin	http://marianina.com/blog
Web Analytics Tool Time by Jesse Gross (Semphonic)	http://tooltime.typepad.com
Web Analytics World by Manoj Jasra	http://www.webanalyticsworld.net
WebAnalyticsBook	http://www.webanalyticsbook.com
WebMetricsGuru by Marshall Sponder	http://www.webmetricsguru.com
Web Strategy by Jeremiah Owyang	http://www.web-strategist.com/blog

Index

Google Analytics Individual Qualification Test Coupon

The Google Analytics Individual Qualification Test (GA IQ for short) allows individuals to demonstrate proficiency in Google Analytics.

The curriculum was developed by Google Analytics experts and is continually updated by Google to ensure that it is in synch with the latest Google Analytics features.

Free online training and access to the GA IQ test can be accessed by visiting www.conversionuniversity.com. Agencies, Certified Partners, and other organizations can point their staff to the GA IQ training and the GA IQ exam to verify their proficiency. Students can also benefit from the free training and then prove their proficiency by taking the test.

We hope that readers of this book will want to further their knowledge of Google Analytics by accessing the online training materials at www.conversionuniversity.com. We are happy to offer a 50% coupon to the first 10,000 people who wish to take the GA IQ test afterward. To redeem this offer, just enter **BrianCliftonBook2010** in the shopping cart's Promotional Code box and then click "Add" when purchasing the Google Analytics Individual Qualification test.

Happy Testing!

—Eva Woo
    Product Marketing Manager, Google Global Certified Partners